Recht und Digitalisierung | Digitization and the Law

Herausgegeben von | Edited by

Prof. Dr. Roland Broemel
Jun.-Prof. Dr. Lea Katharina Kumkar
Prof. Dr. Jörn Lüdemann
Prof. Dr. Rupprecht Podszun
Prof. Dr. Heike Schweitzer †

Volume 26

Sergio Valente

Digital Government in Brazil

Legal-institutional Dimension

Nomos

The Deutsche Nationalbibliothek lists this publication in the Deutsche Nationalbibliografie; detailed bibliographic data are available on the Internet at http://dnb.d-nb.de

a.t.: Hamburg, Univ., Diss., 2025

Original title: Digital Government in Brazil: legal-institutional dimension

ISBN 978-3-7560-3563-2 (Print)
ISBN 978-3-7489-6623-4 (ePDF)

Onlineversion
Inlibra

1st Edition 2026

In memory of Marcelo Pereira Longo.

Acknowledgments

Many people and institutions have contributed to the final result of this work. The list of acknowledgments is only surpassed by the certainty that important people will unintentionally be omitted and that injustices may be committed. I hope, however, to express my gratitude to some of those whose support remains most vivid at this final moment, within the limits of memory and without my words being able to fully convey the true feeling of gratitude and the relevance of their contributions to this work. Without those mentioned here bearing any responsibility for mistakes or inaccuracies, all of them have in some way left their mark or influenced my way of thinking and conducting this dissertation.

First of all, I would like to thank Professor Maria Paula Dallari Bucci for her always attentive and careful guidance, and for the trust she has placed in me throughout this journey, which has been going on since the beginning of my master's degree 10 years ago. I would also like to thank Professor Hans-Heinrich Trute, who made it possible for me to stay in Germany as a student at the University of Hamburg and to take part in activities at the Albrecht Mendelssohn Bartholdy Graduate School of Law. Few people can have a *Doktormutter* and a *Doktorvater* of such academic stature. In addition to their precise guidance, both were instrumental in the challenging task of formalizing a joint doctorate between universities in different countries.

Thanks also to the University of São Paulo (USP) and the University of Hamburg (UHH), two public institutions with a high level of academic excellence, for all the support offered to my research through their libraries, classes, and activities in general. To the German Academic Exchange Service (DAAD), for financial support during 2022 and for fostering environments conducive to the integration of researchers from all over the world, whose ideas inspire and stimulate the creative process. To CAPES - *Coordenação de Aperfeiçoamento de Pessoal de Nível Superior* (Brazilian Federal Agency for Support and Evaluation of Graduate Education), which participated in the process as evaluator of my research project, thanks for trusting my idea and recommending funding. To the Albrecht Mendelssohn Bartholdy Graduate School of Law - AMBSL, and its coordinator Dr. Ülkü Sezgi Sözen, for providing a welcoming, international and interdisciplinary study atmosphere.

To Professors Ana Carla Bliacheriene and Vitor Rhein Schirato, for their careful reading of an initial version of the research project and for their comments during the intermediate qualification exam.

To Davi Tangerino (UERJ), Carolina Gabas Stuchi (UFABC), and Murilo Gaspardo (UNESP), former classmates and now professors with brilliant careers, I would like to thank you for the letters of recommendation needed to make funding and various research-related opportunities possible. I would especially like to thank Davi for giving up some of his time to show me the "ropes" of studying in Germany. To Marcelo Pereira Longo (*in memoriam*), not only for the letter of recommendation, but also for his constant support and, above all, for the fraternal friendship that life's circumstances interrupted all too soon.

To Juliana Costa Hashimoto Bertin Stamm, Father Júlio Lancellotti, and Pedro Abramovay, for the letters of recommendation they gave me for various purposes.

To Professors Diogo Rosenthal Coutinho and José Eduardo Campos de Oliveira Faria, from USP, who, while I was still studying for my master's degree, had an impact on the way I thought about the foundations of this research, as well as making time for specific conversations on the subject.

To Professor Carlos Ari Sundfeld, for welcoming me for a conversation even before the project topic was defined, in which the importance of the themes of innovation and experimentalism in public administration became clearer to me.

To Professors Markus Kotzur, Stefan Oeter, and Karl-Heinz Ladeur, and to Professor Mareike Schmidt, for their constant interaction in UHH classes and events, which enriched the universe of ideas under which this work was written. To Professors Stefan Voigt and Georg Ringe, for providing access to classes and events at the Institute of Law and Economics at UHH on topics that were useful to the research. To Professor Scott Brewer from Harvard University, whose AMBSL Workshop provided me with new insights into common law legal thinking and valuable perspectives for my research

To Judith Legies, Eva Leptien, Linda Dammermann, Jan Frömming, from the University of Hamburg, and to José Antonio Capellari and Camila Rodrigues Pereira da Silva, from the Faculty of Law at the University of São Paulo, for the steps they took to make the joint PhD agreement a reality. Special thanks to Daniella Rodrigues, from USP's Graduate Dean's Office, for her guidance and help with this tortuous process, without which the signing of the agreement would not have been possible, and also to

Professor Fernando Facury Scaff, who was always available as chairman of the Graduate Committee to help with the process.

To Villa Vigoni - German-Italian Centre for the European Dialogue, Dott.ssa Annalisa Grazian and Dr. Matteo Scotto, for the opportunity to participate in the Autumn School in European Studies in 2023, an experience that greatly contributed inspiration and ideas for the work.

To Andreas Knobelsdorf, who gave me remote access to the University of Hamburg library and its systems before I arrived. To Claudia Zavala and Christiane Andresen, for their help with issues about the rules and procedures for admission to the doctoral program at the UHH Faculty of Law.

To all my German teachers, who were many and will probably never be enough, but thanks to whom I was able to open a new door of possibilities for research and knowledge in the language of the "poets and thinkers". Special thanks to José da Silva Simões and Nora Machalous, who, as well as being my teachers and helping me with recommendations for German courses in Hamburg, have inspiring academic careers of their own.

To Kseniia Pershina for her help in translating and understanding Russian texts. To Robin Dudda, for proofreading the German version of the abstract.

To Renata Moura Sena, for proofreading the first versions of the research proposal. To Renato Sano Coelho, for proofreading a first version of the research proposal in English. To Kinan Sabbagh, for his comments on the presentation of the research project at the AMBSL Colloquium.

To Professor Francesco Pallante from the University of Turin, who gave me access to one of his works cited in this paper. To professors Wolfgang Schulz, Marina Fontão Zago, and once again Stefan Oeter and Vitor Schirato, for their participation as members of the evaluation committee and for their critical and attentive comments during the dissertation defense.

To Danilo Marasca Bertazzi and Enzo Mayer Tessarolo, from the Special Office for Federative Cooperation in Management and Digital Government of the Ministry of Management and Innovation in Public Services, and Everson Lopes de Aguiar, from the Digital Government Secretariat, for welcoming me to Brasília and presenting the Federal Government's current initiatives in the area, which provided several insights for the research, enabling a better understanding of the practice of policy formulation.

To my parents, Maria Elvira Polimeni Valente and Francisco Valente, and my sisters, Fernanda Valente Burmeister and Luciana Polimeni Valente, for their constant support.

To Heidi Steepe and Peter Steepe, who together with Claudia Evans, Kerstin Düwel, Jan Steepe, Julian Evans, André Düwel, Kirsten Steepe, Luisa, and Linnea are my second family in Hamburg. Thank you for all your support over the last three years.

To Fernando Simões Paes, for making it possible for me to combine my professional activities in Brasília with the start of my doctoral studies in São Paulo, and also to Ellen Capistrano Martins, Mauro Rodrigues Uchôa, Heider Gomes, Ticiano Bragatto, and Mariana Zenni, who contributed directly to this process. I would also like to thank Ticiano for the exchange of ideas on decision automation and artificial intelligence.

To Rodrigo Pires da Cunha Boldrini, a frequent interlocutor on the topics of state theory and jurisprudence, for his constant support and for the constant exchange of ideas on topics related to research.

To Professors Carlos de Brito Pereira and Flavia Mori Sarti, friends that the legal practice has brought me, for exchanging ideas on economics and for kindly giving me books on the American legal tradition that were useful in the research process.

To Marcos Chucralla Moherdaui Blasi, for his help in obtaining some texts on intellectual property and innovation and for the constant support. To Douglas Borges de Vasconcelos, for always sending me news and interesting material on my topic. To Artur Ferrari de Almeida, for sending me some important German articles for the initial preparation of the research proposal. To Guilherme Alberto Almeida de Almeida, for giving me tips and guidance on the topics of innovation and digital government, which were important for the initial choice of the subject of the study.

To Roberto Zaclis, Cândido Pinheiro de Oliveira, Felipe Amante, Raquel Kaori Yamakami Câmara, Patricia Siano, and Ricardo Milo, for their constant encouragement and for the light and welcoming atmosphere they always provide me with in São Paulo. To Flávio Couto Bernardes, for his contributions to my way of thinking about legal practice and the law over the years.

To the Graduate Student Representation of the USP Law School, especially Isabela Ruiz and Fernanda Vick, who helped me enormously with issues related to deadlines and fulfilling requirements for the joint doctoral agreement. To Gabriela Azevedo Campos Sales and Alexandra Fuchs de Araújo, for their always very judicious ideas and suggestions.

To the *DAAD Freundeskreis Hamburg*, who made it possible for me to meet people from different parts of the world who became friends and frequent interlocutors, such as Kseniia, Anton, Alena, Navai, Mehin, Shams, and Jika, among many others.

To Maria da Conceição Figueiredo, "Conceição" (*in memoriam*), who was responsible for awakening my taste for scientific research when I was a child at *Colégio Humboldt* in São Paulo.

To Christian Bickel, Rodrigo de Oliveira e Souza Wenzel, Luis Eduardo Prado Pfingsten, Bruno Tateo, Maia Burmeister, Thomas Langer, and again to Renato Sano Coelho, for their long-standing friendship, in the hope that they will never refuse to lend me money.

To the "spirit of Malente" that I was able to share with my colleagues and classmates from UHH during a writing retreat in that city, where some of my favorite parts of this text were drafted.

Thanks also to Daniel Campos de Carvalho, Luis Fernando Silveira Beraldo, Vinicius Spaggiari (*in memoriam*), Thiago Lobo Bianconi, Rafael Gandara D'Amico, Valdemar Bragheto Junqueira, Carlos Alberto Pereira Leitão Junior, Frederico Haddad, Osvaldo Alves de Castro Filho, Luiz Gustavo Bambini de Assis, Douglas Ribeiro, Ana Luiza Krüger, Ditha and Christiano Ernesto Burmeister, Ana Priscila Teixeira, Jana von Dach, Senana Lucia Brugger, Neelamma Doddannavar, Haruka Nakamura, Caio Cordeiro, Bruno Passadore, Eros Frederico da Silva, Giovanna Maísa Gamba, Luzardo Faria, Mariana Alves Araújo Lopes, Andreas Burmeister, Cesar Prado, Mauro Bellasque, and Ana Lúcia Bellasque, each with their own place in the challenging trajectory of these years.

Finally, I would like to thank Coffea Arabica, my companion of every morning, many afternoons, and some nights, without "whom" this work would have taken twice as long to complete.

Table of Contents

no fundo, no fundo,
bem lá no fundo,
a gente gostaria
de ver nossos problemas
resolvidos por decreto
a partir desta data,
aquela mágoa sem remédio
é considerada nula
e sobre ela — silêncio perpétuo
extinto por lei todo o remorso,
maldito seja quem olhar pra trás,
lá pra trás não há nada,
e nada mais
mas problemas não se resolvem,
problemas têm família grande,
e aos domingos saem todos passear
o problema, sua senhora
e outros pequenos probleminhas

deep down, deep down,
very deep down,
we would like
to see our problems
solved by decree
as of this date,
that unresolved grievance
is considered null and void
and on it - perpetual silence
all remorse is extinguished by law,
cursed be whoever looks back,
there is nothing behind,
and nothing more
but problems are not solved,
problems have big families,
and on Sundays they all go for a walk
the problem, his old lady
and other tiny little problems

(Paulo Leminski)

Wer sagt denn das?
ich alles, was ich brauch', in meinem Computer krieg'?
(Wer sagt denn, dass) nicht Arbeit sondern Freizeit unsere Zukunft ist?
(Wer sagt denn, dass) viele Klicks Qualität bedeuten
Und wir mit Optimieren nicht nur unsere Zeit vergeuden?

Who said that?
I get everything I need in my computer?
(Who says that) our future is not work but leisure?
(Who says that) many clicks mean quality
And that we don't just waste our time optimizing?

(Deichkind)

...la pittura e scultura è la medesima cosa: e perché ella fussi tenuta così, non doverebbe ogni pittore far manco di scultura che di pittura; e 'l simile, lo scultore di pittura che di scultura. io intendo scultura, quella che si fa per forza di levare: quella che si fa per via di porre, è simile alla pittura: basta, che venendo l'una e l'altra da una medesima intelligenza, cioè scultura e pittura, si può far fare loro una buona pace insieme, e lasciar tante dispute; perché vi va più tempo, che a far le figure.

...painting and sculpture are one identical thing; and since it is so concluded, every painter ought to do no less sculpture than painting, and likewise the sculptors as much painting as sculpture. I mean by sculpture what is done by main force in cutting off; what is done by adding is similar to painting; it is enough that since the one and the other come from the same intelligence, that is, sculpture and painting, they can make peace together between themselves and leave such disputes behind, for more time goes into them than into making figures.

(Michelangelo)

Introduction

A. Overview

Public policies are multidisciplinary phenomena and can be studied from the perspective of different scientific fields. Each area of knowledge has its own way of dealing with the problems arising from the subject, depending on its objects and the material content of the policies studied. A common characteristic of public policies is that they are structured through legally regulated processes,[1] making them particularly appealing to legal scholars. In this sense, the legal elements can be analyzed in isolation in those disciplines that deal with each of the processes involved in the elaboration and implementation of the life cycle of public policies and that deal with more or less inert branches of law, from the perspective of decidability and problem-solving - dear to legal dogmatics. These are the traditional approaches to public law, such as administrative law, financial law, constitutional law and procedural law, for example. Within law itself, the visions of each of these branches are often combined, and although there are integration challenges, there is an implicit coherence due to a recognition that this is a separation for predominantly didactic purposes.

However, if the aim is to understand how a public policy works as a whole and how the legal element interacts to produce its effects, the investigation must incorporate interdisciplinarity into the method, making the scientific fields communicate beyond references to isolated, self-contained subjects. This integration requires that the focus sometimes extends beyond the traditional boundaries of jurisprudence, entering other fields of knowledge and necessitating a distinct methodological effort.[2]

Digital transformation constantly alters various aspects of life in society and is, therefore, a fruitful subject for scientific research in the human sciences. Its most significant expression in the public sector - Digital Government - has the peculiar characteristic of being a policy about policies,

1 BUCCI, Maria Paula Dallari. *Fundamentos para uma teoria jurídica das políticas públicas*. São Paulo: Saraiva, 2013, p. 145–146.

2 On the distinction between interdisciplinarity and multidisciplinarity see ALVAR-GONZÁLEZ, David. Multidisciplinarity, Interdisciplinarity, Transdisciplinarity, and the Sciences. *International Studies in the Philosophy of Science*, v. 25, n. 4, p. 387–403, 2011.

in other words, a set of programs for incorporating information technology into the structures of the state without a specific finality (as in the case of health, education, and security policies) and which permeates all other policies by modifying the structures in which the administration operates and the forms of relationship between citizens and the government. Digital Government is also part of the notion of modernizing the state, characteristically identified with major institutional reforms that are usually preceded by crises but which, in this case, take on the appearance of a continuous and permanent activity. In this sense, it should be seen as the set of structures and institutional arrangements through which the state continually incorporates developments in information technology to achieve its goals. It is, therefore, an issue intrinsically linked to the concept of innovation, whether through the generation of knowledge around technology and its application to public interest purposes, or through the adaptation of the state's own legal and political structures to the swift and appropriate incorporation of technology into its administrative apparatus.

The use of the term "Digital Government" to refer to a concept that is often also referred to as "Digital Administration", "digital transformation in the public sector", or "Digital Governance" highlights the political element of this technological structure that mediates the exercise of state power as an important part of the realization of the democratic project. In this way, in addition to the legally regulated processes that structure it, Digital Government is also made up of political impulses, institutions of various kinds, and a constellation of actors who act according to preferences, interests, incentives, and cognitive-cultural molds provided by the environment and a trajectory of evolution of multiple factors.

Based on this, the research aims to investigate the phenomenon of Digital Government as a public policy, seeking to understand the factors that contribute to its degree of evolution in Brazil, how it fits into the broader context of the welfare state, and its implications for the relationship between civil society and the state concerning national development, from an interdisciplinary perspective based on law. As a result, it also seeks to explore alternative institutional paths in order to contribute with reflections and suggestions for the development of dynamic state capabilities through effective digital transformation.

We also hope to contribute to developing a model for the interdisciplinary analysis of public policies that can be applied to any other international experiences of Digital Government or even to any complex, multidisciplinary, or transversal policies.

B. Social and political context

The continuous development of information technology affects political, social, and legal institutions in ways that are not yet fully understood. From the point of view of the law, scholars and legislators have been addressing the need for strong regulation of some private activities that were previously almost completely free, whether from the point of view of state intervention in the way internet services are provided or in relation to the economic concentration seen in information technology business clusters.[3] In this context, various works and initiatives[4] seek to offer a response presented as a reaction to a process of accelerated evolution that is difficult to control and potentially harmful to fundamental rights.[5]

Law, as is known, pursues social facts, seeking to reach and regulate them. However, in this case, there is no certainty that it will achieve its objective of effectively disciplining human action. Therefore, when we see the emergence of large economic groups based on information technology, with massive use of artificial intelligence, big data, and other technologies in their rapidly changing transnational business models, the concern is heightened that the promise of stabilizing expectations through legal instruments may not be fully realized, because the social fact changes faster than normative movements are able to assimilate.[6] This is a problem in which the state sphere is pitted against the private sphere, with the former trying

---

3 FUKUYAMA, Francis; RICHMAN, Barak; GOEL, Ashish. How to Save Democracy from Technology. *Foreign Affairs*, v. 100, n. 1, p. 98–110, 2021.

4 For instance, the "Digital Markets Act". See GIELEN, Nico; UPHUES, Steffen. Digital Markets Act und Digital Services Act Regulierung von Markt- und Meinungsmacht durch die Europäische Union. *Europäische Zeitschrift für Wirtschaftsrecht*, n. 14, p. 627–637, 2021, p. 630, "Die Zeit des laissez faire ist vorbei. Mithilfe einer harmonisierenden Gesetzgebung möchte die EU den großen US-Plattformen Paroli bieten und den EU-Binnenmarkt wettbewerbsfähiger machen". ("The time for laissez faire is over. With the help of harmonizing legislation, the EU wants to stand up to the big US platforms and make the EU internal market more competitive".); See also DIETRICH, Michael; VINJE, Thomas. The European Commission's proposal for a Digital Markets Act — In search of a 'golden standard' for appropriate ex ante regulation of large digital players. *Computer Law Review International*, v. 22, n. 2, p. 33–38, 2021.

5 On this subject, see JØRGENSEN, Rikke Frank (Org.). *Human rights in the age of platforms*. Cambridge, Massachusetts: The MIT Press, 2019.

6 Take, for example, the role of Whastapp in spreading false information in the 2018 presidential elections in Brazil, as can be seen in MACHADO, Caio *et al.* A study of misinformation in whatsapp groups with a focus on the brazilian presidential elections. *In: The Web Conference 2019 - Companion of the World Wide Web Conference, WWW 2019*. New York: Association for Computing Machinery, Inc, 2019, p. 1013–1019.

to curb abuses in a digital market hitherto subject to little control, and the latter constantly testing and pushing the limits of legal regulation.

Nevertheless, if, on the one hand, there is the scenario of a digital market that is moving at a rapid pace, with the law looking for ways to catch up, on the other hand, there is a diametrically opposite situation, in which the use of technology in the state is moving at a slower pace than it could and in which the role of the law is not to catch up, but to propel, to foster transformation. Not only does the accelerated technological evolution in the private sector create problems for the effectiveness of existing legal norms, but also the excessively slow assimilation of technologies by public services creates lost opportunities for the realization of rights and the achievement of the state's purposes.

The problem of regulating private digital activities and the problem of promoting public digital activities, although different objects of study, are closely related. Compared to the slow progress of digitalization in governments, the accelerated development of the digital market makes it possible for companies to advance into typically state areas and functions, occupying public spaces for which they have no "vocation" or legitimacy. This phenomenon has implications for understanding the concept of the state and the quality of democracy to the extent that the mechanisms for legitimizing the regulation of social relations are weakened or lose their scope.

The Big Techs, large transnational technology companies that dominate the world market in the areas where they operate,[7] concentrate economic power that stands up to many countries. They change the natural location of a series of citizen activities to environments of their influence or domain, becoming mediators of the public sphere. This is the phenomenon of the transgression of spheres, in which, through the legitimate exercise of private activities, there is illegitimate access to and control over countless aspects of political life that are typically collective and public.[8] Decisions on the

7 The Big Five or "Frightful Five" are usually referred to as such: Microsoft, Amazon, Apple, Google and Facebook, but Chinese giants such as Alibaba, Tencent, Baidu and Xiaomi are also part of this group, as are several US-based internet companies such as X Corp, Netflix, eBay, Uber, Salesforce and Airbnb. See TENNER, Edward. Who's Afraid of the Frightful Five? Monopoly and Culture in the Digital Age. *Hedgehog Review*, v. 20, n. 1, p. 68–77, 2018; e VAN DER AALST, Wil; HINZ, Oliver; WEINHARDT, Christof. Big Digital Platforms: Growth, Impact, and Challenges. *Business and Information Systems Engineering*, v. 61, n. 6, p. 645–648, 2019.

8 On this, SHARON, Tamar. Blind-sided by privacy? Digital contact tracing, the Apple/Google API and big tech's newfound role as global health policy makers. *Ethics*

scope of freedom of expression, for example, which would be a typical function of the Judiciary, have their practical regulation shifted to the terms of use and consent of social media platforms, which, in part, end up deciding on a day-to-day basis what is allowed or forbidden to say and do, applying sanctions almost instantaneously, according to their own criteria and methods. When it comes to people's access to information and culture, we can see that it is becoming less and less the subject of public policy and more and more dependent on what the social media algorithm[9] offers its users, who are spending more and more time on the platforms. Even essentially governmental functions, such as providing citizens with a legally valid documentary identity or issuing currency, are gradually being invaded by market initiatives, such as cryptocurrencies[10] and digital identity cards[11]. In the same way, some public services, such as passenger transportation, suffer from competition from private transportation apps,[12] sometimes in a way that harms the service's universality and economic sustainability, due

---

and Information Technology, v. 23, n. Suppl 1, p. 45–57, 2021, p. 50, 54. With emphasis on the following excerpt: "Each of these transgressions presents its own risks. Namely, a crowding out of essential spherical expertise, new dependencies on corporate actors for the delivery of essential, public goods, the shaping of (global) public policy by non-representative, private actors and ultimately, the accumulation of decision-making power across multiple spheres".

9 The public interest that permeates such private activities even prompts proposals to treat them as "public utilities", as is the case with monopoly railways and other types of basic services. For instance, SIMONS, Josh; GHOSH, Dipayan. *Utilities for Democracy: Why and How the Algorithmic Infrastructure of Facebook and Google Must Be Regulated.* Washington, DC: Brookings Institution, 2020.

10 The rise of cryptocurrencies brought back the classic debate about the nature of money and its origin, with emphasis on the theory that highlights the legal aspects that constitute currency (KNAPP) and the theory that highlights the aptitude of a certain commodity to appear as a medium of exchange (MENGER). See MENGER, Karl. On the Origin of Money. *The Economic Journal*, v. 2, n. 6, p. 239–255, 1892; and KNAPP, Georg Friedrich. *The State theory of money*. London: Macmillan & Co, 1925; For an overview of the current debate about the nature of cryptocurrencies, see BJERG, Ole. How is Bitcoin Money? *Theory, Culture & Society*, v. 33, n. 1, p. 53–72, 2016.

11 In 2022, the state of Arizona, USA, in partnership with Apple, launched a model of identity and driver's license directly through the application, with full legal validity. See *Apple Wallet ID - Your Arizona ID in Apple Wallet | ADOT*. Available at <https://azdot.gov/applewallet>. Accessed 3 Jun. 2022.

12 MOROZOV, Evgeny. *Big Tech - a ascensão dos dados e a morte da política.* São Paulo: Ubu, 2018, p. 146.

to abusive practices like cream skimming[13]. In addition, various activities in people's daily lives are subsidized by technology companies by providing "free" services, creating a kind of private and invisible "welfare state" as opposed to the public one,[14] which some authors consider to be a kind of benevolent feudalism.[15]

The most recent developments in information technology generate value and efficiency. Still, the scenario that emerges is one of timid appropriation of the positive externalities of this process by the community in favor of a few intermediary players in the private world[16] who begin to concentrate greater power and influence, causing the new digital market to start to take a leading role in various areas of human life, without, however, the same guarantees, protections, and submission to the democratic pact that govern the relations of public life in the state sphere. Private companies are also becoming primarily responsible for implementing public values in digital societies,[17] outside the boundaries of legitimacy in collective decision-making and in subversion of the postulate of popular sovereignty·

Digital progress, with the significant increase in freedoms and possibilities for personal development through technology, is also a promise of liberal democracies today.[18] The big companies in the digital market, which openly collect and process personal data - sometimes making it the core of their business model[19] - indirectly contribute to frustrating this promise, because the processing of data by artificial intelligence programs is based on

---

13 Situations in which those who operate an activity choose only the most profitable consumers and situations, to the detriment of poorer users or those who are more geographically dispersed. BALDWIN, Robert; CAVE, Martin; LODGE, Martin. *Understanding Regulation*. New York: Oxford University Press, 2012, p. 19.

14 MOROZOV, *op. cit.*, p. 146.

15 *Ibid.*, p. 171.

16 MARCIANO, Alain; NICITA, Antonio; RAMELLO, Giovanni Battista. Big data and big techs: understanding the value of information in platform capitalism. *European Journal of Law and Economics*, v. 50, n. 3, p. 345–358, 2020, p. 346.

17 VAN DIJCK, José. Governing digital societies: Private platforms, public values. *Computer Law and Security Review*, v. 36, p. 4, 2020.

18 SÜẞ, Rahel Sophia. Demokratie ist radikaler Experimentalismus. *In*: RAJAL, Elke *et al* (Orgs.). *Making Democracy - Aushandlungen von Freiheit, Gleichheit und Solidarität im Alltag*. Bielefeld, Germany: transcript Verlag, 2020, v. 94, p. 196.

19 FUKUYAMA, Francis; RICHMAN, Barak; GOEL, Ashish. How to Save Democracy from Technology. *Foreign Affairs*, v. 100, n. 1, p. 98–110, 2021, p. 100. "It is true that digital markets exhibit certain features that distinguish them from conventional ones. For one thing, the coin of the realm is data. Once a company such as Amazon or Google has amassed data on hundreds of millions of users, it can move into completely new markets and beat established firms that lack similar knowledge".

past inputs and outputs to generate future results, stabilizing undesirable social situations, such as structural social discrimination.[20]

In this scenario, regulatory initiatives are important moves as attempts to limit and discipline the power of the digital market, but they start from the assumption that the problem lies only outside the state and that the solution lies in forms of interventionism to solve market failures through regulation, removing its dysfunctionality and rescuing its contribution to the common good. However, this view fails to consider the need for the state to change and correct its own failings, to adapt internally in order to "compete" with the digital market in relation to public interests and to take back the political direction of community life in what it has a vocation and legitimacy to do, especially when it comes to mediating interests and resources in social dynamics involving redistributive conflicts. In addition to the concern about putting the brakes on the extraordinary economic power of large corporations resulting from disproportionate productivity gains due to the application of technology, we must ask how governments are organizing themselves to assimilate these gains at a similar pace and allocate them to the benefit of the community through typically state functions. The state can and must reduce the gap in the creation and incorporation of innovation into its structures to regain the leading role in mediating social relations, interests, and forces, since it is, until now, the concentrator of political legitimacy for decisions that affect the community and the institutional presupposition of the democratic regime and public rights and freedoms. This implies the development of government structures that are shaped, molded, and situated by public law formulations but allow innovation, experimental thinking, and controlled risk-taking to be part of the day-to-day running of public power in an adaptive continuum. To this end, legal-institutional arrangements are needed, which, in addition to mitigating rights violations, enhance the opportunities available to the administration to achieve the state's goals and objectives and create an environment conducive to continuous innovation.

In addition to the state/market dichotomy, in which there is a competition between visions of the boundaries of public and private, there is also a geopolitical arena in which civilizational visions and cultures clash, especially less or more democratic political regimes. The disconnection between state and citizens has long been pointed out as a weakness of democratic regimes, which were originally designed to involve the population efficient-

20 SÜß, *op. cit.*, p. 196.

ly[21] in the exercise of power. It is no coincidence that the crisis of political representativeness in democracy contributes to the rise of populist leaders with an authoritarian vocation in various parts of the world.[22]

Democracy is justified by its value attributes linked to popular sovereignty and the degree of freedom and equality it guarantees, in an ethic of intrinsic value. However, democracy can also translate into a competitive advantage for countries that adopt it, from the point of view of their development. It is possible to argue that authoritarian and centralizing governments have generally proved less efficient from the point of view of the practical results they produce, including economic ones,[23] which is a strong incentive to defend democracy beyond its values and ideals. Although the direct relationship between democracy and economic growth is still controversial,[24] the advantages of democratic regimes can be pointed to in terms of human development indicators and the indirect positive repercussions of the impact on human capital on economic indicators.[25]

However, the massive adoption of information technology by non-democratic governments and, in particular, autocracies, opens up the possibility of this premise being questioned because the efficiency gains provided by the handling of large amounts of data can hypothetically neutralize information asymmetries and the traditional limitations of excessively centralized command. Thus, we must admit the hypothesis that democracy may lose one of its main competitive advantages related to efficiency, competing for cultural hegemony on a less favored basis. And just as social dumping

---

21 The ideal representative democracy would be, according to Stuart Mill and based on Bentham's utilitarianism, an optimization of political institutions aimed at an idea of efficiency oriented towards these decision-making criteria. See MILL, John Stuart. *Considerations on Representative Government.* Cambridge: Cambridge University Press, 2010; BENTHAM, Jeremy. *An introduction to the Principles of Morals and Legislation.* Kitchener: Batoche Books, 2000.

22 THORNHILL, Christopher. *Democratic Crisis and Global Constitutional Law.* Cambridge: Cambridge University Press, 2021, p. 187–190.

23 BROWN, Archie. *The myth of the strong leader: political leadership in modern politics.* New York: Basic Books, 2014.

24 With opposing positions, DOUCOULIAGOS, Hristos; ULUBAŞOĞLU, Mehmet Ali. Democracy and Economic Growth: A Meta-Analysis. *American Journal of Political Science*, v. 52, n. 1, p. 61–83, 2008, p. 63–64; GERRING, John *et al.* Democracy and Economic Growth: A Historical Perspective. *World Politics*, v. 57, n. 3, p. 323–364, 2005, p. 356.

25 BAUM, Matthew A.; LAKE, David A. The Political Economy of Growth: Democracy and Human Capital. *American Journal of Political Science*, v. 47, n. 2, p. 333–347, 2003, p. 343.

can lead to a general lowering of social standards,[26] "democratic dumping" can also pose a threat to the survival of democracies as a whole around the world.

In this context, the digital transformation of the state is both a risk and an opportunity. As a risk, it can provide the necessary tools to perpetuate an authoritarian regime or even legitimize it among the governed due to better material results, while also contributing to the degeneration of full democracies if it is adopted without the necessary safeguards to prevent its abuse. As an opportunity, it can represent the chance to energize democracy's social and political relations, directing efficiency gains towards the realization of rights and the democratic project. The risk-opportunity binomial of digital transformation is modulated by institutions in a context in which law and politics relate in such a way as to restrict powers and, at the same time, create possibilities, to the extent that the means and ends of the state and democracy are appropriate. This relationship guides the understanding of the studied object and is a fundamental element of the legal-institutional view proposed for the analysis of digital government public policies.

C. Research question, objectives, justification, and methodology

In the context presented above, the following research question was formulated: how can legal institutions contribute to the development of Digital Government in Brazil in order to improve its efficiency, transparency, and social participation and make the evolution of the state faster and less dependent on crises? In tackling this question, we must also ask what political and legal conditions or configurations can lead the Brazilian state to adapt more quickly to technological innovation applicable to public service, as well as how it is possible to ensure that this evolution generates positive effects for the realization of social rights and not the creation of a digital red tape or instruments of oppression.

To this end, the general objective is to identify legal-institutional obstacles to the development of Digital Government in Brazil and possible solutions to overcome them, with the potential to have a practical impact on the relationship between government and citizens and on the realization

26 BERNACIAK, Magdalena. *Social Dumping: Political Catchphrase or Threat to Labour Standards?* Working Paper 2012.06. Brussels: European Trade Union Institute, 2012, p. 32.

of rights. The specific objectives are to contextualize the problem within the scope of State Law and current academic debates; develop a theoretical basis for the analysis of Digital Government as a public policy; map the legal-institutional arrangements on Digital Government and on the adoption of technologies by the state in Brazil; map the institutional arrangements of international experiences for comparison purposes; identify the risks that the adoption of technology by governments brings to fundamental rights and the quality of democracy in Brazil, and how to mitigate them; identify the opportunities that the development of Digital Government brings to the exercise of rights and the vitality of democracy and how to enhance them; and carry out the exercise of institutional imagination to propose changes in legal institutions and practice.

Considering the problem of development in Brazil in particular, the proposed topic is highly relevant and topical. The Brazilian state is constantly under pressure to increase its efficiency in the provision of services and the challenge of providing the material conditions for the realization of constitutionally provided social rights, which contrast with extreme inequality and the exclusion of a large part of the population from access to basic items of life in society. The full digitalization of government action is one way of responding to these adversities, but not without other challenges, including adapting legal-institutional structures to innovation and making transformations compatible with the guarantee of fundamental rights. Examining these challenges related to the effectiveness of Digital Government and its ability to improve the quality of relations between citizens and government, with a focus on legal-institutional aspects, favors the search for solutions for the future, with a significant potential impact on the quality of democracy and citizens' way of life.

The work predominantly uses the exploratory qualitative research method,[27] examining the literature on the subject, complemented by the non-quantitative empirical method, especially when examining normative texts and legal-institutional designs of Digital Government initiatives. To some extent, the dialectical method will also be used for specific issues, the historical method for identifying important factors in the institutional trajectory, and the comparative method for investigating the issue's international dimension to better understand Brazil's internal dynamics.

In this respect, the experiences of the German Digital Government and the policies to promote the digitalization of the public sector within the

27 GIL, Antônio Carlos. *Métodos e técnicas de pesquisa social.* São Paulo: Atlas, 1999, p. 13, 16, 27.

European Union were chosen. These cases were part of the daily life of this researcher, who spent the last three years of the research in the city of Hamburg, immersed in public discussions on the subject and in the day-to-day life of German society. In addition, the cases reveal challenges similar to Brazil's in terms of the complexity of federal structures and tackling regional inequalities, which provide important input for a broader understanding of the issue.

Despite the non-dogmatic nature of the proposed research, legal dogmatics has its own place and is an essential tool for understanding and criticizing the legal relationships that operate within institutional arrangements, functioning as an analytical toolbox[28]. On the other hand, interdisciplinarity, which refers more specifically to the penetration of concepts, ideas, and postulates from other areas into legal studies, will be present, especially, in categories from political science, economics, and sociology.

As previously mentioned, the aim is to identify and tackle the political and legal challenges of Digital Government in Brazil by critically analyzing the current legal-institutional arrangements and outlining their political and legal effects. This dissertation aims to highlight the need for the adoption of a legal framework that introduces a culture of innovation and responsible experimental democratic practice within the state, resulting in a qualitative leap in the provision of public services and in society's participation in the objectives of the state, thereby facilitating a significant transformation in the relationship with citizens through Digital Government. The aim is also to contribute with proposals for changing the current situation to make the state more effective in generating value and efficiency by promoting internal technological innovation within the administration and the realization of social rights, as well as the adoption of permanent experimental practices, towards the realization of a digital welfare state in Brazil.

D. Digital government as an object of study

Before embarking on institutional analysis under the proposed interdisciplinary approach, it is necessary to understand the object of study as it presents itself externally, not only to clarify the scope of the research but also to establish a basic alignment of expectations regarding the terms,

28 RIBEIRO, Leonardo Coelho. O direito administrativo como caixa de ferramentas e suas estratégias. *Revista de Direito Administrativo*, v. 272, p. 209, 2016.

concepts, and characteristics of what is referred to here as Digital Government.

For decades now, countries have been looking for ways to intensify the use of information and communication technology to improve public administration performance. Governments have come to see these technologies as a solution that could solve the problem of a lack of congruence and effectiveness in public service delivery and, at the same time, save and free up resources through efficiency and productivity gains.[29] Technology incorporated into government has emerged as a promise of increased economies of scale in the provision of services to citizens, improved democratic participation, and intensified public transparency and accountability.[30] Although this process is part of the third industrial revolution, which produced computers and digital information networks,[31] the issue has taken on new contours and possibilities with the advent of the fourth industrial revolution, which combines artificial intelligence and the analysis of large amounts of data, among other components.[32]

Initially, the use of information technology in administrations consisted of what is known as electronic government, or *e-government*. The notion arose from the need to implement information systems to deal more efficiently with the demands of citizens and businesses in a dynamic environment.[33] This scenario was inspired by the transformation of traditional private business into online business, initially aimed at improving business productivity. E-government was seen as the government's version of e-commerce.[34] The concept initially referred only to the idea of improving organizational efficiency by computerizing and making certain services and information available to the public online. Generally speaking, e-gov-

29 OECD. *Rethinking E-government Services: User-centred Approaches*. Paris: OECD Publishing, 2009.

30 AHN, Michael J.; BRETSCHNEIDER, Stuart. Politics of E-Government: E-Government and the Political Control of Bureaucracy. *Public Administration Review*, v. 71, n. 3, p. 414–424, 2011.

31 PHILBECK, Thomas; DAVIS, Nicholas. The Fourth Industrial Revolution: Shaping a New Era. *Journal of International Affairs*, v. 72, n. 1, p. 17–22, 2018, p. 19–20.

32 XU, Li Da; XU, Eric L.; LI, Ling. Industry 4.0: State of the art and future trends. *International Journal of Production Research*, v. 56, n. 8, p. 2941–2962, 2018.

33 BOUNABAT, Bouchaïb. From e-Government to digital Government: Stakes and Evolution Models. *Electronic Journal of Information Technology*, n. 10, p. 8–21, 2017, p. 8–10.

34 FOUNTAIN, Jane E. *Building the virtual state: information technology and institutional change*. Washington, D.C: Brookings Institution Press, 2001, p. 21.

ernment would be the use of information technology to ensure access to information and services, to increase efficiency in delivery and mitigate various management problems.[35] At the same time, there was also the idea of *e-governance*, which would also encompass forms of democratic participation in the direction of public policies and the improvement of administrative efficiency and transparency in a much wider range of formal and informal institutions. It would also comprise instruments for direct participation in the process of drafting laws and regulations, including citizens voting on the direction of these initiatives.[36]

More recently, the concept of e-government has evolved into what is known as *Digital Government*,[37] which is an updated paradigm for the incorporation of information technology in the public sphere. The OECD (Organization for Economic Cooperation and Development), for example, discontinued its series of studies on electronic government, replacing it in 2015 with the OECD Digital Government Studies, which follows this new concept. In the early stages of digitizing public services, the aim was to computerize offices internally, swapping paper for computers, improving the efficiency and productivity of civil servants by incorporating technology in the form of online information provision and basic interaction, but without transforming the essential processes of public service activity and the traditional forms of public relations and citizen service.[38] In the evolution towards Digital Government, not only are the way of working and the internal processes of the offices optimized by technology, but the services themselves are also profoundly altered, including the elimination of stages, requirements, and service structures.[39] The assumptions and objectives of e-government are expanded, following some specific guidelines and foundations that have already been incorporated. The scope of these initiatives goes far beyond the idea of an electronic administration system

35 For several different definitions of e-government according to the paradigm of the time, see BOUNABAT, *op. cit.*, p. 9.

36 *Ibid.*, p. 8–10.

37 VIANA, Ana Cristina Aguilar. Digital transformation in public administration: From e-government to digital government. *Revista Eurolatinoamericana de Derecho Administrativo*, v. 8, n. 1, p. 115–136, 2021.

38 BOUNABAT, *op. cit.*, p. 14.

39 TANGI, Luca *et al.* Digital government transformation: A structural equation modelling analysis of driving and impeding factors. *International Journal of Information Management*, v. 60, p. 10, 2021, p. 10.

that concentrates online services based on a portal,[40] although this remains important. Today's technologies lay the foundations for a transformational government by enabling real-time solutions that foster collaboration and change public policy-making for the better.

Digital Government, in its most recent conception, encompasses five logical stages: e-government itself, open government, data-centric government, fully transformed government and smart government.[41] The first, as mentioned, is the digitization of traditional services into online form, with a view to greater savings in financial resources. The second, called open government, basically encompasses the ideas of government transparency, fostering participation and collaboration,[42] but can also include derived notions, such as Open Source, Open Standards, and Open Policy-Cycle, among others.[43] Data-centric government consists of a change in position with regard to data and information, moving from a more passive stance to one in which the administration proactively explores the possibilities arising from collaboration and participation.[44] In this model, data is not only used to provide related services but also as a source of policy knowledge, guiding the formulation of new public policies.[45] In fully transformed government, the organization or administrative entity is fully engaged in the dynamics of proactive use of data, and in smart government, this practice is ingrained in all public spheres, with the innovative process being an integral and functional part of government action, ready to provide rapid responses even in scenarios of abrupt or disruptive change.[46]

As these stages are not isolated and can also coexist in some cases or simply serve as indicators of maturity, the term Digital Government is more

---

40 WAJSMAN, Samuel ZUCCARO; BLIACHERIENE, Ana Carla. Access to information, transparency and social control in Brazil. *International Journal of Open Governments*, v. 9, p. 165–190, 2020, p. 171.

41 WILLIAMS, Mark; VALAYER, Clementine. *Digital Government Benchmark. Study on Digital Government Transformation*. Brussels: DG Joint Research Centre. European Commission, 2018, p. 16.

42 MCDERMOTT, Patrice. Building open government. *Government Information Quarterly*, v. 27, n. 4, p. 401–413, 2010, p. 401–402.

43 GEIGER, Christian Philipp; LUCKE, Jörn von. Open Government and (Linked) (Open) (Government) (Data). *JeDEM - eJournal of eDemocracy and Open Government*, v. 4, n. 2, p. 265–278, 2012, p. 266.

44 WILLIAMS; VALAYER, *op. cit.*, p. 16.

45 LEONI, Francesco *et al.* Data-centric public services as potential source of policy knowledge. Can "design for policy" help? *Transforming Government: People, Process and Policy*, v. 17, n. 3, p. 399–411, 2023, p. 401.

46 WILLIAMS; VALAYER, *op. cit.*, p. 16.

suitable for the object of study than e-government or other variants, as it is an umbrella term that incorporates all these characteristics, depending on the political, social and economic context of a country or region.[47]

It should be noted that this contradiction - the coexistence of more and less advanced levels - often occurs in practice. At the same time as we are still discussing the implementation of services based on technologies from the early 1990s, such as the digitization of documents, sending information over the internet, and common databases, other technologies are emerging and generating new demands for modernization in the administration. We live with the need to overcome backwardness and, at the same time, create institutions to anticipate the future. This challenges the state's ability to adapt quickly to innovation from outside but also to foster innovation within its own structures. Even when delays are identified in the basic computerization of governments, such as common administrative acts and processes, the most important concern, at the risk of perpetuating the backwardness, is how to bring the culture of efficient, fast, and democratic values-oriented innovation to the state, and how to institutionalize this culture to integrate it into the policy cycle. Although many offices are still struggling to implement the most basic standards of computerization, focusing on the new and preparing for the future are necessary, especially in order to stay connected with the trends and habits of citizens living in the digital market.[48] Therefore, Digital Government should not be considered as an applied set of specific technologies. Otherwise, the reflections on the subject will already be dated and obsolete, and the pace of progress will be lost. It is, in fact, a reinterpretation of public administration based on its adaptation to existing information technology and local social reality in the light of fundamental rights and democracy.[49]

In 2014, the OECD adopted a definition of Digital Government as "the use of digital technologies, as an integrated part of governments' modernization strategies, to create public value".[50] What is not always evident in

47 It should be noted, however, that e-government continues to be the term used by a large number of scholars in Germany, along with *Digitale Verwaltung*.

48 MEHR, Hila. *Artificial Intelligence for Citizen Services and Government*. Cambridge: Harvard Ash Center Technology & Democracy, 2017.

49 REYNA, Justo; GABARDO, Emerson; SANTOS, Fabio de Sousa. Electronic government, digital invisibility and fundamental social rights. *Seqüência: Estudos Jurídicos e Políticos*, v. 41, n. 85, p. 30–50, 2020, p. 43–44.

50 OECD. *Recommendation on Digital Government Strategies*. Paris: Public Governance and Territorial Development Directorate, 2014, p. 6.

definitions like this, although it is implicit, is that Digital Government should always be seen as a kind of innovation,[51] understood as the continuous incorporation, in the public sector, of state-of-the-art technology with the greatest possible potential for realizing opportunities for democracy and state purposes. Many times, especially when using the term "digitization" or "digital transformation" in the public sector, there is the impression that it is a process with a beginning, middle, and end. As a result, an illusion is created that a conclusion is possible, as if Digital Government meant the implementation of a common reform. In addition to creating unrealistic expectations about the outcome of this transformation, this vision limits the potential of Digital Government and also distorts perceptions about the priority and importance of investments and continued dedication to the issue.

It should also be noted that some authors propose adopting the term digital "governance".[52] Governance, according to this line of thought, would be a more appropriate term because it includes processes that are not necessarily state-run, with horizontal and non-institutionalized decision-making structures, in which there is the participation of public actors, but also private ones, such as companies and representatives of civil society.[53] However, besides the fact that the term Digital Government is more widely used in the literature and official documents from governments and international organizations, it is believed that there is a meaningful implication when the definition of government is denied the characteristic of dealing with horizontalized decision-making processes or incorporating the participation of non-state actors. For those who defend an ultra-liberal anti-state agenda, this is a symbolic subterfuge to diminish the importance of government and the state in social life by seeing important policy-making processes as non-public. For those with a radicalized, anti-market statist vision, it is an equally fallacious reinforcement that does not admit private collaboration and the participation of economic power in government issues. For these reasons, the term Digital Government is used to designate the object under study, with an emphasis on the innovative essence of the continuous

51 See CHUNG, Choong Sik. *Developing digital governance: South Korea as a global digital government leader*. London and New York: Routledge, 2020, p. 177.

52 See, for instance, ERKUT, Burak. From digital government to digital governance: Are we there yet? *Sustainability*, v. 12, n. 3, p. 1–13, 2020.

53 VON LUCKE, Jörn; GOLLASCH, Katja. *Open Government: Offenes Regierungs- und Verwaltungshandeln – Leitbilder, Ziele und Methoden*. Wiesbaden: Springer Fachmedien, 2022, p. 3.

transformation of administrative structures and on the classic element of government as the exercise of political power and the determination of the political orientation of a society,[54] even though it is concentrated in the Executive Branch.

In material terms, Digital Government has some contours and characteristics commonly mentioned in works from different disciplines, comprising a set of relevant descriptive elements. In this sense, the OECD drew up the Digital Government Policy Framework (DGPF) as a tool to help governments "identify key determinants for effective design and implementation of strategic approaches for the transition towards digital maturity of their public sectors".[55] Despite its instrumental nature, the framework objectively brings together these essential characteristics of what is generally understood as Digital Government, dividing it into six dimensions: 1. Digital by design; 2. Data-driven public sector; 3. Government as a platform; 4. Open by default; 5. User-driven; and 6. Proactiveness. Exploring them briefly gives an initial overview of the material scope of the studied object, as well as some of its key concepts and terms that will appear repeatedly throughout the work and are often used in specialized literature.

In this way, *digital by design* refers to the incorporation of "digital" into the public policy cycle, which presupposes technological standards, interoperability of systems, formulators and implementers trained in their use (in addition to IT specialists as part of the civil service or hired under other regimes), and political leadership aware of the importance of technology and its transformative potential.[56] The idea that all public services that can be provided digitally should be so guides new government actions and the very creation of new services, rather than being merely a change of channel from the traditional ways of viewing the relationship between government and citizens.[57] This guideline is also referred to as digital by default or digital first.[58]

---

54 BOBBIO, Norberto; MATTEUCCI, Nicola; PASQUINO, Gianfranco (Orgs.). *Dizionario di politica*. 2. ed. Torino: UTET, 1983, p. 489.

55 OECD. *The OECD digital government policy framework: Six dimensions of a digital government*. Paris: OECD Publishing, 2020, p. 6.

56 *Ibid.*, p. 10.

57 BATISTA, André Pereira; CRUZ, Cláudia Ferreira da. Digital by Default: O uso de canais de serviço por cidadãos em cidades. *In*: *XLIII Encontro da ANPAD - EnANPAD*. São Paulo: ANPAD, 2019, p. 1–17.

58 As can be seen, respectively, in MARTI, Michael D.; ESTERMANN, Beat; NEURONI, Alessia C. Die Tallinn-Prinzipien als Wegbereiter der digitalen Transformation des öffentlichen Sektors in der Schweiz. *In*: PLEGER, Lyn Ellen;

Data-driven or data-centric[59] public sector is about recognizing that data is a strategic asset for the government when it comes to planning, implementing, and evaluating public policies. It moves from the idea of a data-informed government, in which data is used in the decision-making process as an accessory element in policy formulation, to the idea that data and how it is handled are the most important elements for the functions of government. This vision includes evidence-based decision-making and the consequent permanent link between government practice and scientific knowledge.[60]

Government as a platform means providing the citizen user with a transparent base of tools, information, and software to meet their needs, in order to bring together, under a public infrastructure, the various solutions and services offered by different entities and organizations.[61]

Open by default means "communicating, informing, consulting and engaging with external and internal actors to co-create public value, crowdsource collective knowledge and build up public sector intelligence based on a design-led culture."[62] With the availability of a vast amount of open data, a more participatory and transparent way of governing is fostered to the extent that citizens and companies can analyze and process the available information and provide feedback either on the adequacy of the government's response to a given issue, or on the development of complementary solutions to public policies. Open data presupposes broad access to government information, except for information that involves some kind

---

MERTES, Alexander (Orgs.). *Digitale Transformation der öffentlichen Verwaltung in der Schweiz: Stand, Entwicklungslinien und Praxisbeispiele.* Wiesbaden: Springer Fachmedien, 2022, p. 306; WIMMER, Maria A. Once-Only und Digital First als Gestaltungsprinzipien der vernetzten Verwaltung von morgen. *In*: SECKELMANN, Margrit; BRUNZEL, Marco (Orgs.). *Handbuch Onlinezugangsgesetz: Potenziale - Synergien - Herausforderungen.* Berlin, Heidelberg: Springer, 2021, p. 147.

59 Some authors distinguish between these two concepts, considering data-centric as a more advanced stage; however, in this context, they will be considered to have the same meaning. DRAHEIM, Dirk; KRIMMER, Robert; TAMMET, Tanel. On State-Level Architecture of Digital Government Ecosystems: From ICT-Driven to Data-Centric. *In*: HAMEURLAIN, Abdelkader; TJOA, A. Min (Orgs.). *Transactions on Large-Scale Data- and Knowledge-Centered Systems XLVIII.* Berlin, Heidelberg: Springer, 2021, p. 168.

60 *Ibid.*, p. 168.

61 OECD, *op. cit.*, p. 21.

62 *Ibid.*, p. 24.

of well-founded secrecy or protection of privacy and personal data.[63] Thus, open data is the starting point for a series of possibilities, whether simply to improve people's experience of government, or to enable new businesses that meet public policy objectives. This is because open data also fosters the vision of government as a platform for new businesses and GovTech companies that develop projects based on open data. Despite being private, these applications are based on the provision of an Application Programming Interface (API) for access to service data collected and processed instantly. The symbiosis between companies that take advantage of business opportunities generated by government actions to make data available or eminently public competencies brings very significant possibilities and can lead to leaps in productivity and efficiency compared to the other two possible ways of organizing services - purely state or purely private.

User-driven means that technology, as a facilitator of relations and public service provision, must be citizen-oriented, i.e., beyond the technical possibilities of improving the efficiency of service provision, it provides and enables means for the active participation of citizens as co-designers and co-creators of public services, inserting them into contexts of participatory processes in real time as joint formulators of public policies.[64] The transparent and active relationship between government and citizens promotes the effectiveness of policies and strengthens citizen confidence in their relationship with the government. This context also includes the Once Only Principle, which states that, ideally, information or documents should only be requested once by the administration from the citizen. In other words, it is required that "information about a citizen or business can be transferred relatively seamlessly from one administration to another, in order to permit that information to be reused, thus relieving the citizen from a tedious burden while increasing efficiency and reducing errors"[65]. The Once Only Principle calls for integration between various state bodies and entities and, consequently, an environment of mutual trust between institutions that share this data, as well as trust between citizens and the government with

63 BOUNABAT, Bouchaïb. From e-Government to digital Government: Stakes and Evolution Models. *Electronic Journal of Information Technology*, n. 10, p. 8–21, 2017, p. 16.

64 *Ibid.*

65 GRAUX, Hans. The Single Digital Gateway Regulation as an Enabler and Constraint of Once-Only in Europe. *In*: KRIMMER, Robert; PRENTZA, Andriana; MAMROT, Szymon (Orgs.). *The Once-Only Principle: The TOOP Project.* Cham: Springer International Publishing, 2021, p. 83.

regard to the processing of personal data in accordance with fundamental rights.

Finally, *proactiveness* refers to the quality of being able to anticipate citizens' needs, in particular, to prevent them from having to take unnecessary and costly action, offering the best possible experience in the combination of the other five dimensions, also playing a relevant role in increasing the level of trust in government.[66]

Each of these digital government guidelines has more refined manifestations and implications, which will be addressed throughout the dissertation in order to relate them to specific legal and political elements, aiming to clarify the less obvious contours of their expressions. The general and summarized view of these characteristics, however, serves as a basis for contextualizing future problematization within the general framework of the idea of Digital Government.

E. Dissertation structure

The dissertation is structured in four chapters. Chapter 1 provides the primary theoretical basis for the proposed analysis, presenting the legal-institutional view and the most important aspects of the method, including how to handle the interdisciplinary research categories and a proposal for the subsequent applied analysis. This section will explain how the Digital Government will be studied as a public policy and how the legal element relates to the political element to form a heuristic analysis model that will be used in the following chapters. These aspects are explored in detail because they form the lens through which all the subsequent applied research was carried out, from the selection of sources to the final arguments. Thus, it is deemed necessary to introduce the reader to the abstract references that make up the concrete examination of policies carried out in the following chapters and which permeate the dissertation's reasoning and narrative, sometimes more visibly, sometimes implicitly, making up the set of contributions that are intended to be original and can also be applied to other public policies.

Chapter 2 will look at the institutionalization of the Brazilian Digital Government, with a critical examination of its institutional trajectory over the years, passing through an analysis of the legislation that forms the legal

66 OECD, *op. cit.*, p. 35.

basis of the arrangement and ending with general critical considerations about the current framework. Although it also has a purposeful descriptive function to inform the reader about the general framework of the Brazilian Digital Government, the idea is to discuss issues that are sensitive to the digitalization of the public sector during the examination of the legislation, and at the end to conclude with an analysis that outlines the main critical factors in determining the current state of affairs and which, in the following chapters, will be explored comparatively and within the larger context of the development of the welfare state.

Chapter 3 discusses the case studies selected to support the arguments of the dissertation and the proposal of alternatives, initially examining three cases of digital transformation in the Brazilian public sector outside the strict idea of government, namely: electronic elections, electronic judicial proceedings, and the Internet governance model. Next, we explore how Digital Government is dealt with in the European Union and, at national level, in Germany. The critical account of these experiences will allow for the comparison of their trajectories with that of the Brazilian Digital Government, thereby laying the groundwork for an exercise in institutional imagination in the final part of the work.

The fourth and final chapter looks at the Digital Government as an expression of the welfare state in Brazil, emphasizing its role in developing the dynamic state capabilities needed to meet the challenges of its consolidation and reconstruction, and exploring alternative institutional paths for these capabilities to be achieved by the Brazilian state through digital transformation.

1 The legal-institutional view as a model for analyzing Digital Government

This chapter introduces the theoretical approach to the legal-institutional view used to achieve the research objectives. In the following sections, the theoretical foundations of the analysis of Digital Government as a public policy will be presented, as well as how politics, law, and legal dogmatics relate to public policies and how the handling of interdisciplinary elements increases the critical potential of the research. Emphasis is placed on the institutional component, in addition to the legal one, since "institutions are most important factors in explaining how information technology is being adopted and used in government".[67] A set of elements specifically designed for the case will also be presented and explored as a heuristic, i.e., a conceptual construction to help in the understanding of what is being studied, as discovery tools that allow us to see new aspects of the phenomenon of interest.[68]

1.1 Digital Government as a public policy

Digital Government is a multidisciplinary and cross-cutting phenomenon and can, therefore, be examined from the perspective of various areas of theoretical and applied knowledge, such as administration, economics, engineering, computing, and political science. As far as law is concerned, various issues related to the topic are dealt with from a dogmatic point of view, in the sense of identifying and solving problems arising from the interpretation and application of normative texts. Also in the dogmatic sphere, the emphasis can be on finding practical problems involving antinomies or gaps in rules, contrasting them with legally qualified social facts in judgments about their adequacy or inadequacy, or even about

67 YANG, Kaifeng. Neoinstitutionalism and E-Government: Beyond Jane Fountain. *Social Science Computer Review*, v. 21, n. 4, p. 432–442, 2003, p. 440; The author also refers to FOUNTAIN, Jane E. *Building the virtual state: information technology and institutional change.* Washington, D.C: Brookings Institution Press, 2001.

68 SWEDBERG, Richard. On the Heuristic Role of Concepts in Theorizing. *In*: *Theory in Action. Theoretical Constructionism.* Leiden: Brill, 2017, p. 24, 36.

their suitability for producing certain desired or teleologically inferred legal effects. This is what can be observed in most of the legal literature on the subject, and works along these lines tend to focus on finely clipped topics, given the immensity of legally relevant subjects on the most diverse issues, norms, and technologies that make up the world of Digital Government. Some current examples are the legal repercussions of the use of artificial intelligence in public administration, data protection in the spheres of government, the digital administrative process, and racial discrimination by state biometric recognition systems, among others. Within each topic such as these, there are other ramifications of issues involving the relationship between law, technology, and government, as well as the application of the law to specific cases and its sufficiency in adequately resolving relevant conflicts generated in this fertile space.

Another approach to the same object is to see the Digital Government as a public policy, as a government action linked to a political agenda, structured by legal and non-legal elements, with actors performing in an arena formed and mediated by legal-institutional arrangements, containing predefined objectives related to the realization of abstractly positive rights. Seen as a public policy, its study assumes different objectives and methods - although sometimes intersecting - from those involved in the aforementioned legal-dogmatic analyses. The concern is less the subsumption of situations to norms and the relationship between legal antecedents and consequents with a view to a decision, and more the relationship between political, economic, and sociological antecedents and consequents, in the light of the law, always oriented towards a regime of maximum effectiveness, considering agenda, means and ends. In this sense, a "policy-oriented approach examines public decision-making from the viewpoint of what concrete actions come out of the political realm".[69]

It is no coincidence that the study of public policy has developed in areas such as economics, political science, sociology, and administration, with a focus on solving problems or understanding implemented actions, intending to improve them or better design future policies that will succeed them, as well as sharing learning for the creation of public policies in other areas, to benefit the generation of this knowledge. In other words, it's

---

69 JOHN, Peter. *Analyzing Public Policy*. 2. ed. London and New York: Routledge, 2013, p. 11.

about seeking to generalize discoveries[70] in order to anticipate and avoid future practical difficulties - in fact, one of the main characteristics of policy sciences.

Policy sciences have been distinguished over the years by three essential characteristics. Firstly, they are problem-oriented, not concerned with a particular phenomenon in itself, but with its impact on the real world. Secondly, they are essentially multidisciplinary, occupying positions in various areas of research. Finally, they are value-oriented, i.e., they recognize in every social problem object a value component and the subject's own values in relation to that object.[71]

Over the years, much of the research in this area has focused on political science, which is a natural consequence of the fact that public policies operate within the framework of the state, with their stages and components permeated by political elements of all kinds, especially in parliaments (major political decision-makers) and governments, and their implementation is related to managers elected by vote or endowed with some form of political legitimacy to carry out their duties. It is particularly characteristic of political science analysis to be concerned with the form of interaction and negotiation between actors and also, fundamentally, to understand the institutional dimension of public policies, their design and their instruments.[72] Even constructs developed in other branches of science have been incorporated in a central way, given the scope and prestige assumed by political scientists on the subject, such as, for example, the discussion on the contexts of organizations in sociology or the economic rationality of agents in economics. An important part of institutional theories in political science is rooted in sociological, economic, and other types of thought,[73] especially the neoinstitutionalist currents,[74] but they tend to neglect the legal aspect of the subject. This does not occur due to a methodological flaw:

---

70 A good example can be seen in SCHARPF, Fritz W. The Joint-Decision Trap: Lessons from German Federalism and European Integration. *Public Administration*, v. 66, n. 3, p. 239–278, 1988, p. 271–273. By identifying a certain set of consequences related to the decision-making process, the author reflects on the possibility of universalizing the findings for institutions other than those specifically studied.

71 DELEON, Peter; MARTELL, Christine R. The Policy Sciences: Past, Present, and Future. *In*: PETERS, B.; PIERRE, Jon (Eds.). *Handbook of Public Policy*. London: SAGE Publications, 2006, p. 32.

72 PIERRE, Jon. Disciplinary Perspectives. *In*: PETERS, Guy; PIERRE, Jon (Orgs.). *Handbook of Public Policy*. London: SAGE Publications, 2006, p. 483, 484.

73 *Ibid.*, p. 486.

74 HALL, Peter A.; TAYLOR, Rosemary C. R. Political Science and the Three New Institutionalisms. *Political Studies*, v. 44, n. 5, p. 936–957, 1996, p. 955.

a conscious delimitation is made and work is done with the consolidated tools in the respective fields of knowledge within the established objectives. On the one hand, this preserves the rigor of the method and the reliability of the results, and on the other, it provides an opportunity for parts of these constructions to be combined with legal categories to expand the epistemological scope of the research.

In this sense, the legal-institutional dimension of a public policy such as the Digital Government refers to a vision that seeks to bring together different aspects of the object of study, but which are closely related and do not rest entirely under any epistemological umbrella. Even so, the proposed investigation belongs essentially to the field of law, despite the intensive use of interdisciplinary resources to extend the possibilities and potential results compared to an analysis restricted to dogmatics.

Without neglecting the usefulness of legal-dogmatic analysis, by extending the method towards the institutional component of the object, the aim is to adopt an objective similar to that of *policy sciences*, especially the problem-oriented view, guided by the objective of understanding the object for practical purposes. As a result of this perspective, values are reaffirmed in the form of rights, such as democracy and development, which sometimes find themselves in delicate contexts, balancing on foundations that are constantly being constructed and deconstructed.

While the "legal" qualification of the legal-institutional dimension is located within the jurisprudence (or, more specifically, in *legal science*, in the civil law tradition), the "institutional" component has a multidisciplinary relationship, just like *policy sciences* in general, which will be dealt with below.

1.2 Policy sciences and the institutionalist contribution

When it comes to social action with collective characteristics or repercussions, references to *institutions*, whether legal, social or economic, are recurrent. Sometimes, they denote organizations, such as universities, foundations, companies, political parties, etc. Other times, they refer to state political bodies, such as parliaments, public administration bodies, and the Judiciary. On other occasions, they refer to abstract sets of rules and relationships repeated over time, such as marriage, the family, and the market. They produce rules, mediate actors' behavior, interact themselves as collective actors in arenas of interest disputes, and relate to each other in intricate webs of arrangements to produce certain results. As already pointed out, digital transformation is conditioned by institutions of various kinds, and understanding them requires examining them from a legal perspective. To do this, however, we must first get to know the traditional institutional approaches, which pave the way for the interdisciplinary analysis of Digital Government as a public policy.

The roots of the institutional view go back to the classical authors of political philosophy. Aristotle, for example, already identified abstract categories such as the polis, the market, and currency as institutions[75] whose performance he analyzed to draw up recommendations and ideas for other institutions.[76] These roots can still be seen, in some way, in various other traditional authors at the base of political science and state theory. Thomas Hobbes, influenced by the political disorganization caused by the English Civil War, called for strong institutions that could protect men from themselves, while John Locke, also in his efforts to develop theories to justify political power, sought to outline liberal structures that anticipated a more democratic path.[77] Montesquieu, for his part, elevated the law, as an abstract entity, to a central element of the state, replacing individual virtues in directing the course of society[78] and, therefore, guiding behavior in a predictable and stable way.

An even more distinctive character of the institutional approach can be seen in Rousseau's work, in that he sees institutions as limiting and corrupting human behavior, while at the same time it is through them that human beings achieve what he calls civil liberty. They do not alter human nature but induce certain behaviors, and, as they are the work of human action, they can also be modified by politics.[79] Tocqueville also observed institutional dynamics, especially the relationship between behavioral cultural elements and institutions. He recognized, for example, that in stable social conditions, institutions tended to prevail over cultural factors when it came to influencing human behavior, while in unstable environments,

75 CRESPO, Ricardo F. Aristotle on agency, habits and institutions. *Journal of Institutional Economics*, v. 12, n. 4, p. 867–884, 2016, p. 874–879.

76 PETERS, B. Guy. *Institutional theory in political science: the new institutionalism.* 4. ed. Northampton, MA: Edward Elgar Pub, 2019, p. 4.

77 *Ibid.*, p. 4.

78 MONTESQUIEU, Charles L. de Secondat, Baron de La Brède et de. *O espírito das Leis.* 4. ed. São Paulo: Martins Fontes, 2000, p. 36.

79 IMMERGUT, ELLEN M. The Theoretical Core of the New Institutionalism. *Politics & Society*, v. 26, n. 1, p. 5–34, 1998, p. 9.

such as the rise of a new order, cultural factors prevailed over institutions.[80] In his best-known work, about the then newly-founded democracy in the United States, in addition to describing in detail the American institutional environment and the factors for its success, he also suggested that, despite differences in nature, habits, and customs between nations, the same democratic institutions could have similar success if transposed to other countries, with the necessary adaptations and precautions,[81] which denotes the thought that institutional conformation plays a central role in conditioning behavioral changes.

In trying to explain the exercise of political power, its origin, and moral justifications, these classical thinkers identified and described the institutions that make up the public aspects of society, culminating in what is now called "old institutionalism" - the root of institutional thinking in political science, and which in the United States produced works focusing on the state, despite the non-statist American political tradition of the time.[82] Old institutionalism also stood out in a relevant way in the field of economics, not as a school of thought, but as an approach characterized by its emphasis on the constitutive aspects of institutions, with considerable practical influence in the interwar period, especially in shaping social and economic policies such as the New Deal.[83]

From the 1940s onwards, behavioralism prevailed in policy analysis, focusing on the behavior of individuals rather than institutions, and considering that the economy and society influenced political institutions in a causal, one-way street. While the old institutionalism left out important political behavioral aspects from analysis, behavioralism did the opposite: it disregarded institutions as the main determining factor in government actions.[84] Behavioralism was notable for its concern with methodology, with great emphasis on quantifying data and bringing its practices closer

80 MEYER, Heinz-Dieter. Tocqueville's Cultural Institutionalism: Reconciling Collective Culture and Methodological Individualism. *Journal of Classical Sociology*, v. 3, n. 2, p. 197–220, 2003, p. 201–202.

81 TOCQUEVILLE, Alexis de. *De la démocratie en Amérique*. Paris: Institut Coppet, 2012, p. 302.

82 PETERS, *op. cit.*, p. 6. The author mentions Woodrow Wilson's "The State: Elements of Historical and Practical Politics: A Sketch of Institutional History and Administration" as an example.

83 COUTINHO, Diogo R. Direito e institucionalismo econômico: apontamentos sobre uma fértil agenda de pesquisa. *Brazilian Journal of Political Economy*, v. 37, p. 565–586, 2017, p. 568–570.

84 PETERS, *op. cit.*, p. 16.

to the objective approaches of the natural sciences to explain political behavior.[85] Post-behaviouralist movements, on the other hand, came to recognize that objectivity and abstraction ended up concealing "the brute realities of politics" and contributing to a kind of social conservatism, and sought to introduce the consideration of ideological biases in the context of the factual analysis of formerly neutral claims.[86]

Another influential line of theory in the following decades is *rational choice theory*, which assumes the rationality of individuals and their search for the best way to achieve their goals and pursue their interests, with the combination of rational actions by the various actors resulting in a balance reflected in the aggregate result.[87] This theory shares with behavioralism the same central premises about the lesser weight given to institutions in determining political and social outcomes, emphasizing, however, that the political behavior of individuals and groups does not stem solely from social and psychological attributes but rather from the propensity to maximize gains according to a rational economic calculation.[88] Objective observation of the behavior of individuals remains important for explaining political outcomes and can be applied to some extent in the case of Digital Government policies, since digital transformation is also influenced and carried out by people, with their own behavioral modes and patterns. However, this view is insufficient to explain certain phenomena without a broader consideration of the structures that shape them, and which may be conditioning or even determining the practical effects,[89] as will be explored later.

Interest in institutions and their roles and dynamics in conditioning human behavior and policy results (outcomes) began to grow again in the

85 SPIRO, Herbert J. Critique of Behavioralism in Political Science. *In*: VON BEYME, Klaus (Org.). *Theory and Politics/Theorie und Politik: Festschrift zum 70. Geburtstag für Carl Joachim Friedrich*. Dordrecht: Springer Netherlands, 1971, p. 319–321.

86 EASTON, David. The New Revolution in Political Science. *The American Political Science Review*, v. 63, n. 4, p. 1051–1061, 1969, p. 69.

87 OSTROM, Elinor. Rational Choice Theory and Institutional Analysis: Toward Complementarity. *The American Political Science Review*, v. 85, n. 1, p. 237–243, 1991, p. 238.

88 PETERS, *op. cit.*, p. 15.

89 As a study on the factors that influenced health system reforms in Europe after World War II has shown: IMMERGUT, Ellen M. The rules of the game: The logic of health policy-making in France, Switzerland, and Sweden. *In*: STEINMO, Sven; THELEN, Kathleen; LONGSTRETH, Frank (Orgs.). *Structuring Politics: Historical Institutionalism in Comparative Analysis*. Cambridge: Cambridge University, 1992, p. 57–89.

1970s. Ronald Coase, Douglass North, and Oliver Williamson developed theories that reflect on some of the premises of institutionalism, placing them as representatives of an "economic new institutionalism", although they do not derive directly from the original institutionalism, notably because they do not adopt dogmas such as the total rejection of neoclassical economic theory.[90]

In political science, the term neoinstitutionalism (or new institutionalism) was coined by March and Olsen in the early 1980s, and broadly included various approaches that revived the idea of the centrality of institutions in understanding public policies and social phenomena.[91] They argued that the concern with organizations and collective decision-making processes had been supplanted by methodological visions centred on the individual, which were insufficient to answer the questions of political life, since the values dear to it emanated from the organizations themselves.[92] Neoinstitutionalism is not simply a return to the old ideas of traditional institutionalism but a "re-reading" of these ideas based on studies that focused on the behavioral and rational aspects of actors and their limitations for understanding certain political phenomena.[93] When we talk about neoinstitutionalism, we are talking about methods of analyzing policies or social and political phenomena that have been developed independently and, therefore, have their own particularities but are characterized by a set of premises and converging aspects, especially the incorporation of the institutional element as the analytical core in reaction to approaches that focus on the behavior of individuals. The approaches most often cited by scholars are the historical, sociological and those that incorporate elements

90 PETROVIĆ, Dragan; STEFANOVIĆ, Zoran. Methodological position(s) of institutional economics. *Facta universitatis - Series: Economics and Organization*, v. 6, n. 2, p. 105–114, 2009, p. 105–106.

91 IMMERGUT, Ellen M. Historical-Institutionalism in Political Science and the Problem of Change. *In*: WIMMER, Andreas; KÖSSLER, Reinhart (Orgs.). *Understanding Change*. London: Palgrave Macmillan UK, 2006, p. 240.

92 PETERS, *op. cit.*, p. 30.

93 MARCH, James G.; OLSEN, Johan P. The New Institutionalism: Organizational Factors in Political Life. *The American Political Science Review*, v. 78, n. 3, p. 734–749, 1984. "By labeling the collection of ideas 'the new institutionalism,' we mean to note the fact that there was indeed an 'old institutionalism,' that cycles in ideas have brought us back to considerations that typified earlier forms of theory in political science. We do not mean to suggest, however, that the new and the old are identical. It would probably be more accurate to describe recent thinking as blending elements of an old institutionalism into the non-institutionalist styles of recent theories of politics."

of rational choice theory. In addition to these, we can also mention the normative, empirical, discursive, constructivist,[94] and actor-centered[95], whose differences and contributions are equally important for the purposes of this work.

From these theoretical strands and the analytical models they have produced, categories and ideas will be extracted which, combined with the tools of legal dogmatics, will serve as a model for analyzing the Brazilian Digital Government and the other national and international experiences examined. Each line of thought, the result of a series of studies applied to various public policies, contributes slightly to the interdisciplinary instrumental framework used in the investigation into digital transformations in the public sector in the following chapters, and for this reason, a brief explanation of each of them is in order.

The normative strand reflects a revisiting of the tradition of institutional theory in political science, which advocates, in short, that institutions have a greater effect on behavior than the characteristics of individuals. According to this view, institutions represent a set of interrelated norms and routines that define actions, considering roles and situations.[96] There is a logic of appropriateness that governs the relationship between organizations and individuals, and the latter's participation is conformed to their integration into this system of rules and routines, which shape their participants by providing systems of meaning for social and political life.[97] In other words, there is an important emphasis on the norms and values that exist in institutions in terms of their relevance to explaining behavior.[98] In summary, it can be said that normative neoinstitutionalism "emphasizes the behavioral impact of standards of appropriateness established by the community's normative and policy commitments".[99] Institutional rules and processes tend to have more influence on individuals' decisions than their personal beliefs, resulting in a kind of loyalty of the person to the institution, which

94 PETERS, *op. cit.*, p. 30–164.

95 See MAYNTZ, Renate; SCHARPF, Fritz W. Der Ansatz des akteurzentrierten Institutionalismus. *In*: MAYNTZ, Renate; SCHARPF, Fritz W. (Orgs.). *Gesellschaftliche Selbstregelung und politische Steuerung.* Frankfurt/New York: Campus Verlag, 1995, p. 39–72.

96 PETERS, *op. cit.*, p. 35.

97 *Ibid.*, p. 31–32.

98 *Ibid.*, p. 31.

99 THOMAS, Daniel C. Explaining the negotiation of EU foreign policy: Normative institutionalism and alternative approaches. *International Politics*, v. 46, n. 4, p. 339–357, 2009, p. 343.

subverts the logic of individual rationality and the search for the maximization of one's interest or worldview. For example, the behavior of a person who is involved in the vote-counting process will tend to be more "loyal" to defending the integrity of the vote than to favoring a candidate of their personal preference.[100] This logic also explains heterogeneous day-to-day political positions, such as that of an ultraliberal who defends the public university because he is part of its teaching staff, or a doctor who defends the minimal state while at the same time recognizing the importance of the Unified Health System[101] in which he practices medicine.

Of course, social culture also plays an important role in the type of process described above. In this regard, the cultural element is emphasized by the sociological strand, especially that influenced by organization theory. Unlike some traditional sociological theories, which sought to see reflected in institutions a kind of ideal rational model of organization of the Weberian bureaucracy, institutional practices reflect, for this strand, a kind of culture, understood here as a set of rituals present in societies in general. Thus, instead of the rational element justifying why an institution and its actors act in a certain way, the explanation lies in the cultural habits of these entities. Institutions then provide cognitive models and schemas that are indispensable for interpreting the behavior of actors, offering meanings to social life and influencing not only the calculated decisions of individuals according to their interests, but also their subjective preferences.[102] These aspects will be explored more specifically in the context of the research in section 1.9.6 below.

Historical neoinstitutionalism, on the other hand, emphasizes the institutional trajectory as relevant to political choices and directions. For public policy, history determines the institutional contexts in which actors make their decisions but also influences the preferences and beliefs of these actors when faced with their choices.[103] Path dependence is emphasized in the studies and has become a characteristic element of them, although it also

100 HOEFER, Richard. Institutionalism as a Theory for Understanding Policy Creation: an Underused Resource. *Journal of Policy Practice and Research*, v. 3, n. 2, p. 71–76, 2022, p. 72.

101 The Unified Health System (SUS) is Brazil's public, free and universal health system, inspired by the British system and introduced in the country by the 1988 Constitution.

102 HALL, Peter A.; TAYLOR, Rosemary C. R. Political Science and the Three New Institutionalisms. *Political Studies*, v. 44, n. 5, p. 936–957, 1996, p. 946–949.

103 STEINMO, Sven. Historical institutionalism and experimental methods. *The Oxford handbook of historical institutionalism*, p. 108–124, 2016, p. 108–109.

borrows its origins from the economic literature on technological evolution, with the important difference that the notions of conflict and power are given prominence in the historical perspective.[104] Another notable element of this strand is the importance given to the veto opportunities provided to certain actors by the institutional designs of policies or policy-making institutions. In addition, the assertion that institutions distribute power unequally is an essential premise of this view, i.e., political conflicts between actors and interest groups are the focus, not only those mediated by institutions but mainly those that are conditioned or shaped by them, to the extent that the choices reflected in institutional designs serve certain interests to the detriment of others in a zero-sum game.[105] Some of the contributions of this line of theory are particularly important for understanding the evolution of digital transformation public policies and the role of law in this process, and will be detailed in the following sections, 1.9.8 and 1.9.9 below.

Rational choice neoinstitutionalism, on the other hand, originated in studies that analyzed political behavior in the United States Congress, and arose to explain an apparent paradox in the application of rational choice theory to understanding that dynamic: according to its logic, one would observe the formation of new legislative majorities in continuous cycles of preference that would tend to instability of decisions, to the extent that a new formation would tend to suppress the determinations made by the previous formation; but what was observed, on the contrary, was considerable stability.[106] The new view of the problem then starts from the same premise of the rationality of the agents of rational choice theory and introduces the institutional element as an important factor in these decision-making processes. Institutions are considered to be a set of rules that generate incentives and disincentives for certain behaviors and which, added to the behavior of the actors to maximize their gains, condition the results in a different way from the equilibrium of initiatives.[107] This approach emphasizes the decision-making process, and its application is usually seen in the analysis of problems involving collective action, such

104 THELEN, Kathleen. Historical Institutionalism in Comparative Politics. *Annual Review of Political Science*, v. 2, n. 1, p. 369–404, 1999, p. 387.

105 HALL; TAYLOR, *op. cit.*, p. 941.

106 *Ibid.*, p. 942–943.

107 PETERS, Guy. Institutional theory. *In*: ANSELL, Christopher; TORFING, Jacob (Orgs.). *Handbook on Theories of Governance*. 2. ed. Cheltenham, Northampton: Edward Elgar Publishing, 2022, p. 326.

as the governance of natural resources.[108] The contributions of this neoinstitutionalist approach are important for understanding the dynamics of incentives present in the general framework of Digital Government policies and, as will be elaborated on later in section 1.9.5 of its legal aspects.

An interesting contribution from German political science is actor-centered neoinstitutionalism, which focuses on how actors - state and non-state - behave in a plural environment and act to shape the institutions with which they relate, beyond being subject to them as mere products of evolution, historical factors or a given structure. Factors in an institutional context interact with other non-institutional factors in a constellation of actors and, through the mediation of different types of interaction, the result is modified action, which in turn feeds back into the cycle.[109] In this sense, this analytical approach seeks to "capture theoretically relevant aspects of the constellations of actors that encompass an entire sector", not limiting itself to political actors and institutions, but including "all those relevant to the respective fields of social regulation".[110] This view also differs from perspectives that see the social environments subject to regulation as amorphous or passive, seeking to highlight how actors interact within institutional structures.[111] In the specific case of Digital Government, the identification of the actors, the legal possibilities and limits of their competences, and the way in which their modes of interaction are legally regulated are useful for composing the applied analysis model, which will be dealt with more specifically in section 1.9.7.

Another important line of analysis, especially when it comes to understanding political dynamics within the government, is the discursive or

108 *Ibid.*, p. 326.

109 MAYNTZ, Renate; SCHARPF, Fritz W. Der Ansatz des akteurzentrierten Institutionalismus. *In*: MAYNTZ, Renate; SCHARPF, Fritz W. (Orgs.). *Gesellschaftliche Selbstregelung und politische Steuerung.* Frankfurt/New York: Campus Verlag, 1995, p. 45.

110 *Ibid.*, p. 44. In the original, "Im akteurzentrierten Institutionalismus wird dagegen versucht, analytische Kategorien für die Erfassung theoretisch relevanter Aspekte der einen ganzen Sektor umfassenden Akteurkonstellationen zu entwickeln. Dabei können wir uns nicht auf politische Institutionen (oder Akteure) beschränken, sondern beziehen alle relevanten Akteure in den jeweiligen gesellschaftlichen Regelungsfeldernmit ein. Damit wird zugleich die >Gesetzgeberperspektive< vieler politikwissenschaftlicher Untersuchungen vermieden, für die die gesellschaftlichen Regelungsfelder mehr oder weniger amorphe und passive Umwelt bleiben; statt dessen wird die Einbindung staatlicher und nichtstaatlicher Akteure in Strukturen betont, die ihr Handeln prägen."

111 *Ibid.*

constructivist line.[112] The objects of this approach are both ideas and discourse.[113] Through discourse, actors engage in processes of elaboration, legitimization, and processing of ideas in institutional contexts. Institutions not only play the role of a structure for restricting or conditioning behavior (incentives, historical paths, normative or cultural frameworks) but also allow actors, through a logic of communication, to position themselves critically in discourse about the institutions themselves and thus contribute to the process of transforming them.[114] Formal structures end up being secondary, in favor of the ideas that members manage and communicate among themselves and with other social actors from outside. Institutional change occurs, in this sense, by changing the very ideas inherent in institutions.[115] The importance of observing ideas and discourses in the context of institutional arrangements and environments is explained further below in section 1.9.10.

Finally, the empirical line of neoinstitutionalism is characterized by the identification of formal rules as determinants of different policy styles, in a comparative context, considering various political systems.[116] The clearest example is the differentiation between parliamentary and presidential systems and the determination of their concrete impacts, including empirical verifications of the political and social effects of each set of rules in a given context.[117] Although it focuses predominantly on macro elements of public policy, its influence can be seen in the comparative parts of this work and in the case studies, especially in chapter 3, which explores very specific cases of digital transformation in the public sector in Brazil and internationally.

It is important to bear in mind that, although there are debates about the advantages and disadvantages of one or other neoinstitutionalist approach,

---

112 Strictly speaking, these are two distinct lines of approach, but they are differentiated by issues whose relevance to this work does not justify detailing them. As such, they will only be treated as a discursive perspective, a more recent development that has permeated more of the researcher's analysis in recent times, according to PETERS, B. Guy. *Institutional theory in political science: the new institutionalism.* 4. ed. Northampton, MA: Edward Elgar Pub, 2019, p. 127.

113 SCHMIDT, Vivien. Discursive Institutionalism: The Explanatory Power of Ideas and Discourse. *Annual Review of Political Science*, v. 11, 2008, p. 321.

114 SCHMIDT, Vivien A. Reconciling Ideas and Institutions through Discursive Institutionalism. *In*: BÉLAND, Daniel; COX, Robert Henry (Orgs.). *Ideas and politics in social science research.* Oxford and New York: Oxford University Press, 2011, p. 48.

115 PETERS, *op. cit.*, p. 129.

116 CAIRNEY, Paul. *Understanding public policy: theories and issues.* London: Bloomsbury Publishing, 2019.

117 PETERS, *op. cit.*, p. 106.

there is nothing to prevent them from being combined[118] depending on the objective of application, or from identifying elements and tools specific to each of them that can be useful in a concomitant way for tackling a problem. This is what Elinor Ostrom does, for example, when dealing with the issue of natural resource governance, combining strategies from various neoinstitutionalist lines of policy analysis to develop a theory of self-organized collective action.[119]

It should also be noted that the contours and essences of the different neoinstitutionalist approaches become more difficult to understand in the abstract, since these methods are intrinsically related to applied policy analysis, so that their postulates, concepts, and differences emerge from research practices and results in the concrete case, and not the other way around. Thus, for example, actor-centered neoinstitutionalism, described in theoretical terms by Renate Mayntz and Fritz Scharpf in 1995.[120] stems from a research model carried out over the previous two decades in the form of attempts to explain different policy choices made by European governments in the economic and employment areas.[121]

In the same way, various notions, tools, and categories that make up these theoretical understandings, although they arise from observing the results of applied research in policy analysis, once they are established in abstract terms, can be applied *a priori* in new concrete analyses, as small hypotheses or as analytical tools that simply help, from the outset, to better understand the object of study. For example, the notion of a veto point, characteristic of historical neoinstitutionalism, was conceived by the comparative observational practice of different legislative systems during concrete policy-making processes and, once assimilated as a category described theoretically as an analytical instrument, it is used as an *a priori* tool: if, at the outset, an observation of policies was carried out and a certain phenomenon or outcome was named as a veto point, in other works, one starts to deliberately look for these veto points as a way

118 SCHMIDT, *op. cit.*, p. 314.

119 OSTROM, Elinor. *Governing the Commons: The Evolution of Institutions for Collective Action.* Cambridge: Cambridge University Press, 2015.

120 MAYNTZ, Renate; SCHARPF, Fritz W. Der Ansatz des akteurzentrierten Institutionalismus. *In*: MAYNTZ, Renate; SCHARPF, Fritz W. (Orgs.). *Gesellschaftliche Selbstregelung und politische Steuerung.* Frankfurt/New York: Campus Verlag, 1995, p. 39–72.

121 SCHARPF, Fritz Wilhelm. *Games real actors play: actor-centered institutionalism in policy research.* Boulder, CO: Westview Press, 1997, p. 36–37.

of diagnosing a dysfunctional problem or outcome. This is also one of the proposals made here, with the interdisciplinary addition of borrowing some of the premises, tools, and categories theorized by political science, based on a vast accumulation of applied work, for use in an eminently legal analysis, with the legal-normative element as a medial point. There are even analyses of digital government policies that are predominantly based on neo-institutionalist models. Mention should be made of the pioneering work of Jane E. Fountain in the early years of the digital transformation of the state[122] and, more recently, Yan Vaslavskiy and Soslan Gabuev, who deal specifically with the neoinstitutionalist approach as a methodological basis for digital government research and its vocation for identifying factors that hinder the incorporation of information technology innovations in the public sector,[123] emphasizing that

> The need to consider neoinstitutionalism as a methodological basis for the study of e-government is based on the institutional nature of the phenomenon of e-government itself, the need to take into account a set of formal and informal conditions of its implementation, which determine the effectiveness of e-government implementation in a particular institutional environment.[124]

These works, however, are exclusively in the field of political science, and do not explore the relationship between political and legal elements, contrary to what is proposed here and will be discussed in detail later.

Nevertheless, before dealing with the relationship of exchange and assimilation of borrowed categories for the objective purposes of understanding and criticizing the legal-institutional dimension of Digital Government, we will contextualize the notion of institution, a component of traditional legal thought itself, especially in public law and the philosophy of law, as a way of establishing a dialogue between the two sciences on a more judicious basis.

---

122 FOUNTAIN, Jane E. *Building the virtual state: information technology and institutional change*. Washington, D.C: Brookings Institution Press, 2001.

123 ВАСЛАВСКИЙ, Ян И.; ГАБУЕВ, С. В. Неоинституциональный подход как методологическая основа исследования электронного правительства. *Вестник МГИМО-Университета*, n. 6(51), p. 60–75, 2016, p. 73.

124 *Ibid.*, p. 61. In the original, "Потребность в рассмотрении неоинституционализма как методологической базы исследования электронного правительства основана на институциональной природе самого явления электронного правительства, необходимости учёта совокупности формальных и неформальных условий его внедрения, которые определяют эффективность реализации электронного правительства в конкретной институциональной среде."

1.3 Institutionalism in the legal world

At the end of the 19th century and the beginning of the 20th century, a line of legal thought emerged as a response to the two dominant currents of the time: legal positivism and jusnaturalism. It began to be developed relatively independently by various scholars with some characteristics in common, including the rejection of the volitional element as essential in law and the consideration of its social character.[125] This view was called legal institutionalism.[126] As part of a broad current of rejection of formalism, it sought to find a solution to the problems created by a conception of law as something imposed from above by a "political superior" and of legal science as the pure and simple management of a logical system of norms and concepts.[127]

In France, the thinking of Maurice Hauriou stands out within this perspective, for whom institutions are ideas that are legally realized and for which the powers necessary for their realization are organized, such as the structuring of bodies. Hauriou conceived of an institutional life cycle through which there is a legally qualified birth, development, and death, always oriented towards the *guiding idea* or work that gives meaning to its existence, supported by an organizational apparatus that allows the exercise of powers necessary for its full realization.[128] For him, the great foundation of public law was not the state, contracts, or the rule of law but corporate institutions, which even had their own internal constitutions and from which positive law emanated.[129] Hauriou's ideas were later developed by his disciples Georges Renard and Georges Gurvitch, who shared the same basic postulates of his institutionalism.[130]

In Italy, Santi Romano drew up the first broad version of an institutionalist theory of law, equating the legal order with an institution, as an organized social form, rejecting the positivist idea of purely state sources of law

---

125 PINTORE, Anna. Institutionalism in law. *In*: *Routledge Encyclopedia of Philosophy*. 1. ed. London: Routledge, 2016.

126 VEITCH, Scott; CHRISTODOULIDIS, Emilios A.; GOLDONI, Marco. *Jurisprudence: themes and concepts*. 3. ed. London and New York: Routledge, 2018, p. 290.

127 LA TORRE, Massimo. Teorías institucionalistas del Derecho (esbozo de una voz de enciclopedia). *Derechos y Libertades*, v. 11, n. 14, p. 103–112, 2006, p. 104.

128 HAURIOU, Maurice. *Aux sources du droit: le pouvoir, l'ordre et la liberté*. Paris, France: Bloud et Gay, 1933, p. 96–98.

129 HAURIOU, Maurice. An Interpretation of the Principles of Public Law. *Harvard Law Review*, v. 31, n. 6, p. 813–821, 1918, p. 815, 817.

130 PINTORE, *op. cit.*

and defending the idea of the spontaneous creation of law in the context of social relations.[131] In Germany, Carl Schmitt, reinterpreting Santi Romano's pluralist vision, considered the state to be an "institution of institutions" in his legal thinking, with the function of protecting and regulating other non-state institutions.[132]

Decades later, in Austria, Ota Weinberger revived the institutional element in his philosophical view, in direct counterpoint to the consolidated theories of the time, such as Hans Kelsen's Pure Theory. Law taken as an institutional fact brings together various elements and characteristics of its own, being at the same time an order of norms, a tangle of legal relationships dependent on it, a system of "real" institutions such as the state and its normative creation activity, and the legal science itself and its dogmatic disciplines.[133] The author named his vision legal neoinstitutionalism, precisely to distinguish it from the traditional legal institutionalism of Maurice Hauriou, Santi Romano, and Carl Schmitt. In Weinberger's view, institutions are structures for action and cooperation between people, bringing together an informational and orientational core about how human action should take place and expectations about the judgment that should be made about them.[134] In this context, institutional facts are distinguished from "brute" facts because of the institutional structure in which they are formed, which assigns them a specific function and meaning according to the set of information it contains. The example cited by the author is that of a coin, which is physically a "brute" fact but becomes an institutional fact when one observes how the object is used within the normative structure of the financial system.[135] In a neoinstitutional theory of law, legal rules do not exist in isolation, but only as part of functional apparatuses. And their very foundation of validity depends on institutional factors (and not

131 LA TORRE, *op. cit.*, p. 104–105.

132 DE WILDE, Marc. The dark side of institutionalism: Carl Schmitt reading Santi Romano. *Ethics & Global Politics*, v. 11, n. 2, p. 12–24, 2018, p. 20. The peculiar use of the idea of "concrete order", and the idea of a political function of guarding the Constitution, served for the jurist to justify the authoritarian legal order of the Nazi regime, but this will not be examined here.

133 WEINBERGER, Ota. Das Recht als Institutionelle Tatsache: Gleichzeitig eine Uberlegung uber den Begriff des Positiven Rechts Abhandlungen und Aufsatze. *Rechtstheorie*, v. 11, n. 4, p. 427–442, 1980, p. 440–442.

134 WEINBERGER, Ota. Neo-Institutionalism: My Views on the Philosophy of Law. *In*: WINTGENS, Luc J. (Org.). *The Law in Philosophical Perspectives: My Philosophy of Law*. Dordrecht: Springer Netherlands, 1999, p. 255.

135 *Ibid.*, p. 256.

transcendental presuppositions), which represents the theory's main point of fracture in relation to Kelsen's Pure Theory of Law. In this sense:

> Neo-institutionalism holds the view that to the realm of valid law belong not only rules of behaviour, power conferring rules, teleological rules and individual norms arising out of processes of norm creation dependent on these rules, but also the system of established legal principles. Valid law is not only what has been explicitly stated by norm creating act, but also what is de facto institutionalized implicitly.[136]

Weinberger later developed work along neoinstitutionalist legal lines together with Neil MacCormick, which he called *Institutionalistischer Rechtspositivismus* (Institutionalist Legal Positivism).[137] Also seeking to break the boundaries of jurisprudence and enter the field of dogmatic disciplines, legal neoinstitutionalism was understood by the author to formulate a neoinstitutionalist constitutionalism, that is, a theory of the constitution from the neoinstitutional legal point of view. On this basis, he explored problems such as the contradictions and dysfunctions of the democratic system and the relationship between the forms of decision-making and the ideals that guide them.[138]

Even though he was not a lawyer by training, Helmut Schelsky, a sociologist, can also be mentioned among the institutionalists. His normative theory brought him closer to the current of legal realism,[139] which can be

136 *Ibid.*, p. 263.

137 MACCORMICK, Donald Neil; WEINBERGER, Ota. *Grundlagen des institutionalistischen Rechtspositivismus.* Berlin: Duncker & Humblot, 1985.

138 WEINBERGER, Ota. Verfassungstheorie vom Standpunkt des neuen Institutionalismus. *ARSP: Archiv für Rechts- und Sozialphilosophie*, v. 76, n. 1, p. 100–118, 1990, p. 118. In the original, "Aufgrund der institutionalistischen Auffassung kann eine gewisse Antwort auf das Problem der Beziehung zwischen den Formen der demokratischen Willensbildung und den materiellen demokratischen Idealen gefunden werden. Die materiellen Prinzipien der Demokratie können als eine Art von Leitideen der demokratischen Institutionen angesehen werden. Sie sind nicht strikte Verhaltensregeln, sondern Zielvorstellungen und regulative Ideen, die in konkreten Analysen entwickelt werden. Sie sind richtungsweisend für die Wertung der Organisation und für die Beurteilung der Funktionalität der Institutionen. Eine angemessene Berücksichtigung der materiellen Grandsätze ist nur dann gewährleistet, wenn man die Demokratie als Beratung, Diskussion und Kritik, und nicht nur als Kampf um Mehrheiten versteht".

139 KRAWIETZ, Werner. Ansätze zu einem Neuen Institutionalismus in der modernen Rechtstheorie der Gegenwart. *JuristenZeitung*, v. 40, n. 15/16, p. 706–714, 1985, p. 708.

considered a form of neoinstitutionalism within the jurisprudence, more distant from Kelsenian thinking compared to Weinberger's approach.[140]

From a different tradition but with relevant influence, the so-called lines of democratic experimentalism by Michael Dorf and Charles Sabel - and more intensely, the version professed by Roberto Mangabeira Unger - can also be cited as institutionalist approaches to the problem of the relationship between law and democracy. Sabel and Dorf analyze US democratic institutions from the point of view of law and democracy. Intending to promote ideas inspired by scientific pragmatism for improving and re-signifying the structures of the relationship between state and society, they present proposals for new mechanisms and institutional interpretations to reaffirm the values and promises of constitutionalism.[141] Unger, for his part, deals in many of his works with the need for and development of legal-institutional analysis methods aimed at what he calls "institutional imagination", a way of redesigning or reinterpreting state institutions with a view to realizing the democratic ideal and citizenship.[142]

Also noteworthy are contemporary legal thinkers who focus on the problems of development, such as the *law and development* movement, as well as studies of comparative institutional analysis in the field of *law and economics*, by scholars linked or not to these movements, including Katharina Pistor and her practice of "institutional autopsies" of different legal systems in order to establish correlations and causalities between the specific functioning of certain institutions and the results of a country's greater or lesser economic and social development. Her work resembles, to a certain extent, the work of economic institutionalists such as North, Coase, and Williamson, but with an emphasis on the legal perspective of the approach, breaking with the traditional inference of simple causality between legal quality and economic development.[143]

As Francesco Pallante points out, classical legal institutionalism was not able to supplant the dominant legal positivism, and several of the ideas it

---

140 WERNER, Petra. *Die Normentheorie Helmut Schelskys als Form eines Neuen Institutionalismus.* 1. ed. Berlin: Duncker & Humblot, 1995.

141 DORF, Michael C.; SABEL, Charles F. A constitution of democratic experimentalism. *Columbia Law Review*, v. 98, n. 2, p. 267–473, 1998.

142 See, for instance, UNGER, Roberto Mangabeira. Legal Analysis as Institutional Imagination. *The Modern Law Review*, v. 59, n. 1, p. 1–23, 1996.

143 See, for instance, MILHAUPT, Curtis J.; PISTOR, Katharina. *Law and capitalism: what corporate crises reveal about legal systems and economic development around the world.* Chicago: University of Chicago Press, 2008.

criticized remain highly influential in the way law is conceived today.[144] That doesn't mean, however, that it hasn't left an important legacy, especially by providing a greater opening for conceptions of law that are less centered on the normative texts, by highlighting the limits of formalism and by emphasizing the problem of the effectiveness of law as central to its understanding, with the idea that the legal order can only be understood in its relationship with the social order.[145] Legal neoinstitutionalism, on the other hand, contributes to the idea that validity is somehow related to recognition by citizens, as a practice of looking to constitutions for answers not only to the interpretation of the law, but also to the problems of collective life.[146]

Although they share similarities and there can sometimes be some conceptual overlap, legal institutionalism is not to be confused with the legal-institutional view we want to apply here. The latter does not aim to incorporate the institutional element into the core of legal thinking but rather to use legal-dogmatic instruments to extend the possibilities of institutional analysis, or else to use categories and elements from institutional theories in political science and economics to increase the usefulness of legal instruments. It must be admitted, however, that the maxim "institutions

144 PALLANTE, Francesco. *Il neoistituzionalismo nel pensiero giuridico contemporaneo*. Napoli: Jovene, 2008, p. 81. "The ideas of order as a product of the command of the sovereign, of sanction as a distinguishing feature of law, of the pre-eminence of the state over society, of the unity, coherence and completeness of the legal system, of the personification of the legislature, of the law as an expression of the general will formed through representation, of interpretation as a return to the intentions of the historical legislator, of judgment as the application of the general and abstract rule to the concrete case, of the strict separation of law and morality . ..., are all elements that, especially when rigidly understood, represented the polemical target of institutionalist arguments". In the original, "Le idee dell'ordine come prodotto del comando del sovrano, della sanzione come tratto distintivo del diritto, della preminenza dello Stato sulla società, dell'unitarietà, coerenza e completezza dell'ordinamento giuridico, della personificazione del legislatore, della legge come espressione della volontà generale formatasi attraverso la rappresentanza, dell'interpretazione come ritorno alle intenzioni del legislatore storico, del giudizio come applicazione al caso concreto della regola generale e astratta, della rigorosa separazione tra diritto e morale ..., sono tutti elementi che, specie se rigidamente intesi, rappresentarono il bersaglio polemico delle argomentazioni istituzionaliste".

145 *Ibid.*, p. 83.

146 *Ibid.*, p. 234. It should also be noted that the author places Herbert Hart among the theorists with some identification with legal neoinstitutionalism, among other reasons because of the idea of the norm of recognition.

matter"[147] conditions the way public policies are legally thought about when institutional expressions in the legal world are highlighted. This can be seen to some extent in the more recent manifestations of legal institutionalism mentioned above and in some of their interpretations, especially the comparative and prospective ones. In the effort to understand how legal and non-legal institutions interact and function to produce the current Digital Government framework in Brazil, the institutional component will always be present, including in processes of legal interpretation, even if we try to organize this process methodologically. The following topics will explain how we intend to relate the institutionalist approaches of political science and law for the purposes of this work, as well as outlining the limits and criteria of interdisciplinarity that will guide the analysis of public policies related to the development of Digital Government.

1.4 From policy sciences to law

Just as different methods can be combined in the analysis of public policy from the perspective of political scientists, some of these elements can also be used, with discretion, in the field of legal studies. This is particularly true for studies focused on analyzing public policies and their components, as these elements can help broaden the understanding of the political-legal effects of the structuring norms of government action.

Analytical approaches, although they have theoretical orientations and premises, are sets of elements and general categories aimed at explaining phenomena, and their practical applicability is the advantage of identifying and ordering empirical facts in relation to the object of investigation.[148] This approach seeks to combine interdisciplinary elements from neoinstitutionalism with the legal view, considering the characteristics of the object of study (the legal-institutional dimension of Digital Government) within the contours of the general theory of the state. The choice is not arbitrary because it stems from the realization that a complex, multidisciplinary

147 DIMAGGIO, Paul. The New Institutionalisms: Avenues of Collaboration. *Journal of Institutional and Theoretical Economics (JITE) / Zeitschrift für die gesamte Staatswissenschaft*, v. 154, n. 4, p. 696–705, 1998, p. 699.

148 MAYNTZ, Renate; SCHARPF, Fritz W. Der Ansatz des akteurzentrierten Institutionalismus. *In*: MAYNTZ, Renate; SCHARPF, Fritz W. (Orgs.). *Gesellschaftliche Selbstregelung und politische Steuerung*. Frankfurt/New York: Campus Verlag, 1995, p. 40.

phenomenon that is essentially structured by political and legal elements, such as Digital Government, demands this type of analysis.

The relationship between (neo)institutionalism and law can be inferred, at first, from a representation of the binomial of law and politics, considered to be the "primeval interdisciplinarity".[149] The study of public policies with a focus on institutions could be promising for increasing the usefulness of the tools of the legal science. In the opposite and complementary way, a precise understanding of the legal elements of these institutions and the political environments and systems in which they are inserted, using the tools of dogmatics, can also serve to complement the political scientist's view of certain phenomena and ensure that more accurate results are obtained.

This field of possibilities is best understood in practice by analyzing some neoinstitutionalist works applied to central institutions of legal thought, such as judicial bodies. Let's take as an example two "pure" works in political science on the role of constitutional courts in Brazil and Italy, respectively.

Firstly, Matthew Taylor analyzes the veto points provided by the structure of the Brazilian judicial organization and how certain specific actors were able to exercise veto opportunities in a privileged manner due to this structure. Consequently, they actively contributed to the termination of two policies (which he considered good ones), even before they could produce effects, due to their foundational norms being declared unconstitutional by the Federal Supreme Court (STF). Taylor examines two measures taken at the initiative of the Brazilian government but passed by the National Congress in the form of a law - subject, therefore, to formal and material constitutionality control. The first refers to an increase in social security contributions on the salaries of civil servants,[150] and the second deals with a set of measures that facilitated the expropriation of land for agrarian reform purposes, but tightened the penalties for trespassing. According to Taylor, both reforms were substantively appropriate. In the first case, the Brazilian state was undergoing a fiscal crisis and required greater funding to sustain important activities. In the second case, there was a need for a

149 BUCCI, Maria Paula Dallari. Law and Public Policy in Brazil and the United States: A North-South Dialogue. *SSRN Electronic Journal*, 2022, p. 8.

150 The author does not mention the case number in his article, but it was found that, in the first situation, it is about Law No. 9,783/1999, dealt with by the Federal Supreme Court in ADI-MC/2010 DF, Rapporteur: Celso de Mello. Judgement Date: 30/09/1999. Full Court.

better resolution of the agrarian issue in the country, aiming to positively and negatively deter land conflicts, such as land occupations by popular movements. The author concludes that, due to the rules of access to the court, certain political actors had privileged access to it and, consequently, to the exercise of veto opportunities that were decisive in stopping the two policies.[151]

Taylor's article has important merits, but he did not try to understand the legal aspects of the two policies in question and the legal fundaments of the decisions that declared them unconstitutional. On the contrary, he took the Court's decisions as purely political actions, even those "privileged" initiatives by political actors to appeal to the Court against the measures. The consequence of this is a loss of opportunity to identify the real extent and influence of this so-called privileged access to the constitutional court, since if the legal element were introduced into the analysis, this variable could be isolated from the rest and the result more precise.[152]

When analyzing the court's decision in the case of the increase in the social security contribution, for example, it can be seen that the grounds for declaring it unconstitutional were the lack of constitutional provision for the possibility of creating progressive rates of social security contributions and the fact that, in the court's opinion, the total sum of the taxation of income violated the principle of the prohibition against confiscatory taxes, both very reasonable arguments with great legal force. Given this, the question arises: if the policies that were the subject of the claim were more in line with Brazil's constitutional text, would the STF have been as inclined to make the decision it did? And would the Brazilian Bar Association (OAB) have proposed the Direct Action for the Declaration of Unconstitutionality (ADI) in the first place? The plausibility of the violation of an important right for the population certainly weighed heavily in the decision to file the suit. If Taylor's article had, for example, made a legal analysis of the plausibility of the right invoked for the declaration of unconstitutionality, it would have obtained a more consistent result on the real impact of the veto points he correctly identified in the Brazilian judicial institutional structure.

---

151 TAYLOR, Matthew M. Veto and Voice in the Courts: Policy Implications of Institutional Design in the Brazilian Judiciary. *Comparative Politics*, v. 38, n. 3, p. 337–355, 2006.

152 A similar observation about the same work, in a different context, was made earlier in VALENTE, Sergio Ruy David Polimeno. *Políticas públicas e a visão jurídico-institucional: o caso do saneamento básico no Brasil.* Master's thesis, University of São Paulo, 2018.

The second example is a study by Mary Volcansek, also in the field of political science, in which she considers European constitutional courts not only as veto points/opportunities to be exercised by external political actors but as real veto players of public policies in themselves, to the extent that the political component motivating their decisions is sometimes underestimated.[153] Unlike Taylor's essay, Volcansek does not ignore the fact that there is an important - and preponderant - legal element to the outcome of judicial action and thus seeks to isolate this variable from the analysis to determine the real extent of the behavior of constitutional courts as political veto players, as common actors in the processes of public policy dynamics. The problem, however, lies in how she does this, using a logic that does not use the tools that legal dogmatics would provide. The following excerpt summarizes the issue well and illustrates this implicit limitation of the vision:

> [...] in his recent exposition of veto player theory, George Tsebelis (1999: 591) argues that 'the fundamental political differences between countries are generated by the number of veto players' and adds that this applies equally to presidential and parliamentary systems. Whereas he only alludes to courts, I have placed them as competitive institutional actors whose veto sets the parameters for legislative-executive bargaining, either tacitly or explicitly, and thereby allows courts to act in concert with other institutional players to block or to achieve policy change. This is distinct from the more typical conception of courts as external to the policy-making process. First, it moves courts from a position external to the process and places them in political space. Second, it rejects the legal model that implies a static, fixed set of legal rules, applied indifferently. The legal model and its translation at the macro level of analysis to courts as posing fixed external points assumes that courts merely follow the law and seek legal accuracy and legal clarity. *Indeed, the legal model undoubtedly animates much of what courts and constitutional courts do, but that implies a consistency in the actions of the court. If the constitution has not changed, how can the guardian of constitutional rules read those rules differently from time to time?* The legal model denies that courts have any discretion or political motivations. Courts constitute fixed pos-

153 VOLCANSEK, Mary L. Constitutional courts as veto players: Divorce and decrees in Italy. *European Journal of Political Research*, v. 39, n. 3, p. 347–372, 2001.

itions only to the extent that other institutional actors involved in making policy do as well.[154] (emphasis added).

The question posed by the author, despite its rhetorical nature, loses consistency in the eyes of jurists, especially constitutionalists who are concerned with explaining and legally justifying the alteration of constitutional precedents in the civil law system. The *theory of constitutional mutation*,[155] for example, is a dogmatic construction which, if mastered by the scholar, would make the analysis much richer and more precise. This theory explains why and how constitutional norms can change even when there is no change in the normative text and, consequently, why a court would decide according to the new meaning of the norm, without necessarily being driven by a political agenda. The concept of constitutional mutation (*Verfassungswandlung*), as opposed to constitutional reform (*Verfassungsänderung*), in which the text is changed, has been known since Jellinek, in the civil law legal tradition.[156] In the common law tradition (except for England, which doesn't have a written constitution as such but a set of constitutional instruments that is inferred from the combination of different texts),[157] this is taken to a broader level when recognizing, for example, the profound American constitutional transformation as a result of the assimilation, in legal thought, of historical processes of social transformation, still informed by eminently political factors, according to Bruce Ackerman,[158] which is not to be confused with political action by a judicial court. Of course, the hypothesis put forward by the author about the preponderantly political motivations of a court can also occur and is more easily identified in these situations, but they certainly do not apply to all circumstances.[159] Mastery of the dogmatic-legal tool, in this case, could help the analyst to separate "the chaff from the wheat", isolating the legal variable in a precise and not

---

154 *Ibid.*, p. 367; In the excerpt, the author cites TSEBELIS, George. Veto Players and Law Production in Parliamentary Democracies: An Empirical Analysis. *American Political Science Review*, v. 93, n. 3, p. 591–608, 1999.

155 As it is known in Brazil, with no precise translation into English.

156 JELLINEK, Georg. *Verfassungsänderung und Verfassungswandlung eine staatsrechtlich-politische Abhandlung*. Berlin: Häring, 1906.

157 BIRKINSHAW, Patrick J. *European Public Law: The Achievement and the Challenge*. 2. ed. Alphen aan den Rijn: Wolters Kluwer Law & Business, 2014, p. 167.

158 ACKERMAN, Bruce. Constitutional Politics/Constitutional Law. *The Yale Law Journal*, v. 99, n. 3, p. 453–547, 1989.

159 This a very current debate, and has been carried out with great intensity over the review of the Roe vs. Wade case in the United States, to cite one example.

fictitious way and tending towards better results, including for the purposes of a study in political science.

But if the text in question unintentionally highlights a flaw or limitation of method in the analysis of situations in which the legal element is relevant, it also has the merit of pointing out the limits and flaws of a purely legal-dogmatic analysis of the actions of constitutional courts, which she calls the "legal model". By ignoring things such as ideology, interests, beliefs, etc., this model is also insufficient to adequately explain the behavior of judicial institutions and the results of their judgments. Volcansek's work, therefore, indirectly and unintentionally points out the limitations of the unidisciplinary approach of both political science and law for the analysis of a multidisciplinarily complex object.

Similar limitations can be seen in empirical studies in political science that seek to explain phenomena with major legal implications. Josephine Andrews and Gabriella Montinola's work examines 35 emerging democracies in terms of the number of veto players and the system of government in order to propose possible causal relationships between these factors and the degree of rule of law in each of these nations. The conclusions are that the greater the number of veto players, the greater the degree of rule of law in a country, and that countries with presidential systems tend to have a lower degree of rule of law compared to parliamentary systems.[160] The analysis ignores elements dear to legal sociology about the preponderance of patrimonialist traditions and their reflection in the public-private socio-legal relations of the 14 Latin American countries included in the sample, or idiosyncratic characteristics of the origin and evolution of the presidential systems of government of many of these nations, from the historical perspective of law or the general theory of the state, as well as purely legal factors that are preponderant in the rule of law indicators used. Although this is a conscious methodological approach, it restricts the article's conclusions to showing a correlation, when it could be a more precise suggestion of causality.

The complex relationship of interdisciplinary elements seems to be better understood in German political science, for example, when Fritz Scharpf suggests that the constitutional courts' monopoly on legal interpretation alters the distribution of power when it comes to formulating public policy

160 ANDREWS, Josephine T.; MONTINOLA, Gabriella R. Veto Players and the Rule of Law in Emerging Democracies. *Comparative Political Studies*, v. 37, n. 1, p. 55–87, 2004.

by creating veto points for parliamentary groups large enough to supplant the quorum for constitutional reform of a decided issue. He also criticizes the limitation of legal discourses themselves, when he says that they lack "the theoretical and methodological tools for a real analysis of the social problems that need regulation or the incentive effect of constitutional decisions on the behavior of political actors".[161] The author also discusses the effects of these limitations, pointing out that jurists end up reinforcing or perpetuating pre-established tendencies, since the deductive logic of legal discourse generalizes the decision-making premises drawn from the *Zeitgeist*, and at the same time protects them against attempts at change that could occur as a result of the constitutional judgment itself.[162]

Mention should also be made of Britta Rehder's work, which provides a detailed analysis of the behavior of the German labor courts in the light of the analytical model of actor-centered neoinstitutionalism, but which differs from traditional works in political science by substantially incorporating the legal element.[163] Part of the book even describes in detail the internal workings of the Federal Labor Court in terms of the rules of judicial organization, as well as clearly presenting aspects of procedural and substantive labor law, and their complex relationship with institutional factors and the orientation and action of the most diverse actors who are in some way involved in the evolution of labor relations in Germany, especially with regard to the law of collective bargaining agreements.[164] The following excerpt illustrates an overview of the object of study, which involves multiple factors:

> The various actors in industrial relations operate within a complex institutional framework that organizes the interaction of four closely intertwined arenas: the company, the collective bargaining arena, the political system, and the legal system. The complexity of the rules means

161 SCHARPF, Fritz W. Recht und Politik in der Reform des deutschen Föderalismus. *In*: BECKER, Michael; ZIMMERLING, Ruth (Eds.). *Politik und Recht.* Wiesbaden: Springer-Verlag, 2006, p. 329. In the original, "Ihnen fehlen die theoretischen und methodischen Instrumente für eine Realanalyse der regelungsbedürftigen gesellschaftlichen Probleme oder der Anreizwirkung verfassungsrechtlicher Entscheidungen auf das Verhalten der politischen Akteure".

162 *Ibid.*, p. 329.

163 REHDER, Britta. *Rechtsprechung als Politik: der Beitrag des Bundesarbeitsgerichts zur Entwicklung der Arbeitsbeziehungen in Deutschland.* Frankfurt am Main: Campus-Verl, 2011.

164 *Ibid.*, p. 93–324.

> that both the distribution of responsibilities between the actors and the scope of the respective legal norms are unclear. In this context, lawyers provide indispensable expertise for all actors, both in interpreting and organizing the rules and in shaping institutions in terms of legal policy. The liberalization of collective labor law and, in this context, the development of the favorability principle (*Günstigkeitsprinzips*) can be described as a process in which various expert groups and their political coalition partners compete for recognition as epistemic communities and shape the political process: by influencing the formation of actor preferences, by supporting (or hindering) coalition building, and by sitting as gatekeepers in crucial positions of power, especially in the ministerial administration and the courts.[165][166]

We should also highlight the work of Ronald Lhotta, a political scientist with a legal background, who also used the analytical approach of neoinstitutionalism (tending towards the normativist and sociological sides) to analyze problems involving legal institutions, in which the field of dogmatics served to enrich its descriptive (problem setting) and prescriptive (in terms of the results obtained) potential. It should be noted that the author has not only written works on political science incorporating the legal

165 *Ibid.*, p. 91 In the original, "Die verschiedenen Akteure der industriellen Beziehungen bewegen sich in einem komplexen institutionellen Regelwerk, das das Zusammenspiel von vier eng verflochtenen Arenen organisiert: Betrieb, tarifpolitische Arena, politisches System und Rechtssystem. Die Komplexität der Regeln führt dazu, dass sowohl die Zuständigkeitsverteilungen zwischen den Akteuren als auch der Geltungsbereich der jeweiligen Rechtsnormen uneindeutig sind. Juristen liefern hier ein für alle Akteure unverzichtbares Expertenwissen, sowohl bei der Interpretation der Regeln und ihrer Ordnung als auch bei der rechtspolitischen Gestaltung der Institutionen. Die Liberalisierung des kollektiven Arbeitsrechts und in diesem Zusammenhang die Entwicklung des Günstigkeitsprinzips können als ein Prozess beschrieben werden, in dem verschiedene Expertengruppen und ihre politischen Koalitionspartner als epistemische Gemeinschaften um Geltung konkurrieren und den politischen Prozess prägen: indem sie die Bildung von Akteurpräferenzen beeinflussen, indem sie die Koalitionsbildung unterstützen (oder behindern) und indem sie als Gatekeeper an entscheidenden Stellen der Macht sitzen, vor allem in der Ministerialverwaltung und an den Gerichten".

166 Another analysis with mixed characteristics, based on the method of historical and sociological neoinstitutionalism, is carried out by Maria Abad Andrade on the structuring of the decision-making process in the Turkish Constitutional Court and the institutional impacts on the material results of the decisions. ANDRADE, Maria Abad. *Verfassungsgerichtliche Entscheidungsfindung und ihre Folgen: Das Türkische Verfassungsgericht zwischen Mehrheitslogik und Konsensverfahren*. Baden-Baden: Nomos, 2020.

element into his analysis but also works on law in which he proposes the use of the categories of neoinstitutionalism for a better understanding of the legal phenomenon.[167] He also deals with the relationship between neoinstitutionalism and public law, as when he compares the normative neoinstitutionalism of March and Olsen with Hermann Heller's general theory of the state, which would have anticipated several of the neoinstitutionalist findings and analytical categories as early as the 1930s.[168]

Advancing the shift from the political to the legal perspective, and within this same interdisciplinary context, the proposal made by Stefan Oeter in the field of international law is noteworthy, as it advocates addressing the issue of the configuration of an international legal order in light of actor-centered neoinstitutionalism. The author emphasizes that the effort does not consist of a social science perspective but of a legal view of the international order enriched by the contributions of these theories.[169] It is a particularly interesting piece of writing because it applies part of the neoinstitutionalist method to a legal study that does not focus on the judicial body but on a governance structure, albeit with the idiosyncrasies of international relations and its polycentric power. Although neoinstitutionalist approaches have already been mentioned in studies of international politics,[170] the combination of the legal and political elements in relations between nations stands out as an innovative way of understanding the subject.

---

167 LHOTTA, Roland. Europäische Mehrebenengovernance und das Bundesverfassungsgericht. *In*: ARNAULD, Andreas von; HUFELD, Ulrich (Orgs.). *Systematischer Kommentar zu den Lissabon-Begleitgesetzen*. 2. ed. Baden-Baden: Nomos, 2018.

168 LHOTTA, Roland. Der Staat in uns: Hermann Hellers etatistischer Neo-Institutionalismus avant la lettre. *In*: FRICK, Verena; LEMBCKE, Oliver W. (Orgs.). *Hermann Hellers demokratischer Konstitutionalismus*. Wiesbaden: Springer Fachmedien, 2022, p. 85–117.

169 OETER, Stefan. *The global legal order: an international lawyers' perspective inspired by institutionalism*. Bremen: University of Bremen, Collaborative Research Center 597: Transformations of the State, 2009, p. 1, 2, 11.

170 See KECK, Otto. Der neue Institutionalismus in der Theorie der Internationalen Politik. *Politische Vierteljahresschrift*, v. 32, n. 4, p. 635–653, 1991. The author discusses the emergence of institutionalist views of international relations and the potential of neoinstitutionalist approaches to overcome some of the impasses between theories such as realism and functionalism in international relations; For a more general overview of neoinstitutionalist theories in international relations, see SCHIEDER, Siegfried. Institutionalismus in den Internationalen Beziehungen. *In*: SAUER, Frank; MASALA, Carlo (Orgs.). *Handbuch Internationale Beziehungen*. Wiesbaden: Springer Fachmedien, 2017, p. 177–214.

In Brazil, a growing number of studies seek to make interdisciplinary categories of analysis compatible with predominantly legal views of state phenomena. The Law and Public Policy approach, emblematic of this trend, is an interdisciplinary method for a legal view of public policies that has developed a lot in recent years and also deals with other centralities than that of the courts. It has been used - and in the process, co-developed - by various applied Brazilian studies, under the theoretical umbrella of a legal view of public policies that does not claim to be an autonomous branch of law but rather an analytical approach, starting from public law and incorporating findings, premises and elements from other fields of knowledge as method resources, while at the same time valuing legal dogmatics as a veritable "toolbox" available to the researcher. Maria Paula Dallari Bucci, in a monograph on the subject, systematized the bases for a general understanding of the approach, proposing the examination of policies from macro, meso and micro-institutional perspectives,[171] and seeing public policies as government action programs made up of various legally regulated processes, including the legislative process and the judicial process, but going further and adding the budgetary, electoral and administrative aspects, among others.[172] In a convergent line, within economic law, Diogo Coutinho outlines the analysis of public policies from the perspective of the development problem.[173]

As already mentioned, the work of American political science on legal systems has the merit of changing the focus of attention from legislative process and power, shifting the gaze to judicial institutions, which are naturally more identified with the field of jurists. Subsequently, the aforementioned works of contemporary German political science demonstrate how the legal element, including the mastery of dogmatics and the handling of hermeneutics on rules of substantive law, can be incorporated into neoinstitutionalist studies to result in richer and more precise analyses of the objects. The law and public policies approach, in turn, completes this journey, extending the analytical vision beyond the Legislative and Judicial Branches, dealing primarily with government action, taken eminently within the scope of the Executive Branches, presupposing scale, regulation by

---

171 BUCCI, Maria Paula Dallari. *Fundamentos para uma teoria jurídica das políticas públicas*. São Paulo: Saraiva, 2013, p. 45–48.

172 *Ibid.*, p. 109–110.

173 COUTINHO, Diogo Rosenthal. O Direito econômico e a construção institucional do Desenvolvimento democrático. *Rei - Revista Estudos Institucionais*, v. 2, n. 1, p. 214, 2016.

legal rules and objectives oriented towards the realization of social rights, but still deeply related to the action of parliaments, courts and various other actors performing within the legally regulated processes characteristic of public policies in general. We can cite three examples of monographs in law that have specifically used historical neoinstitutionalism as support for the legal analysis of public policies: in a previous work by this author, an attempt was made to shed light on the legal-institutional aspects of basic sanitation in Brazil, identifying institutional dysfunctions and bottlenecks;[174] Carlos Toledo examined the trajectory of policies related to teaching careers in Brazil;[175] and Gabriela Sales sought to establish the legal resilience factors of public policies based on systems, comparing three Brazilian social policies.[176]

These works have in common the fact that they have focused on the historical strand of neoinstitutionalism, especially some of its most distinctive characteristics, in addition to the basic premise that institutions condition human behavior: there is a relationship between path dependence and unequal institutional distribution of power. This concentration did not happen by chance, but denotes an essential aptitude of the history line to help understand policies with certain specific characteristics, such as those chosen by the authors: both basic sanitation, the teaching career, and the national health, social assistance and education systems are policies that are the result of a complex and nuanced evolutionary process over the years, which have passed through various political, ideological, electoral and social conjunctures, coups d'état, dictatorship and democracy, a more liberalizing or socializing state and various constitutions and legal orders, being the subject of disputes between interests and organized groups, whether in their creation and reform, or in their interpretation and implementation. An attentive look at the historical trajectory of each of them, with an emphasis on illuminating how various interests confronted and interrelated in the dispute over the direction of public policies, the component arrangements, and the very scope and legal meaning of their formative norms, beyond their formal positivization, has thus proven to be a necessary methodological trait.

---

174 VALENTE, Sergio Ruy David Polimeno. *Políticas públicas e a visão jurídico-institucional: o caso do saneamento básico no Brasil.* Master's thesis, University of São Paulo, 2018.

175 TOLEDO, Carlos José Teixeira de. *Políticas Públicas e Valorização do Professor da Educação Básica.* Belo Horizonte, MG: Fórum, 2022.

176 SALES, Gabriela Azevedo Campos. *Estado social e federalismo: a institucionalização dos sistemas de políticas públicas no Brasil.* Belo Horizonte, MG: Fórum, 2023.

The approach proved to be very appropriate for demonstrating the theses proposed and for clarifying the extent and form of interaction between the legal and political components that made up the critical success or failure factors of the public policies analyzed. This dissertation is based on a similar approach but seeks to develop it in detail in order to format a broad model of analysis to be applied to Digital Government, which, as a policy on policies, multisectoral and transversal, benefits from a more comprehensive vision. This implies the extensive incorporation of the contributions of the neoinstitutionalist lines mentioned in section 1.2 and, in addition, their reception in the field of law, in a different way, but inspired by the visions presented in section 1.3. This is not only so that they make sense to jurists, but also so that they break the epistemological limits of policy science and traditional legal institutionalism. Once the relationship between neoinstitutionalism and the legal view of public policy is clearer, the next topics will explain how law and its dogmatic tools fit into policy analysis from a legal-institutional perspective.

1.5 The role of law in public policy

Joseph Raz[177] lists four primary functions of law, which are: 1) preventing undesirable behavior and, consequently, protecting the desirable; 2) providing the means for private arrangements between individuals; 3) providing services and redistributing goods; and 4) defining disputes.[178] In addition to these, there are two secondary ones, which are the provision of conditions and means for changing the law itself and the regulation of the application of the law by state bodies.[179] One can think of a multitude of other functions, deriving from or complementing those already mentioned, varying according to the nature and point of view of the analysis, but also those that highlight political struggles, such as the maintenance of patriarchy (according to feminist theories of law) or the structure of eco-

177 RAZ, Joseph. *The authority of law. Essays on law and morality.* New York: Oxford University Press, 2009, p. 169–172.

178 The author distinguishes between unregulated disputes and regulated disputes, the first being situations in which the material law is not clear and therefore procedures are established for resolution by courts and bodies, and the second, of clear application, with no possibility of change by courts. The primary function refers only to the first situation, but is not important in the present context.

179 RAZ, *op. cit.*, p. 175.

nomic production and the submission of the proletariat to its conditions (Marxist theories).[180] Or one can start from the view of key institutions of capitalism, such as the market and private property: when the role of the state (and therefore law) in the creation and maintenance of these institutions is highlighted, as opposed to a view that naturalizes them as social facts or presuppositions, contributing to their desacralization and ideally promoting them as objects that can be changed in their essence by political choice.[181] Richard Posner, on the other hand, by identifying the nature of common law with the quest to promote economic efficiency,[182] brings what could be the object of law into the category of presupposition and ethical theory underlying law itself, relegating its function to correcting market failures, such as externalities, instead of enabling its systemic reimagining.

However, it is the effects, combined with the orientations and preferences of the actors involved in its creation, application, and appreciation, that will define the functions of law in a given context.[183] In this sense, research into the function of law with an emphasis on the cause-effect relationship, especially in comparative studies, can shed light on the correlations between different models of society and their degree of development and explain their greater or lesser capacity to respond to social crises and demands.[184]

An important characteristic of law that is particularly relevant to the field of public policy concerns its relationship with politics, both in its restrictive aspect of state power and in its stabilizing character of political choices, especially by "juridifying" these choices, creating norms as products of them. Law has a combined two-sided function: limiting the exercise of

---

180 GREEN, Leslie. The functions of law. *Cogito*, v. 12, n. 2, p. 117–124, 1998.

181 COUTINHO, Diogo R. Direito e institucionalismo econômico: apontamentos sobre uma fértil agenda de pesquisa. *Brazilian Journal of Political Economy*, v. 37, p. 565–586, 2017, on the functions of law in the thought of Thorstein Veblen, Douglass North and Ha-Joon Chang.

182 POSNER, Richard A. *The economics of justice*. Cambridge, Mass: Harvard University Press, 1981, p. 103–106.

183 BURCHARDT, Dana. The Functions of Law and their Challenges: The Differentiated Functionality of International Law. *German Law Journal*, v. 20, n. 4, p. 409–429, 2019, p. 410.

184 See MILHAUPT, Curtis J.; PISTOR, Katharina. *Law and capitalism: what corporate crises reveal about legal systems and economic development around the world*. Chicago: University of Chicago Press, 2008. The authors compare different environments and institutional arrangements in countries such as the USA, Russia, China, Korea, Japan and Germany, in critical situations, emphasizing the functions of law in each of them and contributing to their outcome.

power and promoting the exercise of power,[185] i.e., it simultaneously creates barriers and constraints to the exercise of political power and provides an organizational infrastructure that enables and encourages this exercise on a legitimate basis.[186] Law also has an adjacent function of an expressive nature, with the potential to readjust or reframe social or moral norms whose effectiveness is compromised.[187] Public law has a communicative function regarding the meaning and scope of actions, especially in the government/citizen relationship. It is the language through which the state communicates with those under its jurisdiction, in particular to convey certain incentives and disincentives,[188] prescriptions, sanctions, speeches and exhortations. It is also through a legal mandate that the government communicates to the social sphere the materialization of the structure of conflicts that characterizes the implementation of public policies.[189]

All aspects closely related to the functioning of the state are subject to modification or intensification to the extent that the action and nature of the state itself changes, in historical-evolutionary terms. The different roles played by the social state, in contrast to the liberal state, also require different roles and instrumental uses of law itself. Thus, Norberto Bobbio points out that, considering the state's active role in achieving (and not just creating the conditions for achieving) social objectives, the idea of a purely protective-repressive legal system gives way to a new concept, namely the "promotional"[190] legal system, in which the technique of encouragement stands out, especially through positive legal sanctions, such as "prizes" rather than punishments, or facilitation techniques, which consist of making conduct easier or less difficult beforehand, regardless of reward.[191] It is true that the positive sanction is not an invention of the welfare state

185 This will be further explored in 1.9.1.
186 BURCHARDT, *op. cit.*, p. 414–416.
187 SUNSTEIN, Cass R. On the Expressive Function of Law. *University of Pennsylvania Law Review*, v. 144, n. 5, p. 2021–2053, 1996, p. 2031.
188 The institutional dynamics of incentives will be examined in more detail in section 1.9.5.
189 CLUNE, William H. A Political Model of Implementation and Implications of the Model for Public Policy, Research, and the Changing Roles of Law and Lawyers. *Iowa Law Review*, v. 69, p. 47–125, 1983, p. 58–59.
190 Although this is not the most common expression in English, the terms promotional norm, promotional program, or promotional measures will be used throughout the dissertation to refer to any acts whose primary function is the active promotion of behaviors.
191 BOBBIO, Norberto. *Dalla struttura alla funzione*. Roma-Bari: Laterza, 2007, p. 24–27.

and the legal theories influenced by its ends. Hans Kelsen, for example, in his conception of law as a coercive order, already accepted the ideas of "punishment and reward" as distinct types of sanction but emphasized that the former, the evil applied to the offender, was much more effective, and that rewards were only relevant in private relationships.[192] Therefore, although the coexistence of negative and positive sanctions predates the finalistic perceptions of the legal order identified with the welfare state, the increase and complexification of the state's functions in the active pursuit of material objectives has altered the potential of positive sanctions. Encouragement, in particular, has become an important tool for achieving the objectives of government programs, which have predefined material goals aligned with an active state political agenda. Thus, in addition to repressing undesirable actions (and indirectly protecting interests/rights) and thereby achieving the effects of inhibiting the prohibited act and negatively stimulating the permitted act (by the mere absence of prohibition), the technique of encouragement seeks to make "obligatory acts particularly enticing and prohibited ones particularly repugnant".[193]

The promotional function of the law does not supplant its protective-repressive function; it merely adds different ranges of possibilities suited to the reality of the times, especially considering phenomena such as regulation and public policies, two sides of the same coin, which take into account a constant public-private relationship and new roles for the state in society and the economy. As far as public policy is concerned, this sum of possibilities corresponds directly to the legal *topoi* that affect the various phases[194] of public policy. In this sense, it's about the different ways the law will be used to understand, execute, and legitimize public policy throughout the cycle that starts with defining problems, setting the

192 KELSEN, Hans. *General theory of law and state.* Cambridge, Massachusetts: Harvard University Press, 1949, p. 17–18.

193 BOBBIO, *op. cit.*, p. 15. "On the contrary, the technique of encouragement aims not only to protect but also to provoke the performance of conforming acts, competing in the case of permissible acts with the possibility of doing as opposed to not doing, making obligatory acts particularly enticing and prohibited ones particularly repugnant". In the original, "Al contrario, la tecnica dell'incoraggiamento mira non soltanto a tutelare ma anche a provocare l'esercizio degli atti conformi, spareggiando nel caso di atti permessi la possibilità di fare con quella di non fare rendendo particolarmente allettanti gli atti obbligatori e particolarmente ripugnanti quelli proibiti".

194 According to the classical view of RIPLEY, Randall B. Stages of the policy process. *In*: DANIEL C. MCCOOL (Ed.). *Public policy theories, models, and concepts: an anthology.* New Jersey: Prentice Hall, 1995, p. 158–161.

political direction and agenda, formulating programs, implementation, and subsequent evaluation. This applies to any public policy, regardless of its final content, and therefore, also to policies related to digital transformation and innovation.

Diogo Coutinho presents a typology of the functions of law in public policies, in four dimensions: substantive, structuring, instrumental, and legitimizing. In the substantive dimension, law has the task of crystallizing and formalizing political choices as cogent norms. In the structuring dimension, it defines tasks and means of coordination between public and private actors, and assigns competences, in other words, it forms the institutional arrangement. The instrumental dimension refers to the law as a toolbox available to the administrator to implement the policy and achieve its goals. Finally, the legitimizing dimension deals with ensuring participation, accountability, and mobilization, with the law being a way of vocalizing social demands.[195]

Coutinho points out that there are two not necessarily antagonistic views relating the aims and objectives of public policy to the law: the first sees them as an extra-legal result of the policy, without the jurist's interference in its definition, which would have the role of instrumentalizing the legal framework for its realization; and the second sees them as defining general guidelines for which they serve as a means, like "programmatic" constitutional norms,[196] which, when formalized, are distinguished from a mere intention. In addition, the attribution of cogent features to elements of the agenda by the law gives public policy its official character.[197]

Law as an institutional arrangement, on the other hand, refers to a structuring vision of legal norms in relation to public policies, regulating procedures, defining public and private actors, assigning competences, obligations and faculties, forms of coordination, and the general organization of the actions of the Public Power.[198] Since the state is a system for

195 COUTINHO, Diogo R. O direito nas políticas públicas. *In*: MARQUES, Eduardo Cesar; FARIA, Carlos Aurélio Pimenta de (Orgs.). *A política pública como campo multidisciplinar*. São Paulo: Fiocruz/UNESP, 2013, p. 194–198.

196 It is not discussed here whether or not the programmatic norm can be immediately effective and how, but rather that it fundamentally guides the formation of other normative bases and interpretation, according to FOCACCIA, Gaetano Alberto. Norme costituzionali e norme di legge anteriori. *Il Foro Italiano*, v. 79, p. 61–70, 1956, p. 66.

197 COUTINHO, *op. cit.*, p. 194.

198 *Ibid.*, p. 196.

forming political will, the law can be seen as a means of structuring this function and the actions included in this unit of "organized people".[199]

The doctrinal distinction between institutional arrangement and institutional environment is common. Institutional environment usually refers to the general rules governing the functioning of society, which govern political systems, basic decision-making processes (such as the legislative process), and the distribution of powers between the branches of government.[200] However, in addition to the basic organizational rules of the state, they also involve the rules that govern the institutional bases for society's relationship with the state, as well as the relationships between individuals in society, with substantial and not just procedural content. Examples of the former include constitutional provisions on economic law, such as the degree and form of state intervention in the economy, the limits between economic activity in the strict sense and in the broad sense, constitutional rules on the delegation of services, and also general constitutional guidelines on tax and criminal legislation, as well as fundamental rights and guarantees. Examples of the second type are certain fundamental rights, such as private property, and general rules for applying private law. It should be noted that, although the Brazilian Constitution contains a substantial part of the legal rules that make up the so-called institutional environment, not necessarily all the rules relating to it are of a constitutional nature, such as the general rules on contracts and general principles of private law, which are in the Brazilian Civil Code.

Institutional arrangements are generally referred to as mid-level structures, also known as the meso-institutional level of public policy.[201] While the macro level is precisely the basis for drawing up policies (the institutional environment, in an institutionalist economics approach), the middle level contains the elements that will deal with their effective functioning, still in general and abstract terms, but which concretely define roles, functions, responsibilities, rights and obligations and, consequently, relationships between actors that transcend the universe of the legal relationship, because they pave the way for behavior that reacts to these structures for

199 HENKE, Wilhelm. Wandel der Dogmatik des öffentlichen Rechts. *JuristenZeitung*, v. 47, n. 11, p. 541–548, 1992, p. 541.

200 DAVIS, Lance; NORTH, Douglass. Institutional Change and American Economic Growth: A First Step Towards a Theory of Institutional Innovation. *The Journal of Economic History*, v. 30, n. 1, p. 131–149, 1970, p. 133.

201 BUCCI, Maria Paula Dallari. *Fundamentos para uma teoria jurídica das políticas públicas*. São Paulo: Saraiva, 2013, p. 205.

assigning rights of a political nature, such as claims, qualitative assessments, speeches, electoral platforms, and distributive disputes. The arrangements are responsible for linking actors and general rules, which takes the form of interpretation and implementation processes that shape the framework of possible interactions and fill the space between the macro and micro-institutional levels.[202] The latter, in turn, is the behavior of the different actors directly related to mid-level institutional structures, actions that can be formal or informal, but which have some degree of conditioned constitutivity, that is, whose content determines some change in the factual spheres that are the object of the policy and which derive, in some way, from the distribution of responsibilities and the determination of ends contained in the program guidelines. In particular, this refers to government action at its cutting edge, in the day-to-day acts and practices of policy administration and implementation. It should also be noted that while institutions can be informal and have as much strength as formal institutions,[203] effective institutional arrangements can also escape complete formalization. This is not always an easy concept for jurists to deal with, as they are used to a typology of public law sources that focuses on forms.

The distinction between institutional environment, institutional arrangement, and institutional behavior has a relevant meaning and practical application, in that it creates didactic fields of analysis whose objects can be grouped and studied according to different characteristics, especially with regard to the transformation capacities of institutions in any of these areas and, specifically, in the concrete design of public policies, considering the constraints on actions brought about by the different levels, and the proportional difficulties or requirements for their modification, whether due to political or legal limits. Its usefulness is evident, for example, in comparative analyses of development models, comparative studies in political science and economics, and in the practical processes of transposing policies from other countries or resulting from international pacts.

However, it is safe to say that, for the purposes of analyzing policies that have the legal element as a fundamental interest, the distinction can be counterproductive, as it gives the impression that there are "watertight"

202 MÉNARD, Claude. Meso-institutions: The variety of regulatory arrangements in the water sector. *Utilities Policy*, v. 49, p. 6–19, 2017, p. 7.

203 LOWNDES, Vivien; ROBERTS, Mark. *Why institutions matter: the new institutionalism in political science.* Houndmills, Basingstoke, Hampshire: Palgrave Macmillan, 2013, p. 5.

levels,[204] - and which therefore require watertight interpretative and analytical processes - of the production and interaction of norms and acts, each with its own systemic logic, each of which can be an independent object of reflection and intervention. From a legal point of view, it is argued here that the institutional environment and government action are part of the institutional arrangement, and splitting these elements brings potential epistemological limitations, due to two characteristics that are sometimes seen as contradictory: the chain of validity of legal norms and the polycentrism of the production of legal norms. This is because each legislative provision relating to a public policy, however specific it may be, carries within it not only the explicit meaning of its own content, but also the implicit meaning of the norms which, firstly, confer its validity and, secondly, complete its material content, giving meaning to its interpretation and application.

In the same way, the administrative act, at the cutting edge of government action, carries with it all the authorizing, limiting, and enabling meaning of the mid-level rule, as well as all the material and procedural meaning of the constitutional rules and principles of law. The institutional environment makes up the arrangement not only in terms of conferring existence and validity on a legal level, or as an institutionalization of the act of institutionalizing (by providing for special roles and basic procedural rules),[205] but also in terms of its content, implied by the way its specific rules work, presupposing a set of larger, more general guidelines. The illustrative figure is then less that of a pyramid or chain of elements, and more of a *matryoshka* doll,[206] in which, paradoxically, the micro level contains within itself the meso and macro, and not the other way around.[207]

---

204 This may be more evident from a legal perspective, but it can also be deduced from the conceptual variability between different institutional levels in works of political science, such as when Patrick Dunleavy conceptualizes micro-institution as being essentially the same as macro-institution, but on a much smaller scale, in DUNLEAVY, Patrick. Micro-institutions and Liberal Democracy. *Political Insight*, v. 10, n. 1, p. 35–39, 2019.

205 To use an expression by LUHMANN, Niklas. *Sociologia do direito I*. Rio de Janeiro: Tempo Brasileiro, 1983, p. 109.

206 As suggested conversely by BROMLEY, Daniel W; YAO, Yang. Understanding China's Economic Transformation. *World Economics-Henley on Thames*, v. 7, n. 2, p. 73, 2006, p. 75: "We must see these institutional arrangements as layered or nested - rather like a Russian Matryoshka doll. The Instrumental Rules of the Economy are nested within - are constrained and liberated by - the Constitutional Rules of the Society. The Working Rules of Going Concerns are nested in - are constrained and liberated by - both the Constitutional Rules of the Society and the Instrumental

However, beyond the question of the relationship between institutional levels, the same reasoning applies to the relationship between institutional elements at the same level or, considering a compartmentalized view, between different institutional arrangements for different policies. The simplest case is when different public policies, which are based on independent legal frameworks but at a similar level, interact with each other in a non-explicit but relevant way due, for example, to the principles of "specialty" and "anteriority"[208] (but not only them). This is easy to understand when you take cross-cutting public policies, such as the General Data Protection Law, which will influence the correct understanding of other policies, such as the regulation of artificial intelligence, social benefits, or the provision of health services. Another very peculiar example in Brazilian law is the Law of Introduction to the Norms of Brazilian Law, which provides rules on interpreting other laws, laying down criteria for hermeneutics, and resolving antinomies, which normally exist as doctrine and practice of law. Nevertheless, the influence of one arrangement on the other can also occur when policies are not necessarily transversal, in less obvious but real implications of changing the meaning of applying a normative text by systemic interpretation or simply by joint interpretation with another normative text. The starting point of one arrangement can be the end point of another, and vice versa.

The taxonomic segregation of institutional elements into levels, such as environment, arrangement, and action, despite their inseparability, has, on the other hand, the practical utility of identifying a greater or lesser aptitude of these institutions for change, and consequently, impacting the establishment of priorities for institutional transformation, insofar as it makes the political energy and resources necessary for their modification quantifiable. In this sense, Williamson distinguishes between four levels, each with its own characteristics that make them more or less subject

Rules of the Economy. We see here the multi-layered institutional architecture of an economy".

207 An illustration of this reasoning, although not explicitly referring to institutional arrangements, can be seen in HEALY, Deirdre; GRIFFIN, Diarmuid. Unnesting the Matryoshka Doll: An Ecological Model of Probation and Parole Decision-Making in Ireland. *Journal of Contemporary Criminal Justice*, v. 39, n. 1, p. 75–93, 2023.

208 In the sense that a law with more specific content takes precedence over a law with general content, and a later law takes precedence over an earlier one, in a hermeneutic judgment.

to change, and over a longer or shorter period of time.[209] The first level includes informal institutions, religion, tradition, and customs, all of which have a deep penetration into social structures, low variability, and a low frequency of change, over periods of between a hundred and a thousand years. The second level is the institutional environment and everything related to it: the structures of society that are the product of politics and shape the way economic activity is organized, such as the powers of the state and the bureaucracy, as well as material rules such as property rights. Basically, this level contains all the rules of the game, which vary over periods of ten to a hundred years. On the third level, there are what he calls "institutions of governance", which deal with the game itself, according to the parameters set out in the institutional environment, in other words, the functioning of markets, companies, and agencies, whose frequency of transformation is between one and ten years and where the transaction cost economy operates. Finally, on the fourth level, Williamson places the institutions dear to neoclassical economists, such as prices and their formation, which have an accelerated dynamic and change continuously.[210] Here, there is also a gradient from structure towards agency, from the greater weight of constraint to greater emphasis on human action, albeit within the idea of structure proper to institutional analysis. The classification, although it also takes into account the nature and interaction between the levels, emphasizes the differences in a decreasing way, especially in relation to the degree of "malleability"[211].

We must also consider the role of government action in the constitution of the law itself, in other words, how the "bottom-up" interaction from the micro to the meso and macro levels can affect the meaning and consequences of the interpretation of the law. Firstly, this is due to the fact that, in today's society, it is difficult to conceive of the centralized production of law itself, especially that focused on the actions of the Legislative Branch. Thus, with a perspective of governance penetrating the institutions of administrative law, with the public-private relationship being mediated less by the phenomenon of legislation and more by subordinate regulation, the idea of polycentrism in the production of law is gaining strength and,

209 WILLIAMSON, Oliver E. Transaction Cost Economics: How It Works; Where It is Headed. *De Economist*, v. 146, n. 1, p. 23–58, 1998, p. 26.

210 *Ibid.*, p. 28–29.

211 CORRÊA, Priscilla Pereira da Costa. Direito e desenvolvimento e sua base teórica. *In*: PINHEIRO, Armando Castelar *et al* (Orgs.). *Reflexões sobre direito e economia.* Rio de Janeiro: FGV Direito Rio, 2020, p. 322.

with it, also the constitutive role of the application of law by various actors, alone or in cooperation.[212] A concrete example that can be given is the pioneering regulation of transport apps in the city of São Paulo, which was done through an administrative act, but which, due to the cooperation and acceptance of those involved in the policy, was able to produce important transcendent legal effects, firstly by actually regulating the operation of services in the city and, secondly, by the fact that the material quality of the rules, balancing the public interest with the private ones, contributed to generating a positive social expectation about the services, which invariably influenced the Brazilian higher courts to consider these services as compatible with the legal order, in an environment where the existing laws could easily give rise to a merely prohibitive interpretation.

Working with the vision of environment, arrangement, and action, or macro, meso, and micro levels, while recognizing that they are part of the same objective whole, is essential to correctly understand the institutional legal dimension of Digital Government. Its first expression depends on the major rules of political functioning, such as those governing the federal system, the distribution of attributions between the Union, States and Municipalities, the system for delegating state functions and activities, and the fundamental rights to be protected (mostly individual) and/or promoted (mostly collective). Secondly, Digital Government is materialized in a "web" of rules and mid-level organizations that formulate specific digital transformation policies and coordinate the spheres of bureaucracy and the distribution of political power. And thirdly, part of this configuration are the government actions, which include the performance of actors and day-to-day administrative activity, including what can be called the street-level bureaucracy. This is made up of the civil servants who are at the cutting edge of the implementation process and create their routines and informal standards for dealing with the practical challenges that arise beyond formal institutionalization, especially those related to the scarcity of resources.[213]

All institutional levels function, to some extent, mediated by legal rules which, in addition to their organizational function, also have the function of stabilizing the expectations of actors and therefore, ultimately, the function of supporting decisions (about what to expect, about the path to take,

212 TRUTE, Hans-Heinrich. Die konstitutive Rolle der Rechtsanwendung. *In*: TRUTE, Hans-Heinrich *et al* (Orgs.). *Allgemeines Verwaltungsrecht - zur Tragfähigkeit eines Konzepts*. Tübingen: Mohr Siebeck, 2008, p. 211–232.

213 LIPSKY, Michael. *Street-level bureaucracy: Dilemmas of the individual in public service*. New York: Russell Sage Foundation, 2010, p. 3, 83.

about what should be done, whether or not it can be done, etc.). In this respect, legal dogmatics and its orientation towards decidability are necessary for practical knowledge of how these institutions work. So, having explained the functions of law in public policy, it is now time to explore how legal dogmatics fits into these functions, in other words, the role of dogmatics in the performance of each of these functions.

1.6 Legal dogmatics and its relationship with the political element

Dogmatics can be seen metaphorically as a bridge between legal science and legal practice, with pillars anchored in each of these areas, generalizing concepts, expressions, sentences, and rules from the normative text to law, leading to a teachable ordering context.[214] Schmidt-Aßmann, corroborating the mediating function between practice and science, associated with the task of generalizing decisions, adds that dogmatics is also fundamental for the criticism, structuring, and progress of law, mainly by providing ways of comparing regulatory models and thus revealing alternatives. In this sense, while its function is to stabilize relations, it is also a way of creating and evolving regulations.[215] The decision-making purpose of dogmatics is also very evident, both because of its intrinsic vocation to focus on answers when faced with the need to decide, as opposed to zetetic models of thought[216], and because it creates repositories of mental exercises for easier and reasonably standardized future application. It "stores, analyzes and evaluates the experiences and consequences of the solution models used so far".[217]

214 GRÖSCHNER, Rolf. Rechtsdogmatik. *In*: HILGENDORF, Eric; JOERDEN, Jan C. (Orgs.). *Handbuch Rechtsphilosophie*. Stuttgart: J.B. Metzler, 2021, p. 69–71.

215 SCHMIDT-AßMANN, Eberhard. *Verwaltungsrechtliche Dogmatik: eine Zwischenbilanz zu Entwicklung, Reform und künftigen Aufgaben*. Tübingen: Mohr Siebeck, 2013, p. 5.

216 As proposed by VIEHWEG, Theodor. Systemprobleme in Rechtsdogmatik und Rechtsforschung. *In*: DIEMER, Alwin (Org.). *System und Klassifikation in Wissenschaft und Dokumentation: Vorträge und Diskussionen im April 1967 in Düsseldorf*. Meisenheim am Glan: Hain, 1968, p. 96–104.

217 RÜTHERS, Bernd. *Rechtsdogmatik und Rechtspolitik unter dem Einfluß des Richterrechts*. Trier: Institut für Rechtspolitik an der Universität Trier, 2003, p. 15. In the original, "Die juristische Dogmatik speichert, analysiert und bewertet die Erfahrungen und Folgen der bisher verwendeten Lösungsmodelle."

Dogmatics can be organized under a disciplinary matrix that involves knowledge of the material object of interpretation, a doctrine of the sources of law, the methods of interpretation and systematization, and the values that govern the process, pillars whose interpretations constitute paradigms, as in other scientific areas.[218] The articulation of these dogmatic paradigms is done through dogmatic legal theories, which can be broadly defined as "a cognitive whole which produces substantiated (well-justified) solutions to given juridical problems",[219] containing as elements the factual and evaluative premises about the object, the legal principles, and propositions about the norms regulating the object and systematization guidelines.[220]

Particularly important in this case are the themes of sources of law, legal forms and legal protection. These are classic areas of dogmatics in administrative law[221] that not only explain the legal phenomena of the organization and functioning of the administration - the crux of public policies - but also deal more broadly with the legal relations between the state and civil society. Studying any government activity requires attention to the domains of administration and its legal aspects, and understanding the institutionalization of technological innovation within government, in the context of tensions between the state and the market, also takes into account the instrumental forms of protecting rights and guaranteeing the legitimacy of the exercise of power.

Dogmatics has an obligatory place in the legal-institutional view because, without it, there would be few substantial differences from traditional policy science approaches. In this type of interdisciplinary view, which aims to bring politics and other areas related to the object into the method, the knowledge and handling of law and its doctrine are presuppositions, both of the broad epistemological potential that is intended to be achieved, and of the introduction of other elements and instruments of extra-legal analysis. In this sense, economic, behavioral, empirical, and political studies

218 AARNIO, Aulis. Paradigms in Legal Dogmatics. *In*: PECZENIK, Aleksander; LINDAHL, Lars; ROERMUND, Bert Van (Orgs.). *Theory of Legal Science: Proceedings of the Conference on Legal Theory and Philosopy of Science Lund, Sweden, December 11–14, 1983*. Dordrecht: Springer Netherlands, 1984, p. 28.

219 *Ibid.*, p. 30.

220 *Ibid.*

221 SCHMIDT-AßMANN, Eberhard. *Verwaltungsrechtliche Dogmatik: eine Zwischenbilanz zu Entwicklung, Reform und künftigen Aufgaben*. Tübingen: Mohr Siebeck, 2013, p. 29.

of the law require that we first know what the law says, and that a legal doctrine also describes its propositional results.[222]

Legal dogmatics features prominently in the legal sciences of various countries. It is particularly marked in German law and in other countries with a Roman-Germanic tradition, such as Brazil, but it is also present to some extent in common law countries,[223] although in this system certain propositions traditionally outside its domain, such as those *de lege ferenda*, can occupy areas where it is difficult to distinguish between legal doctrine and legal sociology.[224]

If, in public policies, the law has particularly prominent functions in the substantive, structuring, instrumental, and legitimizing dimensions, the role of dogmatics is also to bridge the gap between this theoretical vision and the practice of designing, implementing, or simply examining a program. From the functional perspective of law in relation to public policies, legal dogmatics will emerge as a "technology" applied to each of these dimensions. When it comes to law as an objective, which makes agenda definitions cogent and crystallizes public choices, dogmatics can try to identify: the exact normative meaning of those provisions, the measure of the normative force of the agenda's goals provisions, who is the holder of a subjective right by virtue of it (and, consequently, to whom the opposite obligation falls), what procedural legal means can be deployed to guarantee the enforcement of these legally qualified objectives, what is the degree and extent of enforceability of these objectives, what legal limits do they represent in concrete terms for the action of the formulator of other policies or what legal authorizations do they confer for the creation of new programs.

With regard to law as an institutional arrangement, the dogmatic-legal view of the structural conformation of public policy and its categorization allows for a more precise knowledge of these structures. Institutional arrangements are relationships between institutions that presuppose the intricate dynamics between "levels", environments, and actions, as well as the form and measure of this intersection, and the way in which the environment affects the functioning of specific rules. Therefore, in order to know their real extent and character, it is vital to have an interpretative

222 SMITS, Jan M. What is legal doctrine? On the aims and methods of legal-dogmatic research. *In*: ROB VAN GESTEL; HANS-W. MICKLITZ; EDWARD L. RUBIN (Orgs.). *Rethinking legal scholarship: a transatlantic dialogue*. New York: Cambridge University Press, 2017, p. 207–228.

223 SCHMIDT-AßMANN, *op. cit.*, p. 5–6.

224 PECZENIK, Aleksander. Empirical Foundations of Legal Dogmatics. *Logique et Analyse*, v. 12, n. 45, p. 32–64, 1969, p. 34.

process that, firstly, identifies which normative texts, inside and outside the official arrangement of a policy, are relevant for extracting meaning from the norm; and secondly, to be able to understand these texts and how the relationship between them and between them and the actions of actors in the world of facts actually takes place. In other words, it is only through a dogmatic hermeneutic process that the design of a policy is fully visualized and understood, with the identification of all its formal elements, the normative force of each of them, the way in which relationships are configured, the actors, the legal competences and the description of their limits, the instruments available to the manager, the fields of discretion and binding nature, and the systemic relationships of different normative texts that are sometimes excessively implicit and beyond the reach of common exegesis.

Legal dogmatics is the main instrument for this portrait of public policy to reveal the implicit element of systematic intertextual relationships that an isolated analysis of texts, normative frameworks, and formal and informal institutional elements cannot clarify. So, for example, in the case of any public policy that has been declared unconstitutional, or that has some element declared unconstitutional by a court of law, a view that disregards the legal element in the shaping of public policies may identify an incompatibility between institutional arrangement and environment, or, from another perspective, may identify the prevalence of one interest over another in the game characteristic of redistributive measures, when in fact the real problem may simply be a design flaw. Or the opposite: when a certain policy result does not correspond to the initial purpose for which it was created, supposedly for legal reasons and limitations, the use of dogmatics in analyzing the problem can isolate the normative variable in such a way as to make clear the real impact of eminently political factors on that dysfunction, making visible an extra-legal problem that was previously camouflaged in the midst of a complex and poorly understood legal apparatus.

The instrumental dimension of law in public policies is perhaps the most useful field for legal dogmatics in this approach. Government action programs are implemented, within the possibilities and constraints of the framework conditions of their structure, through the use of legal instruments such as contracts, agreements, processes, and administrative acts. Even more so in the case of policies such as Digital Government (which transcend federative spheres), they deal with state and private actors, coexist with technological standards and international practices that are consolidated and often also standardized, i.e., highly complex. Considering the multi-procedural nature of public policies and the different regulations that each procedural aspect has, there is a plethora of instruments far beyond administrative law, such as budget laws and financial law mechanisms, tax law concepts concerning funding sources, legal forms of federative coordination, such as public consortia, urban law mechanisms for public policies related to housing and land use, devices inherent in the legislative process for approving regulatory frameworks, among many others.

The legal toolbox will be well handled by the manager to the extent of his understanding of the legal doctrine that underpins its concepts and applications. In the same way, from an analytical point of view, doctrinal knowledge about the concepts and ways of applying the legal instruments available to the actors in a public policy is the first step towards subsequent criticism, whether it reveals extra-legal reasons for making decisions or for certain results, or whether it proposes different uses for the same instruments, or proposes new ones, in which the creative nature of dogmatics will also be present.

With regard to the legitimizing dimension, dogmatics is responsible for establishing and clarifying the limits and forms of assimilation of political interests within the administrative structure of the state, so that this delicate relationship between private interests and the public interest does not subvert the traditional structures of democratic legitimation of the administration, but rather complements it. The law, as a vocalizer of demands, does not replace the institutional forms of legitimation, whose chain of transmission requires a constant link with the people, with stable and less volatile forms, such as those of representative democracy, especially the sovereignty of the popular vote, which is a component of the Executive and Legislative mandates and which is formally passed on through the legislative process. In this context, the reintroduction of politics into autonomous administration through different channels can be a relevant problem[225], so that the various interests that dispute or influence spheres of power in governments also require a rational and isonomic framework through legal instruments that make it possible to reconcile interests that contribute to the structures of the state, and not co-opt them. In this sense, organizing the vocalization

225 TRUTE, Hans-Heinrich. Die demokratische Legitimation der Verwaltung. *In*: HOFFMANN-RIEM, Wolfgang; SCHMIDT-AßMANN, Eberhard; VOSSKUHLE, Andreas (Orgs.). *Grundlagen des Verwaltungsrechts*. 2. ed. München: C. H. Beck, 2012, p. 370–371.

of demands through participatory means is also a way of overcoming information asymmetries, which the legislative processes of representative democracy are not always able to deal with. Procedural rules that deal with the participation and accountability of administrators can also make public policies more democratic, by making them open to the ideas of the most diverse actors, capable of gaining a place in technocratic circles.[226]

However, if the lack of dogmatic tools limits the view of the dynamics of a given policy, the lack of another element, the political, which is sometimes ignored by legal science, also affects the understanding of a given matter, especially with regard to the effects regime. Seeing precisely the delimitation of the legal competences (and therefore the potential for action) of the actors, as well as the completeness of the instruments available for the exercise of these competences (the normative relationships between various texts, institutions, etc.), but disregarding the political element, can also lead to a misunderstanding of how politics works, by assuming that all these instruments will always be used according to their potential and for the specific purposes for which they were created, and that the actors will always act within the limits of their competence or at their maximum potential.

The "living" design of public policies, with the legally designed features being effectively (or not) mobilized, ignored, contested or expressly opposed, is only perceived if the relevant interests, preferences and orientations of the actors, the characteristics of the beneficiaries, and the socio-cultural (and also institutional) frames influencing the human action relevant to the public policy are identified. This would already be valid if we were only considering public administration, but it becomes fundamental in the case of the (digital) government object, which is not only about performing administrative functions but mainly, ultimately, about exercising sovereign power and directing the course of a people. In this sense, the usefulness of legal dogmatics in public policies, in the context of the legal-institutional view and the theory of the state, cannot ignore the political element, on the contrary: the awareness of its omnipresence makes legal dogmatics an important tool for equating non-political variables and thus better understanding the underlying relationships.

226 COUTINHO, Diogo R. O direito nas políticas públicas. *In*: MARQUES, Eduardo Cesar; FARIA, Carlos Aurélio Pimenta de (Orgs.). *A política pública como campo multidisciplinar*. São Paulo: Fiocruz/UNESP, 2013, p. 197–198.

Another related aspect that is often overlooked is that laws are a product of politics and are therefore not a neutral category,[227] making it difficult to classify them solely as "good law" or "bad law" for the consequence of good or bad economic results. It also follows that an analysis that identifies a set of laws as being of high or low quality may in fact simply be failing to see the real problem (or a substantial part of it): the dysfunction of the political processes behind the formulation of the law and in the course of its enforcement. This may sound irrelevant at first because the relationship between the quality of the "law product" and the quality of the policy is quite intuitive and almost obvious, but its importance is revealed when, for example, we try to implement the same type of legislation in one country that "worked" in another, without the same results. This is because the political dynamic influences the enforcement of that arrangement (or implementation of that policy) in a different way, or because the policy has already conditioned in a different way the formulation of the many other legal provisions that form the network of the systemic construction of the meaning of law.

From a doctrinal point of view, the relationship between law and politics is often explored from the perspective of legal decision-making, especially the decision-making process of judges and courts, with a lot of influence from common law systems, where the role of precedents in defining the meaning of the rule is greater and more central than in civil law countries. A common understanding of the permeability of the legal by the political is the vulgar interpretation that is sometimes made of the methods of the school of legal realism, with a reductionist view that the boundaries between the two fields are intertwined because judges are guided by feelings, personal and ideological values rather than following logical hermeneutic processes.[228] Beyond these views, legal realism effectively contributed to the debate, recognizing and admitting certain data from reality as factors

---

227 MILHAUPT, Curtis J.; PISTOR, Katharina. *Law and capitalism: what corporate crises reveal about legal systems and economic development around the world.* Chicago: University of Chicago Press, 2008, p. 22. "As we noted above, economists are fond of saying that the rule of law must be put in place as a precondition of economic growth. We recognize that this is rhetorical shorthand, but it is telling that economists—so meticulous about certain aspects of their analysis—seem uninterested in the process by which countries acquire and use law, even when law is the explanatory variable in their analyses. The bulk of the new empirical literature about corporate governance, for example, treats law as completely exogenous to markets".

228 TAMANAHA, Brian Z. Understanding Legal Realism. *Texas Law Review*, v. 87, n. 4, p. 731–786, 2008, p. 732–733.

influencing the outcome of the decision, in addition to the consideration of legal texts, arguments, and facts, normalizing the concern of judges with the social and political consequences of the decision.[229] The Critical Legal Studies (CLS) movement[230] is considered a successor to legal realism, and both currents of thought have in common the attempt to lay bare the politics embedded in law.[231] Despite its widespread influence on legal thought in general, its premises are also linked to the American common law system and the legal doctrine molded under its institutional environment. Nevertheless, by starting from a critique of legal objectivism and formalism towards a transformative vision of law and society, CLS seeks to make a broad propositional reflection as a new basis for political action.[232]

Some of its postulates, however, seem out of place when thinking about a restructuring of the national (Brazilian) legal scene, perhaps because they already unconsciously permeate the mental models of jurists currently trained in Brazil, but without a schematic organization that can steer them away from squalid subjectivism and the abuse of open legal categories for the defense of common interests disguised as progressivism. Additionally, this scenario, like legal realism, is also focused on major constitutional issues (albeit through local cases). When we move down from the macro to the meso-institutional level, the focus still remains either on society's relationship with the organs of justice or on the constitutionality of government actions and their reinterpretation in the light of more critical and politically sensitive constitutional judgments. Even when analyzing public policy issues, there is the aim of extracting new meanings from the Constitution itself through the outcome of the final situation of the parties involved and the powers of the state themselves after the final definition - who lost, who won, who changed - from the point of view of the institutions at the macro level.

229 *Ibid.*, p. 783.

230 According to KENNEDY, Duncan; KLARE, Karl E. A Bibliography of Critical Legal Studies. *The Yale Law Journal*, v. 94, n. 2, p. 461–490, 1984, p. 461, the Critical Legal Studies movement originated from the meeting of law and social science scholars held in Madison, Wisconsin in 1977, and has continued in the form of an organization supporting jurists, students and professors in a common theoretical line.

231 DORF, Michael C.; SABEL, Charles F. A constitution of democratic experimentalism. *Columbia Law Review*, v. 98, n. 2, p. 267–473, 1998, p. 274.

232 See UNGER, Roberto Mangabeira. The Critical Legal Studies Movement. *Harvard Law Review*, v. 96, n. 3, p. 561–675, 1983.

The legal-institutional approach can be thought of as a successor to these two traditions, with a more analytical meaning: the relationship between law and politics and the way politics permeates law continues to be of interest, but less as a matter of rescuing the social justice of the law, and more as a requirement for understanding the application of the legal norm itself within the scope of government action, as well as for carrying out an adequate mapping of the de facto situation of that set of norms, identifying their legal and extra-legal effects and proposing changes to the framework aimed at the objectives of the original political agenda. In this sense, the vision of politics in law is not aimed at a transformation agenda, necessarily taken as a rescue of the values of law that would have been subverted by the political interests of dominant groups, but rather at understanding the functioning of policies, and the correct targets of any proposed solutions, in a solution-oriented approach that rejects any form of proselytizing.

The emphasis on the relationship between law and politics can even legitimately and instrumentally serve ideological agendas, including those already favored by the design of an arrangement, and which are intended, by political choice, to be favored even more (or, on the contrary, disadvantaged) in a reform process. In this case, Law and Public Policy analysis will shed light on these relationships but not necessarily "denounce" them (legal realism) or propose a reinterpretation of the law in the light of values that are antagonistic to those favored (CLS). In reality, it makes it possible to clarify, qualitatively and quantitatively, the measure and form of this relationship, the interests involved, and the actors who take part in it. It's like making visible elements that are implicitly part of the law, but which are invisible at first or through the exercise of regular hermeneutics. It should be noted that the fact that they are implicit components of the law does not make them any less legitimate: they are also part of the arrangements and are not necessarily something to be combated by means of a progressive (or conservative) interpretation, but to be remedied if they are internally dysfunctional, i.e., detrimental to the functioning of the very policy they form, and therefore contrary to that same law.

Mangabeira Unger, a member of the CLS, has made a unique contribution to this interdisciplinary field when it comes to proposing legal analysis as institutional imagination. This line seeks to identify and resolve the instability characteristic of programmatic positions in law and politics, namely the dichotomy between valuing the definition of ideas and being subject to structures that prevent these ideas from being realized.[233] This is done by critically mapping out the arrangements and exploring in detail the legally defined institutional structure of society, which consists of "an analysis exhibiting the formative institutions of society and its enacted dogmas about human association as a distinct and surprising structure, and, above all, as a structure that can be revised part by part".[234] It makes it possible to reveal the systemic ties that limit the realization of social ideals, clarifying the meanings implicit in this proposed structure.[235] From a political science perspective, Scharpf already stated that it was necessary to map the concrete problem against the respective constellation of actors in order to understand it.[236] From a legal-institutional perspective, a description of the legal relationships that make up the different modes of interaction is added to identify obstacles and flaws, allowing meaningful political projects and actions to be built, breaking with insufficient or palliative ones that are more easily subject to setbacks.[237]

By critically scrutinizing the existing structures of certain arrangements, institutional mapping allows them to be qualified for the formulation of viable alternatives that actually represent transformation. This mapping should consequently result in alternative responses to the operation of the policy being examined, responses that can be tested in a triple-criteria exercise: in the social dimension (leveling expectations around change), in the temporal dimension (broadening the horizon of changes considered possible) and, in particular, in the material dimension, with the ability to speed up collective decision-making, dynamism in the generation of wealth and the quality of the knowledge produced from it.[238]

It is essential to take into account the living aspect of the arrangements, in other words, the dynamics of the legal-institutional structures together with the conduct and relationships of the actors between themselves and with the institutions. After all, "the analysis of structures without reference to actors remains just as deficient as the analysis of actors' actions

---

233 UNGER, Roberto Mangabeira. *What Should Legal Analysis Become?* London: Verso, 1996, p. 129.

234 *Ibid.*, p. 130–131.

235 *Ibid.*, p. 131.

236 SCHARPF, Fritz Wilhelm. *Games real actors play: actor-centered institutionalism in policy research.* Boulder, CO: Westview Press, 1997, p. 45.

237 GASPARDO, Murilo. Democracia participativa e experimentalismo democrático em tempos sombrios. *Estudos Avancados*, v. 32, n. 92, p. 65–88, 2018, p. 83.

238 AMATO, Lucas Fucci. *Construtivismo jurídico: teoria no direito.* Curitiba: Juruá, 2017, p. 254–255.

without reference to structures".[239] To this end, Diogo Coutinho, in the field of Economic Law, proposes *diagnosis* and *improvement* as analytical phases,[240] the first focusing on the given situation and the second focusing on the imaginative exercise of how current institutions should or could be.[241] Coutinho divides diagnosis into four distinct logical stages. The first seeks to identify the legal-institutional arrangements and their respective roles in a given public policy. The second is an effort to understand how the law influences the functioning of the arrangements. The third is to compare the effective role of the arrangements with those formally defined by the rules that structure the policy, identifying mismatches, reasons and consequences. The fourth focuses on identifying what he calls bottlenecks, i.e., which rules, processes or institutions hinder the achievement attributed to the institutional arrangement of the public policy.[242] Bucci and Gaspardo propose an eight-step roadmap for mapping arrangements, consisting of: 1) delimitation of critical junctures and identification of relevant events and legal acts in the political context and in a specific time dimension, with emphasis on turning points in the orientation of the arrangements; 2) selection and static description of the arrangements being studied; 3) respective legal documentation, with identification of the normative bases, design, underlying political composition and the respective analysis of these elements, with a focus that is less descriptive and more on clarifying the underlying relationships; 4) examining the context and the political actors, and classifying them as protagonists and antagonists in the disputes; 5) analyzing motivations and effects, comparing those expected with those obtained; 6) looking at the institutions in motion, i.e., their actual functioning as an arena for disputes and actions; 7) combining the previous stages into a global analysis of the phenomenon being analyzed, using frameworks

239 MAYNTZ, Renate; SCHARPF, Fritz W. Der Ansatz des akteurzentrierten Institutionalismus. *In*: MAYNTZ, Renate; SCHARPF, Fritz W. (Orgs.). *Gesellschaftliche Selbstregelung und politische Steuerung*. Frankfurt/New York: Campus Verlag, 1995, p. 46. In the original, "Die Analyse von Strukturen ohne Bezug auf Akteure bleibt genauso defizitär wie die Analyse von Akteurhandeln ohne Bezug auf Strukturen".

240 In a similar vein, WIENS, David. Prescribing Institutions Without Ideal Theory. *Journal of Political Philosophy*, v. 20, n. 1, p. 45–70, 2012, with his proposal for clinical institutional design.

241 COUTINHO, Diogo Rosenthal. O Direito econômico e a construção institucional do Desenvolvimento democrático. *Rei - Revista Estudos Institucionais*, v. 2, n. 1, p. 214, 2016, p. 247.

242 *Ibid*., p. 247–248.

or models; 8) and, finally, prescriptive derivations, in which institutional alternatives are proposed based on the results obtained so far.[243]

The process of institutional imagination, through which the barrier of rational-legal analysis is broken down to connect politics and law through critical mapping,[244] makes it possible to explore the institutionalized structure of a society in depth and its central point is to produce a detailed, albeit fragmentary, legal-institutional analysis, replacing currently preconceived notions with others. Through mapping, materials are produced to support the activity of critique, which is essential if alternative institutions are to be imagined one step further.[245] And, as Schmidt-Aßmann reminds us, legal dogmatics is part of this process, providing input for the critique of existing structures and the proposal of new paths.[246]

1.7 Analysis frameworks in LPP: the key questions of the legal-institutional view

Institutionalist approaches to public policy are not exactly theories but rather heuristics for explaining concrete situations[247] and cause-and-effect relationships in the formulation and implementation of programs. Certain elements are emphasized in the analysis process in order to give rise to hypotheses or point out greater plausibility among those already known that converge with the researcher's objectives.

The analytical frameworks for public policies[248] are a kind of objective, tailor-made application of some of the categories of the legal-institutional

---

243 BUCCI, Maria Paula Dallari; GASPARDO, Murilo. Mapeamento de arranjos jurídico-institucionais: um roteiro metodológico para estudos das relações entre direito e política. *REI - Revista Estudos Institucionais*, v. 10, n. 1, p. 1–36, 2024, p. 24–30.

244 WALTON, Kevin. A realistic vision? Roberto Unger on law and politics. *Res Publica*, v. 5, n. 2, p. 139–159, 1999, p. 142.

245 UNGER, Roberto Mangabeira. *What Should Legal Analysis Become?* London: Verso, 1996, p. 130.

246 See the beginning of the previous section.

247 BAUMGARTNER, Sabrina. *Die Regierungskommunikation der Schweizer Kantone: Regeln, Organisation, Akteure und Instrumente im Vergleich.* Wiesbaden: VS Verlag für Sozialwissenschaften, 2010, p. 81, also citing; MAYNTZ, Renate; SCHARPF, Fritz W. Der Ansatz des akteurzentrierten Institutionalismus. *In*: MAYNTZ, Renate; SCHARPF, Fritz W. (Orgs.). *Gesellschaftliche Selbstregelung und politische Steuerung.* Frankfurt/New York: Campus Verlag, 1995, p. 39–72.

248 See BUCCI, Maria Paula Dallari. A abordagem DPP no Brasil_Quadros analíticos. *Revista Campo de Públicas: conexões e experiências*, v. 2, n. 1, 2023.

view that derive from the multidisciplinary approach to Law and Public Policies, and vary according to their specific usefulness and the purposes they serve. They have the ability to guide the researcher's gaze in a somewhat Cartesian way in identifying and describing the parts, actions, and relationships involved in the life cycle of a policy, with an emphasis on the relation between legal and political factors. They are also, at the same time, a way of reducing the complexity of an object of study by making it possible to fill in previously established cells of a relational table with descriptions and brief explanations of the key components of the programs, and to add knowledge of the same object, by shedding light on discrete or hidden aspects in the linear reading. In this sense, they also serve as a basis for the construction of institutional mapping and provide the building blocks for comprehensive criticism.

Thus, the *framework of reference* proposed by Bucci seeks to outline an institutional panorama to be added to the procedural dimension of public policies. It identifies and describes the government administration responsible for a given program, which allows the political context to be read; the normative basis, with the main rules, their hierarchies, and legal forms; the legal-institutional design, with the identification of governmental and non-governmental actors, legal mechanisms for political articulation/coordination, the scale and target public of the program, the economic-financial dimension and the implementation strategy; the actual functioning of the policy, which involves comparing the ideal design with the real dynamics; and the critical aspects of the institutional design, i.e., those on which the reasons for the success or failure of a government program rest.[249]

In a complementary way, but presupposing a circumstance of incompleteness or insufficiency of policies, we have Ruiz and Bucci's *framework of problems*, which lists: the problem situation, i.e., the public problem justifying state intervention; the diagnosis of the situation, which characterizes the social, economic, political and cultural context of the public problem; the normative context, formed by the set of normative texts related to the problem situation; the decision-making process through which hypothetical solutions to the problem must pass and its current stage; the institutional arena in which the discussion around the formulation of the

249 BUCCI, Maria Paula Dallari. Quadro de referência de uma política pública: primeiras linhas de uma visão jurídico-institucional. *In*: SMANIO, Gianpaolo Poggio; BERTOLIN, Patrícia Tuma; BRASIL, Patrícia Cristina (Orgs.). *O Direito na Fronteira das Políticas Públicas*. São Paulo: Páginas e Letras, 2015, p. 7–11.

solution will take place; the protagonists, i.e., the actors whose interests favor a certain decision, as well as their respective antagonists; the decision-makers, responsible for the concrete course of tackling the problem, with a description of their attributes and competences; and the bargaining resources used by the actors to influence the decision-making process.[250]

Mention should also be made of the typology of forms of public policy coordination proposed by Carlos Toledo, in which four distinct forms of coordination are identified: absorption (concentrated policy), direction (regulatory policy), induction (promotion policy), and concertation (agreed policy). The author also describes the legal mechanisms for implementation in each case (constitutional changes, regulation by law, incentive measures, terms of cooperation and agreements, etc., in different combinations), as well as the risks and challenges of each form, such as low adherence or effectiveness, political resistance, federative conflict, asymmetry of capacities and inadequacy of the governance structure.[251]

Analytical frameworks for public policies go beyond the legal-institutional perspective and can also be formulated and applied from a legal-procedural perspective, especially when relevant social conflicts related to ongoing policies politically transcend the judicial procedural relationship, so that the judge's proper handling of procedural instruments will also depend on (or benefit from) the formulation of questions that assimilate the contexts, interests and social relations underlying the material and procedural legal context in a methodologically predictable manner. An example of this is the roadmap proposed by Alexandra Fuchs Araújo[252] for the judicial control/review of public policies,[253] based on her practical experience as a judge in court cases involving the right to housing with great conflict and social repercussions. The author identifies the essential questions to guide the judge's legal reasoning and the correct use of procedural legislation

250 RUIZ, Isabela; BUCCI, Maria Paula Dallari. Quadro de problemas de políticas públicas: uma ferramenta para análise jurídico-institucional. *REI - Revista Estudos Institucionais*, v. 5, n. 3, p. 1142–1167, 2019.

251 TOLEDO, Carlos José Teixeira de. *Políticas Públicas e Valorização do Professor da Educação Básica*. Belo Horizonte, MG: Fórum, 2022, p. 246.

252 ARAÚJO, Alexandra Fuchs de. *Políticas Públicas, Poder Judiciário e o Direito à Moradia*. Belo Horizonte: Forum, 2023, p. 243–245.

253 In Brazil, the role and limits of the Judiciary in public policies is a recurring and very topical issue, considering the well-documented phenomenon of the "judicialization of policies", i.e., the interference of the Judiciary in the cycle of formulation and implementation of government action programs, which represents a challenge in terms of how and when rights are guaranteed, access to justice for those involved and the duty to protect rights.

at each stage of the civil process, considering the particular nature of the underlying problems involved in the dispute.

Analytical frameworks are, in essence, a set of relevant questions about the public policies under study, which induce the researcher to relate interdisciplinary elements in the direction of answers that are not always easily visible in linear unidisciplinary readings. As they are not theories, but practical models, they allow the various types of components - political, financial, legal, etc. - to be visually deciphered so that the researcher can then explore and combine them, using the concepts and accumulated knowledge of the various fields, on the one hand reducing the complexity (of the object) and on the other increasing the complexity (of the results). William Clune provides a very illustrative metaphor in this sense when he describes the law as a fortress in which all the rest of reality can be seen through narrow hatches, as if protecting itself through its walls from influence or attacks from outside, while, at the same time, the gates are paradoxically wide open for any intruder or foreigner to enter.[254] One of the uses of the frameworks is to provide ways of broadening this narrow view of all kinds of elements that relate to the legal component of public policies and to provide practical solutions to this contradiction.

The key questions - through which the doors to understanding the object are opened - suggested by the frameworks will also be asked in this work when it comes to examining Digital Government, most of the time implicitly, to guide the search for information and knowledge about Digital Government public policies in Brazil and explain this phenomenon from a legal-political point of view. The questions and paths of the approach are the basic guideline for the applied examination that will follow later. In turn, the heuristic elements of the conjunction of institutional thinking and legal thinking will serve as an analytical resource, instrument, and typology for the elaboration of answers and clarification of the real dynamics of Digital Government. In other words, they will be the tools of a model which, without being a theory, can be applied in a tailor-made way, topically and partially, or broadly, with greater or lesser intensity.

---

254 CLUNE, William H. Legal Disintegration and a Theory of the State. *German Law Journal*, v. 12, n. 1, p. 186–205, 2011, p. 192.

1.8 Digital Government as a metapolicy

Digital Government is a very specific type of public policy, which can transcend all other policies in some way, as well as having cross-cutting subjects if we look at the material content of the interaction between government and citizens and, especially, the large number and types of public services that will benefit from its implementation.

The term metapolicy can be defined as a policy on how to make policies, dealing with structural aspects, standard processes, decision-making systems, personnel, inputs, and desired outputs, as well as strategies, conceptual frameworks, general instruments and inter-policy guidelines.[255] It can be used to designate policies that deal with legislative-regulatory instrumentalization in other policies, such as normative formulation guidelines, comparison, and evaluation[256] , but also with a more prominent material sense of transversality. Digital Government is, in this sense, a metapolicy because it is a set of government actions which, as well as affecting a series of other thematic policies, has a broad penetration in all spheres of government, federal or not, and at all levels of the administration. Strictly speaking, the Digital Government does not have a well-defined beneficiary or a determinable recipient outside the government, such as a social group subject to eligibility criteria. It is a policy aimed both at the state itself and at citizens in general, in all the relationships they may have with the government, especially, but not only, the use of public services. In addition, it is also a strategic metapolicy, since: it deals with national issues of great national relevance; it addresses intersectoral matters and applies to the whole of society; it requires systemic development approaches, adaptive governance and social learning, articulation of uncertainties and processes of engagement of the actors involved; it requires long-term implementation and continuity; it requires vertical and horizontal integration in the implementation phase.[257]

---

255 DROR, Yehezkel. Social science meta-policy: Some concepts and applications. *In*: CHERNS, A. B.; JENKINS, W. I.; SINCLAIR, R. (Orgs.). *Social Science and Government*. London and New York: Routledge, 1972.

256 See DE PAULA, Felipe. Does Brazil have a Legislative Policy? *The Theory and Practice of Legislation*, v. 4, n. 3, p. 329–353, 2016.

257 According to the criteria set by SAMNAKAY, Nadeem. Thinking Strategically in Federal Policy: Defining the Attributes of High-level Policies. *Australian Journal of Public Administration*, v. 76, n. 1, p. 106–121, 2017.

Naturally, different theories have been developed within the institutional view to explain different public policies, but also to explain the same public policies differently, giving rise to debates about greater and lesser suitability. This is why, for example, there are the various types of neoinstitutionalism described briefly in section 1.2 with propositions that differ from one another. But the crux of the reason why there are such differences in approach is precisely the diversity of objects and, one could say, perhaps even the diversity of subjects and research agendas, even considering that their developments have taken place independently of each other, which, given the great general similarities, is also quite surprising.[258] Much more than visions that would compete for a spot of preference or a position of consolidation, they also form a rich set of elements potentially applicable to various situations and with particular uses. If the object of study, as in this case, is so multifaceted, multileveled, and transversal in form and material content, it is acceptable that it can and should be examined according to a broader set of postulates, products of a theoretical construction of the legal-institutional view. For this reason, the following topic and its sub-items will explore specific contributions from the various theoretical lines mentioned, in order to situate them within a legal-institutional analysis model to be used in understanding the structures for incorporating technology into the public sector and the formulation and implementation of related policies.

1.9 A legal-institutional heuristic for examining Digital Government

The different premises and elements of neoinstitutionalist approaches to public policy, when combined or imported into a study with a predominantly legal bias, require some effort to adapt and justify. In fact, it is not new for jurists to work with the notions of actors, incentives, path dependence, among others, without worrying too much about the consequences of this incorporation, neglecting the alien characteristics of these figures or taking them for granted. Other useful notions from neoinstitutionalism, such as strategy, communicative and coordinative discourse, the power of the idea, the veto points, and modes of interaction, appear little in the legal world, perhaps because they have less intuitive meanings or are identified with common sense. But in addition to the risk of jurists working with

258 HALL, Peter A.; TAYLOR, Rosemary C. R. Political Science and the Three New Institutionalisms. *Political Studies*, v. 44, n. 5, p. 936–957, 1996, p. 937.

these categories in the wrong way due to the temptation to use the language of political science, economics, and sociology easily and without greater responsibility, the lack of a proper "translation" to the system of legal production and knowledge limits their use. As Bucci and Gaspardo point out, "the challenge is to overcome customary practices in legal research of using literature from outside the law randomly, *ad hoc*, without the necessary mediations".[259] In the following sections, we will try to deal with these categories, not only by explaining them, but also by transposing them to the legal world and exploring some of their potential, in the construction of a legal-institutional heuristic that will later serve as an informative benchmark for the examination of Digital Government in Brazil and the other experiences selected to contribute to the argument.

1.9.1 Enabling and constraining: the instrumental keying of institutions

The basic premise of the institutional view is that the institutional framework guides human action in a relevant way, shaping behavior in society.[260] The idea that institutions shape the behavior of actors contrasts with the view that the preferences of individuals and their actions, in any procedural dynamic, are the determining or at least preponderant elements of a decision-making process. There are phenomena in which these preferences will be of greater importance by their very nature, such as electoral processes, for example, in which the principle of popular sovereignty should be translated into a minimum of possible rules to avoid abuses of power, and consequently promote maximum freedom for voters to exercise their individual choices - which, collectively considered, will result in the choice of a representative or program. In the field of public policy, where programs are structured to tackle problems, the decision-making dynamic shifts the weight to the institutional sphere and alters the general flow of influences,

259 BUCCI, Maria Paula Dallari; GASPARDO, Murilo. Mapeamento de arranjos jurídico-institucionais: um roteiro metodológico para estudos das relações entre direito e política. *REI - Revista Estudos Institucionais*, v. 10, n. 1, p. 1–36, 2024, p. 5 In The original, ""o desafio é superar práticas costumeiras na pesquisa jurídica, de utilizar literatura externa ao direito de forma aleatória, ad hoc, sem as mediações necessárias".

260 LHOTTA, Roland. Neoinstitutionalismus und Demokratie. *In*: LEMBCKE, Oliver W.; RITZI, Claudia; SCHAAL, Gary S. (Orgs.). *Zeitgenössische Demokratietheorie.* Wiesbaden: Springer Fachmedien, 2016, p. 128.

although there are different types and quantities of processes that are more or less regulated, depending on their nature.

For the jurist, this aspect may sound somewhat obvious because the traditional set of institutions of interest to legal dogmatics is made up of legal norms, in which the coercive element makes it quite clear that they have the ability, or at least the purpose, to condition or even determine behavior. But this understanding should not be limited to the antecedent-consequent equation mediated by the use of force, or even to the semantic aspect of the rules that make up the set.

Institutional structures can be seen as communication between actors, in which a language is shared in the form of limits/opportunities that allow, prescribe or recommend certain actions.[261] They have three functions in relation to influencing human action: the restrictive function, because they constrain individuals and their behavior; the cognitive function, by providing individuals with information that shapes their perception of reality, including the possibilities and probabilities of the actions of others (who are also constrained by the same rules); and the teleological function, by influencing the ends sought by individuals.[262] However, in addition to constraining individuals, the conditioning by institutions is also seen as encouraging or enabling actions, because the rules create possibilities for interaction that enable choices that would not be possible without the existence of these structures.[263] In the classic social science debate about the structure vs. agency dichotomy,[264] while action is characterized by freedom

261 CRAWFORD, Sue E. S.; OSTROM, Elinor. A Grammar of Institutions. *The American Political Science Review*, v. 89, n. 3, p. 582–600, 1995, p. 583.

262 DEQUECH, David. The Demarcation between the "Old" and the "New" Institutional Economics: Recent Complications. *Journal of Economic Issues*, v. 36, n. 2, p. 565–572, 2002, p. 566.

263 HODGSON, Geoffrey M. *The Evolution of Institutional Economics*. London and New York: Routledge, 2004, p. 425.

264 According to COUTINHO, Diogo R. Direito e institucionalismo econômico: apontamentos sobre uma fértil agenda de pesquisa. *Brazilian Journal of Political Economy*, v. 37, p. 565–586, 2017, p. 568, the problem can be summarized as follows: "...do individuals control their acts, actions and destiny or are they subject to the action of circumstances and social structures, which determine their behavior? That is, do individuals have autonomy in their choices or are they, on the contrary, compelled by irresistible social forces, like 'puppets'?". In the original, '...os indivíduos controlam seus atos, ações e destino ou estão sujeitos à ação de circunstâncias e estruturas sociais, que determinam seu comportamento? Isto é: os indivíduos têm autonomia em suas escolhas ou são, ao revés, compelidos por forças sociais irresistíveis, como "fantoches"?'.

and the power to transform, social structure is seen as something that limits it but, at the same time, provides the tools for creation and transformation that make the exercise of freedom possible.[265] The normative idea of constriction, prescription, or permission, added to the more managerial conception of recommendation, takes on the instrumental character of realizing politically guided objectives. Beyond the impact of commands on individual or inter-individual action in the choices that were originally possible, institutional tools create new possibilities and encourage people to follow paths that did not exist before and are essential to any process of change or adaptation, especially those that are continuous, such as the incorporation and use of new technologies. The institutional switch that sometimes enables and sometimes constrains is the building block of digital transformation policy arrangements, and far beyond individual deontic commands specific to the legal view, it guides not only action but the mutual expectations of actors about each other's behavior and their subjective purposes.

1.9.2 Institutions as equilibrium: stabilizing choices and preferences

Institutions can be understood as a balance of preferences shared by actors, which translate into identifiable stable patterns.[266] Institutionalizing means typifying shared habits.[267] Thus, an institution can be described as a set of frozen preferences,[268] or perhaps as a photograph of a given situation or the result of the interaction of preferences translated into choices. Or even, according to Giddens, a set of practices highly sedimented in time and space, long-lasting and widespread among the members of a given community,[269] although his understanding focuses on the behavioral pattern itself, rather than the preferences that define it. They would, therefore, be a "regular behavior pattern sustained by mutual expectations about the actions that

265 HAYS, Sharon. Structure and Agency and the Sticky Problem of Culture. *Sociological Theory*, v. 12, n. 1, p. 57–72, 1994, p. 61.
266 CRAWFORD; OSTROM, *op. cit.*, p. 582.
267 BERGER, Peter L; LUCKMANN, Thomas. *The Social Construction of Reality. A Treatise in the Sociology of Knowledge*. London: Penguin Books, 1991, p. 72.
268 RIKER, William H. Implications from the Disequilibrium of Majority Rule for the Study of Institutions. *The American Political Science Review*, v. 74, n. 2, p. 432–446, 1980, p. 445.
269 GIDDENS, Anthony. *Central Problems in Social Theory: Action, structure and contradiction in social analysis*. London: Macmillan, 1979, p. 80, 97.

others will take".[270] There is a clear distinction here from the behaviouralist view mentioned in section 1.2: the structured collectivization of behaviors (and not the behaviors themselves) is the focus of greater analytical interest. However, the social configuration of tastes and preferences does not obey a situation of equilibrium, and so there are also limitations in the equilibrium represented by the freeze provided by institutions, which is in itself, to a certain degree, unstable.[271]

The distinction between the view of institutions as constraints and as equilibrium is quite clear from the theoretical point of view of the method, but from the practical point of view it may seem unclear or artificial, and its concrete application depends on the specific object,[272] (but the two perspectives may eventually be complementary). Institutions represent an objective and singular reading of an intersubjective and plural situation, stabilizing the scenario through declarations of decisions but, at the same time, initiating a time-sensitive process of destabilization themselves, considering the mutability of the original situation. The institution, by identifying and declaring patterns, acts as a reliever of tensions in an environment of broad freedom but also acts as a focus for new tensions by creating beacons in this environment, as preferences and tastes change and clash with the institutionalized balance. But the tensions created by the institutionalization of preferences are less than the sum of the tensions existing in the context of free interaction, and the difference represents what the neoinstitutionalists of the sociological school point to as the capacity of institutions not only to shape the behavior of actors but their own preferences, as a result of a symbolic function represented by values beyond the meanings of the prescriptions themselves.[273]

In the case of legal institutions, this process is quite identifiable in the phenomenon of constitutionalization, especially when it comes to transitions of political regimes and contrasting social configurations. The Brazilian Constitution of 1988, for example, seeks to stabilize the patterns and

270 CRAWFORD; OSTROM, *op. cit.*, p. 583.

271 RIKER, *op. cit.*, p. 445.

272 DIERMEIER, Daniel; KREHBIEL, Keith. Institutionalism as a Methodology. *Journal of Theoretical Politics*, v. 15, n. 2, p. 123–144, 2003, p. 133.

273 In this sense, PETERS, Guy. Institutional theory. *In*: ANSELL, Christopher; TORFING, Jacob (Orgs.). *Handbook on Theories of Governance*. 2. ed. Cheltenham, Northampton: Edward Elgar Publishing, 2022, p. 324. "The internal logic of this approach is that the preferences of individuals who join an institution are shaped by that institution, and therefore their actions are shaped by the values and symbols within the institution".

preferences of a society in transition from authoritarianism to democracy, but at the same time creates new tensions by establishing the rules of a certain development model linked to the welfare state. The difference between the sum of the tensions managed by the constitutional conformation and those that culminated in the breakdown of the previous political and social regime contributes greatly to the symbolic function of the Constitution itself beyond its normative prescriptions, influencing not only conduct (according to the traditional legal view) but also the preferences and values that precede action (according to the sociological contribution). Or again, according to Luhmann's perspective of legal sociology, through institutionalization we achieve a stabilization of the structures of expectations, supporting them on consensus expected from third parties.[274]

One perspective arising from the idea of institutions as an equilibrium is the idea that they are essentially linked to the set of understandings and preferences of actors, and should not be considered as something totally external to them.[275] From this point of view, in philosophy of law, the link between an institution and a set of preferences and expectations of actors can have repercussions on the levels of legal validity, efficacy and existence. In the first case, this occurs if this link becomes incompatible with the updated set of choices expressed systematically in the legal order, affecting competence, procedure or material compatibility with higher norms. In the second case, if it fails to achieve its intended purpose, regardless of the correct application of enforcement. The third possibility occurs when there is no enforcement at all, i.e., when institutional statements cease to have consequences regardless of the behavior of the actors or their compatibility with the legal system.[276] Consequently, it can be said that adaptability - the ability and need to adapt - is a characteristic based on the essence of institutions as equilibrium, without which they can become dysfunctional, contentious, or simply cease to exist. This is an attribute that links the legal-institutional view with the experimentalist perspective, intensifying when the material content of a public policy involves innovation of any kind or the incorporation of innovation into a consolidated structure. This is the particular case of this dissertation, which deals with the assimilation of information technology by the state and the role of law in this process.

---

274 LUHMANN, Niklas. *Sociologia do direito I.* Rio de Janeiro: Tempo Brasileiro, 1983, p. 109.

275 CRAWFORD; OSTROM, *op. cit.*, p. 583.

276 Using the concepts of existence, validity and efficacy of MUNZER, Stephen. *Legal Validity*. Dordrecht: Springer Netherlands, 1972, p. 29–44.

The essential relationship between institutions and the preferences and expectations of the actors involved also has repercussions in a field other than the legal planes of existence, validity, and efficacy, although it is transversally related to them. In the case of private institutions, this can be measured in the representativeness qualifier, i.e., the extent to which an institution has the power to represent the interests of certain actors - which in itself will have potential impacts on effectiveness. In state institutions, on the other hand, the corresponding qualifier is legitimacy, and the impact will be similarly potential, but especially with regard to validity.

In public policies, the formation of equilibrium is an essential stage to make implementation feasible. The law itself is a normative expression of the balance of forces and interests, which materializes political awards or commitments with the ability to shape behavior.[277]

1.9.3 Strategies and declarations as pre-normative institutions

From a practical point of view, the lens of the institution as equilibrium can explain assertions that take the form of strategies, which presuppose the knowledge and organization of shareable preferences, as well as expectations regarding future action, by the actors themselves or by other actors and institutions, and the means to do so. Strategies can be broken down into three abstract elements, namely: the *attributes of* who is affected, the *conditions* that determine where, when, and how the assertion applies, and the *aim*, which are the actions or results sought as a goal.[278]

Every strategy, despite the use of the term in different fields of knowledge, has a central aspirational and intentional element, which usually stands out in a context of complexity and competition, with the capacity to create power, guide, and systematize.[279] In law, what is usually referred to as legal strategy is the activity of the jurist in relation to concrete cases, in particular the choice and construction of paths, based on technique, for the success of a represented interest, which may focus on persuading the decision maker, putting pressure on the activity of deciding independently

277 CLUNE, William H. A Political Model of Implementation and Implications of the Model for Public Policy, Research, and the Changing Roles of Law and Lawyers. *Iowa Law Review*, v. 69, p. 47–125, 1983, p. 53.

278 CRAWFORD; OSTROM, *op. cit.*, p. 584–586.

279 KHALIFA, Azaddin Salem. Strategy, nonstrategy and no strategy. *Journal of Strategy and Management*, v. 14, n. 1, p. 35–49, 2020, p. 39–42.

of convincing, or constructing alternatives that are independent of the outcome of the decision.[280]

In addition to the insufficient attention paid by legal science (or even jurisprudence) to the very phenomenon of legal strategy[281], it can be seen that law does not deal with the study of strategies (political, administrative, or governmental) as a legal object, and does not do so mainly because they lack deontic elements or because these elements are not essential to them. Thus, the strategies of states, governments, municipalities, regional blocs, etc., are assimilated into the legal world through the study of their forms, the theory of the sources of law, and the material limits of the competences that these forms presuppose in comparison with their content. But strategies, as institutional statements, produce effects which, because they are below what could be considered a norm but above mere legal fact, are both difficult to treat dogmatically and of substantial importance, especially considering the concern with the regime of effects[282] characteristic of public policies.

The same applies to the idea of a plan, although, considering its greater specificity and rigidity in relation to objectives, it can contain concrete tasks and attributions that, individually considered, somehow add the deontic element to the equation, such as functional obligations in conjunction with the prospect of a sanction borne by a public servant considering the consequence of not carrying out a command. Finally, the political statement, as an institutional discourse, fits into the structural model above the idea of fact, but possessing only attributes and targets. Going beyond discursive exhortations or the exercise of domination over masses or collectives, discourses have an important impact on policy analysis because they decisively influence the adoption of certain rules and models,[283] as well as the very construction of norms through the application process. Ultimately, this has a decisive impact on the direction of a given society.

As will be seen below, the subject of digital transformation is full of strategies in the sense of public documents with aspirations and paths, and with the indication of discursive meanings for government action. From

280 For more details, see LOPUCKI, Lynn M.; WEYRAUCH, Walter O. A Theory of Legal Strategy. *Duke Law Journal*, v. 49, n. 6, p. 1405–1486, 2000, p. 1443.

281 See Introduction, BIRD, Robert C. Pathways of Legal Strategy. *Stanford Journal of Law, Business & Finance*, v. 14, n. 1, p. 1–42, 2008.

282 See chapter 3 in BUCCI, Maria Paula Dallari. *Fundamentos para uma teoria jurídica das políticas públicas*. São Paulo: Saraiva, 2013.

283 As mentioned in SCHMIDT, Vivien. Discursive Institutionalism: The Explanatory Power of Ideas and Discourse. *Annual Review of Political Science*, v. 11, 2008, p. 320.

the digital transformation strategies, concrete initiatives and programs are subsequently drawn up to achieve specific objectives. They are a kind of umbrella and point of mediation between idea and action, an intermediate stage in the relationship between the political impulse and the normative structuring of government action. Drawing up digital transformation strategies involves taking on a politically determined mission. Initially, this mission has no expression in technological language, which is, at this intermediate stage, incorporated to specify technical meanings of aspirational and intentional content, but still in a rougher state of public policy, as it lacks the deontic elements that would complete the structuring of legal-institutional arrangements. As will be seen below, the digital transformation and digital government strategies are important as a basis for government action in this area and, despite their limits, produce effects with different repercussions, depending on the broader institutional framework and the potential of the arrangements to manage efforts through the structures of the macro-institutions.

1.9.4 Institutions as norms and rules

When the *deontic element* is added to the equation, along with *attributes*, *aim*, and *conditions*, institutions transcend the nature of a balance of preferences and expectations to also become a set or system of norms. This is the most common and intuitive configuration, and there are understandings to the effect that, without the deontic element, one could not even speak of institutions or institutional facts.[284]

The deontic element, in the institutional model, is that which, according to deontic logic, distinguishes prescriptive statements from non-prescriptive ones and can be summarized, in natural language, in three operators, namely: *may* (authorization), *must* (obligation) and *must not* (prohibition).[285] From a legal point of view, this differentiation can also be described as being explicit/integrated (in which the rule is deduced from the institutional declaration itself), or implicit/systemic (in which the rule is deduced from external elements of the institutional statement). An example of the latter is what Joseph Raz called "laws which are not norms",

284 SEARLE, John R. *Making the social world: the structure of human civilization*. Oxford: Oxford University Press, 2011, p. 91.

285 VON WRIGHT, G. H. Deontic Logic Revisited. *Rechtstheorie*, v. 4, n. 1–2, p. 37–46, 1973, p. 43.

as in the case of the simple positivization of requirements for the validity of documents and legal transactions,[286] considering the paradigm of the protective-repressive legal system. A practical example in public policy, within the idea of a promotional legal system, would be the requirements for participation or eligibility, such as certain "institutional duties" to be fulfilled by entities or companies in order to increase their practical legal capacities, as in the case of the classification of a legal entity as a "startup", allowing it a different legal regime for contracting with the government to supply new technologies.[287]

If *a consequent* is added to the deontic element, the normative character is also expressed in the more fluid form of a rule[288]. The consequent element ("*or else*") is the description of a situation to be carried out when the command is not complied with, i.e., when the combination of the deontic element with the aim and the conditions is confronted by the holders of the attribute. It can take the classic form of punishments but is not limited to them, and can also refer to any type of institutional action.[289] These, in turn, can also be explicit or implicit and stem from the impact of other organizational elements in the institutional arrangement or environment, completing the normative meaning of the institutional statement. Illustratively, we would be facing something similar to what Hart, in jurisprudence, would describe as secondary rules completing primary rules, transforming the pre-legal world into a fully legal one.[290]

In a more reductionist legal view, everything could be summarized more simply as antecedent and consequent. Attributes of those affected, as well as the general conditions, the deontic operator, and its object, all form part of an antecedent normative statement, a description of a typified situation that varies in its degree of abstraction and generality. On the other hand, there is the consequent element (*or else*), which ultimately takes the form of a legal consequence, something that modifies some sphere of rights. But looking beyond the process of legal subsumption can reveal essential complexities in the analysis of public policy problems that are not so obvious in the day-to-day life of the jurist.

---

286 RAZ, Joseph. Legal Principles and the Limits of Law. *Yale Law Journal*, v. 81, n. 5, p. 823–854, 1971, p. 835.
287 According to Complementary Law No. 182, of June 1, 2021
288 Still a rule in the institutional sense, not necessarily in the legal sense.
289 CRAWFORD, Sue E. S.; OSTROM, Elinor. A Grammar of Institutions. *The American Political Science Review*, v. 89, n. 3, p. 582–600, 1995, p. 586.
290 HART, Herbert Lionel Adolphus. *The concept of law*. 2. ed. New York: Oxford University Press, 1994, p. 94.

For the purposes of Crawford and Ostrom's institutional grammar, the distinction between a system of norms and a system of rules (with cumulative elements - the former containing the latter) rests on whether or not there is an explicit consequence for non-compliance. In a crude analogy with legal thinking, this distinction can be compared with the contrast between legal principles and rules, in the sense that a clear consequential element can identify whether the verification of the application of that norm is binary or not, or requires a process of weighing with other norms of a principled order. The comparison is limited for a number of reasons that are not relevant to the object of this study, but it does suggest that, in the same way that jurists find it more difficult to deal with norms that are principles due to their incompleteness of elements in relation to rules, a spectrum of analytical difficulties will arise in legal thinking when dealing with institutions in a broad way, outside of dogmatic thinking, due to the different degree of completeness of elements that institutions have as a strategy, norms or rules. What's more, as the elements are cumulative, institutions as rules never cease to be norms and never cease to be shared strategies. For this reason, the legal and extra-legal effects in each of these perspectives also overlap, something that legal reasoning can level down by focusing only on the explicit consequent, taking it as sufficient to solve the problem and ignoring the effects of the other spheres that require analysis that necessarily includes the political component.

Thus, if the institutional configuration with only three elements (attribute, condition, and aim) is in the field of shared strategies, the addition of the deontic element adds the normative character, and the complete configuration with the five components (attributes, aim, conditions, deontic element and consequent) gives institutional statements the character of a system of rules.[291] In this sense, institutions can be defined as "durable systems of established and embedded social rules that structure social interactions", in other words, "social rulesystems".[292] These rules can be legal or non-legal in nature and make up mechanisms for coordinating actions that form the institutional structure, which in turn provides an environment for actors to behave according to possibilities and, at the

291 Here we are differentiating between norms and rules in terms of the completeness of their elements, but still within the parameters of Crawford and Ostrom's institutional analysis, i.e., without going into the rigor of the idea of a legal rule.

292 HODGSON, Geoffrey M. *The Evolution of Institutional Economics*. London and New York: Routledge, 2004, p. 424.

same time, shape these possibilities through their own actions.[293] In this institutional grammar, the coercive element can be added as a determining factor of distinction, more precisely the explicit or implicit provision for enforcement, here taken as the possibility of resorting to the state's monopolistic apparatus for the use of force, either directly or as a guarantor of compliance with obligations. In summary, the institutional statements, with their complete elements and with the incorporation of legal characteristics, result in the following general picture:

Table 1 - Legal-institutional syntax

<table>
<tr><td colspan="4"></td><td colspan="3">Antecedent</td><td colspan="3">Consequent</td></tr>
<tr><td colspan="4"></td><td>Attribute</td><td>Condition</td><td>Aim</td><td>Deontic Element</td><td>Full consequence</td><td>Enforcement</td></tr>
<tr><td rowspan="7">Institutional statements</td><td rowspan="3">Pre-normative</td><td></td><td>Discourse</td><td>x</td><td></td><td>x</td><td></td><td></td><td></td></tr>
<tr><td></td><td>Shared strategy</td><td>x</td><td>x</td><td>x</td><td></td><td></td><td></td></tr>
<tr><td></td><td>Public strategy</td><td>x</td><td>x</td><td>x</td><td></td><td></td><td>x</td></tr>
<tr><td rowspan="4">Normative</td><td rowspan="2">social</td><td>Social norm</td><td>x</td><td>x</td><td>x</td><td>x</td><td></td><td></td></tr>
<tr><td>Social rule</td><td>x</td><td>x</td><td>x</td><td>x</td><td>x</td><td></td></tr>
<tr><td rowspan="2">legal</td><td>Legal principle</td><td>x</td><td>x</td><td>x</td><td>x</td><td></td><td>x</td></tr>
<tr><td>Legal rule</td><td>x</td><td>x</td><td>x</td><td>x</td><td>x</td><td>x</td></tr>
</table>

Source: Own elaboration, based on Crawford and Ostrom.[294]

Law is not only interested in examining legal norms, since the extra-legal (or non-legal) aspects of institutions, in terms of coordination mechanisms, can be relevant as functional preconditions for successful or unsuccessful coordination of actions.[295] It can also be questioned whether these aspects are truly extra-legal or just overshadowed by a dogmatic view that is excessively dependent on the theory of the sources of law and pre-established forms.

The vision of institutions as systems of rules that are widely considered is an initial step towards situating the very idea of actors in legal analysis,

---

293 TRUTE, Hans-Heinrich. Die konstitutive Rolle der Rechtsanwendung. *In*: TRUTE, Hans-Heinrich *et al* (Orgs.). *Allgemeines Verwaltungsrecht - zur Tragfähigkeit eines Konzepts.* Tübingen: Mohr Siebeck, 2008, p. 224.

294 CRAWFORD; OSTROM, *op. cit.*

295 TRUTE, *op. cit.*, p. 224, when dealing with the approach of Governance as a conceptual framework.

who can either perform acts that have legal meaning and consequences, or ordinary acts outside the world of law and which do not have legal consequences *stricto sensu*, but whose outcomes indirectly or transversally affect a given legal dynamic, as well as the opposite: legal acts can have meanings and consequences beyond the world of law, which in some way can indirectly return as echoes in decision-making processes and in the conditions for their realization. If the search for what is effectively normatively important for the assessment of concrete cases goes beyond legal doctrine even in judicial decision (with realist doctrines of law having achieved some success in the historical transformation of *stricto-sensu* legal reasoning),[296] a broad normative aspect must be considered even more in the case of public policies, whether in their formulation or implementation, since politics and social needs are presented in their cycle in a clear way, leaving aside the clandestinity that legal-dogmatic analyses usually implicitly impute.

1.9.5 The management of incentives and disincentives by institutions

When we talk about incentives and disincentives, we presuppose the idea of rationality, i.e., that individuals act to achieve their interests. In this respect, rationality is interpreted as the logical process of maximizing preferences, whatever they may be, without looking at the rationality of the preferences themselves, i.e., the reasons why individuals developed them in the first place.[297]

In law, the emphasis on how institutions create incentives and disincentives and how they impact legal decisions and legally relevant behavior is explored mainly in the field of law and economics, when postulates from the theory of rational choice are applied to examine issues that go far beyond those directly involving economic problems or commercial issues. The essential idea is that the law assigns "prices" to different behaviors, and decision-makers, in seeking to optimize their gains and minimize their losses, base their choices on these "prices" in the same way that consumers

296 LEITER, Brian. Legal Realism and Legal Doctrine. *University of Pennsylvania Law Review*, v. 163, n. 1975, p. 11, 2015, p. 1983–1984.

297 SATZ, Debra; FEREJOHN, John. Rational Choice and Social Theory. *The Journal of Philosophy*, v. 91, n. 2, p. 71–87, 1994, p. 72–73.

and traders make their decisions in the economy's relative price market.[298] The options, paths, and consequences that laws assign are priced by the actors in legal decision-making. However, they are not limited to branches of law in which economic calculation is commonplace, such as commercial law, civil liability, tort, etc. The same reasoning applies to any branch of law, even in the case of committing crimes, although a "decision-making process" to break the criminal law makes much more sense in the case of crimes against property or financial crimes (premeditated in general) than in those of passion and influenced by issues of other kinds. In any case, the approach is useful in the construction of public policies to combat crime that are sensitive/responsive to the dynamics of incentives and disincentives of an economically quantifiable nature, as well as, because they are public policies, that have the component of public spending as a variable to be considered in the cost/benefit ratio.[299]

It is important to note that this dynamic of generating and managing incentives and disincentives does not only refer to those that are consciously and intentionally created through the law, with the most obvious examples of explicit punishment and explicit reward, but also to incentives and disincentives created inadvertently by legislators and regulators, due to asymmetry of information, political factors, or failure to anticipate future impacts.

Among these categories, the one that stands out the most is certainly the idea of perverse incentives, i.e., a set of results from a policy design that creates incentives exactly opposite to its purpose. This is the so-called "cobra effect", in the terms described by economist Horst Sieber,[300] but which is not always so clearly seen on a day-to-day basis. Mention should be made of the 2006 reform of the Brazilian Drug Law, which reduced the penalty for the crime of possession of narcotics, replacing it with community service in order to spare the user, and increased the penalty for the crime of trafficking. As a result, after years of application, it can be seen that instead of deflating criminal law and focusing the state's punitive power on the most serious conduct, as was the intention of the lawmakers, there has been an increase in the classification as trafficking of conduct that was

298 ULEN, Thomas S. Rational choice theory in law and economics. *Encyclopedia of law and economics*, v. 1, p. 790–818, 1999, p. 797.

299 BECKER, Gary S. Crime and Punishment: An Economic Approach. *Journal of Political Economy*, v. 76, n. 2, p. 169–217, 1968, p. 207.

300 SIEBERT, Horst. *Der Kobra-Effekt wie man Irrwege der Wirtschaftspolitik vermeidet.* Ungekürzte Taschenbuchausg. München/Zürich: Piper, 2003, p. 1–26.

previously only considered to be possession for personal use, due to the vague way in which the law differentiated the two crimes. As a result, more people were classified as the most serious crime, and the proportion of the prison population imprisoned for drug offenses tripled in just ten years.[301]

Recognizing institutions as generators of incentives and disincentives in the field of public policy cannot, therefore, be limited to the idea of pricing conduct and market-like dynamics, as seems to normally be the focus of law and economics analyses. In addition to considering the economic rationality of the individual in maximizing their interests, a view that brings together institutionalism and rational choice recognizes that there are structural factors that influence this process and interactions, such as the positive impacts on transaction costs.[302] There are also two aspects to consider in the context of legal relations. The first is the overlapping of cultural and ideological issues, in the semantic-interpretative milieu of the real assimilation of incentives at the end, i.e., the realization that in this dynamic, the attribution of "prices" to behaviors, and the respective and expected generation of compatible expectations, provide a useful, but not complete, analytical basis. The second is that incentives and disincentives will not always coincide exactly with the sum of the deontic element and the consequent element of the institutional syntax proposed by Crawford and Ostrom from the point of view of political science, or of the protective-repressive or functional orders, from Bobbio's legal perspective. Their meaning is redefined by external influences such as legitimate or illegitimate political interests, as well as the ideological preferences of the actors that are not institutionally crystallized or taken into account when designing the policy, due to informational asymmetry.

The comparison between incentives/disincentives and institutional syntax can indicate, if they coincide, perfect punitive or rewarding sanctions, and therefore good legal technique, or, on the contrary, dysfunctional sanctions, concluding that legal design fails in the formulation processes. These are two aspects that, if taken into account, make the regular postulates of rational choice theory applied to law good tools for analyzing concrete cases, in a similar way to the neoinstitutionalist analyses of rational choice

301 HUMAN RIGHTS WATCH. *World Report 2017*. New York: Seven Stories Press, 2017, p. 140.

302 MAYNTZ, Renate; SCHARPF, Fritz W. Der Ansatz des akteurzentrierten Institutionalismus. *In*: MAYNTZ, Renate; SCHARPF, Fritz W. (Orgs.). *Gesellschaftliche Selbstregelung und politische Steuerung*. Frankfurt/New York: Campus Verlag, 1995, p. 41.

in the field of political science. Even premises that seem questionable, such as that the preferences of the actors are stable and static,[303] can be weighted with other variables or taken "with a grain of salt", maintaining their usefulness, although not sufficient, for explaining phenomena in public policy. After all, as Oeter says, this is an analysis that emphasizes the normative constriction aspects of the decision-making process, as well as legal analysis.[304] In the case of the development of digital government in Brazil and other parts of the world, it will be worth considering how the different forms of institutionalization of digital transformation policies and their interaction with different legal regulations not only generate incentives and disincentives that affect the actors, but also, as regulatory structures for administrative activity, sensitize or desensitize these same actors to other external incentives, such as those represented by injection of financial resources, international practices, cultural trends or chance events.

1.9.6 Institutions as frames of meaning

The ability of institutions to create and manage incentives helps to explain the dynamics of public policies mediated by legal-institutional arrangements to the point where the very idea of formal rationality is sufficient to explain social behavior. Seeing the usefulness of rational choice theories does not, however, prevent us from recognizing that there are situations in which they do not apply, or at least cannot explain social phenomena without the complementation of other types of analysis. This is the case with the paradox of voting, for example, in which people continue to actively participate in the election, despite the fact that the "cost" of voting is always higher than the benefits,[305] since the impact of a single vote on the fate of the elections is insignificant in individual terms.[306] The contradictions may

303 SCHARPF, Fritz Wilhelm. *Games real actors play: actor-centered institutionalism in policy research.* Boulder, CO: Westview Press, 1997, p. 43–44.

304 OETER, Stefan. *The global legal order: an international lawyers' perspective inspired by institutionalism.* Bremen: University of Bremen, Collaborative Research Center 597: Transformations of the State, 2009, p. 4–5.

305 Cost and benefit are understood here in the context of a relationship between the individual effort a person makes in registering and turning up to vote, with the calculated and individualized return on that effort in terms of real influence on the outcome of an election.

306 BOUDON, Raymond. Beyond Rational Choice Theory. *Annual Review of Sociology*, v. 29, n. 1, p. 1–21, 2003, p. 6–7.

lie both in the questioning of the very idea of rationality as the driving force behind human action, with efforts by behavioral economics to establish patterns of predictability of these behaviors,[307] and in the incompleteness of reason in the case of decisions involving deep moral questions. As has already been pointed out, it should be borne in mind that the approaches are not mutually exclusive and can, therefore, be applied in a complementary way. Individuals can act on a notion of principle or moral commitment that does not presuppose formal rationality, but does not exclude it either.[308]

In this sense - and here again the difference between purely behaviouralist and neoinstitutionalist views is highlighted - institutions provide hermeneutic guidelines for actors aiming to act well, assigning specific meanings to acts according to their character and function, and through a set of instructions aimed at living together in a society oriented towards certain values, such as democracy.[309] It is the complementary expression of institutions as a normative order, but instead of operating in the form of incentives, it does so in an area outside them, through a logic of adequacy. As March and Olsen describe, "although self-interest undoubtedly permeates politics, action is often based more on discovering the normatively appropriate behavior than on calculating the return expected from alternative choices".[310] In the same vein, legally relevant institutional dynamics provide legal meanings to certain acts and facts, depending on the active and passive legitimacy of agents and recipients, with instructions to act in accordance with the law, from a perspective of semantic configuration of the social fact, as suggested by Ota Weinberger's institutionalism, or according to the expectations brought about by possible cognitive interpretations in general, or even the legal expectations of actors qualified to affirm the meaning of the norm in the process of application, choosing between

307 THALER, Richard H. Behavioral economics: Past, present, and future. *American economic review*, v. 106, n. 7, p. 1577–1600, 2016, p. 1579–1586.

308 SEN, Amartya K. Rational Fools: A Critique of the Behavioral Foundations of Economic Theory. *Philosophy & Public Affairs*, v. 6, n. 4, p. 317–344, 1977, p. 326, 344.

309 LHOTTA, Roland. Neoinstitutionalismus und Demokratie. *In*: LEMBCKE, Oliver W.; RITZI, Claudia; SCHAAL, Gary S. (Orgs.). *Zeitgenössische Demokratietheorie*. Wiesbaden: Springer Fachmedien, 2016, p. 139.

310 MARCH, James G.; OLSEN, Johan P. The New Institutionalism: Organizational Factors in Political Life. *The American Political Science Review*, v. 78, n. 3, p. 734–749, 1984, p. 744.

the possible results of interpretation, by an act of will of authority, from a Kelsenian perspective.[311]

The provision of cultural and legal meanings by the institutions, especially considering the direction from the macro to the micro levels, is one of the factors conditioning the concrete results in terms of the digitalization of public services.[312] The restrictions created by the institutional environment contribute to the isomorphism of meso and micro digital government institutions, from a coercive perspective, with a conservative bias. On the other hand, in the scenarios of risk and uncertainty that are inherent to technological innovation, isomorphism is also observed in its mimetic sense, since the restrictions of the environment, added to the pressures of society and the need for transformation, result in the incorporation of models and practices from successful organizations, especially at international level, with the importation of solutions. From a normative point of view, isomorphism[313] in digital government policies is very evident in terms of technological standards and technical standardization, but it is not limited to these, as there is a natural mirroring of the technique in its legal treatment, such as data protection, artificial intelligence and digital market regulations, which in Brazil tend to copy consolidated external initiatives. These general isomorphic trends in digital transformation have both positive and negative aspects. On the one hand, they favor the adaptation of the digital transformation to the protection of fundamental individual rights, by making arrangements and environments compatible, and they also favor the possibility of leaps in development by incorporating tried and tested models. On the other hand, they can limit innovation, insofar as it exceeds the adaptation of pre-conceived models, and delay deeper processes of institutional change in the institutional environment itself (and in the corresponding law), which would be necessary or useful for making better use of the potential of technology applied to state activity. This will

311 KELSEN, Hans. *Teoria Pura do Direito*. São Paulo: Martins Fontes, 1998, p. 392–394.

312 See, for instance, the case of digital government in Russia, ВАСЛАВСКИЙ, Ян И.; ГАБУЕВ, С. В. Неоинституциональный подход как методологическая основа исследования электронного правительства. *Вестник МГИМО-Университета*, n. 6(51), p. 60–75, 2016.

313 On the notion of isomorphism and the perspective from which it is being applied here, see DIMAGGIO, Paul J.; POWELL, Walter W. The Iron Cage Revisited: Institutional Isomorphism and Collective Rationality in Organizational Fields. *American Sociological Review*, v. 48, n. 2, p. 147–160, 1983.

be addressed more specifically in the following chapters and in the case analyses.

1.9.7 Actors, constellation of actors, and modes of interaction

The idea of the actor logically derives from the notion of social action, a kind of human action that considers the relationship with the behavior of others. In a broad Weberian conception, the actor is capable of carrying out actions driven by non-rational factors (such as emotions or cultural traditions) and by rational issues (driven by individual values or the pursuit of certain ends).[314] All of them, however, refer to or are oriented towards the behavior of other people, which highlights the social nature of conduct, even individual conduct.[315] In light of this, different conceptions of social action have been developed by various other sociologists as part of their own attempts to explain how society works.[316]

In policy science studies, the term *actor* is used very frequently and for practical purposes that transcend the theoretical discussion of the types, forms, and consequences of social action in theory, being more important to identify and delimit them specifically on a case-by-case basis and their potential to modify the outcome of a public policy. Some distinctions and classifications, however, become even more necessary considering these practical objectives, because on them will depend the analysis of how critical policy decisions are made and the ability of these decisions to generate effects initially intended by the political agenda. From a legal point of view, the classification of actors, their categorization into legal forms, the description of the limits of their competence[317], the legal-institutional forms of interaction, and the validity of their actions are important informative elements for identifying and evaluating the (dys)functionalities of the legal-institutional arrangements of public policies or critical success factors, with great practical prescriptive application to guide the reconfiguration of legal elements to improve the effectiveness of administrative measures in the specific case.

314 WEBER, Max. *Wirtschaft und Gesellschaft: Grundriss der verstehenden Soziologie.* 5. ed. Tübingen: Mohr, 1990, p. 12–16.

315 *Ibid.*

316 See, for example, the debate on the subject in SCHÜTZ, Alfred. *The theory of social action: The correspondence of Alfred Schutz and Talcott Parsons.* Bloomington: Indiana University Press, 1978, p. 8–61.

317 Attribution/jurisdiction.

The actor-centered approach of neoinstitutionalism combines the classic aspects of institutionalism more identified with the legal view and the specific dynamics of interests and preferences.[318] Of particular interest to this work are the dynamics of the constellation of actors in the institutional environment and the very scope of the idea of actors. What essentially characterizes actors are their capacities, perceptions, and preferences.[319] Capacities refer to resources that allow for a certain degree of action, which is naturally a relative concept, especially considering the objectives pursued. These attributes can be of two types: one referring to the subject's own characteristics, such as intelligence and human capital (as assets incorporated into the person[320]), including access to or control of financial resources, military power, technology, and access to information; and the other arising from rules emanating from institutions, which define competences, rights of action and participation and veto.[321]

From the point of view of a legal transposition of this idea, we have that the first group can be included in the world of facts, because it has more to do with what individuals and entities could effectively do independently of the rules that mediate behavior, in a natural limit of possibilities delineated by material or intrinsic characteristics. The second group, on the other hand, refers to two normative aspects of capacities, which vary according to the displacement of the subject on the public-private spectrum: these are notably the rules of competence for action, in the legal sense of the term, i.e., the fraction of political power that the law authorizes to be exercised by someone, with regard to the purely public spectrum. In addition to these, there are individual rights and duties, in the sense of the rules that authorize someone to exercise a certain positive or negative right vis-à-vis another person (including the state), or that oblige them to do or refrain from doing something. They are therefore aspects of the same element in relation to power - one is a factual expression and the other is a regulatory expression. A substantial part of the *de facto* capacities are neutralized by

318 OETER, Stefan. *The global legal order: an international lawyers' perspective inspired by institutionalism.* Bremen: University of Bremen, Collaborative Research Center 597: Transformations of the State, 2009, p. 11.

319 SCHARPF, Fritz Wilhelm. *Games real actors play: actor-centered institutionalism in policy research.* Boulder, CO: Westview Press, 1997, p. 43.

320 SCHULTZ, Theodore W. Capital Formation by Education. *Journal of Political Economy*, v. 68, n. 6, p. 571–583, 1960.

321 SCHARPF, *op. cit.*, p. 43.

the attribution of competences or obligations,[322] and both the attribution of competences and the form of their exercise are typical functions of law in a context of limitation of power.

Perceptions and preferences, in turn, can be static and stable (as is assumed in rational choice) or vary according to the type of stimulus they are exposed to, such as the definition of a specific problem, exposure to arguments or institutional configuration.[323] This translates into the maxim "Where you stand depends on where you sit", i.e., the actors tend to have their perceptions guided not only by atomized interests but by factors that derive from their structural position in the institutions.[324]

The notion of actor and its essential characteristics of capacities, perceptions, and preferences are a logical starting point insofar as they provide sufficient elements for predicting or explaining a behavior considering an isolated unit: by knowing the capacities and subjective orientations of the actors, as well as having a description of the environment in which they are inserted and the functioning of the laws of causality, one could in theory get closer to a precise answer.[325] But the actors are constantly interacting with each other, and the aforementioned units add up, intersect, and overlap in a dynamic of games, in the form of a constellation that brings together the plurality of those involved in public policy formation processes.[326] The constellations of actors are determined by institutional factors, to the extent that the rules create different competences for each person involved and condition some of their preferences and orientations, but this still refers to a static analysis model. Dynamically, different modes of interaction between actors are identified, which consist of a combination of the form of action and institutional configurations.[327]

Actors can be classified as individuals or composite/complexes[328]. Although social action is ultimately always carried out by the individual, it

322 *Ibid.*, p. 51.

323 *Ibid.*, p. 43–44.

324 FOUNTAIN, Jane E. *Building the virtual state: information technology and institutional change.* Washington, D.C: Brookings Institution Press, 2001, p. 83.

325 SCHARPF, *op. cit.*, p. 44.

326 *Ibid.*

327 The forms of action mentioned by Scharpf are unilateral action, negotiated, hierarchically directed and majority voting, while the institutional settings would be those of the anarchic field, network, association or organizations. *Ibid.*, p. 46.

328 BAUMGARTNER, Sabrina. *Die Regierungskommunikation der Schweizer Kantone: Regeln, Organisation, Akteure und Instrumente im Vergleich.* Wiesbaden: VS Verlag für Sozialwissenschaften, 2010, p. 84.

is reasonable to admit, for practical reasons, that they sometimes act on behalf of others or a group, and therefore sets of individuals can be considered as composite actors, from an external perspective, in order to elucidate certain policy consequences.[329] However, composite actors are made up of individual actors, and although this dimension is usually disregarded for practical reasons, going down to the level of the individual actor may be necessary to explain behaviors that the analysis of the composite actor alone cannot.[330] From an internal perspective, different individuals will interact autonomously within their groups or organizations to achieve a result which, externally, will be observed as the group's unique behavior, but these interactions at the micro level become less relevant for analysis once the action of the composite actor takes shape.[331] There are also situations, especially considering the legal-procedural dimension, in which the link between the composite actor and individual behavior is the subject of a legal presumption, as in the case of representing diffuse interests administratively or judicially.[332]

Composite actors can vary according to their degree of integration.[333] One category is made up of aggregates of actors. These are groups of individuals who act out of individual motivation in a certain direction, but whose choices do not really form a collective choice. The best example of this are groups of voters, but also "rural population", "university students", etc. Although we cannot deduce from their movements a collective choice or even the result of someone's individual choice, these actors can respond in a more or less predictable way to the movements of other actors acting strategically, like coalitions.[334] In this sense, coalitions can be defined as "semipermanent arrangements among actors pursuing separate but, by and large, convergent or compatible purposes and using their separate action resources in coordinated strategies".[335] They differ from aggregates of ac-

329 SCHARPF, *op. cit.*, p. 52.

330 MAYNTZ, Renate; SCHARPF, Fritz W. Der Ansatz des akteurzentrierten Institutionalismus. *In*: MAYNTZ, Renate; SCHARPF, Fritz W. (Orgs.). *Gesellschaftliche Selbstregelung und politische Steuerung*. Frankfurt/New York: Campus Verlag, 1995, p. 50.

331 SCHARPF, *op. cit.*, p. 52.

332 As in Law No. 9,784 of January 29, 1999.

333 SCHARPF, *op. cit.*, p. 54.

334 *Ibid.*

335 *Ibid.*, p. 55.

tors precisely because they have some non-trivial level of organization.[336] They usually act through agreements geared towards the interests of their members, who can also leave the coalition at any time.[337] Movements, on the other hand, have the characteristic of presenting themselves as a sum of voluntary contributions from their members, but unlike coalitions, decision-making processes are hardly defined by agreement or vote, there is no institutionalized leadership or complex decision-making structure, so that consensus-building becomes an essential tool to enable strategic action as a composite actor.[338] Particularly important in the relationship between politics and law are social movements, which are defined by their underlying social conflicts in a clear and well-defined dispute between different interests.[339] Finally, corporate actors bring together entities whose main characteristic is a top-down organization with fairly hierarchical decision-making and which indirectly reflects the interests of an owner, controller, or beneficiary, although there is a distinction between the personal interests of these figures and the interests of the corporation itself.[340] The significantly autonomous mode of organization and decision-making concerning the interests of the populations affected by it allows for a greater degree of effectiveness and efficiency of the measures taken by them, compared to other composite actors, but on the other hand, it allows for the emergence of super-powerful figures who often abuse the powers at their disposal.[341]

336 SABATIER, Paul A.; WEIBLE, Christopher M. The Advocacy Coalition Framework: Innovations and Clarifications. *In*: SABATIER, Paul (Org.). *Theories of the Policy Process*. 2. ed. London and New York: Routledge, 2007, p. 196.

337 SCHARPF, *op. cit.*, p. 55.

338 *Ibid.*, p. 55–56.

339 TOURAINE, Alain. An Introduction to the Study of Social Movements. *Social Research*, v. 52, n. 4, p. 749–787, 1985, p. 772.

340 SCHARPF, *op. cit.*, p. 57.

341 *Ibid.*

Let's return to the idea of modes of interaction mentioned earlier, summarized in the table below:

Table 2 - Modes of interaction

		Institutional setting			
		Anarchic field	Network	Association	Organization
Forms of action	unilateral action	x	x	x	x
	negotiated agreement	(x)	x	x	x
	majority vote	-	-	x	x
	hierarchical direction	-	-	-	x

Source: Adapted from Fritz Scharpf.[342]

The modes of interaction described by Scharpf, if projected as legal forms of interaction, can be combined with the different institutional settings to identify scenarios with different flexibilities and capacities for accommodating arrangements. The institutional configuration of the environment varies on a scale of organizational complexity: from an anarchic environment, in which each individual acts on their own, to orientation in the form of networks, then more structured forms such as associations, and finally the most complex, organizations.[343] Different modes of interaction require different institutional settings for them to be viable, and vice versa, and the concrete problem-solving capacity that results from them changes as the institutional structures change.[344] Modes of interaction and their conditional relationship with models of institutional configuration of complexities are particularly interesting for legal analysis. Unilateral actions, for example, take on different legal forms from negotiated agreements, decisions by vote and hierarchical direction, also varying according to the public and private spectrum. Unilateral actions can be the regular exercise of a subjective right by a private individual, such as a public service user, a company or a consumer, or the performance of an administrative or judicial act. Negotiated agreements, also considering the same spectrum, can be private contracts for carrying out an activity establishing mutual rights and obligations, but also legal forms of public-private relations such as admin-

342 *Ibid.*, p. 47.
343 *Ibid.*, p. 46.
344 *Ibid.*, p. 47.

istrative contracts, or even, in the purest public form, comprising inter-federative and inter-organizational cooperation, such as agreements between the Union, States, and Municipalities. Decision-making by vote can range from the production of a private institutional sectoral decision, such as a union or sectoral entity, or the normative product of a collegiate decision within the scope of a council or board of a public entity with a regulatory function, including agencies and parliaments. Hierarchical direction, in the private sphere, can take the form of the power of corporate control, in the exercise of employers' rights inherent in the employment relationship, and in the public sphere in the exercise of high-ranking executive powers, in municipalities, administrative bodies or state-owned companies.

Institutional settings, on the other hand, also take on different legal forms corresponding to the increasing degree of complexity, the intensity of which conditions the viability of the different modes of interaction and their respective legal expressions. The anarchic field, for example, represents the sphere of the individual as the sole emanator of a decision. In the private sphere, it is the subject of law, and in the public sphere it is the public servant, the manager or the judge. The network, in the private sphere, can be a group of people interacting in a common environment, and in the public sphere an environment of collaborative interaction between entities through voluntary adhesion. The setting in the form of associations and organizations[345] also follows the same increasing scale of sophistication of legal forms and so on.

What we can see is that modes of interaction, combined with institutional settings, generate a range of possibilities for interactions and, consequently, for the choice of legal instruments for government action.[346] Checking how modes and settings present themselves in practice can also indicate an arrangement's greater propensity for adaptation or plasticity and, therefore, for experimental practices and innovation, which are so important for technology-related public policies, especially the digital transformation of the public sector. The potential scope for experimentalism in the practice of public policies is the result of a more or less optimal combination of two factors, namely the legal-institutional setting and the

345 Associations and organizations can be seen as actors in themselves, as mentioned in the previous section, but also as institutional settings for the interaction of other actors.

346 Based on what concludes SCHARPF, *op. cit.*, p. 47, when he states that "What is more interesting, from a theoretical point of view, is the possibility that modes of interaction will change their character—and their capacity for the resolution of policy problems—from one structural setting to another[...]".

legal-institutional modes of interaction, which result in a multiplicity of different scenarios, each with its own implications for the expectations of the actors in relation to the validity and stability of the arrangements.

In a scenario of maximum flexibility, all the degrees of complexity of the institutional setting of the policies converge towards all the degrees of complexity of the legal modes of interaction, giving a great deal of room for choice and action, such as the use of simple instruments for complex configurations and vice versa. Depending on the institutional environment and, in particular, general rules, such as contracting regimes, limitations on competence, etc., scenarios can take on different configurations with greater or lesser versatility, as illustrated graphically below.

Figure 1 - Scenarios of legal-institutional arrangements

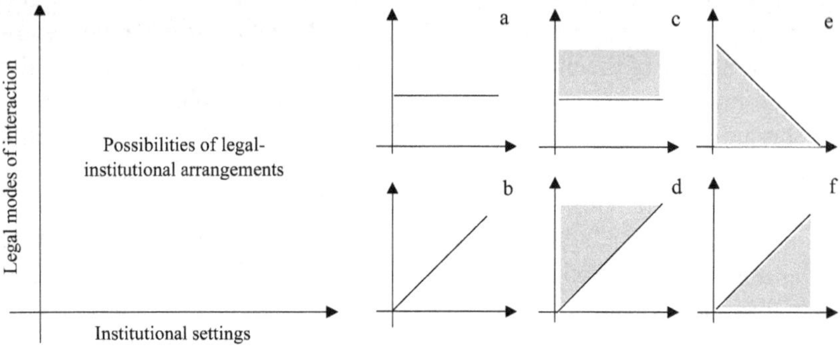

Source: Own elaboration.

Different situations concerning the formulation and implementation of policies can be classified considering the scenarios mentioned to perceive the potential of that arrangement to accommodate innovation. In other words, this also represents different degrees of propensity to isomorphism and the institutional space for action of the most diverse actors involved in the policy-making and implementation process.

1.9.8 Path dependency

As Berger and Luckmann point out, "it is impossible to understand an institution adequately without an understanding of the historical process in which it was produced".[347] In other words, institutions are products and producers of history, and this trajectory is important for understanding the current institutional framework of a society and the possibilities for future transformations.

Path dependency stems from positive feedback mechanisms, such as in the case of policies created and their effects over time on attempts and modifications to the policies themselves.[348] They represent increasing returns concerning the evolution of a given policy, which make it less prone to change due to the incorporation of elements based on pre-established policies, i.e., the cost of adopting alternatives that were foreseen from the outset gradually increases. In the process of increasing returns, "the probability of further steps along the same path increases with each move down that path. This is because the relative benefits of the current activity compared with other possible options increase over time."[349]

What this means in practical terms is that institutions cannot vary at will or randomly depending solely on political initiative or technocratic or voluntarist measures but according to historically solidified constraints that mark their evolutionary path.[350] As path dependency is a factor commonly mentioned in studies on the implementation of digital government,[351] particularly in developing countries, it should also be considered when examining the Brazilian Digital Government.

---

347 BERGER, Peter L; LUCKMANN, Thomas. *The Social Construction of Reality. A Treatise in the Sociology of Knowledge.* London: Penguin Books, 1991, p. 72.

348 See, for example, ZEHAVI, Amos J. Veto Players, Path Dependency, and Reform of Public Aid Policy toward Private Schools: Australia, New Zealand, and the United States. *Comparative Politics*, v. 44, n. 3, p. 311–330, 2012.

349 PIERSON, Paul. Increasing Returns, Path Dependence, and the Study of Politics. *The American Political Science Review*, v. 94, n. 2, p. 251–267, 2000, p. 252.

350 BENZ, Arthur. Themen, Probleme und Perspektiven der vergleichenden Föderalismusforschung. *In*: BENZ, Arthur; LEHMBRUCH, Gerhard (Orgs.). *Föderalismus: Analysen in entwicklungsgeschichtlicher und vergleichender Perspektive.* Wiesbaden: VS Verlag für Sozialwissenschaften, 2002, p. 40.

351 See SENSHAW, Debas; TWINOMURINZI, Hossana. Critical path-dependencies affecting digital government innovation in low-income countries: a case study from Woredas in Ethiopia. *Electronic Government, an International Journal*, v. 20, n. 1, p. 1–19, 2024; PEDERSEN, Keld. E-government transformations: challenges and strategies. *Transforming Government: People, Process and Policy*, v. 12, n. 1, p. 84–109, 2018.

1.9.9 Veto points and enabling points

Veto points are "points of strategic uncertainty that arise from the logic of the decision process itself".[352] The situation caused by the multiple possibility of vetoes in joint decisions requiring unanimity, with its corresponding consequence of political decision-making by the lowest common denominator, was described as a "joint decision trap" (*Politikverflechtungsfalle*) by Fritz Scharpf in 1985.[353] However, it is in Ellen Immergut's work on health system reforms in post-war Europe that these situations are identified as institutional veto points, which, depending on where they are positioned, condition quite different policy outcomes.[354] At the same time, there is also the figure of the veto player, who can be defined as "an individual or collective actor whose agreement is required for a policy decision" according to George Tsebelis.[355] It should be noted, however, that the subjective condition of the veto player is fundamentally dependent on the institutional configuration in which they are inserted, since it is this that transfers to them the meaning and power inherent in their potential action. In this way, veto players will vary as the institutions that mediate their behavior vary, and the qualitative and quantitative examination of the impact of the veto is made by scrutinizing the institutional design, and not by the subjective profile of those who exercise the role institutionally conferred on them.

Naturally, veto points are not determinant of the actions of the actors to whom they confer power, but they create possibilities that tend to be exercised both by the subjects to whom the institutions directly attribute this function, and by actors who orbit the official institutional relationship. Both in situations where actors have privileged access to decision-mak-

352 IMMERGUT, Ellen M. The rules of the game: The logic of health policy-making in France, Switzerland, and Sweden. *In*: STEINMO, Sven; THELEN, Kathleen; LONGSTRETH, Frank (Orgs.). *Structuring Politics: Historical Institutionalism in Comparative Analysis*. Cambridge: Cambridge University, 1992, p. 66.

353 SCHARPF, Fritz W. The Joint-Decision Trap: Lessons from German Federalism and European Integration. *Public Administration*, v. 66, n. 3, p. 239–278, 1988; originally published as SCHARPF, Fritz W. Die Politikverflechtungsfalle: Europäische Politik und deutscher Födemlismus im Vergleich. *Politische Vierteljahresschrift*, v. 26, p. 323–356, 1985.

354 IMMERGUT, *op. cit.*

355 TSEBELIS, George. Veto Players and Law Production in Parliamentary Democracies: An Empirical Analysis. *American Political Science Review*, v. 93, n. 3, p. 591–608, 1999, p. 293.

ers,[356] and in official political dynamics, veto points can explain the degree of influence of interest groups on the course of a public policy and the extent to which certain decision-making structures tend towards certain results.[357] Furthermore, veto points do not appear randomly (as do the actors who exercise them) but come from how the rules establish a decision-making framework. This framework is also indirectly responsible for determining the power of the interest groups that orbit policymaking, much more than their own intrinsic characteristics, such as level of organization and economic power.[358] The identification of legally qualified veto points is a useful tool for examining the functioning of government programs from a Law and Public Policy perspective, and its application can be seen in previous work by this author on basic sanitation in Brazil.[359]

Given the importance of the creative element in public Digital Government policies and innovation in general, the notion of veto points should be complemented with the idea of legally qualified *enabling points*. These are logical consequences of the fact that institutions create and promote initiatives as well as limiting them. Considering the objective of incorporating constant technological innovation that characterizes these policies, their degree and form of distribution in institutional environments and arrangements plays an important role in the state's capacity to develop them.

The act of vetoing is an exclusive power conferred specifically on an actor by previously institutionalized choices; in other words, it is a very particular way in which power has been distributed unequally by institutions. The act of creating, on the other hand, may seem free at first glance, theoretically within anyone's reach and possible in any institutional confluence, since it would not represent a suppressive effect on processes or someone's power over others. However, if it is possible for any actor to have ideas and imagine different ways of solving problems, the materialization of this idea

356 IMMERGUT, Ellen M.; ORLOWSKI, Matthias. Veto Points and the Environment. *In*: ARMINGEON, Klaus (Org.). *Staatstätigkeiten, Parteien und Demokratie: Festschrift für Manfred G. Schmidt.* Wiesbaden: Springer Fachmedien, 2013, p. 205.

357 IMMERGUT, Ellen M. Institutions, Veto Points, and Policy Results: A Comparative Analysis of Health Care. *Journal of Public Policy*, v. 10, n. 4, p. 391–416, 1990.

358 *Ibid.*, p. 397.

359 VALENTE, Sergio Ruy David Polimeno. *Políticas públicas e a visão jurídico-institucional: o caso do saneamento básico no Brasil.* Master's thesis, University of São Paulo, 2018; VALENTE, Sergio Ruy David Polimeno. Direito e políticas públicas: uma visão jurídico-institucional sobre o caso do saneamento básico no Brasil. *Rei - Revista Estudos Institucionais*, v. 5, n. 3, p. 1064–1092, 2019.

as a seed, project, or starting point to have a relevant influence on future decision-making depends on institutional conjunction of various meanings, which can consist of institutionalized ways of collecting and pursuing ideas, material possibilities for continuity, or means of dissemination to enable the idea to be developed by others, and arrangements that enable exchanges of knowledge to make possible an idea that, in isolation, was unfeasible. Enabling points are, therefore, an institutional situation in which an actor has the opportunity to have their idea or initiative echoed and potentially developed by themselves or others; in other words, the institutional set-up that allows actors concrete opportunities to make an objective prosper.

1.9.10 Discourses and ideas in inter- and intra-institutional relations

It is a common observation that ideas affect public policies in different ways, whether in the role of epistemic communities in proposing solutions to problems, in the role of institutions as repositories and propagators of beliefs, or in the institutional dynamics that regulate access to different visions and proposals in the decision-making process.[360] In addition to the very notion of a guiding idea that constitutes the units of organization of law itself (as argued by Hauriou), a discursive neoinstitutionalist perspective advocates that the ideas that permeate public policies can be classified into two types, cognitive and normative. The former respond to questions about the meaning and causality of actions (what it is, what to do), what the problems identified by policies are, and how they propose to solve them; the latter refer to the evaluative element of actions (whether it is good or bad, what should be done), attributing value to political action to legitimize it.[361] The ability of actors to cognitively or normatively influence the preferences of others can be considered a special form of power exercised through persuasion, direct imposition, or altering the contexts in which ideation takes place.[362] The emphasis on ideas, from a static point of view, is close to the sociological approach to the attribution of cultural meanings, but from a dynamic point of view, it shifts attention to the phenomenon of discourse.

---

360 YEE, Albert S. The causal effects of ideas on policies. *International Organization*, v. 50, n. 1, p. 69–108, 1996, p. 86, 88, 92.

361 SCHMIDT, Vivien. Discursive Institutionalism: The Explanatory Power of Ideas and Discourse. *Annual Review of Political Science*, v. 11, 2008, p. 306, 307.

362 CARSTENSEN, Martin B.; SCHMIDT, Vivien A. Power through, over and in ideas: conceptualizing ideational power in discursive institutionalism. *Journal of European Public Policy*, v. 23, n. 3, p. 318–337, 2016, p. 321.

Discourses are not just about ideas, but mainly about the processes by which ideas are managed. They are both structure (because they contain the text - what is said - and also the context - how, when and where), and agency, because they have an author and an addressee.[363] Discourses are important in the dynamics of institutional transformation because of their ability to influence political reality.[364] They can be understood as an exchange of ideas, especially the path from individual thought to collective action.[365] The same can be extended to the legal reality, both in the form of argumentation in the context of power disputes in litigious areas, and in the construction of cognizant legal expectations with society in new or controversial factual situations.

Discourses can be divided into two types. *Coordinative* discourses are those performed between individuals directly involved in the construction of policies, such as civil servants, political agents, public managers, and members of epistemic communities or experts, who exchange normative and cognitive aspects of their views on a problem or subject and generally remain on the sidelines of public debates.[366] In this sense, the more complex the organizational structure (of the state, for example), the more elaborate the coordinative discourse will be.[367] *Communicative* discourses, on the other hand, take place in the sphere of public opinion, and their protagonists, such as political leaders and activists, are responsible for presenting, defending, and legitimizing ideas to the general public, who in turn also contribute to them in some way.[368] The same institutional complexity tends to produce more generic communicative discourses so that exhortations to the public don't interfere with the agreements and adjustments made between the actors at the coordination level.[369]

Discourses can contribute to the success or failure of the ideas they contain, while the formal institutional context conditions the potential success of the discourse insofar as different institutional configurations emphasize different forms of discourse. Simpler or centralized political structures are

---

363 SCHMIDT, *op. cit.*, p. 303.
364 *Ibid.*, p. 306.
365 SCHMIDT, Vivien A. Reconciling Ideas and Institutions through Discursive Institutionalism. *In*: BÉLAND, Daniel; COX, Robert Henry (Orgs.). *Ideas and politics in social science research*. Oxford and New York: Oxford University Press, 2011, p. 56.
366 SCHMIDT, 2008, *op. cit.*, p. 310.
367 SCHMIDT, 2011, *op. cit.*, p. 59.
368 SCHMIDT, 2008, *op. cit.*, p. 310.
369 SCHMIDT, 2011, *op. cit.*, p. 59.

more prone to communicative discourse directly to the masses, while complex and decentralized structures are more prone to the need for a coordinative discourse for integration between the different horizontal actors.[370]

The observation of discourses, their elements, and characteristics in the face of the arrangements given by the context of a given public policy, complements the previous views, especially in order to identify problems in the agenda phase, such as the definition of political priorities or legal means-end relationships concerning the objectives of making social rights effective. The elucidation of questions about public problems that make up the formulation and scrutiny of cognitive and normative ideas involves a prospective judgment of the effectiveness of the ideas in relation to the purposes and, therefore, in relation to their greater ability to maximize the realization of a social right that is the purpose of a program. In this way, the discourse and the ideas it contains, as well as the way it is handled, influence not only the political but also the legal significance of a public policy, such as the adequacy between ends and means (proportionality), the legality of its instruments, and its justification in terms of budgetary priorities in the arena of competition in terms of practical importance to the constitutional program.

1.10 Chapter conclusion

The legal-institutional view of public policies requires compatibility between legal elements of analysis and others related to the study of institutions and is, therefore, an interdisciplinary approach. This does not mean that the legal nature of the research is mitigated. On the contrary, by working with categories developed in other branches of policy sciences, the use of legal science to understand objects of study is maximized. In the same vein, by introducing legal thinking and, in particular, the tools of legal dogmatics, into traditional fields of research in the social sciences, opportunities are created to transcend the epistemological limits of these areas.

This involves looking at the object and identifying the role of law in public policies. As well as regulating the processes that shape them, it has outstanding functions in the substantive, structuring, instrumental, and legitimizing dimensions, in a more promotional and less protective-re-

370 SCHMIDT, 2008, *op. cit.*, p. 311–312.

pressive way. And, in addition to the object, law involves looking at the analytical apparatus used to understand the performance of these functions in concrete cases, in other words, the handling of legal dogmatics, although less concerned with the problem of the decision, and more with the "regime of outcomes/effects".

The incorporation of elements foreign to law into a predominantly legal investigation requires, however, prior conceptual treatment of the premises and categories coming from outside, not only so that their application is more precise, but also to explore how they are expressed in the legal world, which may represent restrictions on the original notions, or possibly expansions. This involves not only explaining concepts from political science, economics and sociology, such as actors, incentives, path dependence, veto points, discourse, among others, and their repercussions in the field of law, but also exploring the normative dimension of institutions from a broader perspective than the traditional legal view. The result is a set of informative elements that make up a proposal for a legal-institutional heuristics to support the study of Digital Government as a public policy.

This conceptual apparatus and its legal developments are added to the collection of key questions extracted from frameworks and models of analysis in Law and Public Policy, which in turn are also, in some sense, the product of the same process of interdisciplinary integration consolidated as a method, the value of which has been previously demonstrated in applied work by other authors.[371]

The application of the conceptual heuristic and the key questions of the legal-institutional view will not be explicit in the analysis of Digital Government policies, as in the form of drawing up charts, tables or clipped comparisons of their elements. It will happen implicitly by informing the line of reasoning and the choices of approaches, comments, and criticisms.

371 Among others, TOLEDO, Carlos José Teixeira de. *Políticas Públicas e Valorização do Professor da Educação Básica.* Belo Horizonte, MG: Fórum, 2022; ARAÚJO, Alexandra Fuchs de. *Políticas Públicas, Poder Judiciário e o Direito à Moradia.* Belo Horizonte: Forum, 2023; GAMBA, Giovanna Maísa. *Estratégia nacional de combate à corrupção e à lavagem de dinheiro: institucionalidade jurídica da política em rede.* Belo Horizonte, MG: Editora Fórum, 2023; CORDEIRO, Caio Barros. *Tecnologia e Estado na era digital: Transformação à luz da abordagem Direito e Políticas Públicas.* Belo Horizonte: Fórum, 2024; SALES, Gabriela Azevedo Campos. *Estado social e federalismo: a institucionalização dos sistemas de políticas públicas no Brasil.* Belo Horizonte, MG: Fórum, 2023; SOUZA, Matheus Silveira de. *Direito, Políticas Públicas e Educação Profissional.* Belo Horizonte, MG: Fórum, 2022; HADDAD, Frederico. *O direito à rua: políticas públicas e a função social das vias urbanas.* Belo Horizonte: Fórum, 2022.

At the same time, an attempt will be made to explore the possibilities offered by this body of information and to stick to its limits. In addition, efforts will be made to ensure that the results, answers, and conclusions of the research are products of the guidelines provided by this structuring of the method.

2 The institutionalization of Digital Government in Brazil

This chapter will explore the institutionalization of Digital Government in Brazil. It will begin by explaining the development of the Brazilian Digital Government as it is understood today, including its trajectory and the key aspects that have shaped the current framework. Next, we will identify and explore the legal bases that make up the Digital Government arrangement and some of its most important characteristics, either because they represent limitations and obstacles to effective implementation or because they consist of elements that should be known as a condition for criticism.

2.1 Overview and institutional trajectory

The first step towards introducing information technology into the Brazilian state took place in 1964 with the creation of the Federal Data Processing Service - SERPRO, a public company whose purpose was all forms of electronic data processing related to ministries and other public entities that contracted its services.[372] SERPRO was responsible for computerizing the back-end of income tax in Brazil in the very first years of its existence, and as early as 1967 tax returns began to be processed with the aid of computers, after receiving physical forms and manually entering data typed in by civil servants.[373] The agency was also responsible for creating the Integrated Financial Administration System of the Federal Government - SIAFI G2G (government-to-government) in 1987, which computerized the management of the federal budget, and in the following years, it also created SISCOMEX, a G2B (*government-to-business*) computerized foreign trade system.[374]

With the beginning of the popularization of the Internet in the 1990s, embryonic and uncoordinated initiatives to computerize channels of interaction with citizens emerged in various public entities and under the

372 Law No. 4,516, of December 1, 1964.

373 LIMA, Weldson Queiroz de. *Contribuições do SERPRO para a formação do Programa de Governo Eletrônico Brasileiro em uma perspectiva fazendária.* Specialization thesis (Public Management), Uniserpro, Porto Alegre, 2014, p. 32.

374 *Ibid.*, p. 35, 38.

influence of the growth of e-commerce.[375] The Brazilian Senate and some federal courts created systems for accessing information and contacting citizens, some states and municipalities developed integrated computerized service centers, and the state and federal tax authorities developed systems for receiving information and providing related services over the internet.[376] Another highlight is the income tax return, which, from 1991, could be submitted electronically (using a magnetic diskette) using software developed by SERPRO in partnership with the Special Department of Federal Revenue of Brazil - SRF. As of 1996, it could also be submitted via the internet,[377] in one of the first national G2C (government-to-citizen) initiatives. By the year 2000, 80% of income tax returns in Brazil were already filed via the internet.[378]

Beyond these one-off initiatives, Digital Government as a nationally conceived policy originated in the late 1990s, in the context of the managerial reform of the Brazilian public administration,[379] influenced by the *new public Management* doctrine, in a scenario of fiscal crisis and demand for structural reforms in various sectors of the Brazilian economy and state. In this scenario, priority was given to policies aimed at reducing public spending and improving the efficiency of government structures, and digitalization represented a promising avenue in this regard.[380] The Master Plan for the Reform of the State Apparatus, a document drawn up in 1995 by the Federal Government and which would guide much of these reforms, included a topic with the embryonic idea of a systematic integration of information, data, and communication between government entities, called *Rede Governo* (Government Network). According to the document, the aim was to

375 RECK, Janriê Rodrigues; HÜBNER, Bruna Henrique. A transformação digital do Estado: digitalização do governo e dos serviços úblicos no Brasil. *Revista Eletrônica Direito e Política*, v. 16, n. 3, p. 1075–1096, 2021, p. 1085.

376 FERREIRA, Antônio Sérgio Seco; NEVES, Sérgio da Cunha. Contribuições para o planejamento da integração e da publicação de informações da administração pública. *Revista de Administração*, v. 37, n. 1, 2002, p. 66.

377 PIETRACCI, Luciano. *Programa gerador de declarações de imposto de renda pessoa jurídica em disquete*. Brasília: ENAP, 1997.

378 GARCIA, Rodrigo-Moreira. Governo eletrônico, informação e competência em informação. *Informação & Sociedade: Estudos*, v. 16, n. 2, 2006, p. 83.

379 SIMÃO, João Batista; RODRIGUES, Georgete. Acessibilidade às informações públicas: uma avaliação do portal de serviços e informações do governo federal. *Ciência da Informação*, v. 34, n. 2, p. 81–92, 2005, p. 81.

380 LAIA, Marconi Martins de *et al.* Electronic government policies in Brazil: Context, ICT management and outcomes. *RAE Revista de Administracao de Empresas*, v. 51, n. 1, p. 43–57, 2011, p. 44.

create a means of sharing public databases between government bodies and to "pass on as much information as possible to society in general and to the government bodies themselves, contributing to better transparency and greater efficiency in the conduct of government business".[381]

The concrete initiative in terms of national public policy dates back to the following year, when the Secretariat of Logistics and Information Technology of the Ministry of Planning, Budget and Management (SLTI) began developing the *Rede Governo Portal* to make information and services available to the administration in a unified way to integrate states and municipalities.[382] While *Rede Governo* was a project designed to integrate the administration internally, envisaged in conjunction with the improvement of public management systems such as the National Treasury's spending register, payroll, budget, planning, supplier registry, etc.,[383] the *Rede Governo Portal* sought to be the integrated electronic form of communication between the state and the citizen. At the time, there were incipient websites of entities and governments, each developed according to different standards and guidelines in specific and uncoordinated initiatives. The idea was for the Federal Government to promote the integration of these, focusing on facilitating user access to information and services. There were innovative features for the time, such as the intention to integrate services, simplify the complex language that prevailed within the state bureaucracy, and establish a clear state policy guideline, signifying that the platform would abstract the elements specific to political administrations in favor of more impersonal and standardized communication.[384] It is important to point out that the project was an internal initiative by civil servants within the bureaucracy of the federal administration, who introduced the idea and its initial outlines within the SLTI, which was later accepted by the administration and imple-

381 BRASIL. *Plano Diretor da Reforma do Aparelho do Estado*. Brasília: Presidência da República, 1995, p. 80. In the original, "... repassar à sociedade em geral e aos próprios órgãos do governo, a maior quantidade possível de informação, contribuindo para melhor transparência e maior eficiência na condução dos negócios do Estado".

382 Information obtained from a report presented at the 7th Innovation in Federal Public Management Competition, in which the project won an award. Available in the repositories of the National School of Public Administration (ENAP), SANTOS, Roberval de Jesus Leone dos. *Rede Governo: o portal de serviços e informações para o cidadão*. Brasília: Escola Nacional de Administração Pública, 2003.

383 BRASIL, *op. cit.*, p. 81.

384 SANTOS, *op. cit.*

mented as a public policy.[385] The portal used resources from the SLTI itself, as well as from the Federal Government for the contract with SERPRO and from the United Nations Development Program (UNDP) for project consultancy.[386]

The *Rede Governo* portal continued to be developed and integrated into a more comprehensive architecture.[387] It was the subject of criticism pointing out deficiencies related to the failure to meet targets, a lack of clarity in distinguishing between services and information, and an unintuitive organization, among others—all attributed to the absence of structured information management policies within the administration.[388] Despite this, *Rede Governo* represented a leap in quality in how the government viewed the relationship with citizens mediated by technology, and many of its foundations and objectives are still valid today. In quantitative terms, by the end of 2002, there were around 1,700 online services listed[389] and 11,000 types of information available on the portal.[390] It functioned less as a portal for direct access to online services and more as an information search index, but despite the limitations of its functionalities, it was a first effort to organize the vast amount of information that the various public bodies published randomly on the internet.[391]

In these early days of structured digital government policies, there was an experimentalist dynamic that provided the basic means for the bureaucracy's ideas and initiatives, even if they followed reformist macro-political guidelines, to take shape and engage institutional resources and efforts. There are multiple factors, however, that contributed to these policies de-

385 The report mentions that the initiative originally came from a single SLTI employee, but this information could not be confirmed by other sources.

386 SANTOS, *op. cit.*

387 In subsequent years, the name "Electronic Government Program" (Programa Governo Eletrônico) was used to refer to this broader vision, and this is the reference in the Annual Budget Laws of the time. See, for example, volume II of the annexes to the Annual Budget Law for 2003, Law No. 10,640, of January 14, 2003.

388 JARDIM, José Maria. Governo eletrônico no Brasil: o portal Rede Governo. *Arquivística.net*, v. 3, n. 1, 2007, p. 34–35.

389 The source consulted refers to online services. However, it was not possible to verify the degree of online functionality.

390 DINIZ, Eduardo Henrique *et al.* O governo eletrônico no Brasil: perspectiva histórica a partir de um modelo estruturado de análise. *Revista de Administração Pública*, v. 43, n. 1, p. 23–48, 2009, p. 36.

391 BITTENCOURT FILHO, Jorge Calmon Moniz de; LOIOLA, Elizabeth R. The Public Services Provided by Brazilian Government Over the Internet. *SSRN Electronic Journal*, 2001, p. 8.

veloping quickly and consistently compared to the standards of the time. Initially, tackling the Year 2000 problem, or "millennium bug", at the end of the 1990s qualified the SLTI as an actor capable of executing the pioneering Digital Government programs and coordinating various actions and actors, since it played a competent role in remedying issues involving sensitive systems, such as tax collection.[392] In addition, the SLTI had the direct involvement and support of the Minister of Planning, especially after the successful adaptations to the aforementioned bug. The minister's involvement was more focused on guaranteeing financial resources and prioritizing the program within the government, which guaranteed SLTI greater autonomy, including adding other important players to the process, such as the Civil House. The Minister of Planning at the time was Pedro Parente, who had great prestige and influence over President Fernando Henrique Cardoso, and his involvement, together with the Civil House, gave the SLTI the political clout it didn't originally have, especially to lobby other ministries.[393] This interaction took place through the Electronic Government Executive Committee (CEGE), which was the inter-ministerial body formally responsible for drawing up e-government policies.[394]

However, there was a major brake on innovation due to the lack of mechanisms and rules that would enable more intense coordination between the various federal government bodies and, more importantly, between the different federal levels. The SLTI was a body within a federal government ministry, with no power to make binding decisions, and any progress depended exclusively on ongoing political efforts. Faced with a situation of cooperation obtained through an initial political effort favored by a good idea and the coordinative discourse that disseminated it as a viable policy, the lack of institutional structures that crystallized a balance of preferences led to a decrease in the mobilization of resources for the project, and the objectives of continuous innovation were cooled.

This was observed from the point of view of human resources, which were demobilized by a loss of political interest and financial resources. In the first case, several factors contributed to this political demobilization. Firstly, the energy crisis in 2001 changed the Civil House's priorities regarding Digital Government programs, and the Minister of Planning became president of the Crisis Management Chamber. As a result, with

392 DINIZ *et al*, *op. cit.*, p. 39.
393 *Ibid.*, p. 40, 41.
394 Decree without number of October 18, 2000.

the absence of the Civil House at CEGE meetings and without the direct involvement of the government's top echelon, the pace of action began to slow down.[395] Added to this was the influence of the election process the following year, in which the low prospects of the government candidate discouraged the teams from structuring long-term projects. The change of government in 2003 caused a temporary discontinuity in CEGE's work, which only resumed effectively in mid-2004, but still with limitations.[396] A comprehensive assessment of the e-government program by the Federal Court of Accounts in 2006 points out that among the difficulties for its continued development was the "loss of political interest in the subject in recent years, which led to a loss of effectiveness of the program's operating structure in the form provided for in the legislation, supported by the CEGE and its TC [Technical Committees]".[397] From the point of view of mobilizing financial resources, it can also be seen that institutional limitations were a major factor, especially the lack of a coordinating body capable of negotiating sufficient budget allocations with the economic area of the Executive Branch.[398] The reported absence of the ministries' Executive Secretaries from committee meetings also indicated the decreasing political priority given to the issue.[399]

The analysis of this initial experience shows that when there are exogenous political impulses and external incentives for the policy to be institutionalized, gains and progress can be maintained consistently even with insufficient or precarious institutionalization, and space can be opened up for experimental attempts with controlled risk-taking aimed at innovation. However, when political priorities change, such as in crisis situations or changes in the political agenda of all kinds, the fragility of the legal-institutional framework contributes to a greater degree to the dysfunctionality of public policy. In this case, the lack of regular CEGE meetings and the deficiency in formalizing and documenting activities meant that the TCs'

395 DINIZ *et al*, *op. cit.*, p. 41.

396 *Ibid.*, p. 42.

397 TCU. *Avaliação do Programa Governo Eletrônico. Tribunal de Contas da União.* Brasília: Secretaria de Fiscalização e Avaliação de Programas de Governo, 2006, p. 17. In the original, "... perda de interesse político no tema nos últimos anos, o que acarretou perda de efetividade da estrutura de funcionamento do Programa na forma prevista na legislação, apoiada no CEGE e em seus CT [Comitês Técnicos]".

398 MEDEIROS, Paulo Henrique Ramos; GUIMARÃES, Tomás De Aquino. A institucionalização do governo eletrônico no Brasil. *Revista de Administração de Empresas,* v. 46, n. 4, p. 1–13, 2006, p. 76.

399 TCU, *op. cit.*, p. 19.

discussions were not transformed into public policy norms and guidelines. Given the lack of clear political direction from the top echelons of the government, problems such as the overlapping roles of administrative bodies and bodies that issue standards on digitization became more acute.[400]

Alongside *Rede Governo*, there was also another set of projects aimed at the digital transformation of Brazilian society in a broader sense: *Sociedade de Informação* (Information Society).[401] The program was the result of efforts made by the National Council for Science and Technology since 1996 and was set up at the end of 1999, coordinated by the Ministry of Science and Technology and bringing together projects already included in the 2000/2003 Multi-Year Plan, with resources in the order of R$3.4 billion at the time.[402] The Program had a strategic objective of coordinating the country's development around communication and information technologies, also with a view to the competitiveness of the national economy, as well as an aspect focused on access to government data and cultural collections of public institutions, for their dissemination.[403]

Also worth mentioning is the "Transparent Brazil" initiative, which brought together a series of measures to make spending and administrative dynamics more transparent, promoting social control over the administration and thus leading to efficiency gains.[404] The initiative stemmed from the results of a working group coordinated by the Ministry of Planning in the second half of 2000 and included measures to develop electronic monitoring of public works and electronic control of government purchases, increase interaction between government and citizens via the Internet, monitor public spending and legal proceedings, as well as publicizing government programs.[405]

These three programs, *Rede Governo* (Government Network), *Sociedade da Informação* (Information Society), and *Brasil Transparente* (Transparent Brazil) represent the *de facto* beginning of a national policy related to Digital Government, and although they started from different and

400 *Ibid.*, p. 18.

401 Decree No. 3,294 of December 15, 1999.

402 FERNANDES, Andréa Gomes; AFONSO, José Roberto Rodrigues. e-Governo no Brasil: Experiências e Perspectivas. *Revista do BNDES*, v. 8, n. 15, 2001, p. 30.

403 MIRANDA, Antonio. Sociedade da informação: globalização, identidade cultural e conteúdos. *Ciência da Informação*, v. 29, n. 2, p. 78–88, 2000, p. 78, 87.

404 FERNANDES; AFONSO, *op. cit.*, p. 32.

405 FERREIRA, Antônio Sérgio Seco; NEVES, Sérgio da Cunha. Contribuições para o planejamento da integração e da publicação de informações da administração pública. *Revista de Administração*, v. 37, n. 1, 2002, p. 66.

separate initiatives, they complemented each other and had a common objective, which was "to change the paradigm from info-exclusion to info-inclusion".[406]

At the same time, at the start of the public sector's digital transformation, the government was faced with the challenge of tackling the digital divide. In a country of continental dimensions like Brazil, where, just a few years earlier, a telephone line had an asset value equivalent to a car or small property, expanding the coverage of a telecommunications access network was a prerequisite for Digital Government policies to be effective. This was to happen mainly with the Telecommunications Services Universalization Fund (FUST), provided for in the General Telecommunications Law (Law No. 9,472/98) and established by Decree No. 3,624/2000. The purpose of the FUST was to universalize telecommunications services in those areas and situations where (newly-established) private operations could not find adequate economic incentives, i.e., it aimed to deal with situations outside the targets imposed on telecommunications service concessionaires, which would be the responsibility of the companies and would have to be financed with their own resources.[407]

However, despite accumulating huge amounts of money, the FUST has been used very little, among other reasons, due to a formalistic and restrictive interpretation by the Federal Court of Accounts of the legal regime for the application of its resources, which would require new processes of delegation of services by the Government and which could not be decentralized to states and municipalities.[408] With regard to the expansion and popularization of telecommunications services in the competitive logic, subject to the operators' mandatory targets, it is clear that they played a decisive role in democratizing access to communications infrastructure. The greatest example is that, shortly after the delegations, the time to obtain a telephone line fell dramatically, and its cost fell to insignificant amounts. On the other hand, the universalization objectives addressed by the FUST were pursued through other institutional channels that did not involve the

406 GONTIJO, Miriam. Análise da proposta brasileira de E-Governo como expressão de uma política de informação a partir do conceito de regime de informação. *Perspectivas em Ciência da Informação*, v. 7, n. 2, 2002, p. 180. In the original, "...a mudança do paradigma de infoexclusão para o da infoinclusão".

407 FERNANDES; AFONSO, *op. cit.*, p. 28.

408 ADAMI, Mateus Piva. *A universalização das telecomunicações no Brasil: uma análise de seus arranjos institucionais.* PhD dissertation (Economic and Financial Law), University of São Paulo, São Paulo, 2021, p. 18, 19, 100.

use of these resources, which does not allow us to say categorically that there was a loss in this process due to the restriction on the use of the fund's resources.[409] At the same time, this provides elements for reflecting on how restrictive legal visions can generate dysfunctions between the desired functioning of an arrangement and its actual ability to deliver results.[410] The telecommunications privatization process will be discussed again in section 3.1.2 on the experience of Brazilian internet governance.

From the point of view of the institutionalization of instances and bodies, the initial kick-off was the creation, in April 2000, of a working group within the Federal Government to "examine and propose policies, guidelines, and standards related to the new electronic forms of interaction", according to the decree that formalized it.[411] However, there was no detailed remit or further provisions on how it would work, just a list of participants from some of the most important ministries in the executive branch at the time. A few months later, in October, the first relevant institutionalization initiative that expressly mentioned the issue of Digital Government took place, namely the creation of the Electronic Government Executive Committee (CEGE), mentioned above. According to the founding decree, this committee was created to "formulate policies, establish guidelines, coordinate and articulate actions for the implementation of Electronic Government, aimed at providing services and information to citizens".[412] The committee comprised the executive secretaries of all the ministries and some additional representatives from the Ministry of Foreign Affairs, Defense, the Presidency of the Republic and its Institutional Security Office, as well as the Federal Attorney General. Two years later, a representative from the Office of the Comptroller General and the National Institute of Information Technology were also included. All of the Committee's members were, therefore, members of the Federal Executive Branch.

The CEGE had a wide-ranging list of duties, such as coordinating the acquisition and use of the federal administration's technology infrastruc-

409 *Ibid.*, p. 197.

410 In this sense, the third and fourth stages of the institutional mapping mentioned at the end of section 1.6.

411 Decree without number of April 3, 2000. In the original, "... examinar e propor políticas, diretrizes e normas relacionadas com as novas formas eletrônicas de interação".

412 Decree without number of October 18, 2000. In the original, "... formular políticas, estabelecer diretrizes, coordenar e articular as ações de implantação do Governo Eletrônico, voltado para a prestação de serviços e informações ao cidadão".

ture, services, and applications, defining service standards and levels by electronic means and establishing guidelines and strategies for ministries to plan and organize their electronic services. Also noteworthy is its express role in the budget process, particularly in expressing its opinion on budget proposals related to investment in information technology, about the bills that establish the Multi-Year Plan and the budgets. The CEGE did not have its own administrative structure, budget or resources, and support for technical-administrative activities was provided by the Ministry of Planning, Budget, and Management. In 2003, the CEGE began to have 8 thematic committees to deal with, respectively, the implementation of free software, digital inclusion, systems integration, legacy systems, and software licenses, website management and online services, network infrastructure, G2G and knowledge management, and strategic information.[413] This was followed by various incremental Digital Government initiatives and programs, such as the publication of interoperability standards based on the low-institutionalization structure, in which CEGE, SLTI, and its new e-Government Department (created in 2004) were central.

Also in 2004, the Transparency Portal was launched by the Office of the Comptroller General (CGU), a body under the Presidency of the Republic, where citizens could follow the financial execution of federal government programs.[414] Later, in 2009, this policy was extended to the entire public administration, introducing the obligation to be transparent by making available "in real time, detailed information on budget and financial execution, in publicly accessible electronic media".[415]

In 2005, the Electronic Auction for public procurement was introduced as a bidding method designed to acquire common goods and services.[416] In 2008, the General Information Technology Strategy (EGTI) was published, with the aim of institutionally improving the use of information technology in the administration's bodies, a strategy that would be updated several times in the following years. From 2007 onwards, the government developed a public software repository platform, where developers, public

413 Decree without number of October 29, 2003.

414 BRAGA, Lamartine Vieira *et al.* O papel do Governo Eletrônico no fortalecimento da governança do setor público. *Revista do Serviço Público*, v. 59, n. 1, p. 5–21, 2008, p. 12.

415 According to Complementary Law No. 131/2009, which amended the Fiscal Responsibility Law. In the original, "... em tempo real, de informações pormenorizadas sobre a execução orçamentária e financeira, em meios eletrônicos de acesso público".

416 Decree No. 5,450 of May 31, 2005.

bodies, and other interested parties could make their software solutions available.

It is worth noting that the Federal Government made the SIASG/Comprasnet portal available to states and municipalities in 2007.[417] SIASG/Comprasnet is a set of tools implemented a few years earlier in the Federal Government that carries out various online procedures related to public procurement, such as registering suppliers, publicizing procurement notices, registering market prices, monitoring contracts, among others.[418] It is a free, standardized management tool that centralizes important registration information nationwide, such as a company's legal suitability to take part in tenders, the existence of penalties, cases of default, etc. As it is a set of modules developed and maintained by the Federal Government, its free use by states and municipalities represents huge economies of scale in terms of the cost-effectiveness of procurement processes. Despite the economic incentive to join SIASG/Comprasnet, it was not compulsory. However, as of 2019, the use of the portal and the "electronic auction/bidding" modality became a condition for municipalities to receive federal funds, and this led to a huge increase in participation. More recently, the Public Procurement Law, Law No. 14,133/2021, provided for the National Public Procurement Portal in its article 174 to integrate the public administration's procurement procedures, with the mandatory disclosure of acts by all federal entities and the optional use for the procurement itself. The information contained in the portal revealed that, even with Comprasnet available free of charge, the majority of contracts (especially in municipalities) are still made using private platforms, which, on the one hand, are sometimes more technologically advanced, but on the other hand, do not always provide the same levels of transparency and compliance with the law, with cases in which the legality of the processes is jeopardized.[419]

In 2011, when the Access to Information Act (LAI) was passed, the government saw the need to adopt a standardized electronic administrative process because, otherwise, it would have difficulties complying with the provisions of the law, especially meeting citizens' requests for information.

---

417 *Compras.gov.br*. Available at <http://www.comprasnet.gov.br/noticias/noticias1.asp?id_noticia=197>. Accessed 8 Apr. 2024.

418 FERNANDES, Ciro Campos Christo. *Sistemas de compras eletrônicas e sua aplicação à administração pública - o caso do SIASG/Comprasnet*. Master's thesis (Business Management), FGV, Brasília, 2003, p. 86–87.

419 According to Ruling 1507/2024 of the Federal Court of Accounts - TCU, full court, Rapporteur Benjamin Zymler, judgment date 31/07/2024.

Thus began the search for a solution for electronic document management, which initially started with a benchmark to find out what solutions were available and in use by various public bodies. After an extensive public consultation process, the SEI - Sistema Eletrônico de Informações (Electronic Information System) software, developed by the Federal Regional Court of the 4th Region, was chosen for implementation by the federal public administration, and the system was gradually adopted as a standard.[420] It should be noted that, although electronic document management was already in place in a large number of agencies, the standardized use of SEI led to a massive adoption of good document management practices, which had previously been subject to the intuitive preferences and conduct of public agents.[421]

In 2011, under Dilma Rouseff's presidency, the government placed great emphasis on increasing the channels and forms of citizen participation in public policy. A national Open Government action plan was set up and the Interministerial Open Government Committee (CIGA) was created.[422] In 2014, the *Participa.br* portal was created to bring together all the social participation channels within the Federal Government.[423] Currently, the *Participa.br* portal has migrated to the unified Gov.br Digital Government website and brings together all the participation processes of the Federal Government bodies, whether they are public hearings, public consultations, or input gathering. In addition to the direct public administration bodies, some other bodies (with a significant degree of autonomy) participate, such as the Central Bank and some Federal Universities. This policy was responsible for Brazil's better position in international Digital Government rankings in the following years.[424] In the same year, the Information Technology

420 SARAIVA, André. *A Implementação do SEI - Sistema Eletrônico de Informações.* Brasília: Enap. Casoteca da Gestão Pública, 2018, p. 4–5.

421 XAVIER, Jean Frederick Brito. *Governo eletrônico: o cidadão e o direito de acesso à informação.* PhD Dissertation (Information Science), University of São Paulo, São Paulo, 2022, p. 119.

422 Decree without number of September 15, 2011.

423 According to Ordinance (Portaria) No. 36, of November 11, 2014, of the Presidency of the Republic.

424 It can be seen that the weight of the digital participation criterion in Brazil's position in the United Nations Digital Government Ranking has been increasing since the 2004 report (when this weight was neutral) until the 2018 report, when it reached its peak. In this report, Brazil ranks 44th in the overall index, and 12th in the *E-participation* index, as can be seen in the interactive reports available at: <https://publicadministration.un.org/egovkb/en-us/Data/Country-Information/id/24-Brazil/dataYear/2018>.

Resources Administration System (SISP) was created, for the "planning, coordination, organization, operation, control and supervision of the information technology resources of the federal public administration bodies and entities", made up of representatives from the information technology administration units of the ministries and other federal public administration entities. Initially, its central body was SLTI, which was replaced over the years by others due to ministerial reforms.[425] In the same vein, in 2015, the Federal Public Administration's Information and Communications Security and Cybersecurity Strategy - 2015/2018 was published.[426]

In 2016, the Digital Governance Policy was established by Decree No. 8,638/2016, article 5 of which provided for the publication of the Federal Public Administration's Digital Governance Strategy (EGD), drawn up and published to coincide with the term of the Multi-Year Plan.[427] The aim of the EGD for the 2016-2019 period was to guide the actions of federal government bodies towards digital transformation. It established strategic objectives in three main areas: access to information, service provision, and social participation. It also established targets and indicators for each of these objectives, with the calculation formula, form of interpretation, body responsible for performance, body responsible for verification, and periodicity of monitoring. Within each objective, several strategic initiatives were also listed, and the bodies responsible for each of them were indicated.[428]

---

425 According to Decree No. 7,579 of October 11, 2011. In the original, "planejamento, a coordenação, a organização, a operação, o controle e a supervisão dos recursos de tecnologia da informação dos órgãos e entidades da administração pública federal".

426 CDN Ordinance No. 14 of May 11, 2015

427 "Art. 5. The Minister of State for Planning, Budget and Management will issue the Digital Governance Strategy - EGD of the federal public administration, a document that will define the strategic objectives, goals, indicators and initiatives of the Digital Governance Policy and guide programs, projects, services, systems and activities related to it. Sole paragraph. The period of validity of the EGD will coincide with the period of validity of the Multi-Year Plan - PPA". In the original, "Art. 5º. O Ministro de Estado do Planejamento, Orçamento e Gestão editará a Estratégia de Governança Digital - EGD da administração pública federal, documento que definirá os objetivos estratégicos, as metas, os indicadores e as iniciativas da Política de Governança Digital e norteará programas, projetos, serviços, sistemas e atividades a ela relacionados. Parágrafo único. O período de vigência da EGD coincidirá com o prazo de vigência do Plano Plurianual – PPA".

428 According to the document Digital Governance Strategy of the Federal Public Administration 2016-19, available on the website of the Ministry of Planning, Budget and Management.

In the same year, now under the Michel Temer government, Decree No. 8,936/2016 established the Digital Citizenship Platform, dealing with the provision of digital public services by the Federal Government. In 2018, the E-Digital - Strategy for Brazilian Digital Transformation - was published, dealing with the digital transformation of society as a whole, not just the government. The Federal Public Administration's Digital Governance Strategy (EGD) was then incorporated into E-digital as a thematic axis. Decree No. 9,319/2018 creates the National System for Digital Transformation (SinDigital) and establishes the governance structure for implementing the Strategy set out in Decree No. 8,638. SinDigital seeks to structurally organize sectors of the Federal Administration to implement the EGD. To this end, it was made up of an Interministerial Committee under the coordination of the Civil House, as well as, originally, a "multisectoral technical body for digital transformation, made up of specialists and people of notorious knowledge representing the scientific community, civil society and the productive sector".[429] Sindigital later became the sum of the Brazilian Strategy for Digital Transformation (E-Digital), and a governance structure in the form of the Interministerial Committee for Digital Transformation - CITDigital, which has representatives from the most relevant ministries and is now coordinated by the Ministry of Science, Technology, Innovation and Communications.

Once the Digital Government strategy from 2016 to 2020 had run its course, Decree No. 10,332/2020 was issued in April 2020, under Jair Bolsonaro's government, with new federal guidelines on the subject and a new Digital Government strategy from 2020 to 2022, later extended to the end of 2023. Although it contained a list of objectives, initiatives, and some targets, the decree was not as detailed as the previous document, nor did it contain indicators or indicate the bodies responsible for fulfilling the items or implementing the measures.[430]

It should be noted that the Digital Government strategies became an integral part of the Brazilian Strategy for Digital Transformation, a broader policy that involves all aspects of the digital transformation of society, not just the government. At the same time, the Gov.br portal was launched, which sought to complete the task of centralizing access to federal public

429 In the original, "instância técnica multissetorial para a transformação digital, composta por especialistas e pessoas de notório saber representantes da comunidade científica, da sociedade civil e do setor produtivo".

430 Decree No. 10,332 of April 28, 2020.

services.[431] This was because, although there had previously been a central portal that derived from the regular development of the former *Rede Governo* (Digital Citizenship Platform)[432], the agencies and entities of the administration (even considering only the Federal Government) still had their own websites and systems for providing services and information, which could be accessed through the central portal, but did not follow the same logic of presentation, login, and terms of use. Gov.br began to integrate all the federal administration's online services under the same access and identification, and also began to count on the voluntary adhesion of states and municipalities to access its services, through agreements.

Nevertheless, digital government public policies have increasingly come to be seen by the government's political leadership as something aimed at generating economic efficiency in a more limited way, in the sense of saving government expenses by eliminating bureaucracy and unnecessary processes, with the strategic and innovative aspects neglected. In this sense, the National Council for Debureaucratization was created in 2017 to recommend priorities and targets for digital transformation strategies.[433] In addition, many of the competences and actions of the Brazilian digital government were subordinated to ministerial bodies and secretariats that took care of reducing state bureaucracy and the so-called modernization of the state, which, after Dilma Rousseff's impeachment, came to mean the increasing implementation of liberal policies and the reduction of the state. This is also evident in the 2020-2023 Multi-Year Plan, in which the "Modernize Brazil" program, whose goal was to improve the E-Government Development Index (EGDI), measured by the UN, and the World Bank's Ease of doing business index,[434] was subordinated to the guideline of "efficiency in public sector action, with the valorization of science and technology

431 Decree No. 9,756, of April 11, 2019.
432 Created by Decree No. 8,936, of December 19, 2016.
433 Decree without number of March 7, 2017.
434 The reports were discontinued after a scandal in which data was manipulated because of ideological preferences. See GRYTSENKO, Ruslan. Why it is so important to keep analytics independent. What are the lessons of the scandal with the Doing Business Report?. *In*: *Proceedings of the 5th International Scientific Conference.* Rome: Publisher.agency, 2023; *World Bank Group to Discontinue Doing Business Report.* World Bank. Available at <https://www.worldbank.org/en/news/statement/2021/09/16/world-bank-group-to-discontinue-doing-business-report>. Accessed 16 Aug. 2024.

and a reduction in state interference in the economy".[435] This emphasis on reducing the size and role of the state, and the linking of the Digital Government as an instrument for achieving it, had not been included in any of the previous multi-year plans.

It should also be noted that the 2016 and 2020 Brazilian Digital Government Strategies have the crucial limitation of covering only the federal administration, without any intention of addressing or even influencing state and municipal public administrations, or the Legislative and Judicial Branches. The 2016 EDG, for example, doesn't mention states and municipalities even once in its 36-page text.[436] In the 2020 to 2022 strategy, the municipalities are mentioned only once, when it comes to creating a voluntary inter-federative collaboration body - the National Digital Government Network - and the states are mentioned once more, when it comes to integrating them into the Gov.br portal.[437] There is yet another problem related to strategies in general that deal with digital transformation: there is a proliferation of different, and sometimes redundant, documents containing plans, strategies, programs, and actions related to digital transformation and related issues, so that this can "blur the institutional Governance" and "limit the efficient allocation of resources to support effective policy implementation".[438] This indicates a lack of institutional political direction around a clear objective, as well as causing practical problems in the formulation of concrete actions.

Despite these limitations, the Federal Government's digital government strategies and programs have been reasonably effective. They fulfill a guiding and organizational function for the federal administration and, by identifying specific objectives and the actions needed to achieve them, they perform a coordinative discursive function in relation to the agencies and ministries, which must draw up their own digital transformation, open data and information technology plans based on these definitions. They are "an essential mechanism to institutionalize policy goals, align priorities

---

435 According to article 3 of Law No. 13,971, of December 27, 2019, the 2020-2023 Multi-Year Plan. In the original, "...eficiência da ação do setor público, com a valorização da ciência e tecnologia e redução da ingerência do Estado na economia".

436 According to the document Digital Governance Strategy of the Federal Public Administration 2016-19, available on the website of the Ministry of Planning, Budget and Management.

437 Decree No. 10,332 of April 28, 2020.

438 OECD. *Digital Government Review of Brazil: Towards the digital transformation of the public sector.* Paris: OECD, 2018, p. 9.

and aggregate coordinated actions."[439] As seen in the previous chapter, in more complex institutional configurations, where there is a multiplicity of actors in the elaboration and implementation of policies, discourse plays an essential role in the horizontal dissemination of ideas and the construction of a focal point for actions, and the legal-formal route for this flow does not require the syntactic elements of complete institutional declarations (with the deontic element and enforcement, besides attributes, conditions, and aim). This is even an advantage: strategies can be developed and modified more freely, without the excessive weight of form or normative force representing points for disputes of interest and the exercise of vetoes by aggrieved actors. Thus, when the objectives and initiatives of the 2020-2023 Digital Government Strategy are compared with a list of digital transformation actions completed by various government bodies,[440] it can be seen that there is a relationship between them that demonstrates the ability of digital government strategies to produce effects, albeit with a pre-normative character and lacking the deontic and enforcement element[441] of the initiatives described.

On the other hand, Brazil's digital government strategies come up against obstacles due to the precarious legal-institutional arrangement where they are embedded, which hinder their effectiveness. In this sense, the Federal Court of Accounts - TCU is right to point out that

> Due to a failure in the internal coordination of federal executive branch bodies, regulations have been issued[442] that assign similar competences on digital transformation to different governance structures, which can lead to fragmentation, overlapping or duplication of efforts in the digital transformation process.[443]

---

439 *Ibid.*, p. 4.

440 See CORDEIRO, Caio Barros. *Desafios do Estado para a transformação digital: uma análise à luz da abordagem Direito e Políticas Públicas.* PhD Dissertation (Law), University of São Paulo, São Paulo, 2023, p. 139–149.

441 On the legal-institutional characteristics of the strategies referred to here, see section1.9.3.

442 The regulations referred to in the report are Decrees 10,609/2021, 9,319/2018 and 9,203/2017, but there are several others, considering not only the Digital Government Strategy, but also other digital transformation policies.

443 According to the follow-up report, Court Ruling 1784/2021, Rapporteur Vital do Rêgo, judgment date 28/07/2021. In the original: "Devido à falha na articulação interna de órgãos do Poder Executivo federal, foram editados normativos que atribuem competências semelhantes sobre transformação digital a estruturas de gov-

Another issue pointed out in the same report relates to the "lack of a systemic vision of digital transformation", which neglects aspects such as the quality and extent of internet access for the most vulnerable populations and the issue of the deficiency of human capital that prevents these populations from using services properly, due to the lack of proper education and training. In this sense, it is also worth remembering that the E-Government Development Index (EGDI) has three basic components: the Online Service Index (OSI), the Telecommunication Infrastructure Index (TII) and the Human Capital Index (HCI). In the OSI, Brazil has an index of 0.8964, while in the TII and HCI the values are much lower, respectively 0.6814 and 0.7953 (according to the 2022 report).[444] In other words, this shows that the 2020 Strategy's priorities of digitizing services to optimize the administration financially, to the detriment of investing in education and infrastructure to promote digital inclusion, are highly questionable.

In a study on the Brazilian Digital Government, the OECD points out institutional dysfunctions in the implementation model adopted by Brazil. Among other issues, the assessment coincides with the TCU's notes on an excess of bodies from which initiatives and decisions emanate, the lack of coordination and articulation between the various actors, and the lack of a clear public policy institutional structure capable of mobilizing stakeholders adequately around advanced objectives.[445]

With regard to Digital Government, the actors can be considered at three levels: the top level of government, a strategic level in which there are highly representative and prominent actors, with great political power and responsible for the major guidelines and public policies; the local top level, which are the heads of institutions responsible for the final areas of the administration, who have a part in the design and monitoring phases of the implementation of Digital Government policies and bridge the communication gap between those technically responsible for implementation in the forwarding of pending issues; and the technical team, a body of civil

ernanças distintas, o que pode levar à fragmentação, sobreposição ou duplicidade de esforços no processo de transformação digital".

444 According to the interactive report available at: <https://publicadministration.un.org/egovkb/en-us/Data/Country-Information/id/24-Brazil/dataYear/2022>.

445 OECD. *Digital Government Review of Brazil: Towards the digital transformation of the public sector*. Paris: OECD, 2018, p. 9.

servants or collaborators with the knowledge of information technology and business, linked to the government or private initiative.[446]

Currently, the following are important actors in the context of Brazilian Digital Government at the federal level: the Digital Government Secretariat of the Ministry of Management and Innovation in Public Services, which is responsible for a series of related functions, such as drawing up Digital Government strategies, coordinating projects, among other duties set out in regulations;[447] and, within the same ministry, the Special Office for Federative Cooperation in Management and Digital Government, which is responsible for liaising with states and municipalities and promoting cooperation between them. In this regard, it should be noted that the Office has played an important role in integrating the other federative levels into the Gov.br platform, since the lack of legislation determining adherence makes the process dependent on the voluntary signing of agreements between the Union and the other entities. The states have all joined the platform, but the challenge today is to integrate the municipalities, especially the smaller ones. In this regard, it should be stressed that states and municipalities are also key actors because it is precisely in their jurisdictions that public policies such as health, education, and security will have their most concrete expression, and they are also the closest point of contact between the population and the state. Likewise, the various ministries of the Federal Government are important actors, as they implement the budgets for digital transformation policies in a fragmented way, albeit under the aegis of individual plans drawn up in accordance with the guidelines of the digital government strategies.

Mention should also be made of SERPRO, a public IT company that develops Digital Government solutions such as ComprasNet, among others, as mentioned above. Since the beginning of digital government in Brazil, SERPRO has been the most well-structured organization around the adoption of technology by the state, and has been responsible for developing most of the systems, as well as having a robust structure: in 2000, it had 9,000 employees spread across 330 cities in Brazil.[448] Today,

---

446 DINIZ, Eduardo Henrique *et al.* O governo eletrônico no Brasil: perspectiva histórica a partir de um modelo estruturado de análise. *Revista de Administração Pública*, v. 43, n. 1, p. 23–48, 2009, p. 32.

447 Decree No. 11,437, of March 17, 2023.

448 TERRA, José Cláudio Cyrineu; GORDON, Cindy. *Realizing the promise of corporate portals: Leveraging knowledge for business success.* Burlington: Butterworth-Heinemann, 2003, p. 315.

there are approximately 7,757 employees in 27 cities, serving 25,000 public and private clients in 16 different countries.[449] It should be noted that SERPRO and DATAPREV, a public company created in 1974[450] responsible for managing the government's social database (such as data from the National Social Security Institute - INSS), were included in the national privatization plan in 2020, i.e., they were destined by the Federal Government to be privatized. This corroborates the argument that the Bolsonaro government's political vision of digital government was limited to an instrument for saving financial resources, in a concept of efficiency that did not go beyond the idea of cutting costs and optimizing expenses. But as well as disregarding important debates on digital sovereignty, the actions of that Administration, especially with regard to the strategic control of states over digital infrastructures, also represented a negligence with regard to respect for the General Data Protection Law and national security. In the first case, an OECD study pointed to concerns that the privatization would violate the privacy rights of citizens who hold the sensitive data that the two companies process.[451] In the second case, the Federal Public Prosecutor's Office drew up a technical note in which it emphasized that privatization would harm the primary objectives of state security, especially since SERPRO is a supplier of digital solutions to the Brazilian Army.[452]

Other relevant actors in the Brazilian digital government arrangement are the private technology companies that provide services to the government or information technology solutions, such as Microsoft, Oracle and IBM, among others, which have large contracts with the government.[453] These players are part of a dispute over the political vision surrounding digital government, notably digital sovereignty and the state's control over the technological means by which it carries out its functions, as well as its control over physical data storage sites and national security. It is what Sergio Amadeu refers to as a "data flow crisis", in the sense that the transnationality of the internet should not imply a normalization around

449 SERPRO. *Relatório Integrado Anual.* Brasília: Escritório de Governança e Estratégia Corporativas, 2022.

450 Law No. 6,125, of November 4, 1974.

451 OECD. *A Caminho da Era Digital no Brasil.* Paris: Organisation for Economic Co-operation and Development, 2020, p. 134.

452 Technical Note GT 2/2021/GTTIC/3ªCCR.

453 According to data contained in an audit report by the Federal Court of Accounts (Ruling 2569/2018), which, although old, reflects the main IT supplier framework.

the storage of citizens' data from one country in another, or by a foreign private company.[454]

The Ministry of Science, Technology and Innovation (MCTI) should also be mentioned. While the Ministry of Management and Innovation in Public Services is responsible for *innovation policies in the public sector*, i.e., innovations in management and public policies, the MCTI is responsible for drawing up *innovation public policies* which, in a different way, aim to promote scientific and technological innovation in society.[455] It is responsible, for example, for the Brazilian Artificial Intelligence Strategy and, more recently, through the National Science and Technology Council (CCT), for an ambitious proposal for investments in the development of artificial intelligence infrastructures and applications, which aim to reduce the country's dependence on systems developed and managed in other countries, in order to strengthen national digital sovereignty. The plan foresees investments of more than 23 billion reais over four years, of which 1.76 billion will go towards implementing artificial intelligence solutions in the public sector, as well as creating "a robust ecosystem of public data in a sovereign cloud, to ensure national technological autonomy, the integrity and security of information and the privacy of citizens".[456] The MCTI also has two subordinate bodies: the Secretariat for Technological Development and Innovation, which focuses on drawing up and supervising national policies for technological development and innovation in general; and the Secretariat for Science and Technology for Digital Transformation, which focuses on digital transformation policies,[457] which add to the complex constellation of public actors.

In 2021, the first legislative framework on Digital Government in Brazil was passed (Law No. 14,129/2021), which structures the organization of the policy on a slightly more solid basis, representing a promise of more robust

454 PADILHA, Felipe; FACIOLI, Lara. Colonialismo tecnológico ou como podemos resistir ao novo eugenismo digital – entrevista com Sérgio Amadeu Silveira. *Estudos de Sociologia*, v. 25, n. 48, p. 363–378, 2020, p. 372.

455 FERRAREZI, Elisabete; ALMEIDA, Guilherme de Almeida. *Laboratórios de inovação: como e por que criá-los*. Brasília: Escola Nacional de Administração Pública - Enap, 2023, p. 17–19.

456 According to the document entitled AI for the Good of All: proposal for a Brazilian Artificial Intelligence Plan 2024-2028, by the National Council for Science and Technology, available on the website of the Ministry of Science, Technology and Innovation. In the original, "... um ecossistema robusto de dados públicos em nuvem soberana, para assegurar a autonomia tecnológica nacional, a integridade e a segurança das informações e a privacidade dos cidadãos".

457 According to the attributions contained in Decree No. 11,493, of April 17, 2023.

conformation of the institutional arrangement of the Brazilian Digital Government. Under the aegis of this framework and already in mid-2024, after a public consultation process, a new Digital Government Strategy for the federal level was drawn up and published (Decree No. 12,198/2024) and also the first National Strategy (Decree No. 12.069/2024 and SGD/MGI Ordinance No. 4.248, of June 26, 2024), the latter an innovation resulting from the new legislative framework.

But can the new legal framework address these challenges of greater clarity of purposes, coordination, and articulation of digital transformation policies in the public sector? A critical analysis of its text, as well as of other important laws for understanding the Brazilian general framework, will be the subject of a separate section.

2.2 Legal basis of the institutional arrangement

The legal basis of the Brazilian Digital Government comprises a relatively recent structuring legal framework (2021), as well as a series of other laws and subordinate legislation that complement each other in the legal-institutional arrangement and guide the actions of state and non-state actors. It is developed based on an institutional environment characterized by a complex federalism with three levels of autonomy in which states and municipalities retain significant legislative and material powers, although these have been adjusted since the 1988 Constitution.[458] Also part of this environment are the constitutional norms that provide for principles of administration (such as the principle of efficiency), an elaborate list of social rights that fulfill the final content of policies, a set of rules regulating fundamental economic law relations (such as the rules on public services), and the legal rules about public servants.

At the same time, some obstacles to the development of the Digital Government are identified, which lie in the way the arrangement was built concerning the environment that contextualizes and integrates it, in the dependence of the programmatic development of initiatives over the years on the institutionalized legal vision, and in the lack of an effective equation of political forces around institutionalization mechanisms capable

458 For example, reforms that took away the power of states to have their own banks issue bonds, which was one of the main limitations of macroeconomic policies at the national level. STEPAN, Alfred. Brazil's Decentralized Federalism: Bringing Government Closer to the Citizens? *Daedalus*, v. 129, n. 2, p. 145–169, 2000, p. 150.

of stabilizing certain expectations around binding decision-making structures. A critical analysis of the main normative elements that make up the arrangement and complete the systematization of the Digital Government policy opens the way to identifying dysfunctions and building prognostic alternatives.

In addition to Law No. 14,129/2021, some other normative texts have been chosen that are considered more important for understanding the digital transformation in the Brazilian government, either because they form a general normative context for digital policies, or because they interact systemically in the legal-institutional arrangement of Digital Government, to change the meaning or practical application of the provisions of the legal framework and government action at the top of the public administration (as explained in sections 1.5 and 1.6). Critical analysis based essentially on examining the normative provisions related to the topic will also be used to introduce some discussions specific to the problems involved in applying the law to the dynamics of digitalization and identifying challenges to be overcome by legal practice or reform. In addition to providing an overview of the legal framework that mediates relations between different actors and interests, the aim is to obtain elements that can provide answers to some of the limitations and obstacles pointed out in the previous section. So, the objective is to pave the way for a more comprehensive reflection on the subject in the following chapters in order to look for institutional alternatives for building a state that is both capable of keeping up with the processes of technological innovation and capable of guaranteeing the protection of rights and the realization of the democratic project.

2.2.1 Law No. 14,129/2021, the Digital Government regulatory framework

Law No. 14,129, of March 29, 2021, known as the Digital Government Law, is the first specific and comprehensive law on the subject in Brazil and seeks to systematize the principles, categories, and instruments of Digital Government that until then had only been part of concrete initiatives or strategies issued by the Federal Government. As Vanice do Valle and Fabrício Motta point out, the Law represents recognition of the multifaceted nature of the administration and an attempt to reconcile the legal rationality that guides administrative structures and processes with management rationality, which focuses on the effectiveness of results.[459]

The law is divided into eight chapters. The first deals with general provisions, such as those that delimit its application to the federal administration and to states and municipalities that expressly issue normative acts in this regard, as well as an extensive list of principles and guidelines. Chapter II deals specifically with the digitization of the public administration and the provision of digital services, and contains most of the rules on procedure and organization. Chapter III deals with Government as a Platform, focusing on aspects of Open Data and interoperability. The remaining chapters contain rules on electronic domicile, innovation laboratories, control, auditing and risk management.

The Digital Government Law is the structuring normative framework for digital transformation in the public sector and is intended to raise the level of institutionalization of the set of initiatives for technological modernization of the state administrative apparatus. For this reason, some of its points are worth highlighting, as they form the basis for understanding the current effects regime.

2.2.1.1 Limited scope: political resistance and regional inequality

Law No. 14,129/2021, as stated in its article 2, does not automatically apply to states and municipalities, in other words, it is only mandatory for federal public administration bodies. The fact that states and municipalities are not obliged to adopt the law, even if there are reasons for that, is a major limitation in terms of its transformative capacity. This limitation originates in the legislative process and reflects the difficulty in dealing with political autonomies and regional interests.

The original bill's text envisaged that the provisions would apply to the entire public administration of all federal entities. The initial idea was, therefore, for a national law with a broad scope. The text went through

459 VALLE, Vanice Regina Lírio do; MOTTA, Fabrício. Governo digital: mapeando possíveis bloqueios institucionais à sua implantação. *In*: VALLE, Vanice Regina Lírio do; MOTTA, Fabrício (Orgs.). *Governo Digital e a Busca por Inovação na Administração Pública*. Kindle. Belo Horizonte: Forum, 2022, p. 58, 74.

several thematic committees[460] of the Chamber of Deputies with this basic configuration and was passed by the Constitution and Justice and Citizenship Committee with similar wording, reaffirming the broad applicability to states and municipalities.

The bill was then sent to the plenary for a vote, and in the opinion presented by the rapporteur, Felipe Rigoni, there was a first and important change regarding the scope of the law. The broad applicability was still maintained, but subject to the absence of a specific rule in other federal entities other than the Union. In other words, it was agreed, in the version sent to the plenary for a vote, that the law would apply equally to all federal levels, but that states and municipalities could approve their own substitute rules, even if they differed from the content of the federal law. Therefore, the law would apply to states and municipalities in the event of inertia on the part of these entities, but it would still be possible for them to pass their own acts regulating the matter differently. This formula is similar to that observed in the interpretation of whether or not the Federal Administrative Procedure Law (Law No. 9,784/1999) is applicable in states and municipalities, with Brazilian courts having built up case law to the effect that it can be applied in the absence of a local rule.[461] The difference is that, in the case of the Digital Government Law, such a command would be explicit, while the Administrative Process Law had nothing on the subject.

Approved by the Chamber of Deputies, the bill went to the Federal Senate for consideration. There, there was a modification to the House text, limiting its applicability to the federal sphere and making its applicability in states and municipalities conditional on the enactment of their own acts, such as state or municipal laws. In other words, if states and municipalities failed to pass similar laws, the Digital Government Act would not apply, and the regulatory gap would continue at municipal and state level. The new text was approved by the Senate and, despite this change, the bill went

460 Committees on Science and Technology, Communication and Informatics; Labor, Administration and Public Service; Finance and Taxation; and Constitution, Justice and Citizenship.

461 In this sense, Precedent 633 of the Superior Court of Justice states: "Law No. 9,784/1999, especially with regard to the limitation period for reviewing administrative acts within the federal public administration, can be applied, in a subsidiary manner, to states and municipalities, if there is no specific local rule governing the matter". In the original, "A Lei 9.784/1999, especialmente no que diz respeito ao prazo decadencial para a revisão de atos administrativos no âmbito da Administração Pública federal, pode ser aplicada, de forma subsidiária, aos estados e municípios, se inexistente norma local e específica que regule a matéria".

straight to the President of the Republic, without returning to the Chamber of Deputies, in violation of the rules of the legislative process.

At this point, it should be clarified that, in the Brazilian legislative process, ordinary bills must pass through both houses of parliament and then be enacted by the President of the Republic, who can veto it if he considers it to be unconstitutional or contrary to the public interest. When a bill begins its passage in one house and is then approved without modification in the other, it is sent directly to the President for signing. However, if the bill is amended in one house, it must be sent back to the other house for these amendments to be accepted or rejected before being sent to the President.[462] But there is an exception to this rule: the so-called "drafting amendments" (*emendas de redação*), which are those that, despite modifying the text, do not alter its substance or meaning. They do not constitute an exception to the constitutional rule but an interpretation that there would be no reason to re-examine a textual modification that does not alter the meaning of the rule.[463] Thus, even if a bill suffers a drafting

---

462 According to article 65 of the Federal Constitution: "Art. 65. The bill approved by one House shall be reviewed by the other, in a single round of discussion and voting, and sent to sanction or promulgation, if the reviewing House approves it, or filed, if it rejects it. Sole paragraph. If the bill is amended, it shall return to the initiating House." In the original, "Art. 65. O projeto de lei aprovado por uma Casa será revisto pela outra, em um só turno de discussão e votação, e enviado à sanção ou promulgação, se a Casa revisora o aprovar, ou arquivado, se o rejeitar. Parágrafo único. Sendo o projeto emendado, voltará à Casa iniciadora".

463 This interpretation can be seen in articles 134 to 136 of National Congress Resolution No. 1 of 1970 (Common Rules of the National Congress), together with articles 118, §8, and 120, §§2 and 3, of Resolution No. 17 of 1989 of the Chamber of Deputies (Internal Rules of the Chamber of Deputies), and articles 323, 325, III, of Federal Senate Resolution No. 93 of 1970 (Internal Rules of the Federal Senate). According to the wording of the provisions: "Art. 134. The bill, once approved in one of the Houses of the National Congress, shall be sent to the other House, in autographs signed by the respective President. Sole Paragraph. The bill shall have a summary and be accompanied by a copy or publication of all documents, votes, and speeches that supported its proceedings. Art. 135. The correction of language inaccuracies made by the reviewing House, as long as it does not alter the meaning of the proposal, does not constitute an amendment that requires its return to the initiating House. Art. 136. If the bill is amended by the reviewing House, it shall be returned to the initiating House, accompanied by the amendments, along with a copy or publication of the documents, votes, and speeches that supported its proceedings". In the original, "Art. 134. O projeto de lei, aprovado em uma das Casas do Congresso Nacional, será enviado à outra Casa, em autógrafos assinados pelo respectivo Presidente. Parágrafo único. O projeto terá uma ementa e será acompanhado de cópia ou publicação de todos os documentos, votos e discursos que o instruíram em sua

amendment in the second house, it can proceed directly to the President of the Republic, since there has been no change in substance.

In the case of the Digital Government Bill, after its approval in the Chamber and Senate, the text went straight to the President for signing, despite the fact that it underwent a modification in the Senate that completely changed its scope. This is because the rapporteur argued that they were only drafting amendments, which would not have the power to change the substance of the bill. According to the rapporteur's justification, the drafting amendment was only intended to clarify one aspect of the proposal, making it compatible with constitutional rules on legislative and administrative competence. The drafting amendment was justified not only by a material correction in itself, but also with what would be its logical compatibility with constitutional rules to the contrary. However, this formal subterfuge to avoid sending the bill back to the Chamber of Deputies has no legal basis because the constitutional rule implicitly limits the scope of a "drafting amendment" to issues that do not alter the normative meaning of the bills under consideration.

Despite the flagrant violation of the legislative process, there was no judicial-legal challenge to the decision, and the bill was sanctioned by the President of the Republic. Even if there had been some kind of challenge, it is worth remembering that, in similar cases, the Brazilian Supreme Court has already dismissed the lawsuit, refusing to assess the merits on the grounds that it is an internal matter (*interna corporis*) of the Legislative Branch, in a highly questionable decision that ignores the fact that it is not the interpretation of an internal regulation, but of the Constitution itself.[464]

---

tramitação. Art. 135. A retificação de incorreções de linguagem, feita pela Câmara revisora, desde que não altere o sentido da proposição, não constitui emenda que exija sua volta à Câmara iniciadora. Art. 136. Emendado o projeto pela Câmara revisora, esta o devolverá à Câmara iniciadora, acompanhado das emendas, com cópia ou publicação dos documentos, votos e discursos que instruíram a sua tramitação".

464 Federal Supreme Court. MS 38339 DF, monocratic decision. Rapporteur: Ricardo Lewandowski, Judgment Date: 20/12/2021, Publication Date: 10/01/2022. "The precedents of this Supreme Court, in observance of the constitutional principle of the separation of powers, is consistent in the sense that the decisions of the National Congress made based on internal rules have an *interna corporis* nature and are, therefore, immune to judicial review. [...] As can be seen, in order to meet the petitioners' request, it would be necessary to examine the internal rules of the Federal Senate and the National Congress, which falls outside, I reiterate, the Judiciary's attributions, according to Article 2 of the Federal Constitution". In the original, "A jurisprudência desta Suprema Corte, em observância ao princípio constitucional da separação dos poderes, é firme no sentido de que as decisões

In this regard, it should be noted that it is not uncommon for this method of *legistic* correction to be used for political strategy purposes,[465] which is encouraged by judicial rulings such as this one.

In this way, the law came into force with the Senate's more timid wording and applicability restricted to the federal administration only, greatly limiting the potential of its effects at the regional level, precisely where most public services are provided and at the points of greatest contact between the state and citizens. The real reasons why the law's national scope was suppressed by the Federal Senate are difficult to reveal, but one hypothesis would be the political resistance of states and municipalities to adopting measures that, despite being modernizing, would demand energy and resources, either because they provide for obligations and standards to be followed internally by civil servants and organizations, or because they provide, on the other hand, for a series of rights for citizens to exercise vis-à-vis the Government. In addition, the dynamics of electoral politics create incentives for states and municipalities to develop their own Digital Government solutions, such as applications, software, etc., at a pace and with priorities politically defined by mayors and governors, generating publicity and electoral dividends and reinforcing the political brands of their administrations. On the other hand, measures for internal organization and standardization or to stimulate continuous innovation have less noticeable effects for the population, which tends to see only the tangible areas of public policy. In the case of municipalities, the issue extends beyond convenience and includes the lack of actual capacity to fulfill obligations, as most municipal public administrations have low institutional capacities or are very diverse.[466] They often operate with very low budgets, precarious structures, and staff who are paid far less than ideal and are less qualified compared to those at the state and especially federal levels, which generally offer better salaries.

---

do Congresso Nacional levadas a efeito com fundamento em normas regimentais possuem natureza *interna corporis*, sendo, portanto, infensas à revisão judicial. [...] Como se pode constatar, para o acolhimento do desiderato dos impetrantes seria necessário proceder-se ao exame de normas regimentais do Senado Federal e do Congresso Nacional, o que refoge, repito, às atribuições do Judiciário, a teor do disposto no art. 2º da Carta da Republica".

465 MANCIO, Sabrina Dominique Dias. *Na guerra entre cotexto e contexto, uma letra faz a diferença: as emendas de redação no texto legislativo.* Specialization thesis (Portuguese language), UniCEUB, Brasília, 2017, p. 26.

466 VELOSO, João Francisco Alves *et al.* Uma visão inicial dos subsistemas da gestão pública municipal. *In*: VELOSO, João Francisco Alves *et al* (Orgs.). *Gestão municipal no Brasil: um retrato das prefeituras.* Brasília: Ipea, 2011, p. 11–40.

Political resistance is a phenomenon that has already been documented in the case of the implementation of Digital Government in the federal public administration.[467] If state actors belonging to the same government unit and subject to the same power of command still manage to exert significant resistance to digital transformation policies, one can imagine how much this is enhanced by the political autonomy of states and municipalities, a scenario accentuated by differences in institutional capacities and, in the case of opposition governors and mayors, by differences in ideological vision. On the other hand, introducing this type of reform compulsorily, as if the chronic and structural problems of states and municipalities could simply be solved with a top-down legislative measure, could encourage widespread non-compliance, turning the law into a dead letter or raising doubts about its constitutionality.[468]

The alternative initially passed by the Chamber of Deputies, namely, the applicability of the law until states and municipalities issue their own acts, would represent an intermediate and good solution. Although it also addresses the inadequacies of state capacities at the regional and local levels, it would create incentives for the entities to enact laws better suited to local realities, thereby provoking debate. The rule would be useful even without explicit consequences, but it could also be accompanied by restrictions on the transfer of voluntary federal funds in case of inaction, which would be within the constitutional competence of the Union. In the end, the option adopted by the legislator is the least likely of all to conform the expectations of the actors at the regional level and to condition their behavior around the goal of completely digitizing the state. The Digital Government Law, despite its merits, reproduces the trajectory of neglecting the regional and local levels precisely at a time when these areas are the most important frontier of public policy. In this case, the path dependency is affirmed by the reproduction of the traditional problems of Brazilian federalism[469]

467 See, for instance, SARAIVA, André. *A Implementação do SEI - Sistema Eletrônico de Informações.* Brasília: Enap. Casoteca da Gestão Pública, 2018, p. 7; FERNANDES, Ciro Campos Christo. *Sistemas de compras eletrônicas e sua aplicação à administração pública - o caso do SIASG/Comprasnet.* Master's thesis (Business Management), FGV, Brasília, 2003, p. 123; JARDIM, José Maria. Governo eletrônico no Brasil: o portal Rede Governo. *Arquivística.net*, v. 3, n. 1, 2007, p. 29.

468 VALLE, Vanice Regina Lírio do; MOTTA, Fabrício. Governo digital: mapeando possíveis bloqueios institucionais à sua implantação. *In*: VALLE, Vanice Regina Lírio do; MOTTA, Fabrício (Orgs.). *Governo Digital e a Busca por Inovação na Administração Pública.* Kindle. Belo Horizonte: Forum, 2022, p. 63.

469 This topic will be revisited at several points later on, particularly in section 4.4.

in the new digital government arrangement, reducing the possibilities for active collaboration and effective coordination, and maintaining an institutional configuration of low flexibility, which limits the modes of interaction between the actors.[470]

Finally, it is also worth highlighting the provision that stipulates the Federal Government's duty to provide technical support to the other federal levels to achieve the digital transformation. This is a recognition of the profound inequality of capacities between Brazil's federal levels, especially in smaller municipalities. However, despite recognizing this fact to the point of prescribing a duty of support on the part of the Union, the law fails to provide mechanisms of actual effectiveness for this to happen, in particular incentives for municipalities to adhere to public Digital Government policies developed externally, or by not providing conditions for such policies to be drawn up originally within the federative units themselves, taking into account specific regional needs. This is compounded by the lack of any repressive mechanisms for states and municipalities. The absence of the latter would be justified by concerns about the effectiveness of the law, but the lack of instruments that make use of the technique of encouraging conduct can be seen as a missed opportunity to contribute to a more vigorous cooperation regime.

2.2.1.2 Low binding nature of rules and lack of division of competences

The Digital Government Law often resorts to authorizing and non-binding commands when it regulates the organization of the state for the implementation and management of Digital Government tools. This is due, in the first place, to the initial characteristics of the bill, which was the initiative of the Legislative Branch and not the Executive Branch, and also reflects the lack of engagement and commitment of government representatives, who left an issue typically of interest to the Executive in the background. The Brazilian Constitution has rules that reserve to the initiative of the President of the Republic bills that establish expenses for the public administration in the form of the creation of positions, new administrative structures, bodies, or legal entities.[471] Therefore, the Digital Government Law could not contain administrative reorganization determinations that

---

470 See section1.9.7.

471 Article 61 §1 of the Constitution.

involved a deeper institutional reformulation, since creating entities and positions would, in this case, be unconstitutional.

It should be noted, however, that it is not any creation of expenditure that is reserved for the legislative initiative of the President of the Republic, but only those that represent the creation of administrative structures or that refer to public servants, as already decided by the Federal Supreme Court.[472] As such, it is understood that, despite the constitutional prohibition on the creation of expenditure structures by laws initiated by the Legislative Branch, the Digital Government Law could have provided more incisively for certain obligations on the Executive Branch, even if this meant creating expenditure, which would have enhanced the effects of the text. Regardless of this, the fact that a policy such as this is not the subject of a leading role and initiative by the Federal Government is quite significant, whether from the point of view of a lack of priority in setting the agenda, considering the political interests of the manager in power at the time, or the care with which the issue is treated in the more technical spheres of the Executive Branch. In addition, the text contains a wide range of principle-based norms or rules with no determinable consequences, the vagueness of which, as well as being ineffective, also leaves room for all kinds of interpretations, not always in favor of the common good.[473]

This does not mean, however, that these principles and guidelines are of no use. They provide a general overview of what the law intends to address and also serve as a guide for the issuing of other subordinate normative texts and for the conduct of administrators, providing meanings that alter

472 Theme/Precedent 917. Leading Case: ARE 878911, Rapporteur Gilmar Mendes. "A law that creates an expense for the Administration, but does not address its structure, the duties of its agencies, or the legal status of public servants (Article 61, § 1, II, 'a', 'c', and 'e', of the Federal Constitution), does not usurp the exclusive competence of the Head of the Executive Branch". In the original, "Não usurpa competência privativa do Chefe do Poder Executivo lei que, embora crie despesa para a Administração, não trata da sua estrutura ou da atribuição de seus órgãos nem do regime jurídico de servidores públicos (art. 61, § 1º, II,"a", "c" e "e", da Constituição Federal)".

473 In this regard, commenting on the list of "principles of public administration" set out in the Federal Law on Administrative Procedure, Carlos Ari Sundfeld sarcastically points out that "If they keep letting administrative law professors make bills, soon there will be no more principles to be discovered in the realm of implicitness!" In the original, "Se continuarem deixando os professores de direito administrativo fazerem projetos de lei, em breve não haverá mais princípios para serem descobertos no reino da implicitude!" SUNDFELD, Carlos Ari. *Direito Administrativo para Céticos.* São Paulo: Malheiros, 2012, p. 65.

the legal expectations of the actors. As Joseph Raz points out, "the law confers certain powers on the agency and directs it to use them to promote certain policy goals in accordance with general principles".[474] In this sense, they are also guidelines for the negative delimitation of conduct, excluding from the scope of legal validity those that are in some way contrary to its content. In other words, even if there are enforcement problems in the event of non-compliance, the existence of the propositions in question, when confronted with conduct, alters expectations and indirectly ends up shaping behavior. This is part of the function of the normative text as an institutional statement, i.e., to provide cultural and legal meanings that condition conduct, regardless of whether it is actually demanded or enforced by a court or authority, along the lines discussed in section 1.9.6 of chapter 1. The provisions also have a communicative and pedagogical function as a discourse that conveys certain ideas developed according to the best administrative and international Digital Government practices to the various actors in the administration, in a kind of coordination of meanings about public policy.

The law is also deficient in that it has not clearly established a division of competences about the tasks and functions necessary to achieve its objectives, which could contribute to better coordination of state actors - a chronic problem even at the federal level.[475] Without the attribution of competences that legally delimit and shape the sphere of preferences and the scope of interests, the programmatic measures contained in the text become excessively dependent on a permanent political impulse to move people and resources. The institutionalization of competences, on the other hand, would require a stronger political impulse at the beginning, but would not require constant reaffirmation. In other words, the lack of competence attribution fails to institutionalize preferences, which means a state of tension arising from the institutional arena is not resolved, and an equilibrium that could stabilize these tensions and prove more fruitful for the continuity of the policy is not achieved.

The law mentions the possibility of the Federal Executive creating knowledge networks. The aim of these networks is to share and generate experiences between federal entities, formulate policies and standards, and

474 RAZ, Joseph. Legal Principles and the Limits of Law. *Yale Law Journal*, v. 81, n. 5, p. 823–854, 1971, p. 841.

475 In this sense, CORDEIRO, Caio Barros. *Desafios do Estado para a transformação digital: uma análise à luz da abordagem Direito e Políticas Públicas*. PhD Dissertation (Law), University of São Paulo, São Paulo, 2023, p. 159.

prospect for new technologies applicable to the administration, consisting of a forum for general debate on the possibilities for the evolution of Digital Government, with the participation of scientific institutions. Knowledge networks were initially mentioned in the 2016 Digital Governance Strategy (Decree 8,638), with an important role in policy formulation. However, they were suppressed in the Strategy published in 2020 (Decree No. 10,332). It is interesting to note that the most important functions for the development of Digital Government in Brazil - (jointly) formulating policies, sharing them, and disseminating state-of-the-art technology with states and municipalities - have been treated superficially and assigned to entities that are created on an optional basis and have a low degree of institutionalization. In this sense, the form of organization and knowledge networks is one of the most important variables for the effectiveness of Digital Government policies.[476] Some of these attributions were repeated when describing the functions of the innovation laboratories, but in this case the focus seems to be more technological than strategic, with policy formulation sidelined.

2.2.1.3 Orientation towards economic efficiency and debureaucratization

The first guideline of the legal text is to "reduce bureaucracy, modernize, strengthen and simplify the relationship between public authorities and society through digital services"[477], and its content is generally geared towards this objective. The idea of bureaucracy, in the pejorative sense of the term (red tape), strongly permeates the citizen's imagination, especially when it comes to issues concerning the state or when they need a service from the state. In this imaginary that makes up the social notion of bureaucracy, there is an excess of paperwork, forms, and documents, redundant requests for information, the need to go to more than one public office to resolve problems and, above all, the impossibility of concretely resolving day-to-day issues that demand energy and time beyond what is reasonable. It is not uncommon for markets to form for intermediaries in the administrative sphere itself, interfering in relations between the government and

476 As indicated, in the context of South Korea LEE, Jooho. Exploring the Role of Knowledge Networks in Perceived e-Government: A Comparative Case Study of two Local Governments in Korea. *American Review of Public Administration*, v. 43, n. 1, p. 89–108, 2013.

477 In the original, "... desburocratização, a modernização, o fortalecimento e a simplificação da relação do poder público com a sociedade, mediante serviços digitais".

the citizen on issues that are theoretically simple but seem insurmountable in practice.[478] Dealing with the state becomes a task only for specialists who know the right "code" for dealing with public administrators, the unwritten rules, the unknown paths, and privileged accesses.

Debureaucratizing and simplifying this relationship involves reducing bureaucracy to the minimum necessary to carry out any service, always with an eye on results, improving communication and making clear the rules and ways to obtain any type of public service. The relationship is strengthened by the reduced need for intermediaries and, above all, by the increase in (mutual) trust between the parties to the relationship, which becomes clearer and more transparent.

The modernization of the relationship between the state and civil society also refers to the social imaginary, referring to the idea of an archaic, outdated administration that can quickly be transformed into something new, better, and more suited to people's needs. This idea of modernity is linked to the fascination with technology as an easy solution to solve chronic and seemingly insurmountable problems. Although, in the first few years, there was less enthusiasm from citizens than from public administrators about Digital Government in countries like the United States,[479] this perception is present in the daily lives of Brazilians. The Digital Government Law itself reproduces this conception to a certain extent by inferring that the modernization of the public administration will be achieved "through digital services".

This is not the wrong direction, but there is one caveat. Just as technology is not an absolute requirement for good administration,[480] there is little point in introducing technological tools without also reviewing and modifying internal processes and the habits of those who carry them out. For example, although the tax collection structure is a pioneer in computerization in Brazil, the country ranks among the bottom in international rankings in terms of ease of paying taxes.[481]

---

478 FREDRIKSSON, Anders. Bureaucracy intermediaries, corruption and red tape. *Journal of Development Economics*, v. 108, p. 256–273, 2014, p. 265.

479 MOON, M. Jae; WELCH, Eric W. Same Bed, Different Dreams? A Comparative Analysis of Citizen and Bureaucrat Perspectives on E-Government. *Review of Public Personnel Administration*, v. 25, n. 3, p. 243–264, 2005, p. 260.

480 For example, the Kanban system developed for Toyota in the late 1940s, based on paper cards. WASSERFALLEN, Antoine. When Asian Industry Influences Western Factories: Kanban Origins. *Ferrum*, n. 82, p. 96–103, 2010, p. 99.

481 WORLD BANK. *Training for Reform*. Washington, DC: World Bank Group, 2019, p. 159.

2.2.1.4 Regulating the digital administrative process

The first section of Chapter II has the function of doing for the administrative process what Law No. 11,419/2006 did for the judicial process,[482] establishing rules on matters ranging from the timeliness of acts and appeals to the form admitted. Although there are already rules on electronic administrative proceedings set out in Decree No. 8,539/2015, the law deals with issues in a more comprehensive way and gives it greater normative force.

Two points can be highlighted. The first is the express provision for the possibility of issuing certificates, diplomas, and supporting documents in general in digital format, as well as the determination of the originality of born-digital documents signed electronically. The express legal provision for validity is a guarantee for the user of public services who holds this type of document, even in the face of third parties who may resist its acceptance, such as employers, universities, and, in particular, other public bodies. Secondly, it is worth highlighting the provision that administrative procedural acts can be carried out in person in cases where it is not feasible to do them online, due to the risk of delays or at the request of the user, demonstrating the concern that digitization should be a means of facilitating and not hindering citizens, also considering the average socio-economic level of the population. This concern appears more than once in the text, in the determination that digital public services be provided by means that are also accessible to the population "on low incomes or living in rural and isolated areas".[483]

2.2.1.5 Components of Digital Government

The law includes a specific section to deal with the "components of Digital Government", namely the User Services Charters, the National Public Services Database and the Digital Government Platforms. It should be noted that the Charters referred to in article 18, II, are the specific subject of another previous law, namely Law No. 13,460/2017, which aims to protect users from the administration in the legal relationship of public service provision in a broader context.

482 This subject will be explored in detail in section 3.1.3.
483 Art. 14. In the original, "de baixa renda ou residente em áreas rurais e isoladas".

The User Services Charter, according to the aforementioned law, has the informative objective of disseminating services to the target public as a kind of "executive summary" of the services offered by a given body, including a list of services, the requirements and necessary measures for access, the form of provision, service times and locations, deadlines, etc. This charter is part of a list of basic rights for users of public services,[484] which has now become an inseparable part of Digital Government. It acts as a practical manual for a given public service, accessible to any user and containing the most important information regarding the activity provided.

The National Services Database and Digital Government Platforms are new features of Law No. 14,129/2021. These are, respectively, a collection of information on public services from each federated entity and a digital means of requesting and following up on services, as well as monitoring their performance.

Despite some redundancy and partial overlap between these three components, they end up complementing each other and having practical relevance when you look at who is responsible for each of them. Dividing the Digital Government into three components is a way of managing the differences and limits arising from the federative nature of the state, but also the characteristics of administrative *deconcentration* and *decentralization*. The Charters are the responsibility of each entity providing the service and serve as an information repository that other elements of Digital Government can leverage. The National Database, on the other hand, aims to bring together this information (as well as the paths and accesses) in one place, in a way of mitigating, for the user, the effects of the fragmentation of the dissemination of information on public services, which invariably results from a complex federalist structure such as the Brazilian one. The Base facilitates comparative analyses of "the flow of delivery of similar public services between various federative levels", as well as their redesign and optimization, between the federated entities around actions that concern common services.[485]

Finally, the Digital Government Platforms aim to unify, at least in each federative entity, the citizen's means of access to digital public services,

484 CARVALHO, André Castro; VENTURINI, Otavio. A função do Código de Defesa do Usuário de Serviços Públicos (Lei nº 13.460/2017) no modelo brasileiro de controle dos serviços públicos. *Revista de Direito Administrativo*, v. 278, n. 1, p. 141–162, 2019, p. 158.

485 ÁVILA, Thiago José Tavares; LANZA, Beatriz Barreto Brasileiro; VALOTTO, Daniel de Souza. Base Nacional de Serviços Públicos do Brasil: sistematização e interoperabilidade de informações para o Governo Digital. *Gestão.org*, v. 19, n. 2,

i.e., they are a single site where they can access not only information but also service and self-service in digital provision. The law thus regulates the configuration of the platforms, introducing the minimum requirements and characteristics that must be included in these instruments. Despite the lack of broad normative force, this regulation serves as a guide for the development of similar tools in the states and municipalities, which can take these legal guidelines as a model for their own planning and implementation.

Providing a single platform for citizens to access information and use public services is also a guideline in line with international best practices and with what has been observed in the implementation of Digital Government in other countries. It is related to the idea of simplification, since single access relieves citizens of multiple registrations, information checks, and the cost of understanding how different systems work to access different public services.

In this regard, Estonia's experience is cited as one of the most successful cases of implementing government as a platform.[486] This small Eastern European country, often referred to as an example of a high degree of development of e-government applications,[487] created a network of online applications in 2001 to share data between agency systems so that all government services are available in one place, called X-Road, which concentrates almost all public services.[488] The development of X-Road and digital government as a whole in Estonia has benefited from multiple factors, such as the existence of advanced human capital resulting from the concentration of investments in computer science in the country since the 1960s (other Soviet republics focused their investments on mathematics and engineering instead) and favorable institutional conditions that reduced transaction costs for the adoption of digital solutions.[489]

It should be noted, however, that perceptions of Estonia's digital government are probably overestimated.[490] In this sense, it should be remembered

---

2021, p. 288. In the original, "...do fluxo de entrega de serviços públicos similares entre vários entes federado".

486 MARGETTS, Helen; NAUMANN, Andre. Government as a platform: What can Estonia show the world. *Research paper, University of Oxford*, 2017, p. 5.

487 ANTHES, Gary. Estonia: A model for e-government. *Communications of the ACM*, v. 58, n. 6, p. 18–20, 2015, p. 18–20.

488 ESTONIAN ICT EXPORT CLUSTER. *X-Road - e-Estonia*. E-Estonia.Com. Available at <https://e-estonia.com/component/x-road/>. Accessed 3 Jan. 2020.

489 KITSING, Meelis. An evaluation of E-government in Estonia. *In*: *Internet, Politics and Policy 2010: An Impact Assessment*. Oxford: Oxford University, 2010.

490 *Ibid.*

that Estonia is a country with a population of around 1,400,000 people, half a million less than the city of Hamburg and almost ten times less than the municipality of São Paulo. The country has approximately 30,000 civil servants in total,[491] 15,000 fewer than Petrobrás, for example, and 300,000 fewer than Deutsche Bahn.[492]

Therefore, although it is interesting to learn about the Estonian experience, thinking about implementing a single, effective digital government platform in a country of continental dimensions like Brazil, with a socially heterogeneous population of more than 210 million people, requires facing challenges that cannot be seen in the case mentioned, especially when considering the issue of federalism. In this sense, it is interesting to note that the single platform, which is one of the foundations of the Digital Government's normative conception, is inconsistent with the aforementioned Brazilian legislative choice not to apply the law automatically to states and municipalities. Of course, this limitation can be legally circumvented by signing agreements between federative entities of different levels or even other types of instruments and solutions, but what can be seen is that it has created, in practice, an additional barrier to be overcome, as well as new arenas for negotiation and new veto points for the policy. Considering that administrative competence in Brazil is divided between the federative entities of different levels and actual service delivery is heavily concentrated in the municipalities, we have the possibility of 5,595 different platforms coexisting in states, municipalities, and the Federal District.

Guaranteeing security on Digital Government platforms is another issue that is growing in importance in this scenario, including from the point of view of national security. Considering that one of the pillars of Digital Government is the unification of citizen access, with the sharing of data and intra-government platforms and the concentration of public services in one place, the management of information security ends up being a critical point, since the potential for damage from a security breach can radiate across several spheres and put the continuity of public services, the privacy of citizens and the essential functioning of the Powers at risk. During the quarantine period of the Covid-19 pandemic, there have been examples of the damaging potential of these events, from invasions of events and meetings of public universities and governments on videoconferencing

491 Data from Statista, available at: <https://www.statista.com/statistics/443785/number-of-employees-administrative-support-estonia/>.

492 Data obtained from the companies' websites.

platforms,[493] to coordinated actions to invade and bring down the entire computer system of the Brazilian Superior Court of Justice for more than a week, culminating, finally, with an attempted attack on the vote counting system in the elections, which touches on the pillars of democracy and could, if successful, undermine the credibility and legitimacy of Brazilian democratic institutions and elections.

2.2.1.6 Creation of a unique identification number

Chapter III of the Law deals with an issue of great importance for the development of Digital Government, which is the establishment of a sufficient number for citizen identification. Article 28 of the Digital Government Law states that the Individual Taxpayer Registry (CPF), created for tax purposes in the 1960s,[494] would become the citizen's identification number for use as a means of accessing digital public services. It can therefore be considered a precursor to a digital identity, which was only regulated later by Decree No. 10,977/2022 and then by Law No. 14,534/2023. The law also determined that the CPF should be included in all registers and documents relating to the citizen, including birth certificates, marriage certificates, the Worker's Identification Number (NIT), the National Health Card, the Work Permit, and passports, among others, totaling 14 different documents.

One of the most surprising facts related to information records in Brazil has always been the lack of standardization around a personal identification document or even a single registration number for the citizen. There have always been different registers in each of the federation states, as well as various other document numbers for specific purposes. The most commonly used identification document, the *Registro Geral* (RG), could, until the beginning of 2024, be issued in multiple numbers, one for each state of the federation. Three laws were passed in the 1980s and 1990s providing for the creation of a single document,[495] but the issue was only resolved recently with the aforementioned Law No. 14,534/2023, providing for the compulsory adoption by the states of a single identification number.

---

493 *Invasão hacker interrompe aula de Lewandowski com mensagens nazistas.* Poder360. Available at <https://www.poder360.com.br/justica/invasao-hacker-interrompe-aula-de-lewandowski-com-mensagens-nazistas/>. Accessed 3 Jan. 2021.

494 Law No. 4,862 of November 29, 1965, amended by Decree-Law No. 401 of December 30, 1968.

495 Laws No. 7,116/1983, No. 9,454/1997 and Federal Law No. 13,444/17.

It should be noted that, although the Digital Government Law pioneered the use of the CPF as citizen identification, influencing the creation of the National Identity Card, there is no possibility for citizens to use it to sign documents, an act that still depends on traditional and problematic forms of digital signatures in Brazil. The development of a complete digital identity that would enable citizens to sign any type of document and carry out the acts of civil life would contribute to a culture of permanent use of the document and, as a consequence, of the digital public services whose access would be linked to it.[496]

In the same vein, there is the "encouragement of the use of electronic signatures" in relations between government bodies and between them and citizens (item XXII). The wording of this section seems timid if we only consider the federal public administration, which has a much higher technical and procedural level than other public administrations in Brazil, so that the systematic and full adoption of digital signatures would be more appropriate. However, this is yet another item designed to be applied to all entities of the Federation and which has its scope and meaning partially undermined by the problematic change in the scope of validity of the text during the legislative process.

2.2.1.7 Standards and rules of interoperability and open data

Interoperability and the promotion of open data policy, mentioned in the law, refer to the challenges of communication and the sharing of efforts between administrative bodies, especially between federal entities. Brazil currently has 26 states and one federal district, and 5,570 municipalities[497] , in addition to the Federal Government. Each of them provides various types of public service and has its own tax authorities to collect the taxes it is responsible for. In addition, each municipality is responsible for managing its own human resources, and even the legal regime/systems of civil servants can vary, with some being statutory, i.e., following their own set of rules contained in a specific municipal statute, and some being "*celetistas*",

496 This function has recently been created within the single digital government platform (as will be seen later), but it is dependent on citizen access to the platform. Moreover, it cannot yet be equated with the highest level of electronic signature security.

497 According to IBGE data, available at: <https://cidades.ibge.gov.br/brasil/panorama>.

i.e. following the legal system of the Consolidation of Labor Laws (CLT) at national level. Social security systems also vary, with some municipalities adhering to the general social security system, managed by the Federal Government, and some having their own social security institutes, responsible for collecting contributions and paying pensions.

Each of these entities can also have different bodies within its administration, such as secretariats and departments. And in the indirect administration, it can have *autarquias*,[498] public companies, mixed-capital companies, and foundations. In the state of São Paulo alone, there are 16 foundations, 6 mixed-capital companies, 13 public companies, and 27 "*autarquias*", including the University of São Paulo.[499]

The interoperability emphasis of open data is also aimed at enhancing the public and private use of information produced by the state. In this sense, the Digital Government Law innovates by determining that public data should be interchangeable, and in this respect it also complements the functions of the 2014 Access to Information Law.[500] There are basically three main reasons for adopting open government data: 1) to increase transparency, and consequently strengthen social and democratic control of the exercise of power by the population; 2) to enhance the generation of social and commercial value, since governments are major producers and collectors of data of various types and origins; and 3) to promote participatory government, since the publication of data can make it easier for citizens to participate directly in the processes of formulating public policies in the day-to-day running of the administration.[501] Open data involves the free use and redistribution of the data produced and made available without discriminating against people or limiting fields of use and with the possibility of being read by machines regardless of platform types.[502]

---

498 The term "*autarquia*" does not have a good correspondence in English, but it is a legal form commonly adopted for indirect administration entities, such as universities and research institutes.

499 According to the official website of the Public Administration Profile on 13/07/2022, available at: <http://perfil.sp.gov.br/admD.asp>.

500 HEINEN, Juliano. Acesso à informação e seus "dois maridos": duas leis em um mesmo tema – transparência e tratamento dos dados públicos. *In*: VALLE, Vanice Regina Lírio do; MOTTA, Fabrício (Orgs.). *Governo Digital e a Busca por Inovação na Administração Pública*. Kindle. Belo Horizonte: Forum, 2022, p. 251, 254.

501 ATTARD, Judie *et al.* A systematic review of open government data initiatives. *Government Information Quarterly*, v. 32, n. 4, p. 399–418, 2015, p. 401.

502 *Ibid.*, p. 402.

When the law deals with interoperability and open data, it is not only restricting itself to the relationship between public entities and the sharing of data between them, but also to the integration of private actors in the dynamics of managing and using this data to generate wealth or social value. This is expressly mentioned in section XXIII of article 3 of the law under analysis which, when dealing with the government as a platform, again emphasizes the use of open data by individuals and companies, with a focus on "public policy making, scientific research, business generation and social control".[503] By not limiting the use of data by field or purpose nor distinguishing the type of person who will have access to it, the law is in line with international best practice. However, when it comes to the use of collected data, especially personal data, there is concern about fundamental issues of privacy and intimacy. Thus, the law conditions the use of data to the protection rights contained in the Brazilian LGPD (General Data Protection Law) and makes it explicit that open data should preferably be anonymized. By opting for the expression "preferably", a minimum burden of justification is created for the public administrator (if there is an intention to use identified data), but without rigidly restricting the possibilities for handling this information.

The policy of open data and interoperability - which presupposes some standardization of the format of this data - also facilitates research in the form of content analysis, including when it comes to automated tools for collecting and interpreting the natural language of acts and decisions, especially useful for the legal professions, but also in the analysis of the regulatory environment and risk for private investment purposes. Content analysis can be defined as "a research technique for making replicable and valid inferences from texts (or other meaningful matter) to the contexts of their use".[504] Although it has existed for many decades, content analysis is gaining greater potential with the application of advanced computers in its realization.[505]

Finally, the law makes a deliberate choice for the preferential adoption of open and free formats in the administration's systems. Although it does not impose mandatory use, this guideline is aimed primarily at managers and planners who are planning and acquiring IT systems for the day-to-

503 In the original, "elaboração de políticas públicas, pesquisas científicas, geração de negócios e controle social".

504 KRIPPENDORFF, Klaus. *Content Analysis: An Introduction to Its Methodology.* 4. ed. Los Angeles: Sage Publications, 2018, p. 24.

505 *Ibid.*, p. 18, 50.

day running of services. In addition to making the administration less dependent on suppliers who own the intellectual property of products and services, this mechanism allows for better adaptability of systems and greater dissemination/standardization among various public bodies, as is the case with the PJE and SaJ in the electronic judicial process.[506] The legal definition of the term "open format" as "free of patents or any other legal restriction on its use",[507] however, is mistaken, because most existing free software license models, despite the fact that their common use by the end user is effectively free of restrictions, contain a prohibition on using the source code to create a new product that has its intellectual property subject to a proprietary license. It is, therefore, a contractual obligation that improvements made by the community are also licensed under the same terms and conditions as the base code, restricting the possibility of restriction.[508] In this sense, it is essential to point out that if the literal inter-

506 This will be discussed in more detail in section 3.1.3.

507 In the original, "livre de patentes ou de qualquer outra restrição legal quanto à sua utilização".

508 A brief explanation of how this question arises in German law can be found in WELSER, Marcus von. Kampf um Linux: Ist die Freiheit der Open-Source-Software bedroht? *Gewerblicher Rechtsschutz und Urheberrecht, Praxis im Immaterialgüter und Wettbewerbsrecht*, n. 7, p. 164–166, 2018, p. 164"According to German legal understanding, the copyright usage rights are granted under a resolutive condition in the sense of § 158 II BGB. If the GPLv2 is not complied with, the usage authorization is no longer applicable". In the original, "Nach deutschem Rechtsverständnis werden die urheberrechtlichen Nutzungsrechte unter einer auflösenden Bedingung im Sinne des § 158 II BGB eingeräumt. Wird die GPLv2 nicht eingehalten, entfällt die Nutzungsberechtigung"; In Brazilian law, especially on the differences between open source and copyleft, see SAKR, Rafael Lima. Do software livre ao desafio informacional: direito e liberdade na sociedade rede. *Revista da Faculdade de Direito, Universidade de São Paulo*, v. 104, p. 617–637, 2009, p. 630: "Despite the differences in value and function, the free software regime and the open source regime have only one irreconcilable difference: the copyleft license. Both regimes grant rights to reproduce, modify and redistribute the programs, but only the free software regime requires the inclusion in these primary norms of a prohibition on altering the usage regime of the original work in derivations developed by third parties. In this way, copyleft consists of a secondary rule that limits the competence of third parties over the disposition of the derivative work. This restriction, provided it is previously and contractually established, does not violate the rights of the authorized author". In the original, "Não obstante as diferenças valorativas e funcionais, o regime de software livre e o regime de código-aberto têm apenas uma divergência inconciliável: a licença copyleft. Ambos os regimes concedem direitos de reproduzir, modificar e redistribuir os programas, porém apenas o regime de software livre exige a inclusão a essas normas primárias da proibição de alterar, nas derivações desenvolvidas por terceiros, o regime de uso da

pretation of the provision prevails, it creates a disincentive to innovation in the public sector by rejecting any traditional open formats, such as those licensed by the General Public License.

2.2.1.8 Duties of the administration and rights of the "user" citizen

The last two sections of Chapter II contain a series of provisions for the organizational duties of the public administration in the context of the provision of digital services and the rights of users in their relationship with the Government. The administration's obligations include eliminating duplicate records and unnecessary demands on citizens, monitoring the quality of services, implementing interoperability, among others. With regard to users' rights, there is an express provision for free access to the platforms, the indication of a preferential channel for citizens to communicate with the public provider, and the right to receive a receipt when attending the service. There is also the presumption of good faith in their actions and the right to enjoy public services by digital means without the need to attend in person, which is implicitly conditional on the existence of conditions to do so.

The provision of the right to face-to-face assistance when necessary is a novelty in the legal system. This provision seeks to offer some response to the phenomenon of digital illiteracy, i.e., the inability or limitation of adults to deal with the technology necessary to carry out the acts of civil life. This provision is also related to the rights of people with disabilities, who cannot be deprived of citizenship due to physical or mental limitations, when there are alternatives to meet their demands. Thus, the text expressly mentions accessibility for people with disabilities and adequate treatment for the elderly, who are particularly affected by digital illiteracy[509] and also by mobility limitations resulting from advancing age.

Digital illiteracy is an obstacle to the development of Digital Government policies because it consists of the low capacity to interpret information by

---

obra original. Dessa forma, o copyleft consiste em uma norma secundária que limita a competência de terceiros acerca da disposição da obra derivada. Essa restrição, desde que prévia e contratualmente estabelecida, não viola os direitos do autor autorizado".

509 DATTA, Arijit *et al.* Bridging the Digital Divide: Challenges in Opening the Digital World to the Elderly, Poor, and Digitally Illiterate. *IEEE Consumer Electronics Magazine*, v. 8, n. 1, p. 78–81, 2019, p. 79.

the people,[510] and this excludes part of the population from the provision of services transformed by innovation, dividing the administration's efforts to the extent that certain activities are also replicated on paper and in person. The higher the rate of digital illiteracy, the greater the scale required for face-to-face and alternative services, and the lower the potential for improving efficiency. There are, therefore, two ways in which the state can tackle this problem. The first, from the point of view of pure and simple efficiency, seeks to promote educational policies that can include the digitally illiterate, developing their skills to the level necessary to enjoy online services. The second, under the aegis of the realization of rights, recognizes that this is a reality for part of the population and that, given this reality, the right and the means must be provided for people to have access to public services regardless of their level of digital education, which the law does correctly in sections II and XVI of article 3 and in article 14.

A related but different concept is that of digital exclusion or *digital divide*, i.e., the lack of access by a given population to digital services and activities that are already generally available. This exclusion can be linked to a lack of infrastructure, such as physical access to the internet, the reach of networks in rural or remote areas, but also to functional digital illiteracy itself, meaning that even when access to the internet and the necessary infrastructure for the proper use of services is available, citizens may not have the necessary notion of the quality of information required to deal with everyday problems and issues, or do not know how to use such means to influence and participate in the actions of the state, in the exercise of "e-citizenship".[511]

In this regard, the law lays down a duty for administrators and civil servants to encourage participation and social control by stimulating educational activities, whether to educate civil servants about the digital environment or to include the population as a whole. These are commands with limited practical effects, but which, as already pointed out, have a symbolic function of affirming public values and prohibiting setbacks.

The law also obliges the administration to use clear language when dealing with citizens, which is especially important in the digital environment,

510 GALLO, Amynthas Jacques de Moraes. Gestão Estratégica da Informação no ambiente do Governo Digital. *Revista Brasileira de Biblioteconomia e Documentação*, v. 6, n. 2, p. 3–19, 2010, p. 10.

511 BARROS, Manoel Joaquim F. de; MELO, Paulo; LEFRANÇOIS, Denise A. E-citizenship: the digital cities program, a tool for a new model of citizenship in Brazil. *Journal on Innovation and Sustainability RISUS*, v. 12, n. 2, p. 30–38, 2021, p. 32, 37.

considering that services are accessed and used directly, without the intermediary of people who, in face-to-face service, can make up for flaws, gaps or excesses in the language of forms and documents. Comprehensibility by "any citizen" is certainly a major challenge, as this includes a significant number of functionally illiterate people.

The requirement to provide information and documents only once, the Once Only Principle, is also part of the set of guidelines that constitute rights. Unfortunately, the law's lack of reach to the other federal levels greatly hinders the realization of this vision of efficiency, since such standardization and intelligent data sharing would be restricted only to the bodies of the federal administration.

2.2.1.9 The balance between formality and risk

When it comes to the relationship between government and citizens, two important notions oppose each other: formality and risk. The aim is to reduce formalities in requirements when their "economic or social cost" outweighs the risk of not requiring them. There are several concrete situations in which this can apply, for example, in personal identification and the presumption of veracity of personal data provided by the citizen.

Concerning identification, there are still risks regarding the security of remote access, i.e., the certainty that, in the digital relationship, those involved are those nominally named as parties to the relationship. The risks are proportional to the type of relationship or legal transaction being carried out. The identification of a party to a real estate purchase contract, for example, requires a greater degree of certainty than the purchase and sale of a low-value asset. In this case, the criterion is economic, i.e., the potential of a fraudulent deal to damage someone's property rights. It can also be inferred from logic that the act of paying a debt constitutes a much lower risk than the act of creating or acknowledging a debt. Thus, for example, in the case of the tax administration, it can be concluded that the act of issuing electronic documents online to settle a tax involves much less risk for the citizen and the administration than the act that formalizes an agreement, transaction, or legal recognition of the tax debt. Under a material criterion, it can be concluded that the identification of a citizen for access to a certificate or declaration regarding specific and isolated personal data (a voting receipt, for example) poses fewer risks than access to their complete medical records.

Regarding the accuracy of personal data, the hypothesis is considered where a citizen submits requests to the state in which their eligibility must be assessed for inclusion as a beneficiary in a certain public policy or the assignment of some direct and individual consequence, such as an error in the collection of a tax or the imposition of an administrative sanction.

Despite the indeterminacy of what the "economic or social costs" to which the law refers are, the administrator is called upon to make a judgment of reasonableness when comparing, especially when formulating policies, the level and quantity of formal requirements and the possible harmful consequences to be avoided by that procedure. The aforementioned costs can also be mitigated by the intelligent use of Digital Government tools and, in a preventive manner, by the automatic cross-checking of data between the various databases held by the public administration. In other words, the development of technologically integrated government structures reduces this variable, so that, in the equation that aims to establish what would be reasonable in terms of requirements and formalities, the contrast becomes more visible, allowing for more permissive measures.

The potential of this can be explained by using a Brazilian example. During the Covid-19 pandemic, the National Congress passed the creation of a policy of emergency financial aid for people whose incomes were suddenly cut or reduced as a result of the health measures adopted to contain the spread of the disease. Beneficiaries had to meet various eligibility requirements, including not having an active formal job and having a personal and family income limited to half a minimum wage and three minimum wages, respectively.[512] Given the urgency of the measure and its gigantic scale, it is natural that its implementation would be based on the mitigation of requirements and formalities in favor of greater speed. However, the lack of preventive integration among various pieces of information already held by the public administration, combined with the political decision not to utilize the extensive registry of social benefit users created in previous administrations, resulted in the occurrence of trivial and avoidable frauds, such as the improper inclusion of public servants as beneficiaries of the measure. Despite the clear text of the law that established the benefit, 680,000 civil servants or pensioners unduly received some portion of the emergency

512 According to article 2 of Federal Law No. 13,982/2020

aid, according to the Office of the Comptroller General (CGU).[513] The investigation was carried out months after the program began, by requesting information from federal entities and cross-checking the data. Particularly striking is the fact that more than 60,000 people who unduly received the aid are federal civil servants or federal military personnel, i.e., directly linked to the federal level responsible for implementing the policy and who could easily have been identified. Of course, in an *ex-post* evaluation and audit, these non-conformities were later discovered, also using data analysis tools and cross-checking information. But the opportunity for an automatic analysis at the time of the benefit application was lost, which could have mitigated the economic and social risk involved and prevented a series of repressive, penal, and administrative consequences that are difficult to implement and counterproductive.[514]

In this way, it is clear that the goal of reducing formalities and even weighing them up against risks is not just a guideline that could be applied in a common bureaucratic reform, but essentially involves, in the context of the Digital Government Law, the rational use of technology to mitigate risks, especially the legal risks of fraud or forgery[515] in the relationship between citizens and public authorities. This is done with a view to increasing levels of mutual trust and preventing the state from having to deal with non-compliance in a purely repressive manner.

2.2.1.10 Innovation, experimentation, and external control/audit

In its final chapters, Brazil's digital government law deals with two issues of great relevance to the digital transformation of public administration: ways of fostering innovation and governance policies (with risk management and administrative control over actions). With regard to the former, it provides for the possibility of public entities setting up innovation laboratories to

---

513 According to news available at: <https://g1.globo.com/economia/noticia/2020/08/13/cgu-identifica-680-mil-servidores-recebendo-auxilio-emergencial-prejuizo-e-de-quase-r-1-bilhao.ghtml>.

514 In theory, each of these 680,000 people may have committed at least one crime under article 299 of the Brazilian Penal Code by unduly receiving the benefit. Imagine that, in order to investigate and punish each crime, a police investigation and criminal proceedings are required. This mobilizes large amounts of resources with questionable practical effects, when the situation could have been prevented by better integration and information management.

515 Crimes provided for in articles 297 and 298 of the Brazilian Penal Code.

> [...] the development and experimentation of innovative concepts, tools and methods for public management, the provision of public services, the processing of data produced by public authorities and citizen participation in the control of public administration.[516]

These laboratories are part of a larger genre of "public innovation sites", which are environments for authorized and controlled experimentation and the development of innovations.[517] Examples of innovation labs include the pioneering Danish Mindlab, conceived in 2001,[518] and the Brazilian GNova, the result of cooperation between Mindlab and the National School of Public Administration (ENAP), a Brazilian government school for continuous learning for public managers and civil servants.[519]

Innovation sites in the public sector are a way of mitigating barriers to innovation that are characteristic of the administration. These include the political system's lack of incentives for knowledge sharing and collaboration, an "anti-innovation DNA" present in the institutional set-up based on hierarchy, and the aversion to divergent ideas and change in general, as well as the low capacity to generalize and increase the scale of innovations diffusely created .[520] In this respect, it is only natural that there are substantial differences in how the public and private sectors deal with risky activities and change, with the state, as the guardian of fundamental rights and the foundation of public order, acting cautiously and guided by a traditional legal rationality. The one-dimensionality and linearity of this process leaves out unforeseen, surprising or unplanned elements, which facilitates

516 According to article 44 of the law in question. In the original, "[...] o desenvolvimento e a experimentação de conceitos, de ferramentas e de métodos inovadores para a gestão pública, a prestação de serviços públicos, o tratamento de dados produzidos pelo poder público e a participação do cidadão no controle da administração pública".

517 FERRAREZI, Elisabete; ALMEIDA, Guilherme de Almeida. *Laboratórios de inovação: como e por que criá-los.* Brasília: Escola Nacional de Administração Pública - Enap, 2023, p. 22.

518 LEE, Celia; MA, Liang. The Role of Policy Labs in Policy Experiment and Knowledge Transfer: A Comparison across the UK, Denmark, and Singapore. *Journal of Comparative Policy Analysis: Research and Practice*, v. 22, n. 4, p. 281–297, 2020, p. 287.

519 Ver BRANDALISE, Isabella; FERRAREZI, Elisabete; LEMOS, Joselene. *Colaboração internacional para inovação: o caso do gnova e mindlab.* Brasília: Enap, 2018.

520 CARSTENSEN, Helle Vibeke; BASON, Christian. Powering collaborative policy innovation: Can innovation labs help? *The Innovation Journal*, v. 17, n. 1, p. 2, 2012, p. 4–5.

administrative activity in a certain sense but can favor path dependency in the course of a policy,[521] and thus be another vector inhibiting change.

When it comes to experimentation environments or investment in the creation and adoption of innovations in general, the logic of progress is guided by the profusion of failures in much greater numbers than successes. In the private sector, entrepreneurship is a force linked to risk and, moreover, significantly characterized by the succession of unsuccessful experiences that often accumulate losses and only generate learning, and whose return in future attempts may or may not materialize or be consolidated. It is in the nature of innovation processes that few of them turn into major success stories and financial returns, especially when we think of startups, which have extremely high "mortality" rates, with 25% closing in the first year, 45% by the fifth year and 80% by the tenth year in the United States[522] - figures that are similar to those of Brazilian companies.[523] This becomes even more extreme when it comes to technological products or services. Technology investors invest a lot of resources in inventions and projects, knowing that only a tiny fraction of them will yield a return, especially since the potential for profitability on a global scale is enormous. In this scenario, Google, Apple, and Facebook are just a few examples of very successful companies that are among the most valuable in the world, among hundreds or thousands of others in the same industry that have not prospered in the same way. These companies often work with disruptive technologies (as opposed to incremental ones), which involve greater risks and are characterized by more short-term failures but have the potential to generate much greater value if they consolidate.[524]

However, the logic of trial and error, in which failures play a central role in the process of creation and innovation, faces challenges when applied to the administration. In part, this is because the public sector does not have to deal with risk in the same way as the private sector, due to its nature, and in part also due to excesses on the part of control/audit bodies, whose supervisory activity sometimes generates unwanted results, in the sense of

521 HILL, Hermann. Die Kunst des Entscheidens. *Die öffentliche Verwaltung*, v. 70, n. 11, p. 433–443, 2017, p. 436.

522 D'AVINO, Marco *et al.* Guidelines for e-startup promotion strategy. *Journal of Technology Management and Innovation*, v. 10, n. 1, p. 1–16, 2015.

523 BEDÊ, Marco Aurélio. *Sobrevivência das Empresas no Brasil.* Brasília: SEBRAE, 2016.

524 CHRISTENSEN, Clayton M. *The Innovator's Dilemma: When New Technologies Cause Great Firms to Fail.* Boston: Harvard Business School Press, 1997.

inhibiting good initiatives by public servants and managers.[525] The problem can be even greater if there is no pre-established law or rule that provides security and clear guidelines for adopting that transformation, along with the need for rapid implementation of technologies due to the process of obsolescence and the risk of failure or setback. Decision-making processes that need to go beyond the rigid specifications of specialized bureaucracy thus encounter cultural, financial, and legal obstacles that make the public service less inclined to a culture of error and learning.[526] Lucas Borges de Carvalho summarizes the reasoning along the same lines:

> The innovation required by the digital government model demands a legal and institutional structure that, instead of the traditional reactive stance of public managers, induces and encourages proactive behavior, focusing on long-term results and enabling the public administration to anticipate trends and social demands, always with the support of new technologies.[527]

In addition to this habitual inertia, Brazil's control and audit structures, such as the Courts of Accounts and the Public Prosecutor's Office, have evolved over time towards a mostly repressive role concerning assessing the legal adequacy of the administrative acts of public managers, in addition to entering into typical public policy and regulatory issues, including those with a high degree of discretion. There are historical and social reasons for this, such as the high prestige that these institutions enjoy in society, together with the high technical capacity provided by well-paid positions and expensive physical structures, in contrast, on the other hand, with the discredit of the political class among the population, together with the precariousness of administrations at municipal and state level, permeated by a lack of resources, improvisations, and a less qualified and worse paid staff.

---

525 CAMPANA, Priscilla de Souza Pestana. A cultura do medo na Administração Pública e a ineficiência gerada pelo atual sistema de controle. *Revista de Direito - Viçosa*, v. 9, n. 1, p. 189–216, 2017.

526 HILL, *op. cit.*, p. 442.

527 CARVALHO, Lucas Borges de. Governo digital e direito administrativo: entre a burocracia, a confiança e a inovação. *Revista de Direito Administrativo*, v. 279, n. 3, p. 115–148, 2020, p. 129. In the original, "A inovação exigida pelo modelo do governo digital demanda uma estrutura jurídica e institucional que, em substituição à tradicional postura reativa dos gestores públicos, induza e incentive comportamentos proativos, com foco nos resultados de longo prazo e que permitam à administração pública se antecipar às tendências e às demandas sociais, sempre com o amparo das novas tecnologias".

There are also aspects of a functional nature that are worth highlighting here. In their control/audit activities, the well-structured Courts of Accounts and Public Prosecutors' Offices, with their technical staff selected and trained to find faults, errors and disparities, have had great success in identifying illegalities, non-compliance and inefficiencies in the entities they audit. This is exacerbated by increased social demands that fall on governments and managers, rather than auditors. Their success in identifying cases of corruption, impropriety and administrative malfeasance of all kinds is widely echoed in the media and enjoys great support and sympathy from citizens.

This repressive empowerment of the administration's external control/audit bodies, which often occurs through a broadening of the self-interpretation of their competences, often ends up frustrating their original objective of serving to improve the administration by carrying out audits and consequent recommendations that can "influence the management of public governance in a systemic way, with a view to constant improvement".[528] Distortions in this beneficial function can be a source of disincentives or perverse incentives for public managers, with counterproductive effects on the quality of the administration and politics. Firstly, there is a severe adverse selection of public administrators, since it becomes part of the manager's life to answer lawsuits, with a high risk of financial liability, and the need to bear the costs of defense regardless of whether the case is dismissed. Thus, especially in municipalities, there is a disincentive for capable and well-intentioned people from civil society to take on positions of trust and responsibility, such as heads or secretariats, while ill-intentioned people ("who have nothing to lose") or less qualified people end up being favored in occupying these positions and functions. Secondly, this represents a severe indirect disincentive to any innovative practice in public administration - already naturally more subject to risks - which the servant doesn't feel comfortable bearing because they will be personally liable for failures that are often part of a process of creating alternatives and innovation.

528 SUNDFELD, Carlos Ari. Como tornar o controle eficiente? Definindo os limites do papel do Ministério Público e dos Tribunais de Contas. *In*: GIAMBIAGI, F.; FERREIRA, S.G.; HOELZ, A.A.M. (Orgs.). *Reforma do Estado Brasileiro - Transformando a Atuação do Governo*. Rio de Janeiro: GEN Atlas, 2020, p. 292. In the original, "influir de modo sistêmico na gestão, com visão de melhoria constante, de governança pública".

There is important empirical evidence that, when it comes to innovation, the relationship between the control/audit bodies and the public administration can have a negative impact when there is too much interference in the policy formulation processes. Take, for example, a study that analyzed concession contracts drawn up by governments and regulatory agencies, identifying the role of the Federal Court of Accounts - TCU in each of them and concluding, after careful statistical analysis, that the greater degree of interventionism by the TCU negatively affects the number of innovations introduced by the agencies in concession contracts. In other words, the content of the control/audit body's decisions, with recommendations regarding the legal modeling of concessions, created an environment that inhibited innovation, which was concretely reflected in how contracts were generally drawn up.[529]

On the other hand, there is also a positive aspect to the intervention of control/audit bodies when it is carried out to the right extent, and can contribute to innovative processes in public administration. This happens, for example, by pushing the administrator to improve their performance on a daily basis, or, more directly, by requiring the administrator to implement some concrete measure of an innovative nature.[530] In this sense, we highlight the monitoring and auditing activities that generate studies and reports, such as the TCU's Digital Government monitoring reports, which provide good input for policy makers.

The Digital Government Law dedicates a specific chapter to governance and risk management mechanisms, determining procedures for constant monitoring of actions, with a view to continuous improvement. By determining that the authorities responsible for digital Government policies create internal control structures for risk assessment and management, this could theoretically contribute to greater efficiency in the control system as a whole, leading to a reduction in the concern of supervisory/control bodies with the individual conduct of managers. The focus would then be on monitoring the implementation and proper functioning of the internal control and risk management mechanisms of administrative bodies, from a compliance perspective. This reinforces the autonomy of administrative

---

529 BRAGA, André de Castro Oliveira Pereira. *O Tribunal de Contas da União inibe inovações em concessões públicas?* Master's thesis (Public Administration), FGV, Rio de Janeiro, 2015, p. 76.

530 JORDÃO, Eduardo. A relação entre inovação e controle da administração pública. *A&C - Revista de Direito Administrativo & Constitucional,* v. 18, n. 72, p. 133–146, 2018, p. 144–145.

bodies to manage their risk policies, enabling institutions to provide a safer environment for managers and civil servants to innovate while preserving the role of external control in overseeing administrative activity. However, this requires a culture change, so the control/audit bodies interpret the law this way.

With regard to legal certainty for individual managers, other initiatives in recent years have sought to remedy distortions in the actions of the Courts of Accounts and Public Prosecutors' Offices, such as the reform of the Law of Introduction to the Norms of Brazilian Law in 2018, and the new Law on Administrative Improbity in 2021. Finally, the weight of the doctrinal discussion on the subject that exists in Brazil today, together with legislative reactions and reforms, will also have some impact on changing the culture of administrative control formalism to an extent that cannot yet be assessed.

2.2.2 Other laws and regulations comprising the arrangement

Several important issues for an overview of the Digital Government arrangement are dealt with in specific laws. Matters such as data protection, access to information, basic rules for the use of the internet, digital signatures, and the regulation of public records, among others, have their own systems and form intersections with digital government rules. Therefore, they will be addressed below.

2.2.2.1 Access to Information Act (LAI)

Brazil's Access to Information Law (Law No. 12,527/2011) established a new system of transparency in the administration by guaranteeing anyone the right to access public information. By making it easier for citizens to monitor and question government actions, the law has become an essential instrument for strengthening democratic relations. The law acts as a driving force behind digitization initiatives, since the obligation of the public authorities to provide all kinds of information in a relatively short time involves the need for internal organization that considers the adoption of electronic data formats that can be easily managed, distributed, and reused.

Not only is this incentive for internal reorganization an effect of the law, but also the availability of information in advance on portals and platforms, which anticipate citizens' most common demands and prevent managers from spending time and resources answering requests individually. In this way, the LAI also creates incentives for civil society to participate more in government, becoming better informed about management through digital channels, which contributes to public engagement.

The LAI also encourages innovation in general by providing increasingly comprehensive and machine-readable data sets, which enables their use by public administrators from different bodies to support the development of public policies and, more specifically, digital applications, as well as the use of data by companies to develop solutions that create economic value and potentially improve public services.

The LAI also brings important challenges for the administration, such as the need for efficient cybersecurity management in a context of integration between data produced and made publicly available and vulnerability to attacks and undue modifications, as well as the complexity of information management considering personal data and confidential information. In addition, it is not uncommon for public managers to abuse the interpretation of the exceptions and hypotheses for classifying information as secret that the LAI provides for, which hinders public access and generates legal challenges, which create liabilities for the state and take resources from interested citizens.

2.2.2.2 Law No. 12,682/2012 on electronic documents

Law No. 12,682/2012 established rules on the digitization of physical documents and the storage of digitized documents. However, the President of the Republic vetoed 3 articles of the bill approved by Congress, in particular the one that equated scanned documents with the originals for the purposes of legal validity,[531] a measure that was only reintroduced into the text of the law seven years later.[532]

By regulating issues such as how to convert to electronic format, the preservation of integrity, legal validity and probative value, the law represented a step forward in a broader process of digitization of the administra-

531 IOCKEN, Sabrina Nunes; GARCIA, Rodrigo Guerra. A Lei no 14.129/21 como facilitadora normativa para transformação digital e gestão do conhecimento nas organizações públicas. *In*: VALLE, Vanice Regina Lírio do; MOTTA, Fabrício (Orgs.). *Governo Digital e a Busca por Inovação na Administração Pública*. Kindle. Belo Horizonte: Forum, 2022, p. 87.

532 Law No. 13,874, of September 20, 2019.

tion that would later involve the procedural aspect. Digitizing documents modernizes the administration's document management and reduces direct costs by reducing the need for physical space to store paper files, as well as enabling easier and more agile access in the case of searches and information retrieval. It is also a prerequisite for integrating services between different administration bodies in interoperable environments.

However, one cannot fail to point out an important gap in the public document management system, which is the lack of control and criteria on the publication and removal of official documents from government websites. While official acts such as laws, decrees, and other provisions are published in the official gazette and remain available in archives (just as physical publications are cataloged and stored in libraries), various digital documents, such as studies, reports, plans, etc., which are important for the ongoing formulation of policies and for government transparency, are taken offline without any formalities, often for political-ideological reasons. Take, for example, a set of environmental reports and studies that disappeared from the website of the Ministry of the Environment between 2019 and 2023, during the administration of President Jair Bolsonaro,[533] characterized by his anti-environmental and climate crisis denialist speeches and practices. Maintaining digital materials and making them available for consultation, considering the lack of physical archives for these documents, requires specific regulations that currently do not exist beyond the incidence of norms such as the principle of publicity and the duties of transparency, without which even scientific research is hampered.[534]

2.2.2.3 Civil Rights Framework for the Internet

Law No. 12,965/2014, known as the *Marco Civil da Internet*, is a law passed in 2014 that establishes principles, guarantees, rights, and duties of various actors about the Internet in Brazil, seeking to regulate the responsibilities

533 As reported in *Ministério do Meio Ambiente de Bolsonaro apagou 30 anos de documentos | Metrópoles*. Available at <https://www.metropoles.com/colunas/guilherme-amado/ministerio-do-meio-ambiente-de-bolsonaro-apagou-30-anos-de-documentos>. Accessed 21 Aug. 2024.

534 On this point, it should be noted that several documents on digital government policies cited in older scientific articles are no longer available at their original addresses, or even anywhere on the internet, making it very difficult for researchers to understand some of the relationships and evolutionary processes of Brazil's digital transformation.

of the parties involved in the relationship of Internet access and use. One of the main measures included in the law is the establishment of the principle of net neutrality, which ensures that data traffic is treated equally by connection providers without discrimination based on content or origin.

The Brazilian Civil Rights Framework for the Internet also establishes rules on the collection, use and storage of data recording access to content by users and the hypotheses for holding access and application providers liable. This point is currently the subject of intense debate, since the requirements for holding application providers liable set out in the law were not designed to deal with the phenomenon of mass disinformation. Article 19 of the law provides that platforms will only be held liable for damages caused by third-party content if they fail to comply with a court order ordering the removal of content deemed offensive. STF Justice Alexandre de Moraes argues that this provision of the law should be interpreted in conjunction with the principles and objectives of the Republic contained in Articles 1, 2 and 3 of the Brazilian Constitution, recognizing a broader responsibility of online service platforms due to their role as beneficiaries of the monetization of this content and their power to control the algorithms that distribute the content among users.[535] It should also be noted that, since 2018, the constitutionality of article 19 has been under consideration by the Federal Supreme Court in Extraordinary Appeal 103396, which is still pending a decision.

It is also worth mentioning criticism of the redundancy of several of the provisions of Law No. 12,965/2014 in relation to the Constitution and other existing laws, as well as the fact that it has removed the old Civil Code rule applicable to application providers, which provided for joint liability *ex delicto* and thus imposed a duty of vigilance on providers.[536] In this sense, before the law was passed, Brazilian courts recognized the liability of internet application providers for third-party content but applied the "notice and takedown" theory inspired by the copyright law governed by the Digital Millennium Copyright Act in the United States. This understanding excluded the liability of platforms in cases where they were notified by the

535 MORAES, Alexandre de. *O direito eleitoral e o novo populismo digital. Liberdade de escolha do eleitor e a promoção da Democracia*. Thesis for full professorship (Law), University of São Paulo, São Paulo, 2024, p. 59.

536 TOMASEVICIUS FILHO, Eduardo. Marco Civil da Internet: uma lei sem conteúdo normativo. *Estudos Avançados*, v. 30, n. 86, p. 269–285, 2016, p. 280–282.

holders of the infringed right and responded promptly to the demand to remove the content.[537]

On the other hand, it is important to bear in mind that the *Marco Civil da Internet*, when passed, represented an important measure for protecting the freedom of internet users in general, by establishing stricter requirements for a publication to be taken down, and this consisted of incentives for the decentralized production of content and lower barriers to entry in these markets. In the same vein, it also established strict requirements for access to user data and records, such as browsing history, which are not accessible by any authority, except through judicial authorization. For this reason, some say that those in favor of making Article 19 more flexible naively want to combat fake news by destroying rights.[538]

Regardless of this discussion, part of the issue of regulating Big Techs that will be addressed later in sections 4.2 and 4.3, the establishment of a more predictable environment for the use of the internet and the limits of responsibility of connection providers, application providers, and users, as well as the certainty of equal treatment of data traffic, contributes to creating a safe environment that is conducive to the development of content and applications, and also able to mediate commercial and personal relationships. In the same way, neutrality helps to avoid creating artificial barriers to the entry of new players into the market, such as start-ups, which stimulates innovation. By establishing a legal basis for the protection of personal data and equal conditions for data traffic, the law provides essential elements for the relationship of trust on which the provision of digital public services is based.

2.2.2.4 General Data Protection Law

The Brazilian General Data Protection Law of 2018 (LGPD) came into force in September 2020 and aims to comprehensively regulate the use of personal data in Brazil by the public and private sectors. It was strongly

537 SCHREIBER, Anderson. Marco Civil da Internet: avanço ou retrocesso? A responsabilidade civil por dano derivado do conteúdo gerado por terceiro. *In*: LUCCA, Newton de; FILHO, Adalberto Simão; LIMA, Cíntia Rosa Pereira de (Orgs.). *Direito & Internet*. São Paulo: Quartier Latin, 2015, v. 2, p. 277–305.

538 PADILHA, Felipe; FACIOLI, Lara. Colonialismo tecnológico ou como podemos resistir ao novo eugenismo digital – entrevista com Sérgio Amadeu Silveira. *Estudos de Sociologia*, v. 25, n. 48, p. 363–378, 2020, p. 371.

inspired by the text of the European GDPR and, therefore, has a systemic identity with its terms, albeit with differences in the treatment of some issues. It is interesting to note that the protection of personal data in Brazil was only elevated to a constitutional provision in 2022, with the approval of Constitutional Amendment 115/2020, which included, in the list of fundamental rights in Article 5, the provision that "the right to the protection of personal data, including in digital media, is ensured, under the terms of the law".[539]

The LGPD plays a fundamental role in the development of Digital Government, especially since it presupposes a relationship of mutual trust between government and citizens, and this involves the expectation of respect for the right to privacy and intimacy, and the guarantee that personal data and information will always be used in accordance with the law and for the benefit of the individual. In this sense, the LGPD tends to generate expectations in private actors in order to increase their trust in digital services by establishing legal rights and guarantees, as well as clear procedures regarding the use of the data provided when using the services. A personal data protection system, of which the general law is the central element, is fundamental to enabling Open Government efforts and the dynamics of data interoperability, shielding them from the risks of abuse and violation of fundamental rights.[540] Widespread leaks of personal data, such as the one that happened in Brazil in 2021,[541] favor the occurrence of internet scams, including those in which criminals falsify official government correspondence. In this way, an effective system for protecting personal data prevents people from losing trust in electronic means of interacting with the government. From the administration's point of view, managers and public servants in general can also benefit from a clearer and more robust regulatory framework concerning data, which encourages the responsible adoption of digital solutions that are hampered in environments of low legal certainty and regulatory uncertainty.

The LGPD, however, can be a challenge and sometimes an obstacle to the proper development of Digital Government policies. Adapting to its rules generates costs and demands continuous effort on the part of the ad-

539 In the original, "...é assegurado, nos termos da lei, o direito à proteção dos dados pessoais, inclusive nos meios digitais".

540 OECD. *Digital Government Review of Brazil: Towards the digital transformation of the public sector.* Paris: OECD, 2018, p. 20.

541 *Entire population of Brazil possibly exposed in massive data leak.* Cybernews. Available at <https://cybernews.com/security/brazil-data-leak-cpf-card/>. Accessed 16 Aug. 2024.

ministration, since dealing with large amounts of data under strict rules and with the prospect of sanctions requires modern systems and well-trained and up-to-date civil servants. Furthermore, as in Europe, the LGPD can sometimes lead to difficulties in implementing services that involve the use and sharing of data, in the context of the tension between improving digital public services and the danger of state surveillance and totalitarianism. Another issue, more specific to the Brazilian reality, is the abuse of the interpretation of certain provisions of the LGPD to justify denials of requests made under the Access to Information Law. The rejection of requests on the grounds that the information requested contained personal data protected by the LGPD is an example of this, leading to a reduction in public transparency and stimulating legal disputes that demand resources from the state and the citizens concerned - just as happens with the abuse of the legal hypotheses of secrecy contained in the LAI.

2.2.2.5 Digital signature regulations

Law No. 14,063/2020 created a new system for digital signatures in Brazil, partially breaking with the previous system based on certifying authorities, provided for in Provisional Measure No. 2.200-2/2001. The break is only partial because the new regulation applies only to interactions with public entities, i.e., it provides for the digital signature of citizens when carrying out acts with governments and also on intra- and intergovernmental acts carried out by public servants, excluding interaction with the Judiciary, which would continue to follow its own specific rules.

This change arose from the need to simplify people's access to digital public services in the context of the Covid-19 pandemic, considering the real danger that face-to-face interactions represented at the time. It is worth noting that, unlike the Digital Government Law, this piece of legislation extends its scope not only to the entities and bodies that make up the federal public administration, but also to the administrations of the states and municipalities, by virtue of what is expressly stated in Article 2.

The point is to classify digital signatures into three different types. The first is called the simple electronic signature, which allows the signatory to be identified and their data to be attached or associated in an expeditious manner, without greater degrees of security. The second, the advanced electronic signature, uses certificates and means of unambiguous proof of authorship, which allow subsequent alterations to be detected, but which are different from the certifications issued by ICP-Brasil. The third classification, called qualified electronic signature, uses the digital certificate provided for in Provisional Measure 2.200-2/2001.

The idea of creating signatures that are different in terms of complexity and security is to make it easier for citizens to carry out simple acts that do not involve high-value legal assets. In this sense, for example, although personal data is a relevant asset and therefore subject to careful protection by the state and legal rules, there is no justification for citizens having to use a complex and expensive form of signature to access a vaccination certificate online, especially during the pandemic, when vaccination was extremely encouraged and even required to enter some establishments and perform certain acts of civil life.

As far as the most secure level is concerned, it can be seen that the digital certificate system adopted in Brazil in 2001[542] is currently the most anachronistic form of digital identity, too complex for the average citizen to use on a daily basis, as well as extremely expensive, at a level that is incompatible with the average national income, especially for the sections of the population most in need of public services. The digital certificate has to be issued in person, renewed every 3 years, and has a cost that prevents its popularization, considering that around 50% of the Brazilian population lives monthly on a per capita income of R$413.00,[543] and the cost of the certificate can be on average R$200.00. Currently, the system is mostly used by those who are obliged to do so to carry out their qualified professional duties, such as lawyers in court and accountants and companies in their dealings with the Federal and State Tax Authorities. It should also be noted that this system requires the use of a card or pen-drive, i.e., it was designed to be used only on a computer with a USB port, whereas nowadays the use of smartphones is much more widespread, including for government applications.

At the beginning of 2024, the Gov.br website, Brazil's single digital government platform, began offering a digital signature service for documents with a high level of security, which could mean that the digital certificate-based system is used less and less. In addition, bills are currently being considered in Congress to increase the validity and legal acceptance of this type of signature.[544]

542 Provisional Measure 2200-2/2001.
543 According to IBGE's Continuous National Household Sample Survey, 2018.
544 For example, Senate Bill 4187 of 2023.

2.2.2.6 Electronic Public Records System (Serp)

Law No. 14,382/2022 created the Electronic Public Registry System (SERP). It is an elaboration and transformation of the provision for an Electronic Registration System originally brought in by article 37 of Law No. 11,977/2009, which had as its specific object a large housing and urban land regularization program ("*Minha Casa, Minha Vida*" Program). This is a large-scale housing public policy aimed at the acquisition of homes by the poorest sections of the population, in the order of 7 million homes delivered to date.[545] This magnitude of scale required efforts to increase the efficiency of bureaucratic real estate registration procedures, as well as reducing the costs of these acts, since, in the context of a public policy that involved subsidies from the state for the acquisition of these properties, the value of costs and emoluments ceased to be a matter of general interest to society and citizens who acquire properties autonomously and privately, and became an informing element of the policy itself.

The computerization of notary offices in Brazil, of course, did not begin with the 2022 law, nor with the 2009 law,[546] and the scenario under analysis is explained by the very nature of the provision of notary services and their form of organization. In Brazil, notary offices, real estate registries, civil registries, etc., are public service delegations whose activity is carried out privately and for life by individuals after passing a public tender. There is a great discrepancy in profitability in the private operation of the activity of notaries, varying according to the type and location, with a great variation also in price and operating regulations, according to each state of the federation.

However, the regulatory model is not based on the establishment of a rate of return, nor does it follow the logic of an administrative concession contract preceded by a bidding process and the best proposal, so the logic of the economic-financial balance of the delegation relationship is quite different. In this sense, the first efforts to computerize registry offices in Brazil came from the initiative of the agents themselves, either by creating and operating internal systems to replace the use of paper and speed up service (as far as the law allowed), or by associating and creating electronic

545 According to data released by the government in 2024, available at <https://agenciagov.ebc.com.br/noticias/202403/minha-casa-minha-vida-completa-15-anos-abrindo-portas-para-novos-sonhos-de-conquista-da-casa-propria>.

546 Mention should also be made of Law No. 13,465/17, which created a specific register for real estate.

systems shared by several registry offices. The main incentive for this was the possibility of incorporating productivity gains for greater profitability in the activity, considering that competition is restricted to only part of the activities, such as drawing up deeds and notarial minutes, in which, as a rule, the prices of services are set by the regulatory body.

The one-off initiatives of notary publics were accompanied by acts and regulations from the government, which initially sought, much more than promoting a leap in quality and an effective digital transformation of processes, to create rules that would guarantee some standardization for the computerization of services from the user's point of view, such as regulating the issuing of online certificates and similar issues. Over time, due specifically to the work of the National Council of Justice - CNJ, these incremental measures have taken on a more robust and integrated form (along the lines of the digitization of court proceedings), but their predominant character has not changed. Although the efficiency gains from digitalization could be partly appropriated by users and society in general, due to speed, ease of service, and improved security, decentralization and digitalization still tended to generate gains that were mostly appropriated by the notaries, consisting of a combination of very limited incentives for transformation: any aspect of the transformation that could make some services unnecessary, or that could justify the unification of providers, or that could represent a gain in productivity, leading society to rethink its own way of operating the activity, had no incentive. In reality, the opposite was true: since the full digitalization of public records could represent, in theory, a threat to the "business model" that guarantees the private management of registry offices, this becomes a potential focus of resistance for these actors.[547]

Law No. 14,382/2022 represented a change in the way this process evolved. It was initially configured as a provisional measure, drafted by the Executive Branch, which was later converted into law by Congress. Considering its legal form originated as an act of the President of the Republic, one can readily infer that it is a set of rules drawn up by a small universe of authors (especially those most influential within the government) on measures aimed at improving efficiency and reducing bureaucracy, linked directly to the Ministry of Economy.

Two relevant interests related to the issue of public registers were opposed, even though the field of dispute was only related to real estate

547 OECD. *Digital Government Review of Brazil: Towards the digital transformation of the public sector*. Paris: OECD, 2018, p. 20.

registry rules. On the one hand, the interests of the registry offices in maintaining the status quo of the regulation of the activity, which would guarantee greater control and autonomy for the delegates/operators in the discussions and implementation of digitalization systems for their services. On the other hand, financial institutions such as banks, interested in making registry systems and the management of contractual guarantees cheaper and more useful for their real estate financing activities, elements closely linked to the profitability of lending activities for the acquisition of properties.

In this dispute, the interests of the financial institutions prevailed in favor of a form of digitalization of the real estate financing process that lowered costs and benefited the banking activity, but harmed (slightly) the economic interests of notaries and real estate registry officers.

2.2.2.7 Legal Framework for Startups, Govtechs and sandboxes

Complementary Law No. 182 of 2021, known as the Legal Framework for Startups, is relevant for Digital Government as it introduces a new simplified form of technology procurement into the legal system, which facilitates the relationship between technology startups and the state, fostering arrangements in which Govtechs create business models based on their interaction with the Government. Also of particular interest is article 11, which provides that any public administration bodies with regulatory powers can waive some of their rules within the scope of an experimental regulatory environment (sandbox) program to promote innovation.

Regulatory sandboxes first emerged as an initiative of the UK's Financial Conduct Authority (FCA) so that innovations in the fintech market - the use of new technologies in the financial sector - could be tested in a safe and more loosely regulated environment.[548] They came to be used by various monetary authorities around the world, including Brazil, to provide a simplified and more permissive set of rules so that innovative technological solutions could be tested in real time in a controlled manner. Over time, other sectors created their own sandboxes, as was the case in the regulation of land transportation, insurance, and energy in Brazil shortly after the Brazilian Central Bank adopted them.

548 FENWICK, Mark; KAAL, Wulf A.; VERMEULEN, Erik P. M. Regulation Tomorrow: What Happens When Technology Is Faster than the Law. *American University Business Law Review*, v. 6, n. 3, p. 561–594, 2016, p. 591.

However, as well as making it possible to test innovations generated in the market, sandboxes also have a great potential to test new forms of regulation. They are opportunities for regulators to test new ideas and approaches on a small scale, which can be widely adopted in the future if they have good results. In this sense, the regulatory sandbox is also a sandbox for regulation.[549] This theme will be mentioned again in section 4.5 of chapter 4, when we discuss how public administration can regulate itself to keep pace with innovation.

2.3 Chapter conclusion

There are three stages in the institutionalization process.[550] The first is the pre-institutionalization phase, in which the reiteration of habits causes certain arrangements to emerge in response to specific organizational problems. At this stage, there may be similar expressions of institutionalization in different places, but with their own idiosyncrasies, and the adopters of these structures rarely have relevant knowledge about the structures of others.[551] When these arrangements go through a process of objectification and diffusion, which involves "some degree of social consensus among organizational decision-makers concerning the value of a structure, and the increasing adoption by organizations on the basis of that consensus",[552] the stage of semi-institutionalization is reached. Full institutionalization is only achieved when there is a process of sedimentation of these expectations, which involves the historical continuity of structures and a resistance to the renewal of their frameworks.[553]

Digital Government in Brazil has never left the semi-institutionalization phase, even after a federal law was passed on the subject. Although its importance cannot be overlooked, the law has not substantially altered the institutional scenario of Digital Government and has not sufficiently responded to the main current challenge of the matter, which is integration

549 ALLEN, Hilary J. Regulatory Sandboxes. *George Washington Law Review*, v. 87, n. 3, p. 579–645, 2019, p. 641–643.

550 TOLBERT, Pamela S.; ZUCKER, Lynne G. The Institutionalization of Institutional Theory. *In*: CLEGG, Stewart R.; HARDY, Cynthia (Orgs.). *Studying Organization: Theory & Method*. London: SAGE Publications, 1999, p. 180–184.

551 *Ibid.*, p. 181.

552 *Ibid.*, p. 182.

553 *Ibid.*, p. 184.

between the Union, States, and Municipalities, with the consequent expansion of the offer of digital services to the regional and municipal levels.

In the last 20 years, there have been many changes related to the committees and secretariats responsible for Digital Government in Brazil, which makes it difficult even to have a consistent narrative about the evolution of the Executive's organization around this issue. Key bodies at the beginning of the policy, such as CEGE, no longer exist - or have changed their name or the ministry to which they are attached. This is a symptom of one of the main problems related to this public policy in Brazil, namely fragmentation and low institutionalization.[554] The existing structures have limitations that prevent them from efficiently conditioning the behavior of all the actors involved in the process and exercising effective coordination.

Over the years, it can be seen that the improvement in Brazil's position in the international Digital Government rankings coincides with the moments when the issue entered the agenda of priorities and had the involvement of the top echelon of the government, especially the Ministry of Planning and Management.[555] This pattern is repeated because the level and form of institutionalization have remained practically the same as those defined in the early 2000s, with bodies without their own autonomy, linked to the Federal Government, and with limited competence, which depend on external political forces for engagement and continuity of actions. At the same time, this same semi-institutionalized structure has largely neglected the state and municipal spheres.

Regarding the municipal level, a mapping carried out in 2022 to assess the maturity of Digital Government in 155 Brazilian cities with more than 200,000 inhabitants revealed that, although municipalities have improved their information technology infrastructure, problems persist, such as poor integration of information and systems, and a lack of transparency.[556] In addition, most of the resources for digital transformation are internal, from tax collection itself, with a minority of municipalities also adding funding from BNDES programs to their processes, such as the Program for the

554 LAIA, Marconi Martins de *et al.* Electronic government policies in Brazil: Context, ICT management and outcomes. *RAE Revista de Administracao de Empresas*, v. 51, n. 1, p. 43–57, 2011.

555 MUSAFIR, Valeria Esther Nigri; FREITAS, Christiana Soares de. Strategies, Policies and Evaluations of Brazilian Electronic Government. *Electronic Journal of e-Government*, v. 13, n. 2, p. 136-149, 2015, p. 142–146.

556 BRASIL. *Mapa de Governo Digital.* Brasília: Secretaria de Governo Digital, 2022, p. 6.

Modernization of Tax Administration and Management of Basic Social Sectors (PMAT) and the National Program to Support the Administrative and Fiscal Modernization of Brazilian Municipalities (PNAFM).[557]

The report also points to some positive trends, such as the organization of planning and management instruments for implementing policies, reflecting some degree of progressive institutionalization, as well as the intensification of digital means of communication and relationships with residents more broadly, such as presence on social networks and the structuring of digital channels for social participation. However, it should be noted that the evaluation paradigm still seems to be that of *e-government*, from the first phase of digitalization of the administration, since the indicators highlighted deal with services such as issuing certificates, procedural consultations, tax collection, and access to documents and information,[558] not covering aspects of Digital Government that are characteristic of the local municipal reality of proximity to the citizen, such as the urban policies that characterize smart cities, for example, and the overt use of data. As Pedro Demo says, citizens don't live in the state or the Union, but in the municipality, which should originally be responsible for implementing most policies, with decentralization being an expression of the "citizenship project",[559] and this aspect is very rarely present in current structures.

To date, the rationale behind the implementation of Digital Government in Brazil has been the search for economic efficiency, and this explains why there has been important progress in this field, even considering the precarious economic-financial dimension and the deficient legal-institutional arrangement of semi-institutionalization and compartmentalization within the members of the Federation. The incentives provided by this line of political direction, however, are insufficient to continue the development of the Digital Government towards a deeper transformation aimed at the full realization of rights and the energization of the relationship between citizens and the government. There is clearly an exhaustion of this model, and the current institutional structures, which have been effective to a certain extent for some progress, will gradually cease to produce good results if they do not undergo consistent modification.

In addition, it should be borne in mind that Digital Government is a policy that has no visibility, precisely because it is not tangible. Citizens

557 *Ibid.*, p. 6, 20.

558 *Ibid.*, p. 33.

559 DEMO, Pedro. Educação na nova Constituição - qualidade e democratização. *Em Aberto*, v. 7, n. 39, 1988, p. 12–13.

are politically sensitive to government deliveries related to tangible policies, such as health, education, and security, without perceiving the impact of digitalization on their results. And, unlike other policies that are also not very sensitive to the electoral issue, such as those related to the treatment of collected sewage, for example, they don't even move the local economy of cities because they don't generate work or local hiring services. There are also difficulties in convincing mayors and governors to join the Gov.br platform due to the issue of trust between the federative levels and also because each politician has an interest in creating their own applications to leave their political mark.

In Digital Government, the fact that there is no obvious clash of interests and redistributive disputes is a problem, as there is no political driving force behind its development, either to put it on the agenda or to compete with other policies for the resources and means needed to implement it. Thus, the dispute between groups and organized interests takes place less within the field and object of the Digital Government public policy and more in relation to the lobbying of other public policies. The game of interests will appear, but discreetly, when it comes to sub-policies, such as the issue of digital signatures, which today generate an important market for certification bodies, or even when it comes to Brazilian public registries, which are currently carried out through private delegation and which in many cases become disproportionate sources of income.

The state bureaucracy (technical civil servants working in the administration) also has its own agenda, which usually complements those of the government and the state, and can be responsible for driving innovation, as the *Rede Governo* project demonstrated in the early 2000s. This independent agenda, however, seems to occupy an underused limbo, due to the lack of institutionalization of regular paths. The agenda of the federal bureaucracy, although set in a less than conducive environment, has tried to develop digital transformation policies to the limit of their weak institutional potential (albeit in a positive manner). However, precisely because of this limited institutional potential, they have taken on the characteristics of a proliferation of texts and documents with limited scope and impact.

As already pointed out, Digital Government in Brazil had a considerable initial boost at the turn of the century, in the wake of the popularization of the internet in Brazil and the growth of e-commerce. This impetus was spearheaded by the Federal Government, in particular the SLTI of the Ministry of Planning, and the CEGE, which provided an inter-ministerial structure for coordinating initiatives between the various government bodies. This semi-institutionalized structure at the federal level, the strong economic incentives to computerize the state and the direct involvement of the political leadership in coordination efforts created an environment conducive to the first initiatives. They emerged as experimental ideas within the government bureaucracy, in the context of a political directive to reform the state, and were disseminated internally by the coordinative discourse of authorities with enough political clout to deal with resistance to their implementation.

As the government's priorities have changed due to the political context, the lower level of leadership engagement has impacted the pace of innovation. However, the degree of institutionalization, albeit partial, achieved by the CEGE as an inter-ministerial body and the consolidation of the SLTI as a developer of digitalization policies ensured a continuity in the development of Digital Government policies within the Federal Government. The change of political administrations, which on the one hand can lead to problems of continuity in the policy cycle, on the other hand also contributes to the introduction of new agenda elements and the renewal of priorities, such as the emphasis on the implementation of online tools for social participation and control and transparency observed in a given period.

Over the years, there has also been an evolution in the structuring of Digital Government policies, which have come to rely on management instruments mainly laid out in the strategies launched by the government, such as the establishment of targets and indicators, even though their economic and financial dimension has had almost no prominence, with no specific funding effort beyond the budgets of the various bodies with varying final competences. However, these strategies are limited by the institutional environment, especially how competences are distributed, which makes the planning and execution of Digital Government policies compartmentalized, confined to the various entities, and with a greater concentration at the federal level. These limitations can be seen even in the National Digital Government Strategy, a document provided for in Law No. 14,129/2021 and published for the first time in 2024. The National Strategy has the merit of being the first more elaborate initiative to involve states and municipalities in the joint formulation of policies, in particular by detailing the functioning of the National Digital Government Network, the only instance of meeting and joint participation of federative entities of different levels. However, membership in the Network is optional, and it does not have a dedicated structure and funding, so its ability to produce satisfactory results will continue to depend on continuous political impetus. In circumstances where it does exist, as can be seen, for example, in the efforts of the Ministry of Management and Innovation in Public Services to integrate municipalities into the Gov.br platform, the National Network could become a useful instrument for disseminating experiences and integrating digital public infrastructures. Without these conditions, it will be nothing more than a set of ineffective provisions.

The vocation of digital government policies to improve the efficiency of the administration, especially the aspect of reducing administrative costs, has also ensured the continuity of the digital transformation throughout administrations with very different political ideologies. During the 2018-2022 period, for example, the vision of Digital Government as a pure expression of efficiency in public spending was at its peak, as Caio Cordeiro points out when he highlights the Minister of Economy's statement that civil servants who retired would not be replaced by the government, because the reduction in the civil service would be offset by the productivity gains provided by digitalization.[560] The common and permanent line of optimizing public spending was important for digitalization, at least at the federal level, to reach high levels, as in the World Bank's evaluation, in which Brazil appears in the top positions.[561]

However, the predominant focus on optimizing public spending has its limitations. Given the compartmentalization of budgets in the federative structure, the vision of Digital Government as optimizing spending translates into incentives to improve processes and services within the Federal Government structure, while integration between the federative levels and, above all, the maturity of Digital Governments in state and municipal public administrations is less attractive to political actors, being beyond the reach of what the federal bureaucracy can achieve on its own.

The approval of a nationwide Digital Government law could represent a change in this scenario if it created sufficiently institutionalized mechanisms for coordination between federal entities and assigned clearer competences that would facilitate the coordination of efforts around the formulation and implementation of policies.

---

560 CORDEIRO, Caio Barros. *Desafios do Estado para a transformação digital: uma análise à luz da abordagem Direito e Políticas Públicas.* PhD Dissertation (Law), University of São Paulo, São Paulo, 2023, p. 156.

561 *GovTech Maturity Index (GTMI) Data Dashboard.* World Bank. Available at <https://www.worldbank.org/en/data/interactive/2022/10/21/govtech-maturity-index-gtmi-data-dashboard>. Accessed 20 Apr. 2024.

However, what can be seen from the Brazilian Digital Government Law is the reproduction of existing structures within the Federal Government, created at the discretion of the public administration over the years. This is partly due to factors related to path dependency, since the institutional evolution of the Brazilian Digital Government with a focus on the Federal Government has an impact on the conception and vision of political and technical actors. In part, this is also due to political factors, such as the government's lack of interest in passing a law that transcends the desired optimization benefits within the limits of the federal budget, in light of the political efforts required to reach an agreement with states and municipalities around a mutually agreed-upon text. And finally, this scenario is also the result of purely legal factors, such as the interpretation that the broad scope (the applicability of the law to states and municipalities) could be unconstitutional, combined with the restriction on creating structures that represent new expenses because the bill originated in the Legislative Branch and not the Executive.

3 Experiences and cases of digital transformation

This chapter will present some case studies that provide useful elements for a more comprehensive understanding of the Digital Government phenomenon in Brazil and, in particular, for building alternatives for its improvement. Initially, three cases of digital transformation in the Brazilian public sector will be examined, which, although on the fringes of what is considered government in the strict sense, provide indications of the critical factors in the process of public innovation and the use of information technology in the state. The digital government policies of the European Union and Germany will then be discussed for comparative purposes.

3.1 Digital Government beyond government: cases of digital transformation in Brazil

The continuous adoption of technological innovation within the administration for the purpose of realizing rights characterizes Digital Government beyond digitization or optimization processes. As already mentioned, the concept does not refer to the application of a specific technology, but to the constant adaptation of the structures of the bureaucracy (and the legal norms that conform them) to the state of the art of information technology, politically oriented towards the achievement of constitutionally stabilized material objectives. By this conception, the realm of Digital Government becomes something about which definitive knowledge has not yet been established. In this way, the state should not always wait for external production of knowledge about the application of technological resources in government action, otherwise development objectives will be jeopardized by delays or missed opportunities. Knowledge can often be generated in administrative and political practice itself in order to take advantage of the benefits that only pioneering offers.

This presents a major challenge or even a contradiction for public administration as we know it. On the one hand, how the administration is organized - translated into legal rules aimed at the Administrator that allow certain behaviors or, if not allowed, prohibit them - can represent an obstacle to any kind of change in procedure and, consequently, to the modification of public activities inherent to the state. Not only can rules eventually form inflexible institutional arrangements, with little adaptability to unforeseen or unanticipated situations, but they can also require extremely complex, time-consuming and uncertain procedures for their modification, the greatest example being the legislative process. On the other hand, these same legal rules offer the only guarantees we are accustomed to against arbitrariness and abuse of power by those in any position of command within the administration. They also provide a degree of stability in the knowledge necessary for the day-to-day implementation of actions by civil servants, who are often unaccustomed to change and unprepared to handle situations outside the instruction manual (or administrative law manual). In a conception of Digital Government that aims to tackle public backwardness in the use of state-of-the-art technology, we need to reflect on the legal-institutional structures of the state and the political conditions that enable responsible experimental practices. Within the state, experimenting also has a strong political meaning, relating to the possibilities of action in a given situation aimed at change, even without certainty about the outcomes.[562] However, what we see in the structures of today's democracies are disincentives to experimentation, which represents a loss of possibilities for the future.[563]

This limitation has, among other things, a political cause: administrators and elected leaders commit themselves in advance to the correctness and effectiveness of their proposals, and learning from mistakes is no longer seen as a natural process.[564] This does not mean an irresponsible adoption of trial and error, because, as in empirical science, every precaution must be taken to avoid things getting out of hand, making it possible to enjoy the positive effects of the generalization of experiments in the creation of a "socialized intelligence" for tackling real-world problems, as is typical of the practices of scientific communities.[565] However, experimentation is not as clearly present in the democratic imaginary as the consolidated

562 SÜß, Rahel Sophia. Demokratie ist radikaler Experimentalismus. *In*: RAJAL, Elke *et al* (Orgs.). *Making Democracy - Aushandlungen von Freiheit, Gleichheit und Solidarität im Alltag*. Bielefeld, Germany: transcript Verlag, 2020, v. 94, p. 195.

563 *Ibid.*, p. 193, 194.

564 CAMPBELL, Donald T. Reforms as experiments. *American Psychologist*, v. 24, n. 4, p. 409–429, 1969, p. 410.

565 BRUNKHORST, Hauke. Demokratischer Experimentalismus. *In*: BRUNKHORST, Hauke (Org.). *Demokratischer Experimentalismus: Politik in der komplexen Gesellschaft*. Frankfurt am Main: Suhrkamp, 1998, p. 10, 11.

concepts of freedom, equality, etc., even though all political action today is a form of experimentation. Experimentalism presupposes dealing with the consequences of social activity with a view to transformation, with the constant "reinvention" of the state, based on empiricism and evidence, but recognizing the political nature of choices.[566] This does not mean adopting technocratic visions, but observing and learning[567] within the political process.

So that the adoption of technologies in the public sphere is not always slow and traumatic, their application can be experimented with in the actual functioning of the bureaucracy, just as normative evolution can be experimented with if the technology applied has the potential to change the very structures of the administration. The following topics will examine three emblematic cases of digital transformation in the Brazilian public sector in which this type of experimentation can be observed. These are: the implementation of electronic elections, the digitalization of the Judiciary, and Internet governance policies. Particularly noteworthy are the various ways in which the state has dealt with innovation or generated it quickly and how legal structures have been both the driving force and the object of change in virtuous adaptations. They provide important indications of the conditions that make transformations possible.

3.1.1 Electronic elections

Since 1932, Brazilian elections have been organized by the Judiciary, more specifically by the Electoral Justice, which is made up of 27 Regional Electoral Courts (one for each state) and local electoral judges attached to them, as well as a Superior Electoral Court (TSE), with national jurisdiction.[568] All elective positions in Brazil are elected every four years, with

566 BUTLER, Brian E. *The Democratic Constitution: Experimentalism and Interpretation.* Chicago and London: University of Chicago Press, 2017, p. 27.

567 DEWEY, John. *The public and its problems: An essay in political inquiry.* Chicago: Gateway Books, 1946, p. 202–203.

568 This was due to the history of fraud and manipulation during the period known as the 'Coffee with Milk Politics,' during which candidates from the states of São Paulo and Minas Gerais alternated the presidency of the Republic. After the 1930 Revolution, Getúlio Vargas, head of the provisional government, issued Decree No. 21,076 on February 24, 1932, establishing the Electoral Code and rules for the organization of elections. Since then, the Electoral Court has been responsible for conducting elections—an atypical function that is at odds with international

the choice of municipal positions (mayors and councillors) and state and national positions (state governor, state and federal deputies and senators) alternating every two years. It should be noted that today, according to the 1988 Constitution, in addition to the jurisdictional function and the responsibility for organizing the elections, the Electoral Justice, through the TSE, also has the regulatory competence to issue rules on the organization of the elections themselves, complementary to the constitutional and legal rules, which gives it a considerable concentration of powers.

The computerization of Brazilian elections dates back to the 1970s, when computers began to be used to tally the votes cast on paper ballots, as in the 1974 elections in the state of Minas Gerais, where an IBM computer that took up half a room was used.[569] Until then, there was no national voter register in the country, and that left room for fraud involving the manipulation of registers of citizens eligible to vote in each region, which were conceived and managed in a fragmented and distinct way. As a result, a national voter register was created which, from 1985, consolidated the data of the 70 million voters in Brazil at the time in a computerized way.[570] This prevented voters from being registered in more than one place, since the system connected all 2,900 electoral zones and the 27 Regional Electoral Courts.[571]

The first introductions of information technology in elections took place in the 1982 vote tallying in the states of Rio Grande do Sul and Rio de Janeiro. The initiatives suffered from the same problem of fragmented records, which, combined with a lack of transparency and the particular immaturity of the systems in one of the cases,[572] gave rise to what became widely known at the time as an attempt to rig the 1982 elections for gover-

---

practice—and this responsibility has persisted whenever elections have been held for any elective office, even during periods of authoritarian rule, in those elections permitted by the regime, especially local ones.

569 ALVIM, Frederico Franco; NETO, Jaime Barreiros; SANTIAGO, Marta Cristina Jesus (Orgs.). *25 Anos da Urna Eletrônica: Tecnologia e Integridade nas eleições brasileiras*. Salvador: Tribunal Regional Eleitoral da Bahia, 2021, p. 16.

570 FERRÃO, Isadora Garcia *et al.* Urnas Eletrônicas no Brasil: linha do tempo, evolução e falhas e desafios de segurança. *Revista Brasileira de Computação Aplicada*, v. 11, n. 2, p. 1–12, 2019.

571 AVGEROU, Chrisanthi. Explaining Trust in IT-Mediated Elections: A Case Study of E-Voting in Brazil. *Journal of the Association for Information Systems*, v. 14, n. 8, p. 420–451, 2013, p. 432–433.

572 BRUNAZO FILHO, Amilcar; MARCACINI, Augusto Tavares Rosa. Legal aspects of e-voting in Brazil. *In*: MAURER, Ardita Driza; BARRAT, Jordi (Orgs.). *E-Voting Case Law: A Comparative Analysis*. Burlington: Ashgate, 2016, p. 69.

nor of the state of Rio de Janeiro, by manipulating the software used to record the votes counted, an episode known as the "Proconsult Case".[573] After 17 years without free elections for governor and still under the Brazilian military dictatorship, elections were held in which two main candidates of conflicting profiles and origins competed in Rio de Janeiro: one opposed to the military regime, and the other supported by the dictatorship. Through parallel counts carried out by press outlets, it was discovered that there was a distortion in the computer programs of the private company hired to do the electronic tallying of the votes (Proconsult), transferring blank and null votes to the candidate supported by the government.[574]

At the end of the 1980s, and given that elections were organized locally by the Regional Electoral Courts with some administrative autonomy, there were some isolated attempts to implement a "voting machine" in Brazil, such as the initiative by the state of Santa Catarina in 1989. These attempts began to draw the TSE's attention to the advantages of adopting e-voting on a large scale.[575] In 1994, the Superior Electoral Court took an important step in this direction, computerizing the tallying of votes in each locality, which were then encrypted and transmitted to the TSE server for final counting. Although voting still took place using paper ballots, it is considered that this measure was the first in the direction of the general digitalization of elections.[576]

However, the main motivation for the Brazilian authorities to speed up the implementation of technology in elections was the widespread fraud in the paper ballot elections in Rio de Janeiro, which forced the TSE to annul the 1994 elections and call a new one, prompting the court to react quickly to the crisis.[577] The following year, the TSE set up a task force made up of its own staff and those of the Regional Courts to begin studies into the implementation of a comprehensive system of electronic elections in Brazil,

573 OLIVEIRA, Evandro Luiz de. Voto Eletrônico - Processo Eleitoral Brasileiro. *IP-Informática Pública*, v. 3, n. 1, p. 17–28, 2001.

574 ARCOLEZE, Conrado Ferreira. O Caso Proconsult não morreu: *Faces da História*, v. 7, n. 1, p. 400–419, 2020, p. 403–405.

575 OLIVEIRA, *op. cit.*

576 AVGEROU, *op. cit.*, p. 433.

577 FREITAS, Jorge Lheureux de; MACADAR, Marie Anne. The Brazilian Electronic Voting System: evolution and challenges. *In*: KRIMMER, Robert *et al* (Orgs.). *2nd Joint International Conference on Electronic Voting*. Lochau/Bregenz: TUT Press, 2017, p. 61–62.

with the support and funding of the World Bank.[578] The aim of the measure was both to eliminate electoral fraud and to increase popular participation, which until then had also been limited due to illiteracy.[579]

At the end of August, this commission for the digitalization of elections, made up of lawyers and systems analysts, presented the foundations for the initial electronic voting machine project (or electronic ballot box, as it became known in Brazil) and, at the same time, drafted a bill with rules for the 1996 municipal elections - among them, the first legal provisions on computerized voting and counting[580] of elections. The bill was passed the following month in both houses of parliament, giving rise to Federal Law No. 9,100 of September 29, 1996, containing a specific and brief chapter on electronic voting with a centralized structure. At its core was the legal provision that the TSE could authorize the TREs to use an electronic voting system, as well as the provision of basic characteristics coinciding with the guidelines of the system being developed by the TSE itself, such as voting by typing in the candidate's number and the appearance of the name and image on the screen before confirmation.

The chapter also provided for rules allowing "broad supervision" by political parties, such as guaranteed access to the computer programs used, and reaffirmed the concern with the secrecy and inviolability of votes, which had to be observed by the system. Once the law was passed, the TSE created a technical group of specialists from the Space Research Institute, the Aeronautics Technology Institute, the Armed Forces, Telebrás (the former state telephone company), as well as administrators and IT specialists from the Court itself. The group was tasked with drawing up the bidding documents for the manufacture of the electronic voting machine, with a basic project and all the technical specifications compatible with the original concept. After a competition between three companies, the winner was Unisys.[581]

---

578 AVGEROU, Chrisanthi *et al.* ICT and citizens' trust in government: lessons from electronic voting in Brazil. *In*: *Proceedings of the 9th conference on social implications of computers in developing countries.* São Paulo: IFIP, 2007.

579 ABEL, Luiz Fernando. Trust in ICT for the public sector: e-voting in Brazil's 2014 election. *Planejamento e Políticas Públicas*, n. 50, 2018, p. 386.

580 CAMARÃO, Paulo Cesar Bhering. Urna eletrônica brasileira: um projeto de sucesso. *In*: ALVIM, Frederico Franco; NETO, Jaime Barreiros; SANTIAGO, Marta Cristina Jesus (Orgs.). *25 Anos da Urna Eletrônica: Tecnologia e Integridade nas eleições brasileiras.* Salvador: Tribunal Regional Eleitoral da Bahia, 2021, p. 31.

581 *Ibid.*, p. 32.

The voting machine developed by the court consists of a DRE (direct-recording electronic) system, in which the votes are recorded on electronic media inside the equipment, which is then physically taken to the Electoral Justice premises and connected to the server for tallying. At the end of voting, each voting machine prints a paper bulletin with all the votes cast, which is displayed in front of the polling stations for interested parties and candidates to check, as well as for any parallel counting, since the bulletin accurately reflects the data contained on the electronic media. Voter access to the electronic voting machine is via a terminal located in front of the polling station attendants, and is authorized by typing in the citizen's voter registration number after checking the identity document provided and signing the attendance book. The original operating system was Microsoft Windows, but it was changed to Linux as it evolved, and the voting software was developed by the court itself. A parallel ballot printing system, for deposit in a normal ballot box and eventual verification in the event of a recount or by sampling, was foreseen in the design of the project and in the rules of the 1996 election, and was even applied to part of the voting machines in the 2002 election. However, in the following years, the TSE abandoned the idea because it felt that it could lead to insecurity and complexity in the process.[582] Among the problems reported in the places where the printed ballot was tested were difficulties for the voter to finish voting and problems with the external printing module, which led to an increase in queues, a greater number of blank votes, and a greater number of defective machines.[583]

The electronic voting machine was then used in the 1996 elections in all cities with more than 200,000 inhabitants, around 33% of the country's total votes. That year's elections were chosen because, in the case of municipal elections, voters would only vote twice, for mayor and councillor, which would minimize the problems of people adapting to the new system. In 1998, more than two-thirds of voters voted electronically and, in the 2000 elections, the system was used in 100% of the electoral zones, making Brazil the first country in the world to carry out all stages of the elections, from

582 BRUNAZO FILHO, Amilcar; MARCACINI, Augusto Tavares Rosa. Legal aspects of e-voting in Brazil. *In*: MAURER, Ardita Driza; BARRAT, Jordi (Orgs.). *E-Voting Case Law: A Comparative Analysis*. Burlington: Ashgate, 2016, p. 72.

583 TSE. *Relatório das Eleições 2002*. Brasília: Tribunal Superior Eleitoral, 2003, p. 20–22.

the act of voting to the counting and dissemination of the result, by fully automatic and digitalized means.[584]

Electronic voting machines can be considered a success in Brazil for three main reasons. The first concerns the speed of counting and determining the result, which went from days (or weeks, in the case of a recount) to a few hours, with the result of the election being known on the same day as the vote. The second, and most important, concerns the elimination of the traditionally known frauds that occurred in the counting, with votes being totaled incorrectly, or with the inclusion of false ballots, among others. The third concerns the inclusion of a considerable portion of the population that was previously excluded from the electoral process for practical reasons related to illiteracy, since paper ballots required the voter to be able to read the candidate's name, in the case of elections to the Executive Branch, and to write the candidate's name in the case of the election of representatives to the Legislative Branch. In this sense, the voting machine, by having a keypad similar to a telephone handset and showing the candidate's photo before confirming the vote, facilitated the electoral participation of this part of the population. This has increased the percentage of valid votes from around 75% to 90%, i.e., almost 15% of the electorate, who used to unintentionally cancel their vote due to the mishandling of paper ballots, now have their vote correctly cast and counted.[585] Another direct effect of electronic voting is the inclusion of visually impaired people, who can vote using the Braille markings on the ballot box, also an important accessibility achievement.

As indirect and not initially foreseen effects, specialized literature has demonstrated the impact of electronic voting on the formulation of social policies and on social statistics, such as the increase in health policies aimed at the poorest population, resulting directly from their greater inclusion in the electoral process, and the reduction in violent crime.[586] In the latter case, a study showed that "enhanced accountability and increased rotation

584 BRUNAZO FILHO; MARCACINI, *op. cit.*, p. 70.

585 FUJIWARA, Thomas. Voting Technology, Political Responsiveness, and Infant Health: Evidence from Brazil. *Econometrica*, v. 83, n. 2, p. 423–464, 2015, p. 433–435.

586 These two studies demonstrate with careful data analysis not only a correlation, but also causality between the introduction of electronic voting and socially assessable results. NIETO-MATIZ, Camilo; SKIGIN, Natán. The Unintended Consequences of Democratic Reforms: Electronic Voting and Criminal Violence in Brazil. *APSA Preprints*, 2020; FUJIWARA, *op. cit.*

in office likely dismantled criminal networks formed by hegemonic local elites with connections to the national politics".[587]

Despite this, since the beginning of its adoption, the Brazilian electronic voting machine has suffered criticisms related to the security of the system and the auditability of electoral results, typical of DRE systems, in which the digital expression of the vote is the only form of verification, with no possibility of alternative verification of the correctness of the record of the voter's intention from the act of typing to the record on the media to be used for transfer in the tally.[588] Some of the criticisms and comments on ballot box security suggest the adoption of simultaneous printing of the vote and deposit in a parallel physical ballot box, for eventual verification by sampling or in the event of the need for a recount,[589] and there are not insignificant arguments in academic circles for the need for a more in-depth debate on the security risks of the system and the adoption of more effective solutions based on a sober debate in the light of policy sciences.[590]

It is important to note in this regard that, in addition to the test carried out by the TSE in 2002 on its own initiative, the adoption of ballot printing was even passed into law by the Brazilian Congress but had its unconstitutionality declared by the Federal Supreme Court - STF, initially in an injunction in June 2018, and then confirmed by the full court in 2020.[591]

The discussion around the security of the electronic voting machine and measures to strengthen it has a healthy role to play in times of democratic normality, but it has taken on very different contours, especially since 2018, when Brazilian far-right movements began to intensely and lightly question the results of elections, including those in which their candidates were victorious, claiming that the machines would be rigged to their disadvantage. These movements, supported by the far-right government elected in 2018, began to put pressure on Congress to pass an amendment to

587 NIETO-MATIZ; SKIGIN, *op. cit.*, p. 31.

588 MARCACINI, Augusto Tavares Rosa; JUNIOR, Irineu Francisco Barreto. Aspectos jurídicos, políticos e técnicos sobre sistemas eletrônicos de votação e a urna eletrônica brasileira. *Revista Brasileira de Estudos Políticos*, n. 118, 2019.

589 FERRÃO, Isadora Garcia *et al.* Urnas Eletrônicas no Brasil: linha do tempo, evolução e falhas e desafios de segurança. *Revista Brasileira de Computação Aplicada*, v. 11, n. 2, p. 1–12, 2019.

590 SANTANO, Ana. As narrativas e as necessidades: o sistema eletrônico de votação brasileiro a partir de uma análise de política pública. *A&C - Revista de Direito Administrativo & Constitucional*, v. 22, n. 88, p. 75, 2022.

591 Direct Action for the Declaration of Unconstitutionality (ADI) No. 5889.

the Constitution to make the printed vote compulsory, circumventing the STF's decision by constitutionalizing the new rules. Originally a measure conceived under legitimate arguments to make the outcome of elections directly auditable and more secure, the printing of votes has become the main instrument of anti-democratic movements to deliberately undermine public confidence in the voting system and the legitimacy of elections.

In addition, considering several episodes during the 2018 and 2020 elections, in which far-right voters simulated situations of fraud or simply vandalized the equipment, the main concern became that, in the event of the approval and concrete adoption of parallel vote printing, such movements could also simulate disparities between the vote on the equipment's screen and the printed vote, intentionally causing the annulment of the votes of entire sections, discrediting and destabilizing the elections as a whole. Constitutional Amendment Proposal No. 135/2019, which instituted the "printed vote", was even considered in the Chamber of Deputies, receiving 229 votes in favor and 218 against, thus failing to reach the 308 votes (3/5 of the total 513 deputies) needed to make changes to the Constitution.

It is interesting to note that, in Germany, a voting system similar to the Brazilian electronic voting machine was deemed incompatible with the German Basic Law (*Grundgesetz*) by the Constitutional Court (*Bundesverfassungsgericht*) in 2009,[592] on the grounds that it violated the principle of the public nature of elections contained in Article 38, in conjunction with Articles 20.1 and 20.2. The Court held that for an electronic voting machine to comply with the Constitution, citizens must be able to check all the essential stages of the voting and counting process, without the need for specialized technical knowledge. This meant, in that case, that voting machines that recorded the voter's vote as in the DRE system, without a way for the voter to check for himself that his vote was correctly recorded on the electronic media (such as a paper printout), would not meet the constitutional requirements, even with the guarantee that the equipment is sealed and the contents are not accessible by unauthorized persons.

Of course, the comparison between the two situations must be made with great caution. In the German case, the machines used were a solution developed and marketed by the Dutch company Nedap, whose reliability was shaken by questions raised by the "*Wij vertrouwen stemcomputers niet*" (We do not trust voting computers) movement in the Netherlands. The activists argued that the Dutch government did not have a proper under-

592 BVerfG, Judgment of the Second Senate of 3 March 2009 - 2 BvC 3/07 -, paras. 1-166.

standing of the technology it had contracted for the voting system and that, in practice, the voting and counting system was beyond the control of the public authorities and largely the responsibility of a private company, almost like an outsourcing of the electoral process.[593] And they did this by demonstrating ways of violating the security of the equipment and the voting system, such as altering the software by an external agent, manipulating the voting records, violating voting secrecy by remotely reading the magnetic waves emitted by the ballot boxes, among other means.[594] This sparked an intense debate about electronic voting that led the Netherlands to return to pen and paper voting, which also extended beyond national borders, influencing public opinion in Germany[595] and making up the context in which the decision was made by the German Constitutional Court.

In the case of Brazil, the system was conceived and developed within the Brazilian state and implemented with the great participation of civil society. Although the voting machines were manufactured by a private company, this process was carried out following the parameters and design resulting from the work of the TSE's study commission, using the basic structure of personal computers at the time and an extremely simple configuration. In addition, over the years, the system has been improved with the migration of its operating software to open-source systems such as Linux, with the improvement of rituals, processes, and layers of security, ranging from the examination of the source code prepared by the Court itself by political parties and other interested parties, to the public software compilation section, authentication and "sealing" of the equipment, *hash* generation and verification, parallel voting and auditing with samples of machines drawn and removed the day before the election from polling stations, as well as public security tests, in which interested parties can try to hack the system

593 OOSTVEEN, Anne-Marie. Outsourcing Democracy: Losing Control of e-Voting in the Netherlands. *Policy & Internet*, v. 2, n. 4, p. 201–220, 2010, p. 205, 206, 216.

594 GONGGRIJP, Rop; HENGEVELD, Willem-Jan. Studying the Nedap/Groenendaal ES3B voting computer: a computer security perspective. *In*: *Proceedings of the USENIX Workshop on Accurate Electronic Voting Technology*. USA: USENIX Association, 2007, p. 1.

595 BIEBER, Christoph. Wählen als elektronischer Demokratieprozess? E-Government und E-Voting als Instrumente politischer Modernisierung. *In*: SCHÜNEMANN, Wolf J.; KNEUER, Marianne (Orgs.). *E-Government und Netzpolitik im europäischen Vergleich*. 2. ed. Baden-Baden: Nomos Verlagsgesellschaft mbH & Co. KG, 2019, v. 19, p. 368–369.

for a certain period of time and under certain conditions.[596] This context, added to the practical result of the voting machines in eliminating the fraud that occurred to a greater or lesser extent at the paper ballot counting tables, and reinforced by the speed of the count and the knowledge of the winners, consisted of a huge leap in the efficiency and reliability of the voting system.

One might wonder if the decision of the German Constitutional Court would be the same, or with the same arguments, if the context and institutional path of development and implementation of the system were more similar to those in Brazil. Or one could ask whether its premises and conclusions would suffer any impact from the digital transformation to which Germany, a country traditionally attached to the use of paper, is currently being subjected, especially due to the abrupt change in working conditions during the Covid-19 pandemic, the policies and strategies of the European Union or the change in people's culture in general towards adopting and relying on digital media. It is interesting to note that electronic voting currently has greater potential for development in Germany than in Brazil, due to differences in the secrecy of the vote. In the city of Hamburg, for example, although voting in person for the 2024 elections will have booths that guarantee the secrecy of the vote, it is also possible to vote in advance by post, by filling in the ballot paper and sending it to the electoral office.[597] This would pave the way for more advanced forms of electronic voting, especially internet voting. In Brazil, on the other hand, this would not be possible, because the possibility of remote voting, without the protection of secrecy guaranteed by the polling agents on election day, would inevitably lead to a violation of the secrecy of the vote, especially for socially vulnerable people.

We are also reflecting on whether, in the Brazilian case, idiosyncratic institutional factors also influenced how the Supreme Court ruled on the (un)constitutionality of compulsory printed ballots and the debate

596 The security and inspection procedures for the 2022 election are outlined in Resolution 23.673/21, along with an extensive list of entities authorized to participate in all stages, from testing the hardware to examining the source code, compiling, encrypting, extracting hashes, sealing equipment, conducting parallel voting, and performing integrity tests. These entities include representative institutions such as the National Confederation of Industry, the Brazilian Bar Association, as well as universities and state bodies like the Public Prosecutor's Office, the Federal Court of Accounts, the Federal Police, and the National Congress."

597 As observed during this researcher's participation in the district elections of June 9, 2024 and also for the European Parliament.

surrounding the issue. It is common and true to say that no fraud in the electronic system has ever been proven. Still, it is overlooked that the main criticism refers precisely to the theoretical impossibility of proving certain types of fraud should they ever occur.[598] Three of the seven ministers of the TSE (including its president) are chosen from among the ministers of the STF, with two-year terms that can be extended for a further two years, which means that all the ministers of the Brazilian Supreme Court have either been or will be presidents of the TSE, carrying out the administrative task of organizing the elections and the voting system. This relationship between the two institutions - the one that organizes the electronic elections and develops the systems, and the one that assesses their constitutionality - cannot be overlooked. In this sense, on the possible adoption of the printed ballot in elections, former STF minister and former TSE president Carlos Velloso said: "It's just that backwardness doesn't go well with progress, stupidity abhors intelligence".[599] Since innovation is a continuous process that can also be expressed in the creation or exploitation of unknown vulnerabilities in information technology systems, caution regarding certainties and absolute convictions is a recognized necessity,[600] especially if it involves the most central aspects of the political system and the democratic rule of law.

As of 2021, some Brazilian public universities, such as USP, Unicamp and UFPE, were able to examine the source code not only in the environment provided by the Court, but in their own computer science departments, which is an important reaction to two of the main criticisms leveled at the Court, namely: that public tests with extremely restricted conditions did

598 In this regard, see the interview with Professor Kalinka Castelo Branco from the Department of Computer Systems at the Institute of Mathematical and Computer Sciences (ICMC) of USP, in which she explains that the way data is stored in the electronic voting machine theoretically allows for tampering without the invasion being subsequently detected. *Segurança das urnas eletrônicas é contestada.* Jornal da USP. Available at <https://jornal.usp.br/atualidades/seguranca-das-urnas-eletronicas-e-contestada/>. Accessed 4 Oct. 2023.

599 ALVIM, Frederico Franco; NETO, Jaime Barreiros; SANTIAGO, Marta Cristina Jesus (Orgs.). *25 Anos da Urna Eletrônica: Tecnologia e Integridade nas eleições brasileiras.* Salvador: Tribunal Regional Eleitoral da Bahia, 2021, p. 18. "É que o atraso não combina com o progresso, a burrice abomina a inteligência".

600 See FOUNTAIN, Chris. Famous last words. A collection of inaccurate forecasts about technology that have been made through history. *IPA Review*, v. 49, n. 1, p. 46–48, 1996, especially the famous statement "Everything that can be invented has been invented", which was allegedly said in 1889 by Charles H. Duell, director of the US Patent Office.

not allow the security of the system to be really put to the test, and that public examination of the source code only on the Court's premises and for a short period of time was insufficient for the analysis of millions of lines of code. In addition, various security measures continue to be added to the voting machine to prevent any kind of external attack. It is interesting to note, however, that the specialized literature indicates that the more layers of security are added to prevent outsider attacks, the more the risks related to insiders are proportionally increased, and, consequently, the amount of trust that needs to be placed in the authorities who directly handle the equipment and its software (in this case, Electoral Justice servers) also increases.[601] This is a technology-related fact that implies conscious political choices in the case of its adoption in the electoral process, leading to weaknesses and virtues in terms of transparency and accountability, thus impacting the way the population sees the system.[602]

Despite these considerations, the electronic voting machine can be regarded as a significant triumph in the evolution of election management. It not only yielded positive results but also embodied a set of ideas and actions that uniquely combined extraordinary elements rarely seen together in Brazilian public administration. The program managed to achieve and even surpass the objectives for which it was conceived, handled and created real innovations in a very effective way, and incorporated experimentalist characteristics in a responsible and controlled manner into the administration of elections - all this with extraordinary speed (approximately a year and a half), considering such a large number of actors, institutional layers and policy processes involved. In this respect, several actions were required in sequence, namely: the original political impetus or "political will" to set an agenda; the technical and legal conception of the project; the approval of a law by the two legislative houses to authorize it; the budgetary allocation for the development of the project, involvement and trust-building of the political parties; dealing with the enormous challenge of communication, education and building a relationship of trust with citizens; the training of poll workers and election collaborators; and building

601 GONGGRIJP, Rop; HENGEVELD, Willem-Jan. Studying the Nedap/Groenendaal ES3B voting computer: a computer security perspective. *In*: *Proceedings of the USENIX Workshop on Accurate Electronic Voting Technology*. USA: USENIX Association, 2007, p. 14.

602 SALDANHA, Douglas Morgan Fullin; SILVA, Marcela Barbosa da. Transparência e accountability de algoritmos governamentais: o caso do sistema eletrônico de votação brasileiro. *Cadernos EBAPE.BR*, v. 18, p. 697–712, 2020, p. 709.

the necessary legal relationships with private actors, such as the companies developing the hardware and software solutions.

From a public policy perspective, the rapid and effective conception and implementation of the electronic voting system in Brazil has some characteristics or critical success factors that deserve to be highlighted and show how the legal-institutional set-up can contribute to a greater or lesser degree of innovation at the state level. Firstly, there is the centrality of administrative powers in the Electoral Court and its institutional autonomy to conceive projects of this type, whose creation or imagination phase, even if it depends on resources, does not depend on authorization from the Executive or Legislative Branches. Secondly, despite the centralization and hierarchy, which were decisive for the coordination of means and actions, the decentralized organizational structure of the Regional Electoral Courts played its part, especially in proposing some initiatives, such as the experimental electronic elections in Brusque, Santa Catarina, in 1989, or the initiatives to computerize the tallying of votes in Rio de Janeiro and Rio Grande do Sul a few years earlier. This coordinated decentralization, in which each court answers to the High Court, but has autonomy for certain innovations to fulfill its local administrative competences better, has been responsible for the emergence of smaller and less mature experimental initiatives, but whose implementation or design attracts the attention of the public and the High Court itself. This structure, therefore, creates institutional enabling points that allow initiatives to emerge and affect other actors, not necessarily thriving themselves but having an impact on other creative processes through the propagation of ideas in a coordinative discourse within the Electoral Court. In this sense, there were several poles of controlled experimentation in the Electoral Court at the dawn of the "digital age" in Brazil, enhanced by each individual electoral judge in their district, who also have administrative duties to fulfill and are therefore under endogenous pressure to increase efficiency.

However, all this would be of little use if the leadership didn't have a clearly defined political agenda preceded by a previously identified problem, a political objective to be achieved, and some clarity on the legal-institutional means needed to move the agenda forward. As for the objective, it has a dual political-legal character, even in the case of an organ of the Judiciary: to put an end to fraud in elections, reducing pressure on the Electoral Justice itself and strengthening it institutionally; and to guarantee a fundamental right of the population to democracy, through clean, stable and legitimate elections.

This political agenda was not just about identifying a problem, deciding how to tackle it and organizing and pooling resources to develop solutions. It translated into clearly identifiable political actions that were decisive for the outcome. The President of the Superior Electoral Court at the time, Minister Carlos Velloso, was personally involved in liaising with the Executive Branch to obtain resources for the project, seeking funding and support from the President of the Republic, as well as being responsible for involving external actors, such as the Inter-American Development Bank, with the Ministry of Foreign Affairs also joining in.[603] In addition, it was possible to work together with various institutions and sectors to jointly implement the project, involving technology specialists, lawyers, and political parties, giving technical quality to the system's design and its normative expression. Last but not least, the Legislative Branch was involved in passing a law containing the authorization and rules necessary for the initiative to go ahead. In addition, ambitious communication work was planned and carried out with civil society to build trust in the system, as well as intense educational actions on how the machine works, with television advertising and simulations,[604] in a communicative discourse that spread the idea vertically.

Moreover, a safe environment was guaranteed in which qualified civil servants could give birth to their own ideas with the real potential for them to become future public policy; in other words, opportunities for creation were provided within the Court's institutional structure. In this regard, it should also be pointed out that, as the TSE is the highest body in the electoral justice system, and its composition and presidency always includes ministers from the Supreme Court, it was also possible to guarantee a kind of tranquility for creative administrative action that does not exist in public administrations, especially at municipal level, due to the fear of censure from the control/audit bodies, which are averse to any risk-taking. This also led to a convergence of the agendas of the political leadership (Presidency of the TSE, Presidency of the Republic, Minister of Foreign Affairs, among others) with the political agenda of the bureaucracy (employees of the information technology sectors of the TSE and the entities involved in the ballot box development process), as is evident from the reports on

603 ALVIM; NETO; SANTIAGO (Orgs.), *op. cit.*, p. 26, preface by Ministro Carlos Velloso.

604 One of the actions consisted of a demonstration of how to vote on the electronic voting machine using fictional candidates represented by prominent figures from Brazilian art, such as singer Elis Regina and writer Monteiro Lobato.

the development of the system by the former president of the TSE and employees of the IT sector.[605]

However, some of the factors responsible for the rapid process of innovation may also be responsible for a certain inertia and resistance on the part of the authorities in the face of criticism of the system and requests for improvements, since there are still observations in academic circles about the security aspects of the equipment, which are not always considered in the way their authors would like.[606] The overlapping competences of the Electoral Justice (organization of elections, regulation, jurisdictional function), which provided some of the conditions for radical innovation, now take on a conservative role. However, the system is continually being improved, especially by the TSE's trained technical staff. In addition, the Court has made efforts to involve civil society and academia more in the processes, in the form of agreements with universities and the creation of the Transparency Commission and the Electoral Transparency Observatory.[607]

3.1.2 Internet governance

In Brazil, until 1994, the Internet was practically restricted to academia and, except for the pioneering partnerships between Fapesp and UFRJ with American universities,[608] it was mostly the responsibility of an organization linked to the Federal Government created in 1979, called the National Computer Network Laboratory, renamed ten years later as the National Research Network (RNP), which was tasked with developing the first back-

605 Curiously in this case, the meeting took place literally, with the idea initially being the subject of a conversation during a tennis match between systems analyst and TSE employee Paulo César Camarão and the then Vice-President of the Superior Electoral Court, Minister Carlos Mário da Silva Velloso, according to the preface in ALVIM; NETO; SANTIAGO (Orgs.), *op. cit.*

606 See ARANHA, Diego F.; VAN DE GRAAF, Jeroen. The Good, the Bad, and the Ugly: Two Decades of E-Voting in Brazil. *IEEE Security & Privacy*, v. 16, n. 6, p. 22–30, 2018.

607 TSE Ordinance No. 578/2021.

608 MAYNARD, Dilton C. S. An Introduction to the History of the Internet: A Brazilian Perspective. *In*: PEREIRA NETO, André; FLYNN, Matthew B. (Orgs.). *The Internet and Health in Brazil: Challenges and Trends.* Cham: Springer International Publishing, 2019, p. 21.

bone for network access in the country.[609] The exception was the initiative of the Brazilian Institute of Social and Economic Analyses (IBASE), which began offering Internet access in small-scale communication via e-mail in conjunction with the International Institute for Global Communications (IGC). During the Eco-92 conference in Rio de Janeiro, IBASE provided internet access for all the international delegations, and soon began collaborating with RNP on various related projects, such as connectivity with other UN international conferences outside the country.[610] From 1994 onwards, the Ministry of Science and Technology decided to develop a large backbone to enable broad access to the network for the general public.[611] It should be noted that, at that time, all telecommunications services in Brazil were provided at the federal level by state-owned companies, such as Telebras and its long-distance arm, Embratel, and by state telephone companies at the regional level.

At the end of 1994, Embratel (a subsidiary of Telebras) launched an experimental internet access service, with plans to keep the internet totally under vertical state control,[612] reproducing with the internet the telecommunications monopoly structure that already existed with fixed and mobile telephony. There was a political dispute between different interests as to how the Internet should be developed in the country: on the one hand, there were those who felt that the state and its telephone companies should provide access; on the other, those who believed that access should be provided by private providers using the state's infrastructure backbones.[613]

In 1995, the Internet Steering Committee (CGI) was created through Interministerial Ordinance No. 147 of May 31, 1995, as a joint initiative of the Ministry of Science and Technology and the Ministry of Telecommunications (to which the state-owned Telebras was subordinate). The context at the time was that of a newly-elected government with a view to reforming the state, influenced by the doctrine of new public management, as previously mentioned. Thus, concurrently, the privatization of telecommunications occurred, specifically through the auction of state-owned companies

609 AFONSO, C.A. The Internet and the community in Brazil: background, issues, and options. *IEEE Communications Magazine*, v. 34, n. 7, p. 62–68, 1996, p. 62.

610 *Ibid.*, p. 62–63.

611 For detailed information on the emergence and early years of the internet in Brazil, see CARVALHO, Marcelo Sávio Revoredo de Menezes; CUKIERMAN, Henrique Luiz. The Dawn of the Internet in Brazil. *IEEE Annals of the History of Computing*, v. 37, n. 4, p. 54–63, 2015.

612 AFONSO, *op. cit.*, p. 63.

613 *Ibid.*, p. 67.

and the establishment of public service delegation relationships in these areas. This led to a massive expansion in the availability of telephone lines, which until then had been expensive and scarce. Previously, people even declared telephone lines as assets for income tax purposes, similarly to how they would declare cars and real estate.

The Committee was created to be a focal point for the development and governance of the Brazilian Internet in a context in which it was moving away from purely scientific use to become commercial.[614] The main objectives were to coordinate, integrate, and promote services, as well as promote innovation and the technical quality of the network.[615] The normative form chosen for the creation of the CGI was an interministerial ordinance, which is a normative act of the Executive Branch of government divided between different government sectors - in this case, the Ministry of Communications and the Ministry of Science and Technology. In addition to technical issues, such as coordinating the allocation of IP addresses, registering domain names and recommending operational procedures for networks, the CGI was also tasked with formulating strategies for the deployment and interconnection of networks, evaluating technologies and the functional roles of organizations such as companies and educational and research institutions, recommending technical and ethical standards and procedures for using the Internet, as well as disseminating information about the Internet.

The composition of the body was "multistakeholder" from the outset. It had nine members, representing, respectively, each of the two ministries (Communications and Science and Technology), Telebrás, RNP, and the academic, general business, service provider and user sectors.[616] In 2003, the newly-elected government changed the structure of the CGI through a presidential decree, increasing the number of members to 21, of which 9 were representatives of bodies and entities linked to the government (8 from the Federal Government and 1 from the state governments) and 12 were representatives of civil society, as well as increasing their terms of office. The members linked to civil society were divided into three groups: the business sector, with 4 members (one representing access providers,

614 GLASER, Hartmut; CANABARRO, Diego R. Before and after the WGIG: Twenty Years of Multistakeholder Internet Governance in Brazil. *In*: DRAKE, William J. (Org.). *The Working Group on Internet Governance: 10th anniversary reflections.* Johannesburg: APC, 2016, p. 141.

615 *Ibid.*, p. 142.

616 Interministerial Ordinance No. 147

another infrastructure providers, another the IT industry and another user companies); the academic community, with 3 members; the third sector (non-governmental organizations) with 3 members; as well as one more independent member with notable expertise.[617]

There have also been discreet but important changes to its attributions. The recommendatory nature of its actions has been transformed with the explicit introduction of the function of establishing, and not just suggesting, strategic guidelines for the development of the Brazilian Internet. It was added the task of proposing research programs related to the Committee's object, as well as carrying out studies on various topics within the scope of the dissemination and use of the Internet, with explicit mention of cybersecurity. Two new responsibilities, however, should be highlighted here: the coordination of "actions related to the proposal of rules and procedures regarding the regulation of activities inherent to the Internet"[618] and the possibility of signing contractual instruments, such as agreements and covenants, aimed at managing the Internet and bringing it into line with international standards. It should be noted that these two competences, together with the possibility, also new, of approving its internal regulations, give the CGI a *sui generis* institutional character, which has the official form of a committee (which normally refers to a more precarious order), but adopts the structure and characteristics of a strong administrative body, or even an *autarquia*.[619]

The Internet Steering Committee and the public policy that it both represents and continually formulates, i.e., the governance of the Brazilian Internet, has very innovative characteristics in institutional terms. Since its creation, it has been responsible for coordinating all the actions surrounding the growth and management of the Brazilian Internet, which has taken place in a very robust and organized manner, also considering the enormous speed of growth in demand and the complexity of interests of the constellation of actors involved. The most interesting thing to note is that the CGI emerged as a committee, that is, a gathering of people without legal personality, its own budget, bylaws, and an administrative structure. Despite the precariousness of its legal-institutional form, it established itself as a strong and respected institution with great capacity for achievement.

---

617 Decree N° 4,829/2003

618 In the original, "...ações relativas à proposição de normas e procedimentos relativos à regulamentação das atividades inerentes à Internet"

619 This concept was explained earlier in footnote 497.

Under the umbrella of the CGI, various specialized institutional arms were created and maintained, namely: Registro.br (responsible for registering domains and assigning IP addresses), Cert.br (responsible for dealing with security incidents), Ceptro.br (responsible for projects relating to network technology and its ongoing development), Cetic.br (responsible for carrying out research into Internet use and monitoring the socio-economic impacts of information technology to support the formulation of public policies), Ceweb.br (for promoting new Web technologies and experimentation), Ptt.br (which manages infrastructure connections between networks, the *Internet Exchange Points* - IXPs), Simet (which carries out measurements and evaluations on bandwidth quality to provide information to Internet providers and other actors with a view to improving the Internet) and Nic.br, which is considered to be the "executive arm" of the CGI which, as well as managing the Committee's finances, coordinates all the actions of the aforementioned "agencies" within the CGI at executive level.[620]

Of all these different branches, Nic.br, the CGI's executive arm, stands out the most. In addition to the *sui generis* characteristics of the CGI, Nic.br can also be considered unorthodox in terms of Brazilian administrative law, because its legal nature is that of a civil association, i.e., a legal entity under private law whose founders and associates are members of the CGI, and which has its own bylaws, forms of deliberation and operation, such as a general assembly, board of directors, executive board and collaborators. Despite being linked to the CGI by the composition of its associates, it is subject to a private law legal regime, entering into contracts in the same way as an ordinary non-profit legal entity, with no obligation to hold public tenders or competitions, and with an employee hiring regime governed by the Consolidation of Labor Laws (CLT),[621] and not by the general regime for public servants of the Union (Law No. 8,112/1990). Nic.br was delegated the task of "executing the registration of Domain Names, the allocation of

620 ANASTÁCIO, Kimberly. Brazil's approach to multistakeholderism: multi-participation in the Brazilian Internet Steering Committee (CGI. br). *Berkman Center for Internet & Society at Harvard University*, 2015, p. 6–7.

621 Decree-Law No. 5,452 of May 1, 1943, which generally governs private employment relationships.

IP Addresses (Internet Protocol) and the administration of the Top Level Domain", as authorized by Decree No. 4,829/2003.[622]

The CGI (through Nic.br or any of its "arms") has carried out the duties set out in its current normative decree in a very satisfactory manner, being responsible for mediating the interests and actions of Internet stakeholders in Brazil, i.e., the relevant players in terms of services and information technology applied to public networks in the country. Over the years, it has also conducted various research studies on the use of the Internet, which have supported the thinking of academics and policymakers in the country and abroad and organized events of international relevance.

In the case of the *NETmundial* Meeting, a conference organized at the initiative of the Brazilian government after the negative repercussions of the Edward Snowden case, the CGI not only played an organizing role together with ICANN and other national and international bodies but also set an active agenda in an attempt to improve global internet governance, especially to guarantee and realize the human rights it affects.[623] A short time earlier, Edward Snowden, a former employee of the US National Security Agency (NSA), revealed to the public secret information about a US global espionage and surveillance apparatus on the internet, including involving the communications of heads of government and/or state such as Angela Merkel (Germany) and Dilma Rousseff (Brazil).[624] This leak sparked a global political debate about state surveillance in the context of information technology.[625] Even though the progress of these negotiations at NETMundial has been hindered since then, the event had a great impact internationally and represented a mitigation of the centrality of the United States in this area.[626]

---

622 In the original, "execução do registro de Nomes de Domínio, a alocação de Endereço IP (*Internet Protocol*) e a administração relativa ao Domínio de Primeiro Nível".

623 FRAUNDORFER, Markus. Brazil's Organization of the NETmundial Meeting: Moving Forward in Global Internet Governance. *Global Governance*, v. 23, n. 3, p. 503–522, 2017.

624 LANDAU, Susan. Highlights from Making Sense of Snowden, Part II: What's Significant in the NSA Revelations. *IEEE Security & Privacy*, v. 12, n. 1, p. 62–64, 2014, p. 63.

625 SCHEUERMAN, William E. Whistleblowing as civil disobedience: The case of Edward Snowden. *Philosophy & Social Criticism*, v. 40, n. 7, p. 609–628, 2014.

626 SHEN, Hong. China and global internet governance: toward an alternative analytical framework. *Chinese Journal of Communication*, v. 9, n. 3, p. 304–324, 2016, p. 317.

A particularly important action in the Brazilian political context was the coordination of efforts to draft legislation that would stipulate clearer rules for the use of the Internet, such as basic principles and guarantees, and the attribution of roles, rights, and duties for users, service providers and the state.[627] The drafting of this text became a priority for the Brazilian government after the Edward Snowden scandal[628] (which shook confidence in governance systems and internet companies and servers).[629] It was done in a broadly participatory way during its passage through the National Congress, giving rise to the Marco Civil da Internet, Law No. 12,965, of April 23, 2014 (the Civil Rights Framework for the Internet). The CGI played a leading role in establishing the basic principles for drafting the law, which was then formatted in work carried out by the Ministry of Justice in conjunction with academic institutions and put through a public consultation process to gather suggestions.[630]

The successful trajectory of Brazilian internet governance is not limited to good technical management of access methods, nor to the appropriate distribution of related means and resources, nor even to providing services to the general public—such as domain registration, among other things. It is characterized by an efficient balancing of the various and conflicting political and social interests of diverse actors, especially in the initial period when the future model was undefined and under debate and dispute. It is also notable for its efficient handling of innovation - either by incorporating what was rapidly emerging and evolving from an international technological point of view, or by fostering innovation internally through its own research and development and guidelines for external actors to add their own solutions and adaptations. In addition to the managerial element, important studies have been carried out that have provided information for the creation and planning of government actions, as well as for private actors in the convergence of digital inclusion policies and the strengthening of citizenship.

In a somewhat unusual way, a precarious legal figure (compared to other Brazilian state structures) has been carrying out long-term policies for almost 30 years that transcend governments and contribute to concrete im-

627 BELLI, Luca. A heterostakeholder cooperation for sustainable internet policymaking. *Internet Policy Review*, v. 4, n. 1, p. 1–21, 2015, p. 10.

628 OMARI, Jeffrey. Chronicles of Internet Openness: The Brazilian Case Study Articles and Essays. *Colorado Technology Law Journal*, v. 20, n. 1, p. 85–120, 2022, p. 100.

629 ALMEIDA, Virgilio A. F. The Evolution of Internet Governance: Lessons Learned from NETmundial. *IEEE Internet Computing*, v. 18, n. 5, p. 65–69, 2014, p. 65.

630 OMARI, *op. cit.*, p. 98–99.

provements in the provision of public and private services. When looking at the context of its configuration in the 1990s, in a developing country with accumulated infrastructure problems and issues of population access to telephony, amid a troubled process of legal and operational transition of its telecommunications activities and with a newly established democracy after a long period of military dictatorship, one must recognize the merits of the model.

Some legal-institutional reasons may explain this combination of results, including how disputes of interest between various actors crystallized in the context of an institutional environment undergoing profound changes with the re-democratization: the promulgation of the 1988 Constitution and the first management reforms of the administration that followed; the characteristics of the arrangement, with a multi-sectoral design of the Internet Steering Committee and its "arms"; and the provision of autonomous sources of funding independent of the federal budget, mainly revenue from domain names registrations.

The competing interests and visions of the various actors in the early years were arbitrated and resolved by the strong presence of a government political agenda. At first, at the end of the 1980s, there were opposing centralizing and decentralizing interests regarding the development and use of the first international data connectivity infrastructures. The centralizing project was a remnant of the way telecommunications were developed under the Brazilian military government, in which nationalism, national security, and strict control of policies by the Federal Government were the systemic foundations. In this sense, institutions such as the then powerful Special Secretariat for Information Technology (SEI) and the also powerful state-owned Embratel, which represented bottlenecks to the development of the policy (being responsible, respectively, for authorizing international data connections and supplying and charging for them), lost their strength due to political decisions. The SEI, which wanted to impose the use of the OSI protocol instead of TCP/IP[631] for reasons of national security from a military perspective, was gradually reduced to a less powerful IT department. Embratel, for its part, was compelled to allow the National Research Network access to international data transfer for a fixed price, rather than the old data volume system that would have made the costs

631 OSI and TCP/IP are different technical standards for communication models in computer networks. See ALANI, Mohammed M. *Guide to OSI and TCP/IP Models.* Cham: Springer International Publishing, 2014, p. 5, 6, 19, 20.

unfeasible, following pressure from academia.[632] It was also decided that Embratel would approve and promptly implement any connection request with foreign academic institutions, which was considered a victory for the Brazilian academic community[633] and, consequently, for the decentralizing vision of the model.

Shortly afterwards, when the internet began to be used commercially by the general public, two other conflicting interests were clearly opposed: the statists and the privatists. The former believed that the data transfer and network access service should remain directly in the hands of the state, being provided by the telecommunications companies that had previously offered telephone services. The latter wanted private providers (internet access providers) to have access to the infrastructure so that they themselves could provide services to the general population on a competitive basis, as in the United States. The commercial service began to be provided almost exclusively by Embratel in May 1995, but this monopoly was soon broken by a decision of then Telecommunications Minister Sergio Motta, who opened up the service to private initiative.[634] This decisive arbitration was consistent with the political project that had come to power that year with the election of President Fernando Henrique Cardoso, who was initiating impactful macro and microeconomic reforms in the wake of the so-called Washington Consensus, a list of economic measures recommended to developing countries by international financial institutions, among which were deregulation, privatization of state-owned companies and opening up trade and finance.[635]

The creation of the Internet Steering Committee at the time was part of the crystallization of the prevalence of decentralist and privatist visions in relation to the Internet and telecommunications in general. In the following years, Brazil's state-owned telephone companies were privatized, and there was a leap in the range and quality of services while costs for the end user fell exponentially. Telephone lines, which used to take years to be installed in applicants' homes, or were marketed in parallel at high prices by those who were lucky enough to have been granted one, soon have zero

632 CARVALHO, Marcelo Sávio Revoredo de Menezes; CUKIERMAN, Henrique Luiz. The Dawn of the Internet in Brazil. *IEEE Annals of the History of Computing*, v. 37, n. 4, p. 54–63, 2015, p. 56–58.

633 *Ibid.*

634 *Ibid.*, p. 61.

635 WILLIAMSON, John. A Short History of the Washington Consensus. *Law and Business Review of the Americas*, v. 15, n. 1, p. 7–26, 2009, p. 9–10.

installation costs and immediate availability. The CGI, with the mission of coordinating the management of the enormous growth in the mass of Internet users, the number of network access providers and the demand for IP addresses and domains, was created along the lines of the new public management doctrine, which had four main guidelines: the reduction of the state machine; the privatization or quasi-privatization of services; the use of automation and IT; and the internationalization of public policy agendas with an emphasis on management, design of arrangements and international cooperation.[636]

In 2003, the election and inauguration of President Lula represented a change in the political vision in power, which was critical of the idea of the minimal state and carried a nationalist discourse that could be perceived very clearly in some sectors,[637] and less clearly in others.[638] In the case of telecommunications, this movement did not occur, probably because the privatization of the companies was consolidated and because the leap in the quality and availability of services was undeniable. As far as Internet governance is concerned, the legal-institutional design and the relationship between different actors, such as access providers, telephone companies, and users, were also consolidated not only by the good results of the commercial Internet development process but also by the conformation that the modified institutional environment generated, with telecommunications now being provided by private actors and regulated by public actors. There was also the emergence of legal structures that stabilized these arrangements at the meso and macro level, in particular Law No. 9,472 of 16 July 1997 (the General Telecommunications Law), which created Brazil's first regulatory agency - the National Telecommunications Agency (ANATEL) - and established normative guidelines for the sector.

The change in political outlook in 2003, however, far from a structural change in direction, resulted in an incremental process of improving the CGI's institutional design through Decree No. 4,829. The more pro-state

636 HOOD, Christopher. A Public Management for All Seasons? *Public Administration*, v. 69, n. 1, p. 3–19, 1991, p. 3.

637 For example, in the National Basic Sanitation Policy. See VALENTE, Sergio Ruy David Polimeno. Direito e políticas públicas: uma visão jurídico-institucional sobre o caso do saneamento básico no Brasil. *Rei - Revista Estudos Institucionais*, v. 5, n. 3, p. 1064–1092, 2019, p. 1077.

638 SERAFIM, Milena Pavan; DAGNINO, Renato Peixoto. A política científica e tecnológica e as demandas da inclusão social no governo Lula (2003-2006). *Organizações & Sociedade*, v. 18, n. 58, p. 403–427, 2011.

and nationalist vision of the new government, rather than an unlikely and impossible return to a centralized service provision model, meant a strengthening of the CGI's multistakeholder approach. Its structuring preserved the technical character of the institution while adding significant political powers, such as more explicit responsibilities for coordinating debates around the directions of the Brazilian internet, and the of the entity as a standardizer and regulator, which was well demonstrated in the case of the approval of the *Marco Civil*. The CGI's multisectoral institutional form has served as the inspiration and main model for current proposals to improve global internet governance, such as the establishment of a charter of principles and a roadmap drawn from the 2014 Working Group on Internet Governance.[639]

The legal-institutional structuring of Brazilian internet governance, due to its peculiar characteristic of simple legal forms and unusual arrangements for the administrative tradition, attracted the attention of the Federal Court of Accounts, which, on the initiative of one of its technical departments, the Secretariat for the Supervision of Privatization and Regulation (SEFID), initiated a process to investigate the dynamics of domain registrations and other aspects of internet governance. The case was judged by the Court on May 16, 2012,[640] and is a good illustration of the opposition between two legal views on processes of change and institutional innovation linked to technology and influenced by the speed of its evolution and the urgency of its implementation: legal formalism on the one hand and a kind of legal pragmatism on the other.

Among SEFID's allegations against the CGI and the governance model in general, and which represent the legal formalist view, were the argument that state intervention in Internet administration services would have to be provided for in a law establishing its rules and limits. As there was no law on the subject, the ordinance creating the CGI and Decree No. 4,829/2003 would be null and void on the grounds of unconstitutionality, since the attributions that would give the CGI the character of a regulatory body require the prior existence of a law. In addition, it pointed out that the legal relationship between CGI and Nic has no correspondence in Brazilian administrative dogmatics, since the Government has innovated by creating

639 GLASER, Hartmut; CANABARRO, Diego R. Before and after the WGIG: Twenty Years of Multistakeholder Internet Governance in Brazil. *In*: DRAKE, William J. (Org.). *The Working Group on Internet Governance: 10th anniversary reflections.* Johannesburg: APC, 2016, p. 141.

640 TCU. Ruling 1164/2012 – Full Court, Rapporteur Raimundo Carreiro.

a new entity and/or contractual figure without authorization to do so. Therefore, the general conclusion of SEFID's opinion was that all acts by the CGI and NIC.br to regulate internet services were null and void.

On the other hand, the pragmatic position, opposed to that of the court's technical department, can be seen in the content of the vote by rapporteur Raimundo Carreiro to reject SEFID's requests, which was followed by all the other TCU ministers in a judgment before the full court. In the grounds for the decision, the rapporteur points out that there was a clear intention on the part of the government to hand over management of the internet to a pluralistic committee, in which the state would be just another "actor on the net", without imposing control or regulatory intents. He adds that, with the creation of the CGI, the government wanted to promote the minimum actions necessary for the good and agile development of the Internet, especially considering the dynamism of the sector, and allowing civil society to regulate these relations through a body with government representation and participation was an appropriate way to achieve these objectives. The best demonstration of this would be the fact that, in the chosen arrangement of delegation to a private entity, the NIC.br carried out its functions to the exact extent of Decree 4,829, and that the CGI's role was also carried out as foreseen in controlling tariffs and the application of the funds collected. The Rapporteur also stressed the practical importance that NIC.br and related entities (such as Cert.br, Cetic.br, etc.) have, especially their ability to carry out studies and produce statistics and indicators to support innovation and the universalization of internet services in Brazil. Finally, he also said that the CGI is not a body or a public company and has no legal personality, functioning as a council and being "just a meeting of people", but that it is in line with the best international practices of internet administration that rely on the participation of civil society.

This judgment illustrates some of the resistance to innovation on the part of the formalist legal culture. Although SEFID's legal arguments were defensible in the light of the concepts and rules of administrative law, their rigid application would mean a step backwards in a consolidated policy that was considered successful. In the clash between formalism and pragmatism, the latter prevailed in order to sanction an institutional structure not conventionally understood by traditional administrative law, but which was affirmed by its regime of effects. And although it is hard to imagine that the TCU could actually declare a body like the CGI, (which enjoys great prestige in society and in epistemic communities) illegal, the restrictive rulings that contributed to making it impossible to use FUST funds for the universalization of telecommunication services[641] demonstrate that the risk always remains. This clash can also be seen from the perspective of the role of legal dogmatics in public policies: on the one hand, an instrumental interpretation purely focused on a rigid model of decision and conformity, like a kind of institutional fetishism, which would be less a problem of the institutions themselves and more a defect or limitation of the vision of jurists and political agents, with their watertight and plastered positions on the rules that govern them, their functions and potential.[642] On the other hand, dogmatics was used in the argument to find appropriate ways to deal with an unusual situation, whose atypicality did not necessarily mean unlawfulness.

3.1.3 The electronic judicial process

The first significant initiatives to digitize the judicial process in Brazil were taken by the Federal Regional Court of the 4th Region, when it launched a system for sending pleadings, petitions, appeals, and other procedural acts via the Internet, using a login and password, in 2003.[643] The system was developed by staff from the Federal Court's IT department using free software and became mandatory for all 104 federal civil local courts in the southern region of Brazil four years later.[644] The initial legal basis for the system was §2 of Article 8 of Law No. 10,259/2001, which expressly authorized the courts to organize themselves to receive petitions by electronic means.

The implementation of a broader electronic judicial process in Brazil dates back to the early 2000s, especially the attempts to pass a law on the subject. Its origins can be traced back to a bill initiated by AJUFE - the

641 See section 2.1.

642 According to UNGER, Roberto Mangabeira. *What Should Legal Analysis Become?* London: Verso, 1996, p. 7, institutional fetishism is "the belief that abstract institutional conceptions, like political democracy, the market economy, and a free civil society, have a single natural and necessary institutional expression. Institutional fetishism is a pervasive type of superstition in contemporary culture. It penetrates each of the disciplines mentioned earlier, and it informs the language and debates of ordinary politics".

643 LAZZARI, João Batista. Justiça sem papel: uma realidade dos Juizados Especiais Federais do sul do Brasil. *Revista de Doutrina da 4ª Região. Porto Alegre*, n. 18, 2007.

644 RUSCHEL, Aírton José; LAZZARI, João Batista; ROVER, Aires José. O processo judicial eletrônico no brasil: uma visão geral. *In*: COÊLHO, Marcus Vinicius Furtado; ALLEMAND, Luiz Cláudio (Orgs.). *Processo Judicial Eletrônico*. Brasília: OAB, 2014, p. 17.

Association of Federal Judges of Brazil, which drafted the initial text of the bill and proposed it to the Participatory Legislation Commission of the Chamber of Deputies,[645] a commission created shortly before to deal with legislative initiatives coming from the general population.[646] The proposal was made official in December 2001 as Bill 5.828/2001 and moved swiftly through the Chamber of Deputies, having been unanimously approved in plenary on June 19, 2002.[647]

After being passed, it went to the Federal Senate, where it was not so enthusiastically received, and its processing remained stalled under the Rapporteurship of Senator Magno Malta for three years.

In the meantime, at the end of 2004, Congress passed Constitutional Amendment 45, which reformed the Brazilian Judiciary. The main item of the reform was the creation of the National Council of Justice (CNJ). The CNJ is provided for in article 103-B of the Constitution, is chaired by the president of the Supreme Court, and has 15 members appointed by the president of the Republic after approval by the Federal Senate, divided between ministers (justices) of higher courts, state and federal judges, members of the Public Prosecutor's Office, lawyers, and citizens of notable legal knowledge appointed by the Chamber of Deputies. Judicial reform was one of the main agendas at the start of the Lula administration in 2003, and the creation of the CNJ, which had centralized powers to control the administrative actions of the Judiciary and the functional duties of judges, was met with political resistance from the Judiciary.[648]

---

645 DANTAS, Adriano Mesquita. A evolução do processo brasileiro: história e perspectiva do processo judicial eletrônico. *Revista do Tribunal Regional do Trabalho da 18ª Região*, v. 12, p. 177–192, 2012, p. 180.

646 In the Brazilian legislative process, there is the concept of the popular initiative bill, the requirements for which are set out in article 13 of Law No. 9,709/1998. In practice, however, as the formal requirements are considerably high (a minimum of 1% of the country's electorate and 0.3% of voters from at least 5 states), it is easier for such a bill to be endorsed by a member of parliament or a group of members of parliament as if it were their own initiative. In 2001, the Commission for Participatory Legislation was created with the aim of facilitating this type of participation. In the case of Bill 5828/2001, although, in practice, the initiative came from AJUFE, the official authorship is attributed to the Commission itself, according to the Chamber of Deputies' records.

647 The bill was also the first originating from the Committee for Participatory Legislation to be approved by the Chamber of Deputies.

648 TOMIO, Fabrício Ricardo de Limas; ROBL FILHO, Ilton Norberto. Accountability e independência judiciais: uma análise da competência do Conselho Nacional de Justiça (CNJ). *Revista de Sociologia e Política*, v. 21, n. 45, p. 29–46, 2013, p. 39.

The CNJ played a central role in the resumption of discussions on the regulation of the electronic judicial process, one of its duties being to ensure the administrative efficiency of the courts throughout the country.

Once interest in the issue resumed and after the change of rapporteur to Senator Serys Slhessarenko, the text of Bill 5.828/2001 was passed by the Senate with modifications and then returned to the Chamber of Deputies and, with its final endorsement, became Law No. 11,419/2006, the Law on Computerization of the Judicial Process.

During the course of the discussion of this bill, the decisive role of the recently created CNJ in getting it discussed and passed should be highlighted. There is evidence that the CNJ's work was decisive so that the bill, which had been forgotten in the drawers of the Federal Senate, could be discussed again, properly updated, and approved. In this sense, the statements made by the CNJ's Secretary General at the time, Sérgio Tejada, prove that the Council directly interfered in the resumption of discussion and also in the formatting of the text:

> "In fact, what has been done with information technology to date has been to computerize bureaucracy. What we want now, and especially with Bill 71, is to give justice a new form of computerization. And the council is working on it. This bill will authorize the computerization of the process, the entire process can be virtual, in other words, do away with paper. We'll be able to create an electronic official gazette, which today is very bureaucratic, it's on paper, it takes time, in some more distant parts of the national territory, it takes ten days to arrive."[649]

It can be said that the CNJ played a major role in the issue, setting up a committee on the subject and acting politically in Congress to get the bill passed with modifications. It should be noted that, although the bill itself was not the subject of major political disputes, to the point that it was

649 *Especial CNJ 1 - Conselho Nacional de Justiça desenvolve ações para acelerar processos no Judiciário (07' 00") - Rádio Câmara.* Portal da Câmara dos Deputados. Available at <https://www.camara.leg.br/radio/programas/271167-especial-cnj-1-conselho-nacional-de-justica-desenvolve-acoes-para-acelerar-do-processos-no-judiciario-07-00/>. Accessed 7 May 2024. In the original, "Na verdade, o que se fez com informática até hoje foi informatizar a burocracia. O que se quer agora, e, principalmente, a partir do Projeto de Lei, PL 71, é dar uma nova forma de informatização para a justiça. E o conselho está trabalhando nisso. Esse projeto vai autorizar a informatização do processo, todo o processo pode ser virtual, ou seja, acabar com o papel. Vamos poder criar um diário oficial eletrônico, hoje é muito burocratizado, é em papel, demora, em alguns pontos mais distantes do território nacional, ele leva dez dias para chegar".

unanimously approved in the House and through mutual praise between members of the government and the opposition, the implementation of a law that enables the start of a digital transformation in the Judiciary only came about due to the strength and pressure of an organized entity, newly created as part of the reform of the Judiciary and with the competence and structure to coordinate interests and initiatives in this direction that would benefit various Courts and bodies of Justice spread across the country, with high degrees of autonomy and little coordination or communication.

The law was important in authorizing changes to the rules of Brazilian civil procedure by allowing the state to require the parties to legal proceedings to behave in accordance with digital processes (such as receiving electronic subpoenas and the obligation to carry out procedural acts through the systems), as well as making the electronic form of acts by the parties and the judge compatible with procedural law and its provisions. In fact, a substantial part of the text of the law was enacted as an amendment to the Brazilian Civil Procedure Code, a set of rules that is also applied subsidiarily in labor and criminal proceedings.

However, the law did not include any mechanisms to encourage the development of electronic court proceedings, nor any type of commandment to stimulate their development, create forums for discussion or provide for coordination mechanisms. Thus, the development and implementation of the systems, now authorized and with their own rules, was left to the state and regional courts, which in Brazil enjoyed great autonomy in relation to each other, the other branches of government, and the higher courts.

This scenario has only changed as a result, once again, of the CNJ itself, whose competence as the general administrative body of Brazilian justice has made it possible to act more proactively in promoting digitization. It was through its coordinating and integrating action that progress could be seen. In this sense, the Council identified initiatives in courts or even outside them, such as the Creta and E-Proc and Projudi programs, together with the courts and citizens.[650] Using its prerogative and competence to coordinate and formulate public policies for the Judiciary introduced by the constitutional reform, the CNJ started with a system previously implemented by the Federal Regional Court of the 5th Region[651] and developed an

650 In September 2006, a donation agreement was signed in which the developers of the Prodigicon system transferred to the CNJ the intellectual property rights of the case management software they created.

651 RUSCHEL, Aírton José; LAZZARI, João Batista; ROVER, Aires José. O processo judicial eletrônico no brasil: uma visão geral. *In*: COÊLHO, Marcus Vinicius Furta-

improved version together with other Courts, which was renamed PJ-e,[652] open source, and made available free of charge to any Court and Justice body that wanted to adopt it. Adoption of the PJ-e was not compulsory, but it was strongly encouraged by the Council in the form of incentives. The CNJ's assumption of this role in 2009 was essential to resolving the scenario of a lack of coordination between the courts in the development of systems.[653]

The development and encouragement of the use of the PJ-e essentially took into account the element of scale in its design. By developing the system centrally and offering it to the Courts, the Council discouraged what would be the most natural course of action on the part of each body, i.e., purchasing or developing their own systems individually. Efficiency was thus gained by discouraging the parallel development of systems or the multiple purchase of proprietary code platforms, without the need to use prohibitive measures, since adoption was optional. It was also possible to develop a standard for how judicial information is handled, something that was lacking in the various Brazilian courts, each following a different way of classifying and numbering case files, handling personal data, search systems and cataloging case law and decisions. The CNJ issued a mandatory rule for all courts in order to standardize the handling of information, even among those that adopted other computerization systems or even those that still worked 100% with physical records.[654]

Currently, the system developed by the National Council of Justice is already in use in all the Regional Labor Courts, all the Electoral Courts, and most of the State Courts and Federal Regional Courts,[655] The approval of a federal law on the adoption of electronic proceedings that would apply throughout the country and constitute a standardized guideline for the establishment of structural foundations for digitalization in the Judiciary was fundamental to the success of this policy, as was the coordination of initiatives, best practices, and standards by a centralized body. The high level of institutionalization of the CNJ, its functions and objectives, through

---

do; ALLEMAND, Luiz Cláudio (Orgs.). *Processo Judicial Eletrônico*. Brasília: OAB, 2014, p. 18.

652 Technical cooperation agreement no. 043/2010, available on the CNJ website.

653 ZAMUR FILHO, Jamil. *Processo judicial eletrônico: alcance e efetividade sob a égide da Lei N° 11.419, de 19.12.2006*. PhD Dissertation (Law), University of São Paulo, São Paulo, 2011, p. 41.

654 Resolution 66/2008 and Resolution 12/2006 of the CNJ.

655 According to updated information on the website <http://www.pje.jus.br/wiki/index.php>

Constitutional Amendment 45 of 2004, and the ability to coordinate efforts and discourses around an agenda that this allowed can also be pointed to as a critical success factor.

The CNJ's role, however, is not limited to the development and maintenance of the PJ-e. It is also responsible for coordinating innovation in the Judiciary, which it does by regulating the use of technology and identifying and replicating regional or local solutions at national level.

Among the various thematic commissions that the CNJ currently has, the Permanent Commission on Information Technology and Innovation stands out, whose function, among others, is to submit proposals to the plenary for the regulation of new technologies, including those pertaining to artificial intelligence tools, and oversee the adoption of new technologies within the Judiciary.

In the first case, the CNJ's normative competence is a factor that facilitates innovation and experimentation, because by disciplining basic rules for the use of technology that are applied to the various courts, it creates a safe environment for the development of applications, as well as ensuring that they can be easily replicated and improved. For example, while discussions on the regulation of artificial intelligence are slow in the legislative process and public administrations are using this technology with their own precarious or non-existent regulations, the CNJ has already established rules on this since 2020. Through a resolution that regulates the algorithmic transparency of solutions based on artificial intelligence,[656] the CNJ addressed issues such as auditing results, guaranteeing impartiality, non-discrimination, the use of predictive solutions in calculating sentences, among others, with reference to the principles of the European Charter on the use of AI in the Judiciary.[657]

When it comes to monitoring the implementation of technology within the Judiciary, the CNJ's powers make it possible to explore the experimental potential of the autonomy of the various courts throughout the country. In this sense, take the example of the Sinapses Platform, which aims to use artificial intelligence and machine learning models[658] and officially

656 Resolution no. 332 of 21/08/2020.

657 TEIXEIRA, Lucas De Barros. Transparência algorítmica em soluções utilizadas por governos. *Revista Internacional de Debates da Administração & Públicas - RIDAP*, v. 6, n. 1, p. 1–10, 2021, p. 5.

658 ARAÚJO, Diógenes Carlos *et al.* A Comparison of Classification Methods Applied to Legal Text Data. *In*: *Progress in Artificial Intelligence. EPIA 2021.* Cham: Springer, 2021, p. 69.

consists of a "computational solution, maintained by the National Council of Justice, with the aim of storing, testing, training, distributing and auditing Artificial Intelligence models".[659] The system began to be developed by the Court of Justice of the State of Rondônia (one of the least populous in the country) in 2017, and was then incorporated by the CNJ as a strategic initiative, and began to be developed jointly for implementation at a national level.[660] Today, the platform brings together around 150 artificial intelligence models from 29 courts, and is funded by a partnership between the CNJ and the United Nations Development Program (UNDP).[661]

The CNJ's influence on digitization processes also transcends the sphere of jurisdictional activity in the strict sense, as can be seen in the regulation of the digital transfer of ownership of motor vehicles, to be carried out by civil registry offices in conjunction with the National Traffic Secretariat (Senatran) of the Ministry of Transport.[662]

Finally, it should be noted that the CNJ, as a body presided over by the president of the STF and with members from various Superior Courts, has the autonomy and political strength necessary to provide an environment for creation and experimentation that is less vulnerable to the inhibitory and excessively formalistic and repressive administrative external control sometimes carried out by the Courts of Accounts and the Public Prosecutor's Office. Likewise with the courts, which are administratively answerable to the CNJ itself but have the autonomy necessary to take innovation initiatives that involve some significant degree of risk.

3.2 Digital Government at European level and in Germany

Every country in the world is facing the challenges of digitalization. Each of them, with their different forms of state and systems of government,

659 Resolution no. 332 of 21/08/2020. In the original, "solução computacional, mantida pelo Conselho Nacional de Justiça, com o objetivo de armazenar, testar, treinar, distribuir e auditar modelos de Inteligência Artificial".

660 ABREU, Marjory da Costa; SILVA, Bruno. A critical analysis of "Law 4.0": The use of Automation and Artificial Intelligence and their impact on the judicial landscape of Brazil. *Revista de Direitos Fundamentais e Tributação*, v. 1, n. 3, p. 1–16, 2020, p. 11.

661 *Plataforma Sinapses reúne 150 modelos de inteligência artificial.* UNDP. Available at <https://www.undp.org/pt/brazil/news/plataforma-sinapses-reune-150-modelos-de-inteligencia-artificial>. Accessed 19 Apr. 2024.

662 *Corregedoria autoriza transferência eletrônica de veículos por registro civil.* Portal CNJ. Available at <https://www.cnj.jus.br/corregedoria-autoriza-transferencia-eletronica-de-veiculos-via-registro-civil/>. Accessed 12 Oct. 2024.

have different ways of dealing with the modernization of their institutions and the incorporation of technology in the public sector. This is also why international experiences in Digital Government are quite diverse, as are the degrees of success and the critical factors that determine the results of public policies in this area. The European Union, in this respect, represents a small universe of diversity, with member states at different stages of digital transformation and human development, and a common goal of integration and development forming a comprehensive political project.

Within this universe of 27 different countries, Germany stands out as the strongest economy in the bloc and also the most politically influential nation in the region. Nevertheless, Germany is known for the complexity of its bureaucracy and its digital backwardness. Germany also has a complex, multi-level federalism, which, compared to smaller, unitary states, contributes to change processes taking longer. Despite this, and although Germany does not boast the best digital transformation results in Europe, the way in which the state has mobilized over the years to adapt to innovations in information technology is noteworthy because of its consistent incrementalism and how it seeks to address the difficulties of coordinating and implementing its Digital Government.

The European and German experiences are also part of the day-to-day life and work of this researcher, who over the last three years has been able to follow this process closely, suffer personally from its limitations and also be enthusiastic about the progress made. In addition, of particular interest to this research is how institutions organize themselves around structured programs to promote public policies for digital transformation, in the context of a very assertive political discourse of integration, overcoming regional inequalities and modernization. In this sense, although the research is eminently based on doctrinal sources and the corresponding legislation, we cannot ignore the strong ethnographic inspiration that daily experience in the city of Hamburg has provided over this time. The following topics will analyze how the issue of Digital Government is dealt with by the European Union and Germany, the roles of the institutions in this process, and the repercussions of this for the objectives of this dissertation, identifying insights and key elements that are useful for understanding the Brazilian case and for exercising institutional imagination, in order to draw up, in the final chapter, a prescriptive analysis concerning alternatives for transformation.

3.2.1 The European Union and the digital transformation: cohesion and discourse

The European Union promotes policies aimed at developing Digital Government in its member states based on two broader perspectives, namely: the improvement and administrative integration of Europe as a single market; and the digital transformation of European society in an economic context. The subject initially entered the public debate in the form of actions to digitize the public administration or related acts, from an e-government perspective characteristic of the static understanding of the 1990s and early 2000s,[663] becoming more important as the digital transformation itself demonstrated its economic potential.

The prospects for big leaps in productivity with the intensified use of technology involve many social sectors with remarkable public-private symbiosis, such as energy efficiency, mobility, and health services.[664] Much more than a question of productivity gains, the digital transformation is today seen as a great opportunity to strengthen Europe's socio-economic cohesion, to such an extent that strengthening digital capacities, taking into account the differences in the stage of development of the member states, has become a declared priority.[665]

There are different ways for the EU to foster the development of Digital Government, including *informative* measures, *pre-normative* measures, *normative* measures, and *promotion* programs. Informative measures are studies, benchmark reports, and forums for the exchange of knowledge, which form the basis of ideas and guidelines for institutionalization and support the communicative and coordinative discourse around the implementation of measures.[666] Pre-normative measures are those that aim to condition the behavior of European actors through declarations and strategies, in which the deontic and enforcement elements are absent or discrete, but which have real effectiveness due to the determination of collective

663 BARCEVIČIUS, Egidijus *et al. Exploring digital government transformation in the EU: analysis of the state of the art and review of literature.* Luxembourg: Publications Office of the European Union, 2019, p. 10–12.

664 CODAGNONE, Cristiano *et al. Europe's Digital Decade and autonomy.* Luxembourg: Policy Department for Economic, Scientific and Quality of Life Policies. European Parliament, 2021, p. 13.

665 MILUTINOVIC, Petar. Digital public policy and e-Governance as factors of the enhanced socio-economic cohesion in the European Union. *Kultura Polisa*, v. 19, n. 4, p. 146–166, 2022, p. 151.

666 See sections 1.9.6 and 1.9.10 above.

meanings about the issues dealt with and the alignment of expectations around certain objectives. These are translated into action plans, declarations, and sectoral strategies. As pointed out in 1.9.3, they are intermediate institutional stages in the relationship between the political impulse and the normative structuring of government action, and the absence or lesser preponderance of deontic elements does not detract from their importance, even from the point of view of the law. Normative measures, on the other hand, are aimed at cogent harmonization, establishing rules that are automatically applicable to member states in some cases, or that establish the duty to be incorporated into their legal systems within a certain period of time by issuing national rules. Promotion programs, on the other hand, consist of financially structured action programs with a more direct penetration than declarations, strategies and plans, but still preferring the path of promoting conduct and encouragement. Normative measures and promotion programs are the result of integrating the other elements of institutional grammar into government action, notably the deontic element, but also enforcement, when the structure of competences allows. Below we will mention some of the main pre-normative, normative, informative and promotion measures in the context under analysis, not to explore their content in detail, but to outline a general picture of the initiatives that contribute to an understanding of the way Digital Government is dealt with at European level, serving as input for the subsequent critical considerations.

According to the distribution of competences at European level,[667] issues such as the implementation of Digital Government are mainly the responsibility of national governments, which is why the European Union mainly uses non-binding legal initiatives to achieve digitization objectives in the public sector, since it does not have much scope to legislate directly on the matter.[668] This is done mainly by drawing up strategies and action plans, but also through the mechanism of the European Semester Process, in which the Commission publishes specific recommendations to countries,[669] in addition to other policies and programs that have taken on greater importance, as will be mentioned in due course.

667 Articles 2 to 6 of the Treaty on the Functioning of the European Union (TFEU).

668 VERHEYEN, Sabine; RIEKE, Katharina. E-Government in der Europäischen Union. *In*: STEMBER, Jürgen *et al* (Orgs.). *Handbuch E-Government: Technikinduzierte Verwaltungsentwicklung*. Wiesbaden: Springer Fachmedien, 2019, p. 98.

669 The recommendations for 2023 can be accessed at EUROPEAN UNION. *2023 European Semester: Country Reports - European Commission*. Available at <https://e

In terms of the origins and timeline of these initiatives and strategies on European digital transformation, it can be mentioned that in 2000, the EU drew up an action plan, known as the Lisbon Strategy, for improving the competitiveness of Europe's economy, with a set of initiatives and recommendations to be adopted by member countries in order to achieve the desired objectives by 2010 and make Europe the most competitive region globally. The Strategy was revised in 2005 and, although it does not explicitly deal with Digital Government or digital transformation (it is limited to investment in IT and network access infrastructure), it lays the foundations for Europe's transition to a more dynamic and competitive knowledge-based economy, in which innovation is the driving force behind development.[670] Often considered a failure in terms of economic effects, it succeeded "to change policy thinking and cognitive maps through the introduction in the national debate of EU concepts",[671] i.e., it had an important impact as a communicative discourse to foster institutional change in the national spheres of the member states, albeit indirectly and belatedly. In spite of the lack of political commitment at national level regarding the new economic model to be adopted - enhanced by the characteristics of the open method of coordination decision-making process[672] - the emphasis on the trinomial of research, education and innovation was positive.[673]

In the same vein, the eEurope 2002 action plan was published in 2001, proposing various measures to implement online access to public services in line with the objectives of the Lisbon Strategy, notably the digitization of health and transport systems, as well as providing for a system to monitor

conomy-finance.ec.europa.eu/publications/2023-european-semester-country-reports_en>. Accessed 30 Mar. 2024.

670 RODRIGUEZ, Ricardo; WARMERDAM, John; TRIOMPHE, Claude Emmanuel. *The Lisbon Strategy 2000 – 2010 An analysis and evaluation of the methods used and result.* Brussels: European Parliament, 2010.

671 NATALI, David. The Lisbon strategy a decade on: a critical review of a multi-disciplinary literature. *Transfer: European Review of Labour and Research*, v. 15, n. 1, p. 111–137, 2009, p. 128.

672 AMABLE, Bruno; DEMMOU, Lilas; LEDEZMA, Ivan. The Lisbon strategy and structural reforms in Europe. *Transfer: European Review of Labour and Research*, v. 15, n. 1, p. 33–52, 2009, p. 37.

673 SORIANO, Fernando Hervás; MULATERO, Fulvio. Knowledge Policy in the EU: From the Lisbon Strategy to Europe 2020. *Journal of the Knowledge Economy*, v. 1, n. 4, p. 289–302, 2010, p. 296, 300.

the evolution of these policies at national level.[674] In the same year, the ministers and secretaries of state of the European Council gave high priority to the issue of Digital Government, in particular to encourage citizen participation, with the inclusion of an environment of security and trust, and the promotion of organizational changes in general.[675]

In 2010, the European Commission published the Europe 2020 strategy to succeed the Lisbon Strategy, to achieve sustainable, inclusive, and intelligent economic growth, setting concrete objectives for the European Union to pursue by 2020, such as targets for unemployment rates, investment in technology, among others. The strategy involved improving communication and interconnectivity services, as well as proposing the Digital Agenda for Europe initiative, with measures to stimulate the improvement of digital infrastructure at EU level, and at national level, with the promotion of digital services, including government services.[676]

In 2021, the EU implemented the Digital Compass 2030 initiative, with a vision for Europe by the end of the decade, comprising the outlining of objectives, ways of achieving them, and monitoring tools in a way of examining the pace of change, its gaps, and the concrete implementation of the related standards. Always based on the postulates of solidarity and sustainability, the intention is to provide a sovereign, interconnected, secure, and resilient Digital Europe, while at the same time empowering citizens and businesses.[677] A series of other more or less relevant initiatives or documents, in the form of declarations, strategies, or plans, have been launched over the years on the subject of digitization and related issues, such as the Digital Single Market Strategy for Europe, the Interoperability Action Plan 2016 - 2020, the EU eGovernment Action Plan 2016 - 2020, the

674 COM(2003) 66. Communication from the Commission to the Council, the European Parliament, the Economic and Social Committee and the Committee of the Regions - eEurope 2002 Final Report.

675 Ministerial declaration: eGovernment - a priority for Europe. Available at <https://ec.europa.eu/commission/presscorner/detail/en/IP_01_1704>. Accessed 30 Mar. 2024.

676 COM(2010) 2020. Communication from the Commission. Europe 2020. A strategy for smart, sustainable and inclusive growth, p. 11-12.

677 MILUTINOVIC, Petar. Digital public policy and e-Governance as factors of the enhanced socio-economic cohesion in the European Union. *Kultura Polisa*, v. 19, n. 4, p. 146–166, 2022, p. 152.

Tallinn Declaration on eGovernment and the Berlin Declaration on Digital Society and Value-Based Digital Government, among others.[678]

From a normative point of view, European Union law influences the adoption of Digital Government policies in the member states through the implementation of various initiatives related to the modernization of the public sector and/or the single market, which indirectly contribute to its evolution.[679] Article 41 of the EU Charter of Fundamental Rights provides a basic guideline for these initiatives by mentioning the right to a swift and efficient administrative process within the EU institutions, affirming good administration as a legally protected value. eIDAS (EU Regulation 910/2014), which regulates electronic identification within the EU, has served as the basis for various national digital signature infrastructures.[680] In 2024, this regulation underwent a major overhaul (eIDAS 2.0) to adapt it to the needs and habits of today's citizens, in particular, the creation of EUDI Wallets. These are a more practical way of secure identification and bringing together other digital documents in a single system, and must be adopted by all member states by the beginning of 2027. Directive 2006/123/EC, known as "The Bolkestein directive", created several obligations for states to provide single points or channels of access to information and the interoperability of systems, and remote administrative procedures, among others, and its provisions were subsequently internalized into the administrative laws of the member states.[681] Directive 2014/55/EU brought

678 Such as the Digital Agenda for Europe, the European Cybersecurity Strategy, the European Digitalization Initiative, the Europe Fit for the Digital Age Strategy, the Digital Europe Program, the European Digital Innovation Hubs, the Path to the Digital Decade Program, the Digital Rights and Principles for the Digital Decade, the European Data Strategy, the European innovation scoreboard.

679 EUROPEAN UNION. *eGovernment in the European Union*. Brussels: European Commission, 2017, p. 8.

680 Regulation (EU) 2024/1183 of the European Parliament and of the Council of 11 April 2024 amending Regulation (EU) Nº 910/2014 as regards establishing the European Digital Identity Framework - eIDAS 2.0.

681 SCHULZ, Sönke E. Rechtlicher Rahmen der Digitalisierung und der Online-Dienste. *In*: LÜHR, Hans-Henning; JABKOWSKI, Roland; SMENTEK, Sabine (Orgs.). *Handbuch Digitale Verwaltung*. Wiesbaden: KSV Medien, 2019, p. 160–161. See, for instance, § 71e VwVfG in Germany; VOSS, Vivien C. Die Implementation der Europäischen Dienstleistungsrichtlinie – lessons learned im Hinblick auf das Wirksamwerden der Single Digital Gateway-Verordnung und des Onlinezugangsgesetzes. *In*: SECKELMANN, Margrit; BRUNZEL, Marco (Orgs.). *Handbuch Onlinezugangsgesetz: Potenziale - Synergien - Herausforderungen*. Berlin, Heidelberg: Springer, 2021, p. 203.

in the obligation to introduce electronic invoices, and the public procurement directives brought in the obligation for fully electronic procurement (implemented in Germany, respectively, by §4a EGov G § 97 5 of the GWB).[682]

The adoption of the Once Only Principle by member states is also an important normative influence at European Union level. The Once Only Principle, as already mentioned, presupposes not only integration between various branches, bodies, and entities of the state but, above all, an environment of mutual trust between institutions and, within the European Union, between member states. This environment is only possible through a shared legal basis,[683] which occurred with the publication of the Single Digital Gateway Regulation (Regulation EU 2018/1724 of the European Parliament and of the Council), which not only determined the creation of a single portal for access to European Union information and services,[684] but also regulated in detail the operation of the Once Only Principle in its article 14. The regulation obliges member states to respect this principle and digitize certain services and information, making them available online.[685]

Regulatory measures do not always have the pure character of driving or enabling but can also use constriction as a regulatory technique to build certain institutional balances.[686] For example, the General Data Protection Regulation (GDPR), by creating a consistent data protection system, contributes to an institutional environment in which fundamental rights intrinsically related to the digital world, such as privacy, intimacy, and dignity, are effectively guaranteed, generating stable expectations, trust and legal certainty, all necessary for the expansion of relationships mediated by information technology. At the same time, the GDPR may serve as a dampening factor for some policies, having gained the reputation of being a regulation of the "right to prevent digitalization".[687] This sometimes conflicting relationship between data protection and digitalization, as well as the larger

682 SCHULZ, *op. cit.*, p. 161–162.

683 KRIMMER, Robert *et al.* The Once-Only Principle: A Matter of Trust. *In*: KRIMMER, Robert; PRENTZA, Andriana; MAMROT, Szymon (Orgs.). *The Once-Only Principle: The TOOP Project.* Cham: Springer International Publishing, 2021, p. 2.

684 The portal can be accessed at the following address: *Your Europe*. Your Europe. Available at <https://europa.eu/youreurope/index.htm>. Accessed 30 Mar. 2024.

685 According to article 39 of Regulation (EU) 2018/1724 of the European Parliament and of the Council of 2 October 2018.

686 See sections 1.9.1 and 1.9.2 above.

687 BOTTA, Jonas. Der digitale Staat als gläserner Staat. Transparenz als Bedingung verfassungskonformer Registermodernisierung. *In*: KUHLMANN, Simone *et al*

backdrop of the relationship between the protection of individual rights and the exercise of political power are recurrent in this field, and are dealt with more closely in other passages, such as in section 2.2.2.4 above and 4.2 below.[688]

Concerning the funding programs, the following can be highlighted: ISA (Interoperability Solutions for European Public Administrations), CEF (Connecting Europe Facility), Horizon 2020, European Structural and Investment Funds (ESIF), Structural Reform Support Program (SRSP), Justice Program, The Digital Europe Program, and Next Generation, the latter being at a distinct and more robust level than the others, as will be discussed later.

The ISA, established in 2015 by the European Parliament and the Council, provided an environment for the development of cross-border digital public services jointly by member states, with an investment of 131 million euros from 2016 to 2020.[689] The CEF was an instrument adopted in 2011 by the Commission to improve Europe's transport, energy and digital connection networks, given their strategic importance, and saw investment of 1.14 billion euros in digital services activities and infrastructure from 2014 to 2020.[690] Horizon 2020 is a research and innovation program for implementing the Innovation Union, one of the initiatives for fulfilling the Europe 2020 strategy,[691] and has funded research in various areas related to innovation, including emerging technologies in the public sector, open government, administrative transparency, and applications, with funding of 80 billion euros from 2014 to 2020.[692] There are thousands of funded projects that can be accessed online, more than 4,000 of which are related

(Orgs.). *Transparency or Opacity: A Legal Analysis of the Organization of Information in the Digital World.* Baden-Baden: Nomos, 2023, p. 32.

688 There are a number of other rules within the European Union that relate more or less directly to digitalization issues, but these are the most relevant for understanding the European Union's legal-institutional action on the subject of Digital Government. For a list of these rules, see EUROPEAN UNION. *eGovernment in the European Union.* Brussels: European Commission, 2017, p. 26–35.

689 *Ibid.*, p. 22.

690 *Ibid.*, p. 23.

691 VAN DEN HOVE, Sybille *et al.* The Innovation Union: a perfect means to confused ends? *Environmental Science & Policy*, v. 16, p. 73–80, 2012, p. 74.

692 EUROPEAN UNION, *op. cit.*, p. 23.

to government, most of them dealing with information technologies applicable to the administration.[693]

The ESIF is a broad program, a set of comprehensive instruments that focuses especially on economically disadvantaged areas, also providing funding in the area of Digital Government, given the importance of this type of investment for development. For the years 2021 to 2027, one of the main priorities of the financing funds is a smarter Europe,[694] which includes the issue of digitizing administrations. For its part, the Structural Reform Support Program was a financial support for member states to the implementation of structural administrative and institutional reforms to increase productivity and competitiveness, among other objectives, and had 142.8 million euros from 2017 to 2020.[695]

The NextGenerationEU program is an economic recovery policy in response to the effects of the Covid-19 pandemic, which reverses the logic of fiscal austerity that has prevailed in Europe since the 2008 financial crisis, encompassing investments in the order of 360 billion euros in the form of loans and 390 billion euros in grants,[696] with a substantial part of this going towards digital transformation and, in particular, national Digital Government policies, such as the 3 billion euros earmarked for Germany for this purpose.[697] In addition, after discussion in the European Council, a broad EU funding program called "Digital Agenda" was created, which will fund projects that refer to "supercomputing, artificial intelligence, cybersecurity,

693 According to a search on *Search | CORDIS | European Commission.* Available at <https://cordis.europa.eu/search?q=contenttype%3D%27project%27%20AND%20frameworkProgramme%3D%27H2020%27%20AND%20(%27digital%27)&p=1&num=10&srt=Relevance:decreasing>. Accessed 31 Mar. 2024 (Using the filters "Collection: Projects" and "Framework Program: Horizon 2020", as well as "government").

694 *Inforegio - Priorities for 2021-2027.* Available at <https://ec.europa.eu/regional_policy/policy/how/priorities_en>. Accessed 31 Mar. 2024.

695 *Structural Reform Support Programme (SRSP) - European Commission.* Available at <https://commission.europa.eu/about-european-commission/departments-and-executive-agencies/structural-reform-support/structural-reform-support-programme-srsp_en>. Accessed 31 Mar. 2024.

696 DE LA PORTE, Caroline; JENSEN, Mads Dagnis. The next generation EU: An analysis of the dimensions of conflict behind the deal. *Social Policy & Administration*, v. 55, n. 2, p. 388–402, 2021, p. 389.

697 For a comprehensive overview of the distribution of values across EU countries, see the table in CORDEIRO, Caio Barros. *Desafios do Estado para a transformação digital: uma análise à luz da abordagem Direito e Políticas Públicas.* PhD Dissertation (Law), University of São Paulo, São Paulo, 2023, p. 99.

advanced digital skills, and the broad use of digital technologies across the economy and society" for the period 2021 to 2027.[698] The Digital Europe Program[699] is also part of a list of measures designed to bring about a sustainable economic recovery for the continent after the serious economic and social crisis caused by the Covid-19 pandemic and has resources of around 7.5 billion euros.

Funding programs are powerful inducement mechanisms, as they represent external incentives (in the sense that they do not derive directly or indirectly from the meaning of the rules but from the budgetary dimension of the policies) for digitalization objectives. In this regard, it is worth emphasizing what was mentioned at the end of section 1.9.5 and which will also be dealt with later in section 4.5 about the effects of external incentives, enhanced by an institutional structure that sensitizes the constellation of actors to receiving stimuli of this kind. In other words, the EU's funding programs depend for their success on a legal-institutional arrangement that involves not only the supranational components but also the national components of the member states around guiding ideas and well-defined discourses via pre-normative institutional statements.[700]

Finally, as informative and monitoring measures, in addition to the numerous studies promoted by European Union institutions on digitalization and Digital Government, the E-Government Benchmark Reports, which have been produced since 2003 regarding the status in member states,[701] as well as The Digital Economy and Society Index – DESI, stand out.

In this regard, it should be noted that the DESI is possibly the most relevant indicator of the performance of the digital economy in European countries, with individual and comparative analyses between them capable

698 *Programa Europa Digital – Conselho define a sua posição.* Available at <https://www.consilium.europa.eu/pt/press/press-releases/2018/12/04/digital-europe-programme-council-agrees-its-position/>. Accessed 7 May 2024. In the original, "...supercomputação, inteligência artificial, cibersegurança, competências digitais avançadas, e ampla utilização das tecnologias digitais em toda a economia e sociedade".

699 See Regulation (EU) 2021/694 of the European Parliament and of the Council of 29 April 2021.

700 See section 1.9.3 above.

701 STEMBER, Jürgen; HASENKAMP, Victoria; HABBEL, Franz-Reinhard. E-Government auf den unterschiedlichen administrativen Ebenen in Deutschland. *In*: STEMBER, Jürgen *et al* (Orgs.). *Handbuch E-Government: Technikinduzierte Verwaltungsentwicklung.* Wiesbaden: Springer Fachmedien, 2019, p. 187.

of providing robust elements for policymakers to improve programs.[702] Mention should also be made of the Joinup platform, linked to the European Commission, which individually monitors several of its initiatives,[703] in addition to the public participation mechanisms already mentioned. These initiatives also include official channels for civil society participation in policy-making, such as the eGovernment4EU platform, through which citizens and companies contribute suggestions in a consultation process. The European Commission and the member states periodically evaluate and select the suggestions for later incorporation into EU policies and programs.[704] As of 2021, the platform has been discontinued, but its discussion forums have been incorporated into the Futurium platform, which also discusses other European policies.[705]

In general terms, the EU assumes the role of assisting its member states in the development and implementation of institutional mechanisms for the formulation and implementation of digital public policies, also fostering cooperation between countries, while at the same time its ethical and legal frameworks guarantee standardization and the preservation of fundamental rights.[706]

But perhaps the EU's most significant function in relation to policies of an eminently reformist nature, such as the digital transformation, is to bring together visions and ambitions related to a certain topic that is not yet so well known or assimilated, building a political idea that is democratically forged through supranational procedures and open debate. As a result, there is the consolidation of a common development ideology and a vision of the future, not only through its normative and pre-normative legal-institutional instruments but also through discourse. Coordinative discourse is used to a large extent to harmonize preferences and align institutional actions within its bodies, forums, and instances, as well as legal and procedural rules that allow for the exchange of ideas on common standards and guidelines, consolidating a community ideology. From the point of view of

702 LIU, Tze-Chang. Digital policy in European countries from the perspective of the Digital Economy and Society Index. *Policy & Internet*, v. 14, n. 1, p. 202–218, 2022, p. 203.

703 *Joinup*. Available at <https://joinup.ec.europa.eu/>. Accessed 31 Mar. 2024.

704 STEMBER; HASENKAMP; HABBEL, *op. cit.*, p. 185.

705 *Futurium*. Available at <https://futurium.ec.europa.eu/en/node>. Accessed 31 Mar. 2024.

706 MILUTINOVIC, Petar. Digital public policy and e-Governance as factors of the enhanced socio-economic cohesion in the European Union. *Kultura Polisa*, v. 19, n. 4, p. 146–166, 2022, p. 152.

communicative discourse,[707] EU representatives and authorities emphasize priorities, demonstrate the connection of technical issues with the regular interests of European citizens, and situate choices and visions in the geopolitical scenario. This is a crucial function today, given the rise of the far right, which, while feeding off the real frustrations and disappointments of the population about the state of affairs and the institutions that represent it, also disputes discursive meanings about the perception of the material progress observed in the EU as a whole and the results of public policies.

As seen in 1.9.6, ideas statically assign cultural or legal meanings to certain situations, depending on the position and legitimacy of the actors involved. The processes by which ideas are handled, however, will dynamically define the suitability of discourses for transformation. Considering the highly complex and multi-level structure of the European Union, together with its member states, the coordinative discourse becomes sophisticated or even prolix, permeating strategies, studies, declarations, and legal norms in order to stabilize the expectations of the actors directly involved in the implementation of policies. Despite the huge number of documents and plans, which are often difficult to understand due to the overlapping of subjects and matters, the actors to whom the measures are addressed are people or institutions within the EU's own bureaucracy, which makes them easier to apply. In addition, many of the measures contained in strategies and plans are directly supported by funding programs, which takes the determinations from the plane of ideas to concreteness.

Despite the limits in terms of competence and attribution of the European Union in relation to the member states when it comes to Digital Government, EU policies also play an important role in inducing the overcoming of inequalities and promoting the development of lagging regions, which is directly linked to the issue of European cohesion and, therefore, to its key objective of maintaining and promoting integration. Combating inequalities in the capacity and institutional maturity of the administrations in the member states contributes to strengthening the communicative discourse aimed at the population, also strengthening the political direction, at the same time as it can be favored by this same discourse, in a virtuous circle.

The large number of initiatives and different standards at European Union level has the impact of directly and cogently influencing the digital transformation in member countries in terms of mandatory implementa-

707 On ideas, coordinative and communicative discourse, see section 1.9.10.

tion directives and other rules that must necessarily be observed. And many of these rules, despite not directly dealing with Digital Government matters, act as drivers or facilitators of policies. As facilitators (or enablers), they create institutions that make the development or use of Digital Government itself more attractive from an economic point of view, reducing transaction costs. As drivers (or promoters), they change people's perceptions by attributing new cultural meanings to certain traditional relationships, such as contracts, agreements, forms of communication, and consequently their habits in relation to them, shaping sets of preferences and tending towards new ways of stabilizing them.

When the EU brings in uniform rules on electronic signatures, for example, and as a result member countries are pressured to adopt them in their internal regulations, it speeds up these national procedures that would previously have had their pace dictated by other variables. And when a regulation on the use of electronic signatures is internalized as a result of external pressure, even in a social context where demand for it is low, this reality becomes part of the collective imaginary of citizens, as well as part of the list of legal instruments for creating or improving public policies, which now start from higher levels of evolution.

All these regulatory initiatives as drivers and facilitators, combined with pre-normative initiatives of an attractive nature such as plans, strategies, and qualified declarations, encourage member states, each in their own way, to undertake their initiatives related to digital transformation and public administration. They advance at uneven paces, and in differing quantity and quality, yet demonstrate experiences and cases of success and failure that are multiplied and amplified by the number of member states taking action driven by the EU's political direction. These experiences are inevitably exchanged, whether in the official EU information-sharing forums, through the work of academic researchers who comparatively scrutinize the institutions of the member states, or through official monitoring and indices.

In addition to providing political direction and generating driving and facilitating elements, as well as fostering an environment for sharing experiences, the EU also ends up creating healthy competition in terms of digital transformation in the public sector among its members, due to the rankings and studies it sponsors. This in itself generates new incentives for member states, now on their own momentum, to continue on a constant path of evolution and reflection on the public problems and obstacles surrounding the reform and modernization involved in developing digital states. And all these political and social incentives are, of course, in addition to the direct economic incentives resulting from the EU's recovery and financing plans.

3.2.2 Digital Government in Germany: incrementalism and coordination

It is very common to analyze the trajectory of digitalization in Germany as a succession of failures and dysfunctions, with government measures that, even after years of implementation, still do not have acceptance and usage considered ideal by the Germans.[708] Every foreign resident who has recently moved to the country inevitably identifies with memes and comical pictures on social media satirizing Germany's highly methodical day-to-day bureaucracy, especially the commonplace use of paper and (physical) mail as a means, often obligatory, of communication and the enjoyment of simple services, which could be replaced by an electronic message or even a phone call. The same perception is shared by Germans in general who, whenever asked about the subject, are rigorously assertive in pointing out that digitization is lagging behind in Germany. Not infrequently, this same critical German may also prefer to pay restaurant bills in cash for privacy reasons, use mail and physical forms even when there is no need, and have an extraordinary appreciation for data protection, beyond the expectations of someone from another culture.

The latest report from the *Nationaler Normenkontrollrat* (NKR), the body that carries out assessments of regulatory quality,[709] points out that Digital Government in Germany is progressing at a slow pace and continues to lag behind most European countries, despite important initiatives such as the *Onlinezugangsgesetz* (OZG), which will be discussed later. The reasons for this are, in a nutshell, "a lack of vision, ambition and political will to move forward in big steps and with less consideration for federal and departmental sensitivities",[710] associated with the anachronism

708 These include experiences such as De-Mail, digital identity and the digital health card, which will be discussed later. LÜHR, Henning. Von der Konferenz "Deutschland online" zur föderativen IT-Kooperation – Innovation und Digital Leadership im föderalen Mehrebenensystem in Deutschland. *In*: SECKELMANN, Margrit; BRUNZEL, Marco (Orgs.). *Handbuch Onlinezugangsgesetz: Potenziale - Synergien - Herausforderungen*. Berlin, Heidelberg: Springer, 2021, p. 97.

709 According to the law that created it, Gesetz zur Einsetzung eines Nationalen Normenkontrollrates. *Bundesgesetzblatt Teil I*. n. 39, p. 1866, 2006, §1, (2).

710 NKR. *Jahresbericht 2023 des Nationalen Normenkontrollrates*. Berlin: Bundesministerium der Justiz, 2023, p. 4. In the original, "Es fehlt an Vision, an Ambition und

of public registers. In view of this, the document objectively lists what should be done to remedy these shortcomings: "central basic infrastructures and platforms, binding architecture specifications and standards, faster decision-making processes and easier IT procurement, as well as public implementation monitoring and an effective federal control organization".[711]

It seems quite clear, however, that Germany is making a conscious political choice to be as cautious as possible when it comes to implementing changes to its well-established bureaucracy with bicentennial roots, which, over the decades, has undergone enough reforms to make the country one of the most developed in the world, despite all its problems. "We're doing badly, but at a very high level",[712] would have said Otto Graf Lambsdorff, Germany's former economy minister in the 1980s, about the country's economic situation, and the same logic can be seen with regard to the digital transformation: on the one hand, there is a great deal of backwardness and the challenge of overcoming it, but on the other, Germany remains one of the most prosperous economies in the world and the strongest in Europe.

As far as Digital Government is concerned, moderation and incrementalism, with the careful development and implementation of modernization structures and measures, while carefully preserving fundamental rights, have the advantage of producing institutions that, in the long term, have a good chance of developing sustainably and reflecting good permanent political functioning. Incrementalism usually has the advantage of mitigating the possibility of serious errors in reforms of all kinds,[713] and also represents a way of satisfactorily equalizing the expectations, demands, and resistance created by relevant changes that affect interests. In this sense, as far as impact transformations are concerned, "changing things piece by piece, eventually changing everything, makes it much more difficult to establish the distinction between winning and losing than in the case

---

dem politischen Willen, in großen Schritten und mit weniger Rücksicht auf föderale und ressortegoistische Befindlichkeiten voranzugehen".

711 *Ibid.*, ". In the original, "Zentrale Basisinfrastrukturen und Plattformen, verbindliche Architekturvorgaben und Standards, schnellere Entscheidungsverfahren und leichtere IT-Beschaffung sowie ein öffentliches Umsetzungs-Monitoring und eine schlagkräftige föderale Steuerungsorganisation".

712 JACOBY, Wade; BEHRENS, Martin. Experimentalism as a tool of economic innovation in Germany. *German Politics and Society*, v. 19, n. 3, p. 1–33, 2001, p. 2. In the original, "Uns geht es schlecht aber auf einem sehr hohen Niveau."

713 LINDBLOM, Charles E. The Science of "Muddling Through". *Public Administration Review*, v. 19, n. 2, p. 79–88, 1959, p. 86.

of punctual, once and for all changes".[714] The sequence of incremental gains can mean, even if paradoxically, faster changes, compared to the deadlocked processes common in major reforms, allowing the losers of the political game to assimilate their losses and still continue in the subsequent public debates, which guarantees a convergence of all in relation to some basic values of the democratic process.[715]

However, this does not mean that incremental policies will always be formulated and implemented in the right way or at the right pace. German coordinated capitalism, as reflected in the technological modernization of the state, is progressing more slowly than desired or compared to other countries worldwide. At the same time, it represents steady gains towards increasing digitalization, with the utmost preservation of values cherished by the community, especially the private sphere, and a rejection of any form of totalitarianism. Whether these gains are enough to prevent the economy from losing its dynamism and maintain the important position Germany currently occupies in the world is up for debate. After all, the undeniable digital backwardness does not seem compatible with the foundations of an economy and a welfare state in a society marked by the importance of information technology, and even consistent progress can be unsatisfactory in a globalized and competitive world.

This dissertation does not aim to draw conclusions about the causes of Germany's delay in Digital Government, since the analysis made here is to support the examination of the Brazilian case. However, some critical factors in this scenario are commonly mentioned by specialized literature, including political, social, cultural, and legal barriers. Political and social barriers include issues related to the electoral process and the interests involved, the lack of preparation of the political class to deal with these issues, the lack of clarity about responsibilities and competences in implementation, and concerns about the dangers of automation, violation of privacy, or discrimination. Legal barriers include the lack of certainty regarding data protection rights, the complexity of regulations, and overly rigid German public law. Technical barriers include a lack of appropriate technological know-how, obsolete public IT infrastructure, incompatibility between proprietary systems, and all kinds of deficiencies in information

714 DORF, Michael C.; SABEL, Charles F. A constitution of democratic experimentalism. *Columbia Law Review*, v. 98, n. 2, p. 267–473, 1998, p. 310.

715 LINDBLOM, Charles E. Still Muddling, Not Yet Through. *Public Administration Review*, v. 39, n. 6, p. 517–526, 1979, p. 520.

technology management. Finally, as cultural barriers, there are weak social and organizational incentives, a deficit in learning new technologies, a rigid organizational hierarchy, a typically German bureaucracy (high and complex), and a traditional leadership style in public administration.[716]

Cultural barriers, in particular, should not be underestimated. After all, it's hard to believe that German army officers use fax machines to send documents in the middle of 2024[717] for any other reason than because they want to or because this has always been the way organizations do things. There is also the consideration that perhaps the cost-benefit ratio of changes is hampered by an unconscious perception that the social situation in general and the stage of national development are sufficient for the full enjoyment of life in society. Even the German "analog"/paper bureaucracy, known for being extremely high, complicated, and time-consuming, usually ends up achieving the objectives it sets out to achieve (in the eyes of a foreign researcher), while the analog bureaucracy in countries like Brazil, for example, in addition to its complexity, delay, and cost, presents tangible dysfunctions beyond the cost and time involved. In other words, German bureaucracy, with all its flaws, seems to work in one way or another (at least compared to Brazil), albeit at a high cost and with delays. Meanwhile, bureaucracy in countries with a more precarious level of development often suffers from the same problems, but without presenting an advantage justified by the achievement of its intended purpose. Using the cliché of the boiling frog syndrome[718] as a metaphor to explain the digitalization and efficiency of the German state, it can be said that the frog has been sitting comfortably in the gradually warming water for years, while in countries with a lower level of development, social discomfort is felt more acutely by the general population, and perhaps this is why it provokes stronger reactions (and transformations).

Nevertheless, the German frog began to realize that something was wrong, so that digitalization became a priority issue on the political agenda,

---

716 As mentioned in WIRTZ, Bernd W.; KUBIN, Pascal R. M. E-Government in Deutschland: Entwicklung, Barrieren und Verbesserungsansätze. *VM Verwaltung & Management*, v. 27, n. 6, p. 285–294, 2021, p. 288–290.

717 MICHALLEK, Stefanie. *Funkgeräte aus den 80ern, Dokumentenversand per Fax: Bundeswehr kämpft mit veralteter Technik*. Business Insider. Available at <https://www.businessinsider.de/politik/bundeswehr-nutzt-alte-technik-enorme-investitionen-seien-noetig/>. Accessed 27 Mar. 2024.

718 OFFERMAN, Theo; VAN DER VEEN, Ailko. How to subsidize contributions to public goods: Does the frog jump out of the boiling water? *European Economic Review*, v. 74, p. 96–108, 2015, p. 97.

featuring prominently in the coalition agreements between the parties that form the governing coalitions in the respective legislatures (*Koalitionsverträge*).[719] The issue of Digital Government appeared somewhat timidly in the *Koalitionsvertrag* of the 17th Legislature (2009-2013), but it already mentions the clear intention to pass the Digital Government Act (EGovG), which was accomplished within the period of the legislature. In the following *Koalitionsvertrag* (2013-2017), the issue of digitalization in general is given even more prominence, and a digital agenda is established, with emphasis on the proposal to institutionally concentrate[720] more coordinating functions between the Federal Government and the states for the effective implementation of measures. In the *Koalitionsvertrag* of the 19th Legislature (2018-2021), a specific section on Digital Administration stands out, notably the intention to strengthen federal cooperation around pilot solutions, through a Digital Government agency working together with existing federal coordination bodies. The agency was never created during the parliamentary term, but *Föderale IT-Kooperation* (FITKO), a legal entity providing executive support for federative coordination, was set up with its own structure, budget, and qualified staff. The agreement also provides for the allocation of 500 million euros to support the fulfillment of the OZG's determinations and targets for the digitization of services. As for the *Koalitionsvertrag* (2021-2025), the topic continued to feature prominently, whether from the point of view of digital administration or digital transformation in general. Highlights include the continued implementation of the OZG, the strengthening of FITKO as a flexible focal point for federal cooperation, and the principle that has become known as *Einer-für-alle* (EfA). In this respect, *Einer-für-alle*, which means "one for all", alluding to

719 CDU; CSU; FDP. *Koalitionsvertrag 2009-2013*. Available at <https://www.nachhaltigkeit.info/media/1272874930php6WwCER.pdf>. Accessed 26 Mar. 2024; CDU; CSU; SPD. *Koalitionsvertrag 2013-2017*. Available at <https://archiv.cdu.de/sites/default/files/media/dokumente/koalitionsvertrag.pdf>. Accessed 26 Mar. 2024; CDU; CSU; SPD. *Koalitionsvertrag 2018-2021*. Available at <https://archiv.cdu.de/system/tdf/media/dokumente/koalitionsvertrag_2018.pdf?file=1>. Accessed 26 Mar. 2024; SPD; BÜNDNIS 90/DIE GRÜNEN; FDP. *Koalitionsvertrag 2021-2025*. Available at <https://www.spd.de/fileadmin/Dokumente/Koalitionsvertrag/Koalitionsvertrag_2021-2025.pdf>. Accessed 26 Mar. 2024.

720 The concentration took place in a body called IT-Planungsrat, as will be discussed below.

D'Artagnan's motto,[721] is a very interesting form of cooperation between federal entities for digitization in the context of the OZG. It envisages solutions developed by one state or municipality at a local level being efficiently generalized to others, so as to gain in scale, including mechanisms for financial compensation and concrete collaboration. In addition to the economic and financial dimension of economies of scale and efficiency, the EfA also represents two important characteristics of experimentalism in public administration. The first is protective, in the sense of creating an environment for controlled risk-taking and the promotion of innovation, with a firewall that protects the rest of the administration from failed attempts, and the second is promotional, with the ability to generalize successful innovations quickly to the rest of government institutions.[722]

In terms of its legal-institutional trajectory, the idea of Digital Government in Germany began to take shape after public organizations began to create homepages on the Internet in the 1990s. This was followed by the improvement of communication through electronic mail and the creation of possibilities for interaction through the first digitalized services, which gradually moved away from being an instrument for automation and maximizing administrative efficiency towards a reorientation of the political-administrative system around new technologies, involving the integration of services and processes.[723]

The initial legal basis for the digital transformation of German public administration was §3 of the *Verwaltungsverfahrensgesetz* (VwVfG), the Administrative Procedure Act, introduced by legislative amendment in August 2002.[724] This amendment enabled and regulated the use of electronic communication in government, such as the transmission of documents and the replacement of physical forms with digital ones, referring to the already existing regulations on digital signatures in general, the *Signaturgesetz* (SigG) of 1997, which in turn is regulated by the *Signaturverordnung* (SigV),

721 BERGER, Ariane. Die Entfesselung von D'Artagnan. *In*: SECKELMANN, Margrit; BRUNZEL, Marco (Orgs.). *Handbuch Onlinezugangsgesetz: Potenziale - Synergien - Herausforderungen*. Berlin, Heidelberg: Springer, 2021, p. 76.

722 See JACOBY, Wade; BEHRENS, Martin. Experimentalism as a tool of economic innovation in Germany. *German Politics and Society*, v. 19, n. 3, p. 1–33, 2001, p. 10.

723 STEMBER, Jürgen; HASENKAMP, Victoria. E-Government in Deutschland: Ein Überblick. *In*: STEMBER, Jürgen *et al* (Orgs.). *Handbuch E-Government: Technikinduzierte Verwaltungsentwicklung*. Wiesbaden: Springer Fachmedien, 2019, p. 32, 24.

724 Drittes Gesetz zur Änderung verwaltungsverfahrensrechtlicher Vorschriften. *Bundesgesetzblatt Jahrgang 2002 Teil I* Nr. 60, 27. August 2002, p. 3322.

which was later replaced by the *Vertrauensdienstegesetz* (VDG). Other laws from this period or the years immediately following are also related to the timeline of Digital Government in Germany, albeit indirectly, such as the *Informationsweiterverwendungsgesetz* (IWG), which dealt with the reuse of information between German federal bodies and was passed to implement Directive 2003/98/EC of the European Parliament and Council, and was later replaced by more comprehensive legislation, the *Datennutzungsgesetz* (DNG). In addition, the *Personalausweisgesetz* (PauswG) introduced the electronic identity document and allowed it to validate a person's identification on the internet in the same way that the physical document does in face-to-face situations. The document mixes physical and digital presentation, and its activation, which was initially optional,[725] became automatic in 2017 with a change in the law.[726] Mention should also be made of the *Informationsfreiheitsgesetz* of 2005, the German Access to Information Act.

However, it was in 2009 that the most significant structuring initiative in German digitalization took place. On that occasion, the concern with coordination between federal entities in Germany's complex federalism was elevated to constitutional status with articles 91c and 91d in the Fundamental (or Basic) Law (*Grundgesetz* - GG). The provisions contained guidelines on cooperation between the Federal Government and the states for the creation and operation of information technology systems and technical security standards, through agreements. Article 91c provided for the establishment of a network by the Federal Government to connect and integrate the networks of the states and the Union, while Article 91d dealt with the possibility of jointly carrying out comparative studies on the performance of their administrations. These changes represented the creation of a structural constitutional framework for developing information technology in the German public sector,[727] as well as a clear message that Germany

725 SCHWEIGHOFER, Erich; HÖTZENDORFER, Walter. Electronic identities – public or private. *International Review of Law, Computers & Technology*, v. 27, n. 1–2, p. 230–239, 2013, p. 232–233.

726 HAOUACHE, Gerold. Die rechtliche Erfassung neuer Technologien zur digitalen Aufgabenerledigung der Verwaltung (E-Government/M-Government). *In*: HARTLEB, Torsten; FISCHER, Jürgen (Orgs.). *Innovative Verwaltung in Forschung und Lehre.* Baden-Baden: Nomos, 2020, p. 53.

727 STEMBER; HASENKAMP, *op. cit.*, p. 35. "a constitutional structural framework for information technology". In the original, "ein verfassungsrechtlicher Strukturrahmen für Informationstechnik".

was henceforth attaching more importance to digitalization than could be inferred from previous initiatives and rules.[728]

As a direct result of the new provisions of the *Grundgesezt* and following the logic of this new constitutional framework for the digitalization of the public sector, the states and the Federal Government signed an agreement/treaty for the creation of the *IT-Planungsrat*,[729] a council aimed at centralizing coordination between the federal entities of initiatives related to the technological modernization of the administration. The body is a key player in the development of Digital Government in Germany, and its operation, powers and structure are set out in detail in the agreement. To provide material support for the Council's activities, an office has been established within the structure of the Ministry of the Interior, financed half by the Federal Government and half by the states in accordance with the "*Königsteiner Schlüssel*", a rule that deals with the proportion of the states' contribution to the joint financing of certain activities. This rule originates from a 1949 agreement (*Königsteiner Staatsabkommen*), made to define the distribution of spending by German scientific and research institutions between the states, and is regularly updated by the *Gemeinsame Wissenschaftskonferenz* (GWK), as well as being used for other purposes, such as the distribution of refugees between locations in Germany. The basic logic is a division of responsibilities based on the economic strength of each state, but the population variable is also included in the calculation.[730]

Before the existence of the *IT-Planungsrat*, there was already an inter-federative cooperation body for information technology issues, the KoopA ADV - *Operationsausschuss Automatisierte Datenverarbeitung Bund/ Länder/ Kommunaler Bereich* (Cooperation Committee for Automated Data Processing in the Federal/State/Municipal Sector), founded in 1970, which established common principles on the use of technology by the public sec-

728 WIRTZ, Bernd W.; KUBIN, Pascal R. M. E-Government in Deutschland: Entwicklung, Barrieren und Verbesserungsansätze. *VM Verwaltung & Management*, v. 27, n. 6, p. 285–294, 2021, p. 286.

729 Gesetz zum Vertrag über die Errichtung des IT-Planungsrats und über die Grundlagen der Zusammenarbeit beim Einsatz der Informationstechnologie in den Verwaltungen von Bund und Ländern - Vertrag zur Ausführung von Artikel 91c GG. *Bundesgesetzblatt Teil I*. n. 26, p. 662, 2010.

730 SCHMANDT, Marco; TIELKES, Constantin; WEINHARDT, Felix. Königsteiner Schlüssel verteilt Gelder und Aufgaben zwischen Bundesländern kaum nach Wirtschaftskraft. *DIW Wochenbericht*, v. 90, n. 18, p. 204–209, 2023.

tor at the various administrative levels.[731] The KoopA ADV had important coordinating merits, especially on issues with sufficient convergence level between the participants. However, because it lacked constitutional backing, it had limitations regarding the (non)binding nature of its decisions, which became more evident and problematic as digitization issues became more politically and budgetary relevant, as well as problems regarding the representation of entities and effective operation.[732] As a reaction to these limitations, an coordination body called *Deutschland-Online* (*Arbeitskreis der E-Government Staatssekretär*innen*) was organized in 2002, a working group of secretaries of states involved in e-government from the Ministry of the Interior which, although not endowed with a constitutional institutionality to have binding decisions, represented a leap in quality in the participation and interaction of states and the Union, in particular by subjecting it to a clearer regime of political direction.[733] Various projects were then dealt with jointly in this new arena of cooperation between the various administrative levels.[734]

In 2010, however, the mentioned *IT-Planungsrat*, an institutionally much more complex figure, constitutionally backed and with a more sophisticated and effective governance structure, replaced both coordination committees.[735] From a legal-institutional point of view, the institution of the *IT-Plannungsrat*, supported legally by the constitutional framework and politically by the government coalition agreements, represented an evolution in the composite character of the actors in the collective bodies for formulating digitalization policies, to the detriment of the preponderance of the individual actors who formed them. As mentioned above in section 1.9.7, composite actors, such as legally constituted decision-making bodies or

731 LÜHR, Henning. Von der Konferenz "Deutschland online" zur föderativen IT-Kooperation – Innovation und Digital Leadership im föderalen Mehrebenensystem in Deutschland. *In*: SECKELMANN, Margrit; BRUNZEL, Marco (Orgs.). *Handbuch Onlinezugangsgesetz: Potenziale - Synergien - Herausforderungen*. Berlin, Heidelberg: Springer, 2021, p. 101.

732 *Ibid.*, p. 102.

733 *Ibid.*

734 SIEGFRIED, Tina. E-government in Germany. *In*: NIXON, Paul G.; KOUTRAKOU, Vassiliki N. (Orgs.). *E-government in Europe*. London: Routledge, 2007, p. 92–93.

735 HUSTEDT, Thurid; TREIN, Philipp. Koordination und Integration im E-Government. *In*: KLENK, Tanja; NULLMEIER, Frank; WEWER, Göttrik (Orgs.). *Handbuch Digitalisierung in Staat und Verwaltung*. Wiesbaden: Springer Fachmedien, 2020, p. 05.

instances, are made up of individual actors who have their own preferences. The institutional improvement represented by the *IT-Plannungsrat* makes the preferences of the composite actor prevail over the preferences of its individual component actors in the institutional order of action, through legal binding based on the constitutional framework. This arrangement, however, does not in itself solve the issue of coordination, especially concerning German municipalities. This ends up being done through prior coordination of these demands by the states, with meetings of mid-level managers in "expert conferences", so that the result of these negotiations at sub-state level is then taken by the respective state representative to the *IT-Plannungsrat.*[736]

A year after the creation of *IT-Plannungsrat*, the *De-Mail-Gesetz*[737] was passed, a law that sought to establish a secure system of official communication and sharing of legal documents between citizens, the government, and companies, through the DE-Mail system, provided by a selection of companies, as a communication platform between citizens and the administration.[738] Considered to be an important step in communications security, despite the fact that encryption is not required,[739] the system is not widely used, and the number of providers offering it is decreasing.[740]

In 2013, following the presentation of a bill by the government, the *Bundestag* and *Bundesrat* approved a national law on Digital Government, the aforementioned *Gesetz zur Förderung der elektronischen Verwaltung* (EGovG), which was an important step towards greater institutionalization of the initiatives that had been conceived up until then. This law has the function of standardizing certain procedures, but it also has a clear promotional character, since it also establishes a series of obligations for the administration to achieve an established agenda. The main material points include the obligation for administrative units to have an electronic access

736 MERGEL, Ines. Digital Transformation of the German State. *In*: KUHLMANN, Sabine *et al* (Orgs.). *Public Administration in Germany*. Cham: Springer International Publishing, 2021, p. 334.

737 Gesetz zur Regelung von De-Mail-Diensten und zur Änderung weiterer Vorschriften. *Bundesgesetzblatt Teil I*. n. 19, p. 666, 2011.

738 ROßNAGEL, Alexander *et al*. De-Mail und Bürgerportale. *Datenschutz und Datensicherheit - DuD*, v. 33, n. 12, p. 728–734, 2009.

739 GERLING, Rainer W. De-Mail und E-Mail made in Germany sind ein konsequenter Schritt. *Datenschutz und Datensicherheit - DuD*, v. 38, n. 2, p. 109–111, 2014, p. 110.

740 *De-Mail: Der Telekom-Ausstieg und die Folgen | heise online*. Available at <https://www.heise.de/news/De-Mail-Der-Telekom-Ausstieg-und-die-Folgen-6194853.html>. Accessed 22 Mar. 2024.

channel, rules for managing digital files, measures to adopt and simplify electronic receipts, the obligation to make digital means of payment available in administrative processes, the adoption of digital official gazettes, and rules on the provision of machine-readable data by the administration (Open Data). In addition to establishing a digital access channel, §3 of the law contains basic transparency and information obligations, such as the duty of each authority to provide information on its functions, address, and contact details. Other important provisions contained in §10 and §11 are, respectively, the explicit duty of the Federal Government, through its IT Council (*Rat der IT-Beauftragten der Bundesregierung* - IT-Rat), to follow the determinations of the *IT-Planungsrat* in terms of interoperability and security, and the provision for joint procedures between the various bodies for the automated processing of personal data, under the terms of Regulation (EU) 2016/679 of the Parliament and of the Council, and the Data Protection Directive 95/46/EG. As a final highlight, mention should be made of the norms on data and information supply requirements, in particular the determination that machine-readable document and data formats should be the standard, which paves the way for the implementation of automated procedures.

The EGovG applies primarily to the federal level of government but also to states and local authorities when they apply federal laws. Administrative activities of the Judiciary are also subject to the law when they are subject to review by administrative courts, excluding civil or criminal sanction procedures. Despite its restricted application to the federal sphere or to services that concern issues involving or representing the Federal Government, the law has had an important guiding function for states (*Länder*) in drawing up their regional Digital Government laws, without preventing them from making different regulations, as is the case with the Bavarian e-Government Act.[741]

In this respect, the publication of different Digital Government laws in each of the German states may seem, at first glance, to be a complicating factor in the uniform implementation of a public policy with a national vocation, and this is certainly a point to consider. However, it can also be an example of how federalism can live up to its experimentalist "voca-

741 BECK, Wolfgang. Aktuelle E-Government-Regelungen in Deutschland, Österreich und der Schweiz. *In*: STEMBER, Jürgen *et al* (Orgs.). *Aktuelle Entwicklungen zum E-Government: Neue Impulse und Orientierungen in der digitalen Transformation der öffentlichen Verwaltung*. Wiesbaden: Springer Fachmedien, 2021, p. 14.

tion" and provide a kind of meta-experimentalism in the case of Digital Government. This is because some of the German states, when approving their own regulations, made use of the instrument of the experimental clause, which is "a legal regulation that authorizes the administration to deviate from certain provisions of the applicable law in order to try out new approaches and gain insights from them".[742] This type of legal construction allows solutions to be tested for a short period of time, without the need for major revisions to the rule as a whole, and naturally incorporated definitively or revised once the learning process is over.[743] This clause was widely used during the Covid-19 pandemic to relax certain formal requirements for orders and services so that they could be provided quickly online.[744] Autonomy and legislative freedom within the framework of federalism have, therefore, created the conditions for local political experimentalism to innovate in legal terms, using a different solution to those brought in or standardized at national level - interestingly, a solution that involves in itself experimentalism in the legal-material sense.

In 2017, in another initiative of great relevance for the improvement of the "constitutional framework" of Digital Government, the *Grundgesetz* was amended again to add paragraph 5 to article 91c, providing for the adoption of a federal law to regulate online access to state and federal administrative services by citizens.[745] This represented a centralization of the competence to regulate access to administrative services not only in federal bodies, but also in state and municipal ones. This change was part of a broader reform to reorganize financial relations between the various federal levels.[746] As a result of the new constitutional provision, the Online Access to Public Services Act, *Onlinezugangsgesetz* (OZG), was passed, along with other measures related to federative coordination on various

742 GEIS, Ralf. Das Onlinezugangsgesetz im Rechtsvergleich. *In*: SECKELMANN, Margrit; BRUNZEL, Marco (Orgs.). *Handbuch Onlinezugangsgesetz: Potenziale - Synergien - Herausforderungen*. Berlin, Heidelberg: Springer, 2021, p. 242. In the original, "...eine gesetzliche Regelung, welche die Verwaltung dazu ermächtigt, bei ihrer Tätigkeit von gewissen Bestimmungen des geltenden Rechts abzuweichen, um neue Vorgehensweisen zu erproben und daraus Erkenntnisse zu gewinnen."

743 *Ibid.*, p. 242.

744 *Ibid.*, p. 243.

745 Gesetz zur Änderung des Grundgesetzes (Artikel 90, 91c, 104b, 104c, 107, 108, 109a, 114, 125c, 143d, 143e, 143f, 143g). *Bundesgesetzblatt Teil I*. n. 47, p. 2347, 2017.

746 STEMBER, Jürgen; HASENKAMP, Victoria. E-Government in Deutschland: Ein Überblick. *In*: STEMBER, Jürgen *et al* (Orgs.). *Handbuch E-Government: Technikinduzierte Verwaltungsentwicklung*. Wiesbaden: Springer Fachmedien, 2019, p. 31–52.

issues, most notably the *Konsens-gesetz*, which instituted a program to develop common software for tax administration throughout the country. The main feature of the OZG is the obligation for the Federal Government, states and municipalities to offer all their public services digitally by the end of 2022, in addition to integrating their public service portals into a single access portal. This is clearly established not only as a target, but as an obligation, although the law does not specify the consequences of non-compliance.

There are also several other provisions in the OZG that complement the scope of the E-Government Act, such as §4, which authorizes the Federal Government, after consulting the *IT-Planungsrat*, to take certain initiatives and make choices about the use of technologies without the need to go through the Legislative Branch (in this case, the Bundestag), which gives the bureaucracy flexibility to adapt to new technologies. The same applies to rules and specifications on IT security, which can now be laid down by non-statutory act (*Rechtsverordnung*) without the need to go through the Legislative (in this case, the *Bundesrat*), and with an obligation for states to comply and refrain from regulating in any other way. In addition, the Ministry of the Interior, after consulting the *IT-Planungsrat*, was authorized to establish the technical standards of portal networks, including state ones, also without the need for the consent of the Legislative Branch. Paragraph 8 of the law is also of great importance in the context of the massive digitization of services, because it establishes rules for the processing of user data, also taking into account different levels of authentication confidence.

In 2019, the *eID-Karte-Gesetz* was passed, creating a digital identity document for non-German EU citizens residing in Germany, with the same digital identification functionalities as the German ID, to facilitate their access to digital public services, especially in the context of the OZG. It is important to note that the roll-out of the OZG has gained momentum since 2020. The government's package of measures drawn up as a reaction to the Covid-19 pandemic provided for an extra 3 billion euros just for the implementation of the OZG, notably to pursue the goal of digitizing the 575 administrative services that are part of the target set by the law.[747]

Another major legislative reform, this time at the infraconstitutional level, was carried out with the approval of the *Registermodernisierungsgesetz* - RegMoG, a set of laws with a series of reform measures regarding public

747 SCHULZ, Sönke E. Schulz: Der elektronische Zugang zur Verwaltung. *Recht Digital*, n. 8, p. 377–383, 2021, p. 378.

information registry systems. The aim is to connect the various types of registers in order to enable the exchange of information between them, so as to guarantee the best provision of public services without any related discontinuities or obstacles, also setting the target that by 2025, at least, the most important registration systems will be connected.[748]

The main item of the reform, however, is the Identification Number Act, *Identifikationsnummerngesetz* (IDNrG), which introduces for the first time a widely used identification number, which serves to assign data to a person and to compare and interact data on the person in different registration systems. The identification number is an extension of the function of the existing tax identification number (*Steueridentifikationsnummer*), which was only introduced in 2007 in Germany.[749] In other words, until 2007 there was no taxpayer unified identification number, which had several consequences for the administration in terms of managing information about citizens and the country itself. It is interesting to note, for example, that after the introduction of the tax identification number, the population registers were cleaned up and many registrations were canceled, which even had an impact on the statistics on the total population in 2009.[750]

The citizen identification number is a direct consequence of the package of measures to react to the Covid-19 pandemic in June 2020, which recognized that the lack of a single comprehensive register hindered the implementation of the OZG, especially concerning the Once Only Principle, i.e., the duty of the administration as a whole to request and register data and information from people and companies only once. Thus, as measure number 40 of the package, it was agreed that a bill would be presented in the following months of that year to modernize the registers and create a more comprehensive identification number.[751] It is interesting to compare this issue with the Brazilian case because, as seen in section 2.2.1.6, the problem was quite different: while in Germany there was no identification

748 BOTTA, Jonas. Der digitale Staat als gläserner Staat. Transparenz als Bedingung verfassungskonformer Registermodernisierung. *In*: KUHLMANN, Simone *et al* (Orgs.). *Transparency or Opacity: A Legal Analysis of the Organization of Information in the Digital World*. Baden-Baden: Nomos, 2023, p. 29.

749 Verordnung zur Vergabe steuerlicher Identifikationsnummern (Steueridentifikationsnummerverordnung - StIdV).

750 EHLING, Manfred; SOMMER, Bettina. Struktur und Entwicklung der Bevölkerung in Deutschland. *In*: BADURA, Bernhard *et al* (Orgs.). *Fehlzeiten-Report 2010: Vielfalt managen: Gesundheit fördern — Potenziale nutzen*. Berlin, Heidelberg: Springer, 2010, p. 57.

751 *Corona-Folgen bekämpfen, Wohlstand sichern, Zukunftsfähigkeit stärken Ergebnis Koalitionsausschuss 3. Juni 2020*. Available at <https://www.bmwk.de/Redaktion/D

number, in Brazil there was a multiplicity of them and for the most varied purposes.

The passing of the Identification Number Act is the subject of extensive controversy in Germany, and its critics accuse the measure of paving the way for a panoptic surveillance society that would allow abuses by the state and violations of fundamental rights.[752] This is a sample of the country's appreciation of personal data protection and the underlying conflict between citizens' privacy, dignity, and self-determination, as well as the scope of administrative activity.[753] But the law has brought in well-designed protection mechanisms based on transparency that mitigate this concern, such as the *Datenschutzcockpit* - a mechanism that allows data subjects to access information about how their data is being used and to exercise rights over this process by influencing its use.[754]

All these legislative initiatives, milestones, and normative acts, and their evolution over time, can be seen as push-factors for the development of Digital Government, as they have the dual function of creating opportunities for the actions of administrators and at the same time establishing binding results.[755] From a legal-institutional perspective, the set of normative texts fulfilled the concomitant functions of enabling and constraining. The measures become more significant, however, as soon as the constitutional framework allows it, such as the improvement of the enabling structures and federative coordination after the 2009 reform (EGovG, *IT-Plannungsrat*, etc.), and the establishment of a promotional law and policy experimentation mechanisms, with coordination and generalization of experiences after the second amendment of the *Grundgesetz* in 2017 (OZG and EfA).

E/Downloads/E/eckpunktepapier-corona-folgen-bekaempfen.pdf?__blob=publicationFile&v=6>. Accessed 25 Mar. 2024, p. 10.

752 BOTTA, *op. cit.*, p. 31.

753 One may cite the paradigmatic judgment of the German Constitutional Court regarding the unconstitutionality, in light of Articles 1 and 2 of the Grundgesetz, of the collection and processing of certain data provided for in legislation on the conduct of a demographic census in 1983. BVerfG, Order of the First Senate of 15 December 1983 - 1 BvR 209/83 -, paras. 1-214.

754 BOSSE, Christian K. *et al.* Auf dem Weg zu gebrauchstauglichen Datenschutzlösungen für digitale Ökosysteme. *Datenschutz und Datensicherheit - DuD*, v. 48, n. 2, p. 82–88, 2024, p. 83.

755 STEMBER, Jürgen; HASENKAMP, Victoria. E-Government in Deutschland: Ein Überblick. *In*: STEMBER, Jürgen *et al* (Orgs.). *Handbuch E-Government: Technikinduzierte Verwaltungsentwicklung.* Wiesbaden: Springer Fachmedien, 2019, p. 36.

Among these milestones are also some regulations under European law, such as Directive 2006/123/EC of the European Parliament and of the Council of December 12, 2006 (on services in the internal market), and the directives on concession contracts and public procurement: Directive 2014/25/EU of the European Parliament and of the Council, Directive 2014/24/EU of the European Parliament and of the Council, and Directive 2014/23/EU of the European Parliament and of the Council. Directive 2006/123/EC established administrative simplification as a common objective of the member states, in particular through the creation of a system of digital procedures and formalities for access to services as a condition for the development of the European internal market. The others dealt with common rules on public procurement, which resulted in the implementation of digital procedures in these processes by Germany in 2016, notably expressed in §97 (5) of the *Wettbewerbsbeschränkungen* (GWB) and §9 (1) of the regulation on the award of public contracts, *Vergabeverordnung* - VgV.[756]

Alongside the regulatory measures that Germany has implemented to promote digitization, there is also a set of actions, programs, and frameworks that serve as pull factors[757] in legal forms with a lower level of institutionalization, such as the *Bundonline Program* (*Program BundOnline* 2005), *E-government* 2.0, the National E-government Strategy of 2010, the Digital Agenda 2014-2017, the *Modellkommune E-Government* of 2013/14 and the *Modellkommune Open Government* of 2017/19.

BundOnline 2005 was a Ministry of the Interior program that represented the Federal Government's assumption of responsibility for the digitization of public administration, and aimed to digitize the processes of various federal administration bodies, which until then had been almost entirely analogue. It resulted in a paradigm shift that fostered the first processes of document digitization and the transfer of tax returns, which placed Germany among the Digital Government highlights in international rankings

756 In the original, "(5) Für das Senden, Empfangen, Weiterleiten und Speichern von Daten in einem Vergabeverfahren verwenden Auftraggeber und Unternehmen grundsätzlich elektronische Mittel nach Maßgabe der aufgrund des §113 erlassenen Verordnungen. / (1) Für das Senden, Empfangen, Weiterleiten und Speichern von Daten in einem Vergabeverfahren verwenden der öffentliche Auftraggeber und die Unternehmen grundsätzlich Geräte und Programme für die elektronische Datenübermittlung (elektronische Mittel)".

757 STEMBER; HASENKAMP, *op. cit.*, p. 36.

at the time.[758] This was followed by the *E-Government* 2.0 program, the aim of which was to start implementing some citizen-oriented digital services, such as the *Kindergeld* application. In the same vein, and shortly after the EGovG law was passed, the *BundesGabinet* published the Digital Agenda 2014-2017, the objectives of which, among others, were to improve internet services and digital security infrastructure, with a view to improving user experience and trust.[759] The legislature, through the *Bundestag*, subsequently set up a Digital Agenda Committee to deal with related issues, and soon afterwards a program called Digital Administration 2020 (*Digitale Verwaltung 2020*) was implemented with the mission of implementing the EgovG.[760]

Finally, mention should be made of *E-Government-Modellkommunen*, which was a project launched at the end of 2016 by the Ministry of the Interior, in conjunction with the main associations of municipalities, aimed at exploring the potential of Digital Government initiatives at municipal level and testing the suitability of the conditions for implementation in the day-to-day running of the administration, seeking to produce and share replicable experiences and solutions.[761] Municipalities from all over Germany were invited to present Digital Government projects in a kind of competition, with the selected projects receiving prizes of between 60,000 and 100,000 euros to contribute to their implementation, which was to be followed by a report to be presented to the Ministry and a workshop to be held for other municipalities, in order to pass on the knowledge acquired in the actual implementation and encourage the sharing of ideas.[762] A similar competition was held shortly afterwards on the theme of Open Government, in which 26 municipalities submitted applications and 9 were selected as model projects.[763] Despite their merits, there are doubts about

758 WIRTZ, Bernd W.; KUBIN, Pascal R. M. E-Government in Deutschland: Entwicklung, Barrieren und Verbesserungsansätze. *VM Verwaltung & Management*, v. 27, n. 6, p. 285–294, 2021, p. 286.

759 *Ibid.*, p. 287.

760 *Ibid.*

761 STEMBER, Jürgen; HESSE, Emanuel. Das Projekt E-Government-Modellkommunen des Bundesministeriums des Innern in Deutschland. *In*: STEMBER, Jürgen; EIXELSBERGER, Wolfgang; SPICHIGER, Andreas (Orgs.). *Wirkungen von E-Government: Impulse für eine wirkungsgesteuerte und technikinduzierte Verwaltungsreform*. Wiesbaden: Springer Fachmedien, 2018, p. 347.

762 *Ibid.*, p. 348–349.

763 WEWER, Göttrik. Open Government als Zukunftsvision für Kommunen?. *In*: ROTERS, Wolfgang; GRÄF, Horst; WOLLMANN, Hellmut (Orgs.). *Zukun-*

the relevance of the results of the projects, and a consistent evaluation of the results at municipal level is not yet fully known.[764]

The set of initiatives, norms, and programs described above involves a multiplicity of stakeholders and individual or composite actors who define the institutional framework of these policies and have their scope of action determined by them. This constellation of actors in government actions on Digital Government in Germany is quite complex. In this sense, the *Normenkontrollrat*, the regulatory control board responsible for assisting the government on issues of reducing bureaucracy and the quality of regulation,[765] when drawing up an evaluation study on the state of digitalization in the country, published a table with all the actors involved in the OZG processes with the suggestive and ironic caption "Many people responsible for digitalization and complex implementation structures - Does it work?".[766] In fact, it can be seen that there is a profusion of structures, instances, entities, bodies and councils in the process of drawing up and implementing public Digital Government policies in Germany, and this is also a result of both the complexity of German federalism itself and the timeline of the evolution of the issue within the state, in which instances of interaction are created at the outset, institutionalizing them over time and multiplying them to the extent that the importance and complexity of the material object of the policy also multiplies.

Among the more than 30 relevant actors listed in the table, not counting the individual state and municipal federative entities themselves, the most important should be highlighted. Firstly, there are the actors in the federal structure, which comprises 16 states (*Länder*) and approximately 11,000 municipalities (*Kommunen*), as well as the Federal Government (*Bund*). As Germany is a federal state with at least three very distinct levels,[767] each with its own degree of autonomy, this naturally poses major political and coordination challenges.

---

ft denken und verantworten: Herausforderungen für Politik, Wissenschaft und Gesellschaft im 21. Jahrhundert. Wiesbaden: Springer Fachmedien, 2020, p. 377.

764 *Ibid.*, p. 388.

765 Gesetz zur Einsetzung eines Nationalen Normenkontrollrates. *Bundesgesetzblatt Teil I.* n. 39, p. 1866, 2006, §1, (2).

766 In the original, "Viele Digitalisierungsverantwortliche und komplexe Umsetzungsstrukturen - Funktioniert das?" *Digitale Verwaltung.* Bundesministerium der Justiz. Available at <https://www.normenkontrollrat.bund.de/Webs/NKR/DE/digitaler-und-moderner-staat/digitale-verwaltung/digitale-verwaltung_node.html>. Accessed 26 Mar. 2024.

767 Or four levels, depending on the criteria.

Specifically at the federal level, two institutions stand out. Firstly, the Ministry of the Interior, which since the early days of e-government in Germany has taken on implementation functions, and today is the main actor at federal level, with competences and attributions explicitly conferred by the related normative texts, especially the OZG, which concentrates on it various coordinating functions and policy directives. There is also the *IT-Rat*, which is a strategic political body responsible for clarifying operational issues of Digital Government at federal level, and is a mandatory consultation body in various situations listed in the OZG, as well as the *CIO Board*, which decides operational issues at federal level.

The *IT-Planungsrat*, which is the political steering body for cooperation between states and the Federal Government on Digital Government issues, stands out at the inter-federal level. As already mentioned, it was first created as a result of the amendment of the *Grundgesetz* in 2009 in the context of the federalism reform "*Föderalismusreform II*" and the signing, in 2010, of an agreement between the states and the Federal Government to implement highly institutionalized federal cooperation, as provided for in the constitutional text, replacing the *KoopA ADV*, which was more precariously institutionalized. The *IT-Planungsrat* now has the support of a body, a legal entity under public law, the *Föderale IT-Kooperation* - FITKO, created to be an executive organizational structure jointly funded by the states and the Federal Government. This executive arm is responsible for managing *IT-Planungsrat* projects and the budget earmarked for digitization. This has allowed the *IT-Plannungsrat* to "focus on its political coordination role among the Länder CIOs and leave technical details and implementation issues to FITKO".[768] The *IT-Planungsrat* is tasked with coordinating cooperation efforts between the states and the Federal Government for the implementation of the OZG, managing Digital Government projects arising from the National Strategy, deciding on issues of interoperability of security systems and technical information technology standards applicable to Digital Government. It is not responsible for operationalizing online services, which is the responsibility of the states, municipalities, and the Federal Government, but only for planning and coordinating the different administrative levels, which are detailed and updated frequently in an ac-

768 MERGEL, Ines. Digital Transformation of the German State. *In*: KUHLMANN, Sabine *et al* (Orgs.). *Public Administration in Germany*. Cham: Springer International Publishing, 2021, p. 335.

tion plan.[769] The body is made up of the Federal Government's *Chief Information Officer*, as well as representatives appointed by each of the states, who are usually the secretaries responsible for information technology.[770]

The Ministry of the Interior maintains a progress monitor for the implementation of the OZG target, a dashboard that also has funding from the European Union's Next Generation program.[771] The site has good availability of data broken down by both state and district on interactive maps, as well as information on which states currently have projects following the *Einer für Alle* principle. Together with the Ministry of the Interior, the Ministry of Finance has always played an important role in the digital transformation issue, and should, therefore, be highlighted as an actor at the federal level. *Digitalrat*, meanwhile, is a council of experts appointed from the private sector to make recommendations to the Federal Government on issues relating to digital transformation and policy.

There is also the *Nationaler Normenkontrollrat*, recently attached to the Ministry of Justice, which, as mentioned above, carries out assessments of regulatory quality and aims to reduce bureaucracy and improve regulation in general, which not only assesses certain processes of digital transformation in the state but also works together with the *IT-Planungsrat* on some projects. The constant assessment of the regulatory burden not only contributes to improving the quality of regulations in general, but also raises awareness among the administration of the potential of digitalization to reduce bureaucracy and improve efficiency.[772] In the 2023 Annual Report, the NKR devotes a chapter to examining Digital Government processes in the public administration, under the motto that there is no debureaucratization without digitalization. It also devotes another chapter to the Digital Check

769 LÜHR, Hans-Henning. IT-Planungsrat. *In*: KLENK, Tanja; NULLMEIER, Frank; WEWER, Göttrik (Orgs.). *Handbuch Digitalisierung in Staat und Verwaltung*. Wiesbaden: Springer Fachmedien Wiesbaden, 2020, p. 5–6.

770 RACKWITZ, Maike; HUSTEDT, Thurid; HAMMERSCHMID, Gerhard. Digital transformation: from hierarchy to network-based collaboration? The case of the German "Online Access Act". *dms – der moderne staat – Zeitschrift für Public Policy, Recht und Management*, v. 14, n. 1, 2021, p. 104.

771 *Dashboard Digitale Verwaltung*. Available at <https://dashboard.ozg-umsetzung.de/>. Accessed 26 Mar. 2024.

772 KÜHN, Hannes. Recht als Gestaltungsinstrument einfacher, digitaler Verwaltungsleistungen – Bessere Rechtsetzung als Voraussetzung vollzugs- und digitaltauglicher Gesetze. *In*: SECKELMANN, Margrit; BRUNZEL, Marco (Orgs.). *Handbuch Onlinezugangsgesetz: Potenziale - Synergien - Herausforderungen*. Berlin, Heidelberg: Springer, 2021, p. 27–28.

activity,[773] i.e., assessing the suitability of new bills for the digital reality so as not to create obstacles or backward steps, as legally mandated in 2022.[774]

The *Bundestag*, the German parliament, is also an actor in the Legislative Branch. It represents the political forces from which the coalitions that support the Federal Government emerge and determine the priority political guidelines for the legislature. It can also set up committees to examine public problems and make recommendations, as was the case with the *Enquete-Kommission Internet und digitale Gesellschaft* on the impact of the internet on society.[775] The *Bundesrat*, on the other hand, represents the states and must pass certain measures for approval, in accordance with the *Grundgesetz*.

There are also other composite actors in the constellation, such as the *Deutscher Städtetag*, *Deutscher Landkreistag* (*Zusammenschluss der Landkreise*) and *Deutscher Städte- und Gemeindebund*. Other actors include networks and think tanks of a public nature, such as *Kompetenzzentrum Öffentliche IT*, *Kommunect digital*, *eGov Campus*, as well as others of a private nature, such as *Initiative D21* and *NEGZ*. They are also joined by private technology and information systems companies that supply products and services to the public administration.

Finally, it should be pointed out that the digitization of the justice system is carried out by a different body, called *eJustice-Rat*, which is linked to the *Justizministerkonferenz* (a body which holds regular meetings of the ministers of justice of the German states). Although it has different goals,

---

773 NKR. *Jahresbericht 2023 des Nationalen Normenkontrollrates*. Berlin: Bundesministerium der Justiz, 2023, p. 36–60.

774 Zweites Gesetz zur Änderung des Gesetzes zur Einsetzung eines Nationalen Normenkontrollrates. *Bundesgesetzblatt Teil I*. n. 20, p. 920, 2022. "(3) The review of the National Regulatory Control Council may extend beyond the review pursuant to § 1 paragraph 3 to include an examination of the extent to which the possibilities of digital implementation of new regulations have been examined (digital check)". In the original, "(3) Die Prüfung des Nationalen Normenkontrollrates kann sich über die Prüfung nach § 1 Absatz 3 hinaus ebenso darauf erstrecken, inwieweit die Möglichkeiten der digitalen Ausführung neuer Regelungen geprüft wurden (Digitalcheck)."

775 HARRAẞ, Sven. Liquid Democracy im Feldversuch – Beteiligungsmöglichkeiten in der Enquete-Kommission "Internet und digitale Gesellschaft" des Deutschen Bundestages. *In*: FRIEDRICHSEN, Mike; KOHN, Roland A. (Orgs.). *Digitale Politikvermittlung: Chancen und Risiken interaktiver Medien*. Wiesbaden: Springer Fachmedien, 2015, p. 486–487.

plans, and actions from *IT-PlanungsRat*, it maintains close cooperation with it.[776]

As can be observed, there has been a respectable evolution over the years in the structures for formulating and implementing policies to promote digital transformation in the German public administration. This evolution has also led to the complexity of the constellation of actors, which can be attributed in part to a phenomenon of path dependence, as explained in section 1.9.8 above. To the extent that technological and legislative advances are observed, and new concrete demands are created for technology and its use in the enjoyment of rights and in state activity, public and private organizations are also created to deal with them, in processes that are sometimes historically cumulative. Given the dependence of the actors on the institutional trajectory, it is up to incremental reforms to redistribute power in the form of legal competences or participation rights, in order to avoid deadlock situations such as the "joint decision trap".[777] This beginning of trends can be seen in the strengthening of the *IT-Plannungsrat* and the creation of FITKO, although the NKR points out that a bigger step is needed.

It is also interesting to note the importance of discourses in this process of evolution, and the role of pre-normative institutions in building bridges between the political impetus of the idea and full institutionalization. Virtually all the institutional advances observed in the trajectory of Germany's Digital Government, whether in terms of organizations, entities, or regulations, have as their foundation the political declarations contained in the coalition agreements (*Koalitionsverträge*), which established the necessary political direction for institutional development. As a result, the presence and weight of the digital transformation on the political horizon has been on the rise since 2009. Illustratively, this can be seen in a quantitative analysis of the texts of the coalition agreements. The term "digital" appears 7 times in the 2009-2013 agreement, 125 times in the 2013-2017 agreement, 298 times in the 2018-2021 agreement, and 226 times in the 2021-2025 agreement. In the latter, the term "Digital State" (*Digitaler Staat*) also appears for the first time, denoting a broader vision of the issue than the pure and simple digitalization of the administration. In the new coalition

776 LÜHR, Hans-Henning. IT-Planungsrat. *In*: KLENK, Tanja; NULLMEIER, Frank; WEWER, Göttrik (Orgs.). *Handbuch Digitalisierung in Staat und Verwaltung*. Wiesbaden: Springer Fachmedien Wiesbaden, 2020, p. 6.

777 See sections 1.9.9 and 4.4.

agreement between the CDU, CSU, and SPD in May 2025, the term "digital" appears 187 times, and the issue seems to permeate all other policies in a cross-cutting manner, consolidating the view of the importance of the topic in the functioning of German society as a whole. The Covid-19 pandemic also influenced this process in terms of accelerating the implementation of certain Digital Government measures, as the abrupt social isolation and remote working created additional and stronger incentives for digitalization. However, these external incentives have, to a certain extent, found actors who were already sensitized[778] to the need for technological modernization of the state.

Today, the topic of digital transformation and digital government is undoubtedly at the forefront of public opinion, the media and political speeches. In 2025, with the rise of the new government, a Ministry for Digitalization (Bundesdigitalminister) was even created, which is especially symbolic of the importance that the issue is having on the country's priority agenda. Whether this means that Germany will finally make the leap to the technological forefront in the state and, in addition to compensating for the digitalization gap, catch up with the pace of technological evolution in the digital market, will certainly depend on many other factors and cultural changes that are difficult to predict. The goal of the OZG, to digitize 525 administrative services at various levels by 2022, has not been met. In addition, multiple problems ingrained in the public administration escape monitoring and superficial evaluations of goals and objectives.

For example, there is an initiative called *Bafög* Digital, which is nothing more than the creation of an online means of applying for student financial aid (*BaföG*), which currently benefits around 630,000 people, almost 80% of them university students.[779] However, despite the fact that the application is made digitally by students, the forms are still printed out one by one in public offices for processing, to the point where, in Hamburg, the administration has hired an extraordinary number of trainees to help exclusively with the printing of applications, to reduce the waiting time for approval.[780] This is not only the case with the *BaföG*, but it seems to be an issue in many newly digitized services.[781]

---

778 See section 1.9.5, final part.

779 *BAföG 2022: Durchschnittlicher Förderbetrag um gut 5 % gestiegen.* Statistisches Bundesamt. Available at <https://www.destatis.de/DE/Presse/Pressemitteilungen/2023/08/PD23_307_214.html>. Accessed 28 Mar. 2024.

However, the progress made by the OZG as a result of clear political signaling and a set of reasonably well-structured government actions in the form of national public policy is not insignificant. Despite skepticism, especially about certain legal conditions for the transformation of the administration (such as the rigidity of the form of procedures, mandatory written form, among others[782]), it can be said, as a result of the analysis made, that the country has created the minimum legal-institutional conditions necessary for the state to adapt more easily to innovation compared to the recent past. Of particular note in this regard is the creation of institutional focal points that have neutralized veto opportunities (enhanced by the federative system), through inter-federative coordination and decision-making mechanisms. In addition to these, there has been the creation of enabling points[783] through the promotion of policy experimentation and learning-by-monitoring environments, such as FITKO, *IT-Planungsrat* and the *Einer für Alle* cooperative work principle, as well as activities such as competitions and workshops.

Moreover, the national policy brought in by the OZG continues to be refined, since on July 24, 2024 the *OZG-Änderungsgesetz* came into force, a law that modified the OZG to intensify the pace of digitization of the German public administration.[784] The amendments recognize the digital transformation as an ongoing process and include provisions such as the abolition of the need to sign forms manually and the use of *DeutschlandID* as the citizen's central account for communication with any government body. There are also measures to implement the Once Only Principle throughout the territory and to standardize systems and protocols.

780 TAGESSCHAU. *Wie das BAföG Studierende in den Wahnsinn treibt | akkurat.* Available at <https://www.youtube.com/watch?v=p3nY-pxOsQY>. Accessed 28 Mar. 2024.

781 PROLL, Eva-Charlotte. Die Umsetzung des OZGs in Deutschland. *In*: STEMBER, Jürgen *et al* (Orgs.). *Aktuelle Entwicklungen zum E-Government: Neue Impulse und Orientierungen in der digitalen Transformation der öffentlichen Verwaltung.* Wiesbaden: Springer Fachmedien, 2021, p. 31, 49.

782 SCHULZ, Sönke E. Rechtlicher Rahmen der Digitalisierung und der Online-Dienste. *In*: LÜHR, Hans-Henning; JABKOWSKI, Roland; SMENTEK, Sabine (Orgs.). *Handbuch Digitale Verwaltung.* Wiesbaden: KSV Medien, 2019, p. 183.

783 See 1.9.9 above.

784 Gesetz zur Änderung des Onlinezugangsgesetzes sowie weiterer Vorschriften zur Digitalisierung der Verwaltung (OZG-Änderungsgesetz - OZGÄndG). *Bundesgesetzblatt Teil I.* n. 245, 2024.

The legal-institutional scenario for innovation and self-adaptation, which before 2009 tended to represent a more rigid field of possibilities, has become more flexible with the approval of constitutional reforms, rules, and improved competences and decision-making processes on public policy.[785] Thus, the greater or lesser set of social and economic stimuli and incentives to which they are politically subject, in conjunction with cultural tradition and the protection of individual rights, will dictate the pace of future changes, which, however, given the slow - but solidly developed - legal-institutional bases, are capable of being produced consistently, at greater or lesser speed.

3.3 Chapter conclusion

In the European Union, the digital transformation of society and the state has gained political priority status as a way of guaranteeing the Union's integration and cohesion, as well as representing a path for the continent's geopolitical positioning in the face of global competitiveness challenges. Characteristics of the legal-institutional environment in relation to EU competences mean that pre-normative institutional forms, such as strategies and declarations, are preferably used as the primary means of driving the development of Digital Government at national level. The commitment of the EU institutions to the discourse of digitalization and the modernization of Europe, however, ensures that the strategies and declarations are effective by concretely mobilizing actors for their implementation and financial resources for their funding, resulting in concrete programs and mechanisms for benchmarking and monitoring results. Regardless of whether or not this model is sufficient to promote the modernization of public administrations, the analysis clearly shows the importance of political direction and discourse in the drafting and implementation of policies, as well as the repercussions of this prioritization of the agenda on the economic and financial dimension, which is essential for the implementation of any initiative.

The investigation into the German scenario, on the other hand, despite the situation of backwardness and all the barriers that exist in German society to hinder a faster process of digital transformation of the state, shows an institutional model that was built incrementally and in an excessively re-

785 For the various scenarios, see Figure 1.

sponsive manner, but which today is a reasonably robust legal-institutional arrangement with the potential to deal with the next stages of technological modernization of the administration at a higher level. The logic of coordination, represented mainly by the efforts to implement the OZG jointly with the Federal Government and the States and Municipalities, may not yet have produced the desired results, but it is innovating in that it seeks to rescue the experimentalist vocation of federalism with measures such as *Einer für Alle*. Also essential in this process of incremental evolution of German institutions has been the building of political consensus around the importance of Digital Government, represented by the increasing reproduction of the theme in the coalition agreements of legislatures formed by different parties, which gives the coordinative discourse the necessary strength to break down the political and cultural resistance of the administration and also guarantee resources to finance the process. The complexity of the constellation of actors involved, which seems to stem from the institutional trajectory of the Digital Government in a path dependence process, is pointed out as an obstacle, but the strengthening of some of them by the distribution of competences, made by the sequence of reforms and new normative texts, could neutralize a large part of these effects.

When we compare the cases of Europe and Germany with Brazil, we get some insights that can be explored in greater depth as a prognosis for the next chapter. Europe, in the context of the European Union project and as a factor of internal cohesion and the region's geopolitical positioning in the world, has adopted integration development policies with a clear discourse and political direction around the importance of digitalization and the modernization of the state in general. This goes beyond the mere pursuit of economic efficiency and is part, especially after *NextGeneration*, of a broad economic recovery project based on sustainability and the affirmation of democratic values. Within the limits of its competences, the promotion of Digital Government in the European Union, although it also suffers from problems of overlap and fragmentation, highlights the role of strategies as pre-normative institutional declarations that bridge the gap between the political guideline and the concrete elaboration of programs. The process also provides an institutional framework that in itself encourages the national policies of member states to directly promote digital transformation in their administrations.

In the case of Brazil, in the absence of a structure that institutionally incorporates the function of affirming and disseminating the discourse and the idea, the Digital Government agenda is subject to the initiatives of the state bureaucracy itself or to exogenous political impulses, such as the initiative for the Digital Government Law, which had low participation from the Executive in its drafting, as well as little concrete interest from the government in its approval.[786] And the product of these impulses also tends to suffer from consequent limitations, such as the inability of the proposed policies to transcend the spheres of the proposing entities and, in particular, to address the challenges presented by the federal structure.

In this regard, it is worth highlighting the institutional trajectory of Digital Government in Germany and how, over time, it has evolved towards a structure of (almost) full institutionalization aimed at resolving the federal issue. It is marked by a clearly identifiable flow from political concertation around an agenda, through the development of a constitutional framework to the creation of the basis for a more elaborate mid-level legal-institutional arrangement. Notably, the approval of amendments to the Basic Law both enabled and encouraged the creation of coordinating bodies across federal levels, alongside the passage of the OZG law, which, despite being less comprehensive than desired, represents an important and consistent step of a distinctly promotional nature. To some extent, the four types of public policy coordination described by Carlos Toledo[787], mentioned in section 1.7, can be observed here. The "negotiated policy" occurred through coalition agreements, the "concentrated policy" through the amendment of the *Grundgesetz*, the "regulatory policy" with the approval of the OZG, and the "promotional policy" through national and European Union funding programs. It is noteworthy that the simultaneous adoption of these forms of coordination ended up compensating for the risks of each other, with negotiation mitigating the risks of political blockage and federative conflicts, and the regulatory and concentrated policies mitigating the risk of low adherence and low effectiveness.

In Brazil, on the other hand, as we saw in the previous chapter, the semi-institutionalization of digital government makes it impossible to coordinate effectively between the federal levels and create a binding and consistent national policy. In this case, it wouldn't require a constitutional

786 The Digital Government Bill was, at a certain point, included in a list of priority projects by the Ministry of Economy during the legislative process, mainly due to its potential to accelerate the debureaucratization policies prioritized by the government at the time. However, this had no practical effects and did not result in any significant government action to improve the text.

787 TOLEDO, Carlos José Teixeira de. *Políticas Públicas e Valorização do Professor da Educação Básica.* Belo Horizonte, MG: Fórum, 2022, p. 246.

amendment (although that could be useful) but rather infraconstitutional arrangements that could involve states and municipalities more directly, especially through the technique of encouragement and spaces for interaction that would enhance the experimental vocation of federalism.[788]

It is true, however, that certain arrangements favor this type of dynamic, as can be seen in the case of the Brazilian electronic judicial process. The National Council of Justice, created by constitutional reform, has become a decisive player in achieving the current results of digitalization. This can be seen from its work with Congress to properly format and pass a regulatory framework for the digitization of judicial proceedings, to its day-to-day function of directly regulating the use of innovations in information technology by the courts. In this regard, it is particularly important to highlight the CNJ's role in encouraging experimentation with technological innovations in the courts of each federative entity, quickly identifying success stories and generalizing them to the entire judicial system, gaining scale.

The case of electronic elections, in turn, demonstrates that deep and rapid transformations based on technology are also possible in the Brazilian public sector, including in sensitive areas involving fundamental rights and the foundations of the democratic rule of law. This happens under certain institutional conditions that allow for a confluence between political initiative, the idea coming from the bureaucracy staff, and an environment conducive to experimentation, which quickly transformed the experiment into policy, preserving fundamental rights and increasing the quality of Brazilian democracy.

When we look at the Digital Government, we see a similar dynamic at the beginning, but the differences in terms of the autonomy and institutional strength of the policy-making bodies (the SLTI and, above all, the CEGE) did not guarantee sufficient endogenous impulses so that the continuation of the policies could continue to accelerate. It is true that the challenges of Digital Government are greater than those of electronic elections, especially due to infrastructure issues, digital illiteracy, and digital exclusion, but this would be all the more reason for a permanent and continuous structure for formulating national policies to be established and strengthened.

In this regard, when analyzing the case of the Internet Steering Committee, for example, one can see how this continuous and growing role of a

788 As there are no structured forms of concentrated and regulatory coordination, but only those dependent on pacts and agreements, the risks of low adherence and effectiveness become greater.

policy formulating and evaluating body produces satisfactory results, capable of transcending the mere passive management of the Brazilian Internet to also represent a force of influence not only in national legislation and regulations, but also in the debate on global Internet governance. It is worth highlighting the arrangement's ability to circumvent the path dependency of information technology in Brazil, breaking with the statist and protectionist legacies of a closed market, whose digital infrastructure policies still followed a centralized logic from the time of the military regime. Experience also shows that high-level formal legal institutionalization is not essential for an effective arrangement (although it can be useful), as long as the institutional configuration, even if formally precarious, adequately incorporates the balance of forces and interests of society around the issue. A similar path could have been taken by the CEGE in relation to Digital Government, which, however, ended up being abolished and incorporated into the structure of the federal public administration.

The national and international experiences examined, therefore, offer relevant insights for developing solutions for the Brazilian Digital Government. In the following chapter, these insights will be contextualized in a broader scenario of state institutions, in which Digital Government assumes a more ambitious role, namely that of enabling dynamic state capabilities for the consolidation of the welfare state in Brazil.

4 Digital Government as an expression of the welfare state in Brazil

This chapter deals with the subject of Digital Government in the context of the Brazilian welfare state, as a way of achieving the necessary capacities to face the challenges inherent to it. Firstly, the welfare state and its manifestation in the Brazilian reality will be characterized, followed by the concept of the digital welfare state. It ends by analyzing four key aspects for promoting a welfare state with dynamic capabilities in Brazil, emphasizing the role of political direction, coordination, an institutional environment conducive to state innovation, and new ways of involving citizens in the provision of public services through the use of information technology. In this process, the insights provided by the findings of the previous chapters are used to enable reflection on the conditions necessary for the full development of digitalization in the Brazilian state in order to meet its general objectives and achieve democracy beyond simple optimization or its purely instrumental use.

4.1 The welfare state and the Brazilian situation

The state is the result of historical processes, which include major events such as revolutions, evolutionary leaps in ideas, and their expression in rights.[789] The diachronic analysis of the state and its configurations, therefore, links parallel dimensions, such as the historical events themselves and their motivations, the emerging ideas that make up the political *Zeitgeist,* and the normative dimension translated into legal "documents", major political-normative milestones with relevant consequences.[790] This three-dimensional view is also a way of understanding the concept, configuration, and current challenges of the welfare state, whether in a global context or in the specific case of Brazil, which has relevant idiosyncrasies, as well as from

789 BRESSER-PEREIRA, Luiz Carlos. *Democracy and Public Management Reform: Building the Republican State.* Oxford: Oxford University Press, 2004, p. 14.

790 In this sense and as an example, in several combined passages JELLINEK, Georg. *Allgemeine Staatslehre.* Berlin, Heidelberg: Springer Berlin Heidelberg, 1929, p. 217, 239, 330, 347, 464.

the point of view of a reconfiguration of the welfare state in the future and the role of technology in this process.[791]

The welfare state can be defined as "the orientation of state activities towards the creation of social rights to provide security against social risks in the context of a capitalist market economy"[792] from a functional perspective, or, from an institutional perspective, as "the institutional outcome of the assumption by a society of legal and therefore formal and explicit responsibility for the basic well-being of all of its members".[793] These characteristics are also the result of historical processes that have allowed - or put pressure on - the creation of social rights and their entry onto political agendas, being expressed through the positivization of rights in normative instruments, usually with a high degree of institutionality.

Although the terms "social state" and "welfare state"[794] emerged after the Second World War, the building blocks of this idea have their roots in debates on the social question in the previous century, motivated especially by the efforts of the working class to socialize the means of production.[795] This took place in a context in which old forms of social protection, such as feudal relations, guilds, and charitable organizations, had fallen into decay with the phenomena of industrialization and urbanization.[796] At the end of the 19th century, innovative measures in terms of social policies emerged in

---

791 This relationship constitutes a complex historical and social context with various nuances. Therefore, they should not be viewed as processes of cause and effect or static correlations. In this regard, see the critical comments by STROMBERG, Roland N. The Philosophes and the French Revolution: Reflections on Some Recent Research. *The History Teacher*, v. 21, n. 3, p. 321–339, 1988; e BAUMGOLD, Deborah. Hobbes's and Locke's Contract Theories: Political not Metaphysical. *Critical Review of International Social and Political Philosophy*, v. 8, n. 3, p. 289–308, 2005.

792 NULLMEIER, Frank. Sozialstaat. *In*: ANDERSEN, Uwe *et al* (Orgs.). *Handwörterbuch des politischen Systems der Bundesrepublik Deutschland*. Wiesbaden: Springer Fachmedien, 2021, p. 836. In the original, "die Ausrichtung staatlicher Aktivitäten auf die Schaffung sozialer Rechte zur Sicherung gegen soziale Risiken im Rahmen einer kapitalistischen Marktwirtschaft." .

793 HARRY, Girvetz. Welfare State. *In*: SILLS, David (Org.). *International encyclopedia of the social sciences*. New York: Macmillan, 1968, v. 16, p. 512.

794 On the different terms referring to the Welfare State, their uses and contexts since the 19th century, see the introductory chapter of RITTER, Gerhard A. *Der Sozialstaat: Entstehung und Entwicklung im internationalen Vergleich*. 3. ed. München: Oldenbourg Verlag, 2010, p. 1–29. In this work, the term "Welfare State" will preferably be used as a synonym for Social State, Sozialstaat and État-providence.

795 NULLMEIER, *op. cit.*, p. 837.

796 BÉLAND, Daniel *et al* (Orgs.). *The Oxford Handbook of the Welfare State*. 2. ed. Oxford: Oxford University Press, 2021, p. 2.

various places as a response by "the powers that be" to social pressures and destabilizing threats. In this sense, we can mention the social security legislation promoted in the 1880s by Bismarck in Germany, which, despite being a top-down measure in the context of an authoritarian imperial regime, was also motivated by the need to ensure workers' loyalty to the state, in a context in which protests and freedoms of organization and expression were significantly repressed.[797] From this tradition stems the fact that the term "welfare state" is also used not only to designate a particular model of institution, but also as a synonym for the set of social policies practiced in a given country.[798]

The welfare state is a dynamic concept in itself, not a static end, insofar as people's perception of "welfare" changes and adapts to new conditions. As a dynamic reality, it also relies on a set of broad procedural conditions for its update, especially the general rules that characterize the rule of law and constitutional democracy.[799] Although it originally developed under the aegis of authoritarian regimes (Bismarck's Germany, Von Taaffe's Austria and Napoleon III's France, for example), which had more power to impose taxes and other interventions on the population and elites compared to more democratic countries,[800] various studies point to a direct correlation between the expansion of democratic rights and the development of social policies.[801]

Recent experiences in countries of democratic erosion such as Hungary and Turkey, where the welfare state has undergone transformations due to the autocratic tendency of governments, which at the same time have preserved or expanded social policies in some areas,[802] add complexity to this notion, in addition, of course, to what is being observed today in

---

797 KUHNLE, Stein; SANDER, Anne. The Emergence of The Western Welfare State. *In*: BÉLAND, Daniel *et al* (Orgs.). *The Oxford Handbook of the Welfare State*. 2. ed. Oxford: Oxford University Press, 2021, p. 77.

798 As can be seen in comparative studies such as ALBER, Jens. Der deutsche Sozialstaat im Licht international vergleichender Daten. *Leviathan*, v. 26, n. 2, p. 199–227, 1998.

799 ZACHER, Hans F. Der Sozialstaat als Prozeß. *Zeitschrift für die gesamte Staatswissenschaft*, v. 134, n. 1, p. 15–36, 1978, p. 17, 32.

800 ESPING-ANDERSEN, Gøsta. *The three worlds of welfare capitalism*. Reprint. Cambridge: Polity Press, 2009, p. 15.

801 SKOCPOL, Theda; AMENTA, Edwin. States and Social Policies. *Annual Review of Sociology*, v. 12, p. 131–157, 1986, p. 136–139.

802 SZIKRA, Dorottya; ÖKTEM, Kerem Gabriel. An illiberal welfare state emerging? Welfare efforts and trajectories under democratic backsliding in Hungary and Turkey. *Journal of European Social Policy*, v. 33, n. 2, p. 201–215, 2023, p. 212.

China. Thus, the qualitative classification into three types of welfare state regimes, which is quite widespread in the social sciences - namely, liberals, social democrats, and conservatives[803] - could possibly be expanded to explain new phenomena, or inspire new classifications, such as the one that separates welfare state regimes into institutional, neoliberal, populist and residual.[804]

The welfare state presents itself legally as the institutionalization of a large part of second generation human rights, which are those that require "positive action by the state to be implemented".[805] In concrete terms, we can cite the classic examples of social security and labor legislation. However, the idea of a social law/right transcends the question of the material content of the norms, and is not limited to one or other autonomous field, because it is a different way of structuring rights of all kinds compared to the previous logic; in other words, it means the socialization of the law itself.[806]

Each country, as well as falling into different types of welfare state, also has its own unique trajectory around these configurations, depending on historical events and the way in which conflicting social situations are dealt with. Brazil is part of a particular group of countries referred to as "laggard welfare states", in which the shape of the welfare state took on sharper contours after the 1970s and especially after the processes of redemocratization.[807]

The Brazilian welfare state began to develop most notably during the Vargas era in the 1930s, with the establishment of the primary structures of social security and labor legislation, followed by their expansion to rural workers in the 1960s and reaching its apex after the 1988 Constitution, which introduced the universal and free Unified Health System, as well as

---

803 See ESPING-ANDERSEN, *op. cit.*

804 For an explanation and classification of various nations into these four categories, see YÖRÜK, Erdem; ÖKER, İbrahim; TAFOYA, Gabriela Ramalho. The four global worlds of welfare capitalism: Institutional, neoliberal, populist and residual welfare state regimes. *Journal of European Social Policy*, v. 32, n. 2, p. 119–134, 2022, p. 124–125.

805 VASAK, Karel. A 30-year struggle; the sustained efforts to give force of law to the Universal Declaration of Human Rights. *The Unesco Courier*, p. 29–32, 1977, p. 29.

806 EWALD, François. A Concept of Social Law. *In*: TEUBNER, Gunther (Org.). *Dilemmas of Law in the Welfare State.* Berlin, New York: De Gruyter, 2011, p. 41.

807 BUCCI, Maria Paula Dallari. Estado social: uma sistematização para pensar a reconstrução. *Revista de Ciências do Estado*, v. 8, n. 1, p. 1–31, 2023, p. 8.

a series of other social policies.[808] It is interesting to note that this more robust and complete legal-institutional conception of the Brazilian welfare state coincides with the opposite movement in Europe and the United States, where the crisis of the welfare state had already begun a few years earlier. It also coincides with a particularly unfavorable economic climate for the realization of these rights in Brazil and for the implementation and consolidation of these institutions recently created by the Constitution. In other words, it consolidates itself and at the same time faces the challenge of adaptation and reform.

Lévi-Strauss described the transformation of the environments of the New World as a passage from youth to decrepitude without reaching maturity. He was referring in particular to the development of cities, which had to be renovated as quickly as they appeared. He was impressed by the idea of the lack of consolidation of things, in an early decline of the new, which he referred to as "going from barbarism to decadence, without passing through civilization".[809] Today's Brazil still carries some of this reality, due to the way and time in which it has gone through the various modernization processes: from late industrialization and, at the same time, prematurely atrophied, to population aging at a faster rate than the generation of wealth provided by the demographic window of population youth, to the precariousness of labor relations without there first being an adequate average level of income and conditions. With regard to the welfare state, something similar is happening: it is consolidating itself and already needs to be reformed, and it is declining without having properly matured. The pressures for a liberalizing reform of the state influenced the implementation of the newly-constitutionalized social policies, sometimes frustrating their objectives.[810] On the other hand, these same pressures led to the search for efficiency in state activities and resulted in the managerial reform of the 1990s, which, despite being labeled neoliberal, provided the basis for public services of a strongly social nature to be consolidated,[811] such as the Unified Health System - SUS itself.

---

808 *Ibid.*, p. 25.

809 LÉVI-STRAUSS, Claude. *Tristes tropiques.* Paris: Librairie Plon, 1955, p. 105. In the original, "Um esprit malicieux a défini l'Amérique comme um pays qui a passé de la barbárie à la décadence sans connaître la civilisation."

810 GOMES, Fábio Guedes. Conflito social e welfare state: Estado e desenvolvimento social no Brasil. *Revista de Administração Pública*, v. 40, p. 201–234, 2006, p. 229.

811 BRESSER-PEREIRA, Luiz Carlos. Reforma gerencial e legitimação do estado social. *Revista de Administração Pública*, v. 51, p. 147–156, 2017, p. 151, 152.

Mangabeira Unger argues that the current shape of the state in Brazil is influenced by two traditions in crisis. The first derives from the "proto-democratic" liberal constitutionalism that emerged after US independence,[812] i.e., it is the direct influence of the Madisonian model of organizing and distributing powers[813] on the way Brazilian macro-institutions have been shaped. This tradition is characterized by the fragmentation of power as a form of control (a liberal principle) and mechanisms for slowing down and limiting the potential of politics through constitutional obstacles that inhibit major changes (a conservative principle).[814] These are institutions designed to prevent two distinct types of tyranny, one representing the abuse of power by majority factions over minorities, and the other representing the abuse of power by rulers over the ruled.[815] Over time, the model has been eroded, degenerating into practices that discourage high levels of citizen mobilization in different moments of crisis, such as the configuration of electoral rules and political participation in general, which are insufficient to stimulate change to a satisfactory degree.[816]

The second tradition mentioned by Unger is the late assimilation of Weimar constitutional doctrines.[817] It dates back to the advent of a syntax of constitutionally positive rights, like the first two social constitutions in history,[818] the Weimar Constitution of 1919 in Germany and the Mexican Constitution of 1917. They represent two of the most significant pieces of legislation of this kind among a series of constitutions promulgated in the wake of the First World War.[819] This tradition in Brazil is characterized by the "constitutionalization of social or redistributive expectations", in the form of promises of economic and social rights, without, however, a model

812 UNGER, Roberto Mangabeira. A constituição do experimentalismo democrático. *Revista de Direito Administrativo*, v. 257, p. 57–72, 2011, p. 59.

813 ROSENBLOOM, David H. Public Administration's Legal Dimensions: Three Models. *In*: MENZEL, Donalf C.; WHITE, Harvey L. (Orgs.). *The State of Public Administration: Issues, Challenges and Opportunities.* London and New York: Routledge, 2015, p. 372.

814 UNGER, *op. cit.*, p. 63.

815 CAREY, George W. Separation of Powers and the Madisonian Model: A Reply to the Critics. *American Political Science Review*, v. 72, n. 1, p. 151–164, 1978, p. 154–155.

816 UNGER, *op. cit.*, p. 63.

817 *Ibid.*

818 VIANELLO, Lorenzo Córdova. Liberalismo, democracia, neoliberalismo e ingobernabilidad. *Revista Mexicana de Sociología*, v. 58, n. 4, p. 3–35, 1996, p. 18.

819 MURRAY, Thomas. Socio-Economic Rights Versus Social Revolution? Constitution Making in Germany, Mexico and Ireland, 1917–1923. *Social and Legal Studies*, v. 24, n. 4, p. 487–508, 2015.

of economic order that would ensure the concrete realization of such expectations.[820] This dynamic resulted from a process in which more radical forces in favor of a profound reorganization of the factors of production stopped doing so in exchange for the conservative institutionalization of social expectations in the form of social democracy, whose institutional timidity does not ensure the vaunted results, due to the lack of conditions for new and more radical forms of strategic association between the state and the private productive sector to thrive. According to Unger, this scenario tends to result in a "de-energized" democracy, disfavoring popular engagement and relegating public choices to technical expertise, dissolving the political debate into vague issues with less impact.[821] Flawed practices keep citizens at a low level of mobilization, while rigid institutional arrangements slow down politics through "impasse-favoring or consensus-requiring".[822]

On the one hand, Unger's criticism makes sense in terms of a state of affairs that falls short of what it could be, with a social situation that does not reflect the amount of wealth and material prosperity created by the accumulation of capital in the market economy, and a limitation of individual potential for self-realization and full development, as well as one of the worst social inequalities in the world.[823] No wonder the term "brazilianization" has already been coined to refer to the precariousness of legal and social relations (such as work and social security) in some advanced European countries, in the context of a risk society.[824] In this sense, it can also be said that the criticism of the traditions of the welfare state applies not only to Brazil but also to all modern democracies and is one of the reasons why they are in crisis and under threat from far-right political movements with "anti-system" mottos.

On the other hand, Unger's critique, while inspiring, fails to move beyond the limits of abstraction to propose concrete ways of overcoming and transforming. Furthermore, there is always the danger that this kind

---

820 UNGER, *op. cit.*, p. 64. In the original, "constitucionalização das expectativas sociais ou redistributivas".

821 UNGER, Roberto Mangabeira. *What Should Legal Analysis Become?* London: Verso, 1996, p. 10.

822 *Ibid.*, p. 165.

823 ASSOUAD, Lydia; CHANCEL, Lucas; MORGAN, Marc. Extreme Inequality: Evidence from Brazil, India, the Middle East, and South Africa. *AEA Papers and Proceedings*, v. 108, p. 119–123, 2018.

824 BECK, Ulrich. *Schöne neue Arbeitswelt.* Berlin: Suhrkamp, 2007, p. 28–37.

of iconoclastic vision[825] will serve as a subterfuge for a damaging attack on the institutions that guarantee rights and maintain order and security, in order to weaken democracy and enable the autocratic domination of certain groups of people and interests that are not legitimized by the processes characteristic of the rule of law. It is also possible to lose sight of or underestimate the importance of essential advances made in recent decades, such as the succession of successful elections, or the creation of public policy systems like SUS and SUAS[826], among others. While it is likely that there are structural obstacles to the full realization of the democratic project in Brazil through its welfare state, it also seems right to acknowledge the progress that this structure has made possible over time,[827] albeit along sometimes incongruous and precarious paths, and even at times of economic crisis.[828]

Therefore, the Brazilian welfare state is today presented with all the contradictions arising from its historical process and suffering political pressures as a result of a more unstable scenario at the political level following the crisis in the second Dilma Rousseff government and the rise of the far right to power from 2018 to 2022, and at the economic level, especially due to the Covid-19 pandemic and its impact on the productive and revenue structure. This imposes a double challenge on the reality of this welfare state: its reconstruction,[829] at the same time as its effective affirmation. In both aspects, digitalization plays an important role, both in terms of improving the efficiency of state provision, paving the way for its consolidation, and because it represents possibilities for affirming special dynamic capabilities that will alter its very conception in the future. The establishment of a digital welfare state in Brazil, in a broad sense that

825 AMATO, Lucas Fucci. Justiça Social e Instituições: a visão de Unger comparada ao Liberalismo Igualitário e à Teoria Crítica. *Revista Estudos Políticos*, v. 8, n. 16, p. 90–114, 2019, p. 103.

826 Unified Social Assistance System.

827 See WORLD BANK. *Brazil: Systematic Country Diagnostic.* Washington DC: World Bank Group, 2016.

828 In this sense, it is argued that Brazil managed, at least at a certain historical moment at the beginning of the century, to invert the postulates of the "Kuznets curve", according to which the increase in inequality necessarily precedes economic development and is resolved after its consolidation. FALCÃO, Tiago; COSTA, Patricia Vieira da. Advances and challenges for social development in Brazil. *In*: CASTRO, Ana Célia; FILGUEIRAS, Fernando (Orgs.). *The State in the 21th century.* Brasília: Enap, 2018, p. 334.

829 BUCCI, Maria Paula Dallari. Estado social: uma sistematização para pensar a reconstrução. *Revista de Ciências do Estado*, v. 8, n. 1, p. 1–31, 2023, p. 24.

involves not only the provision of digital services and the optimization of the administration but also the effective rapprochement between the population and governments, with maximum potential for the enjoyment of rights, could be one of the ways to energize Brazilian democracy, in the sense of building a development model based on expanding opportunities to learn, work and produce,[830] in addition to other initiatives and reforms that deal with deeper historical and structural issues.

4.2 Digital welfare state as a state of dynamic capabilities

The state is permanently at the center of an effort to reconcile the idea of established order and change. Understanding the state apparatus as a dynamic whole subject to a system of tensions, and at the same time as an order that maintains the results already achieved, is essential to achieving the goals of freedom and social justice.[831] The state is updated as social (and technological) changes occur, taking on different features throughout history and in the most diverse contexts.

In the wake of the permanent technological evolution that society is going through, what has been called the fourth industrial revolution stands out.[832] The first industrial revolution took place between the second half of the 18th century and the beginning of the 19th century, and consisted of the introduction of mechanized manufacturing systems that used the motive power of water and steam. The second industrial revolution, in the second half of the 19th century, can be represented by mass production driven by the use of electricity. The third revolution, or digital revolution, began in the middle of the last century and introduced automation and microelectronics into manufacturing processes. In general, it encompasses the computer communication technology that we are used to on a daily

830 UNGER, Roberto Mangabeira. A constituição do experimentalismo democrático. *Revista de Direito Administrativo*, v. 257, p. 57–72, 2011, p. 58.

831 DALLARI, Dalmo. *Elementos de Teoria Geral do Estado*. 32. ed. São Paulo: Saraiva, 2013, p. 139.

832 According to PARK, Sang Chul. The Fourth Industrial Revolution and implications for innovative cluster policies. *AI and Society*, v. 33, n. 3, p. 433–445, 2018 the term Industry 4.0, used to refer to the applications of the technologies being developed in the fourth industrial revolution, became known after the 2011 Hannover technology fair, as part of a German government project for high-tech industrial development strategies for 2020.

basis. The fourth industrial revolution brings together innovations such as artificial intelligence, big data, the internet of things, and robotics.[833]

Technology has a substantial impact on the way nations produce and also on the way individuals interact, which in turn alters economic and social relations and puts pressure on the state to change the way it exercises power. The first two phases of industrialization are directly linked to the overcoming of the liberal state model and the pressure to adopt social protection instruments, in the form of rights and apparatuses guaranteeing rights, corresponding to the demands forged in the class struggle characteristic of industrial society. The growth of industrial cities and the precarious situation of the working masses were also succeeded by new laws and changes in the relationship between the population and governments.[834] The third industrial revolution, in turn, laid the foundations for a process of accelerated globalization, with trends towards globally considered problems and solutions and the resulting polycentrism in decision-making leading to further changes in the expression of public power, with its more pronounced insertion into the international order and the emergence of legal constructions with a global vocation, such as the right to a sustainable environment. The fourth industrial revolution brings the idea of a digital society based on data and process automation, with its correspondence in the public sector in the form of a Digital Government on the same basis.

The digital welfare state can refer to two different concepts, one narrower and the other broader. One refers to the digitalization of a country's set of social services and the activities that characterize these services, from an operational perspective. The other refers to the variable of digitalization introduced into the concept of the welfare state as a form of capitalist government that has mechanisms to mitigate crises arising from the processes of capital accumulation.[835] Both understandings are often the subject of skepticism as to their effects on citizens' sphere of rights, whether they are considered in the narrower sense of beneficiaries of social programs or in the idea of citizenship as the relationship between a people and their state, and their sphere of rights in general.

833 XU, Li Da; XU, Eric L.; LI, Ling. Industry 4.0: State of the art and future trends. *International Journal of Production Research*, v. 56, n. 8, p. 2941–2962, 2018.

834 JERATH, Kavita S. *Science, Technology and Modernity: An Interdisciplinary Approach*. Cham: Springer International Publishing, 2021, p. 120.

835 COLLINGTON, Rosie. Disrupting the Welfare State? Digitalisation and the Retrenchment of Public Sector Capacity. *New Political Economy*, v. 27, n. 2, p. 312–328, 2022, p. 313, also citing Claus Offe and Esping-Andersen.

Skepticism arises both in relation to the co-optation of state structures by the market, due to models for contracting and implementing digital solutions, and in relation to the abuse of power by the state and its authorities, due to de facto superpowers caused by the large-scale control and processing of personal data. Existing technologies, such as those that enable government action based on the analysis of large amounts of data, bring opportunities for concrete improvements in human life in the context of a welfare state, and are capable, among other things, of radically transforming transport and healthcare, increasing public safety and providing personalized education.[836] However, the mismatch in the use and standardization of technology in the public sector encourages the latter's dependence on corporations for the implementation of digital solutions, as well as shifting the center of influence in the formulation of public policies towards private actors without political representation/legitimacy.[837] This is the dominant feature of the digitalization of society today, with the increasing prominence of companies not only in terms of economic power but also in the roles traditionally occupied by governments.[838]

Pressured by the effects of austerity policies with limited resources for social policies, governments are resorting to contracts and agreements with technology companies which, due to their massive data mining activity and concentration of information infrastructure, are able to offer services at lower costs. This leads to a future imbalance of power that would favor private agents much more than public ones.[839] Although partnerships between the private sector and governments have great potential to generate beneficial effects for the community and have already proved to be positive in many aspects,[840] it is also necessary to have adequate legal and institu-

836 AROGYASWAMY, Bernard. Big tech and societal sustainability: an ethical framework. *AI and Society*, v. 35, n. 4, p. 829–840, 2020, p. 837.

837 SHARON, Tamar. Blind-sided by privacy? Digital contact tracing, the Apple/Google API and big tech's newfound role as global health policy makers. *Ethics and Information Technology*, v. 23, n. Suppl 1, p. 45–57, 2021.

838 *Ibid.* The aforementioned article observes this phenomenon by analyzing the tracking of Covid-19 cases carried out by two large technology companies, Google and Apple, and emphasizes the relevance of these companies in certain health policies during the pandemic.

839 MOROZOV, Evgeny. *Big Tech - a ascensão dos dados e a morte da política.* São Paulo: Ubu, 2018, p. 168.

840 As in the policies for tackling the Covid-19 pandemic by tracking the outbreaks of the disease and the centers of contamination.

tional structures to deal with the risks this entails in terms of protecting fundamental rights from economic power.[841]

If, on the one hand, there are risks in the interaction between companies and governments in the implementation of digital solutions from the point of view of the legitimacy of influences and the limitation of economic power, there are also risks and problems related to the power of the state in the face of individual rights and the democratic principle. In Denmark, for example, strategies to use artificial intelligence to manage social services involve the overt use of personal data to process benefits and predict the degree of vulnerability of families who are potential targets of policies, even outside the contexts in which they were collected, which maximizes their usefulness but is questioned in the light of the principle of purpose limitation of the European data protection system.[842]

Algorithms and the structure of material and human resources for their development play a central role in the digital welfare state, as they are used for data mining to detect correlations and patterns that support the decision-making process regarding the provision of social services to the population, their best allocation and formulation.[843] The ultimate goal is to equalize the social distribution of risks and the allocation of resources.[844] Much of the debate on the subject is concerned with analyzing how digitalization affects the enjoyment of social rights and the very contours of the welfare state - when, for example, technology solutions are outsourced to private providers,[845] resulting in the risks already mentioned - with a resulting reflection on digital sovereignty and independence.[846]

841 UNITED NATIONS. *E-Government Survey 2020*. New York: Department of Economic and Social Affairs, 2020.

842 JØRGENSEN, Rikke Frank. Data and rights in the digital welfare state: the case of Denmark. *Information, Communication & Society*, v. 26, n. 1, p. 123–138, 2023, p. 132.

843 PEDERSEN, John Storm. The digital welfare state: Dataism versus relationshipism. *In*: PEDERSEN, John Storm; WILKINSON, Adrian (Orgs.). *Big Data: Promise, Application and Pitfalls*. Cheltenham: Edward Elgar Publishing, 2019, p. 302.

844 LARASATI, Zita Wahyu; YUDA, Tauchid Komara; SYAFA'AT, Akbarian Rifki. Digital welfare state and problem arising: an exploration and future research agenda. *International Journal of Sociology and Social Policy*, v. 43, n. 5/6, 2022.

845 For instance, COLLINGTON, Rosie. Disrupting the Welfare State? Digitalisation and the Retrenchment of Public Sector Capacity. *New Political Economy*, v. 27, n. 2, p. 312–328, 2022, p. 319, when she says that "The digitalisation of administration, which has entailed the outsourcing of responsibility for critical infrastructures to the private sector, has not been without its consequences for the realisation of democratically accountable goals in the public's interest".

When dealing with the Danish case, Jørgensen states that there is now a new market for predictive solutions within the public sector, which, unlike what happens in the private sector (with its characteristic orientation towards influencing consumers), would be guided by the collective interest, such as identifying potential targets for public policies. The author argues, however, that this type of practice undermines citizens' sphere of autonomy and diminishes the quality of the relationship between the state and civil society, insofar as a disproportionately high collection of personal data ends up serving specific and minor legitimate purposes.[847] In this sense, Jørgensen concludes that

> While the data harvesting and prediction logic of surveillance capitalism has mostly been associated with the private sector, it is now traveling to the public sector. The developments towards the digital welfare state and its increasing focus on automated solutions as part of delivering public services and controlling welfare benefits effectively deploy the same type of data analytics that tech giants deploy for commercial purposes, to target and influence the behaviour of their users. Likewise, it may lead to similar data maximization, profiling of the individual, invasive means of surveilling and predicting citizens, and ultimately disempowerment - depending on how the public sector develops and deploys its digital welfare project.

The dichotomy between the protection of individual fundamental rights (especially intimacy, privacy, and freedom), which the control of personal data seeks to ensure, and the full digitalization of the state, which involves the use of data to formulate public policies, is actually a re-reading of an older problem of the welfare state. It's about knowing how to balance two principles: the rule of law, which is necessary to protect individuals in an increasingly complex and dangerous world, and the role of the state, because, after all, the "government is a problem-solver, as well as the guardian of law".[848] This balance, however, is shifting due to the pseudo-public arena that the digital market has created, intensified by the massive use

846 BIZER, Johann. Digitale Souveränität – wer steuert, organisiert und kontrolliert die digitale Verwaltung?. *In*: LÜHR, Hans-Henning; JABKOWSKI, Roland; SMENTEK, Sabine (Orgs.). *Handbuch Digitale Verwaltung*. Wiesbaden: KSV Verwaltungspraxis, 2019, p. 23–36.

847 JØRGENSEN, *op. cit.*, p. 132,133.

848 FRIEDMAN, Lawrence M. Legal Culture and the Welfare State. *In*: TEUBNER, Gunther (Org.). *Dilemmas of Law in the Welfare State*. Berlin, New York: De Gruyter, 2011, p. 15.

of technology and personal data to optimize their private businesses. The conservatism of these opinions must be weighed up in the light of the capacities necessary for the welfare state in current times, which does not mean neglecting the protection of fundamental rights, but directing state activity towards legitimate objectives. It is thought that limiting the power of the state, when it comes to the use and processing of data, is a measure that requires as much or more caution and care as initiatives to regulate the digital market, because this invariably also means limiting public opportunities for the realization of the democratic project and the rule of law itself, restricting the possibilities for relationships to be mediated by institutions with the legitimacy that the market does not offer.

The debate about whether a legal decision can be automated is not new and goes back to Leibniz's vision of law and its application in the 17th century. For him, the contradictions of legal decisions and the problem of indeterminacy could be solved by establishing a set of algorithmic rules that would guarantee uniform results, as in a mathematical model.[849] In contemporary terms, this takes the form of decision-making through automated content analysis, which includes processing the natural language of normative texts and narratives of facts and arguments, if there are participants involved in the decision-making. In public administration, for example, this can be translated into decisions about a citizen's eligibility for a particular public policy, deliberations about public transport flow management, or the response that the administration gives in a particular interaction with the citizen in the context of service provision. In this way, an administrative decision can be replaced or strongly instructed by the work of neural networks in conjunction with content analysis.[850]

On the one hand, this can lead to the law becoming more predictable, explicit, and transparent in some cases, as a result of repeated application. On the other hand, in theory, the interpretative or enforcement efficiency of this type of law and computing approach can dispense with the participation of the parties in decision-making, which is procedurally manifested in the adversarial principle (*audiatur et altera pars*) and, in the sphere of government, is still an essential element in the exercise of citizenship. Participation would then no longer be seen as an additional way of improving the quality of decision-making and regulation, by reducing information

849 LIVERMORE, Michael A. Rule by rules. *In*: WHALEN, Ryan (Org.). *Computational Legal Studies. The Promise and Challenge of Data-Driven Research.* Cheltenham and Northampton: Edward Elgar, 2020, p. 238.

850 *Ibid.*, p. 248–252.

asymmetries and increasing the number of people involved in decision-making, but as something to be justified solely by its intrinsic value.

Criticism of digital welfare states based on the overt use of data and automated algorithmic decision-making solutions cannot be reduced to unfounded alarmism or a kind of digital luddism,[851] since the technique does make it possible to create panoptic surveillance structures that are typical instruments of totalitarianism. However, the risk of using these solutions lies not in their implementation per se but in the purposes that guide them, the control of which can be achieved by developing new governance structures[852] or improving existing ones. They can be designed in such a way as to guarantee the necessary legitimacy and security of ways of using data and algorithms that may today appear threatening in light of elements that were not designed to deal with them. In this way, society should not be deprived, as an *ex-ante* rule, of the potential benefits of this use and, furthermore, experimental initiatives within the administration with the potential to reveal new uses are not castrated. General prohibitions or very strict rules can disregard the complexity of the issue without weighing up the pros and cons. Instead, the characteristics of these instruments should be analyzed to determine the appropriateness of their application and the acceptable limit of concrete risks.[853] In addition, both the ways in which algorithms have been programmed and systems have been trained, and the *ex post* elements of their activities should be observed. If today methods are being developed within jurisprudence based on logical analysis to assess the quality of legal arguments and motivations,[854] there would be no reason not to do the same with automated processes. In this way, technology should be used to increase institutional capacities, with the same orientation towards constitutionally protected values that applies to the analog state.

---

851 The original Luddism, in the 19th century, was a movement that sabotaged factory machinery as a way of protesting against the adoption of technologies in the manufacturing process that mischaracterized traditional forms of work. JONES, Steven E. *Against Technology: From the Luddites to Neo-Luddism*. New York: Routledge, 2006, p. 47.

852 MAZZUCATO, Mariana; KATTEL, Rainer. COVID-19 and public-sector capacity. *Oxford Review of Economic Policy*, v. 36, n. S1, p. S256–S269, 2020, p. 264.

853 TRUTE, Hans-Heinrich. Rechtliche Herausforderungen der Digitalisierung: Daten – Algorithmen – Wissen. *In*: BÄR, Christian; GRÄDLER, Thomas; MAYR, Robert (Orgs.). *Digitalisierung im Spannungsfeld von Politik, Wirtschaft, Wissenschaft und Recht*. Berlin, Heidelberg: Springer, 2018, p. 323.

854 For example, the logocratic method, as can be seen in BREWER, Scott. Logocratic method and the analysis of arguments in evidence. *Law, Probability and Risk*, v. 10, n. 3, p. 175–202, 2011.

Rainer Kattel and Mariana Mazzucato claim that there are two cultures when it comes to institutional capacities, which do not communicate much: the culture of *capabilities*, from the Schumpeterian tradition of dynamic capacities of companies to adapt and reconfigure their activities in a changing market; and the culture of *capacities*, from the Weberian tradition, which aims for development by strengthening public bureaucratic structures and meritocratic recruitment of the best talent, with political orientation towards a legitimate and politically defined objective.[855] However, ideally there could be a synthesis of these cultures in the form of *dynamic capabilities* in the public sector.[856] Along these lines, a digital welfare state in Brazil must be translated into the deployment of these dynamic capabilities in an organic way and in accordance with the guidelines laid down in the Constitution, with regard not only to fundamental rights but also to the development model. They are affirmed in part through Digital Government policies and, at the same time, are themselves political-legal conditions for the development of Digital Government, as they involve the creation of environments conducive to innovation and experimentation. In this sense, the state must be able to: 1) adapt and learn; 2) align public services and citizens' needs; 3) govern resilient production systems; and 4) govern data and digital platforms.[857]

Based on the analysis of current Digital Government arrangements carried out above, these capabilities presuppose a clearer political direction in policy formulation, overcoming the limitations of federalism by intensifying its experimentalist vocation, creating an institutional environment that fosters innovation within the public administration, and bringing the government closer to citizens in terms of the provision of public services. These four points will be discussed in more detail below.

4.3 The political direction of Digital Government

Digital transformation is the biggest and most impactful process of change in society in recent decades, judging by its impact on people's way of life

855 KATTEL, Rainer; MAZZUCATO, Mariana. Mission-oriented innovation policy and dynamic capabilities in the public sector. *Industrial and Corporate Change*, v. 27, n. 5, p. 787–801, 2018, p. 795.

856 According to the authors, however, this synthesis differs from proposals along the lines of Public Choice and New Public Management, which would have failed to transfer certain virtues from the private sector to the public sector. *Ibid.*, p. 9, 10.

857 MAZZUCATO; KATTEL, *op. cit.*

and on productive relations. It is, therefore, a topic that is part of the development issue, more central in the case of countries with a social and economic deficit like Brazil, but also present in advanced nations. These countries face their own internal and external challenges aggravated by globalization, whether in guaranteeing and fulfilling the social rights of their original populations and those with a history of migration, or in the very competition of their productive structures in the global trade and production chain scenario. Despite the fact that, today, digitalization is at the heart of the discussion on development, the issue is treated publicly as a neutral, politically sterile technical question: everyone is in favor of the technological modernization of the state, and digitalization is unanimous in public opinion, on both the left and the right.

Of course, like any public policy that involves resources, public procurement, and some degree of change in the sphere of practical enjoyment of rights or the exercise of influence, the interests surrounding digital transformation and, specifically, Digital Government also exist and act. However, unlike public policies such as health and education, conflicts and disputes take place on a more veiled basis. If, on the one hand, as in the case of the national sanitation policy or attempts at tax reform, the dispute between interest groups can be fierce to the point of creating years-long deadlocks, on the other hand, when one or other vision prevails as a result of the victory of a group or political composition, a hegemony is created around an agenda and the political direction of that social objective is strengthened.

In this regard, it is worth mentioning Emiliano Brunet, who points out that some of the categories in Antonio Gramsci's thought are conducive to understanding issues dear to the theory of the state, and therefore to a legal-institutional approach, notably the formation of consensus, political direction and the aptitude of institutions for transformation, regardless of revolutions.[858] In the process of building hegemony (in the sense of the political and cultural direction of one group over others, which permeates all aspects of a society), Gramsci observes that, at first, embryonic ideologies clash and conflict until one of them prevails and spreads throughout society, forming an intellectual and moral amalgam that dictates its economic and political objectives, acting as a universal driving force. The state, although it can be an instrument for the dominant group (as in the Marxist

858 BRUNET, Emiliano. Estado, Poder Político e Direito em uma época de mudanças: por que ler Gramsci? *REI - Revista Estudos Institucionais*, v. 7, n. 3, p. 880–907, 2021, p. 887.

tradition), is guided by hegemony and not the other way around, and "state life is conceived as a continuous formation and overcoming of unstable balances (within the framework of the law) between the interests of the fundamental group and those of subordinate groups".[859]

Hegemony, despite its eminently ethical-political character, then requires the ability to make key economic decisions in a given productive hub.[860] With regard to digital transformations, it can be seen that today this is exercised notably by Big Techs and emerging private companies in general, considering that areas of development such as AI are concentrated in the private sector like never before. Expanding this dialog, we turn to the reflections of Manuel Castells, who states that "the nation-state is increasingly submitted to a more subtle, and more troubling, competition from sources of power that are undefined, and, sometimes, indefinable".[861] The author refers generically to networks of capital, production, communication, crime, military apparatuses, international institutions, even before the popularization of the internet. In this sense, the nation-state is increasingly having to deal with other flows of power that oppose the exercise of its authority. Over time, this prediction has been confirmed with the accentuation of globalization and the advent of innovations such as social networks, as well as huge transnational technology companies.

Octavio Ianni called the *Electronic Prince*[862] the entity that concentrates political, economic, and legal functions[863] in a globalized era, in some

859 GRAMSCI, Antonio. *Quaderni del carcere - Quaderni 12-29*. 2. ed. Torino: Einaudi, 1977, p. 1584. In the original, "...la vita statale viene concepita come un continuo formarsi e superarsi di equilibri instabili (nell'ambito della legge) tra gli interessi del gruppo fon damentale e quelli dei gruppi subordinati..."

860 GRAMSCI, Antonio. *Quaderni del carcere - Quaderni 1 - 5*. 2. ed. Torino: Einaudi, 1977, p. 461; GRAMSCI, *op. cit.*, p. 1591.

861 CASTELLS, Manuel. *The Power of Identity*. 2. ed. Chichester: Wiley-Blackwell, 2010, p. 357.

862 In reference to Machiavelli's Prince. According to the author, "The Electronic Prince, however, is neither a *condottiero* nor a political party, but carries out and goes beyond the insights and activities of these two classic political figures. The electronic prince is a nebulous and active, present and invisible, predominant and ubiquitous entity, continuously permeating all levels of society, locally, nationally, regionally and globally. He is the collective and organic intellectual of the present, predominant and active structures and power blocks on a national, regional and global scale, always in accordance with the different socio-cultural and political-economic contexts drawn on the new map of the world." In the original, "O Príncipe Eletrônico, no entanto, não é nem *condottiero* nem partido político, mas realiza e ultrapassa os descortínios e as atividades dessas duas figuras clássicas da política. O príncipe eletrônico é uma entidade nebulosa e ativa, presente e invisível, predom-

cases blurring the role of constitutional norms in making different systems compatible.[864] At the end of the 1990s, the Electronic Prince was a reality that could be considered alongside the traditional economy and society. With the development of hyperconnectivity and the fourth industrial revolution, the Electronic Prince, who knows no borders or jurisdictions, is tending towards hegemony, supplanting the traditional market and state. This can be seen in the phenomenon of Big Techs, which are bigger than the economies of many countries, and whose decisions, standards, and terms of use end up having more intense practical effects than many national laws. They take on the form of institutions that mix finance, politics, and data, with an aspiration analogous to the "collective and organic intellectual of power structures and blocs" cited by Ianni,[865] in addition to the gigantic concentration of economic power. In 2020, the market value of Apple Inc. exceeded the sum of all the wealth produced in one year in Brazil, to cite just one example.[866] Big Techs grow quickly and aggressively, so that in the end only the leader remains and covers the entire market, making it very difficult for other companies that may enter the market later to compete.[867] Here, the logic of "the winner takes all",[868] in which you don't compete in the market but for the market, is due to the high scalability of the actions and services of these platforms, which benefit from the so-called network effect.[869]

---

inante e ubíqua, permeando continuamente todos os níveis da sociedade, em âmbito local, nacional, regional e mundial. É o intelectual coletivo e orgânico das estruturas e blocos de poder presentes, predominantes e atuantes em escala nacional, regional e mundial, sempre em conformidade com os diferentes contextos sócio-culturais e político-econômicos desenhados no novo mapa do mundo."

863 IANNI, Octavio. O príncipe eletrônico. *Sociologias*, v. 22, n. 1, 1999.

864 Referring to Luhman's sociological view already mentioned.

865 IANNI, *op. cit.*. In the original, "intelectual coletivo e orgânico das estruturas e blocos de poder".

866 *Valor de mercado da Apple ultrapassa o PIB do Brasil de 2019 | Tecnologia | G1*. Available at <https://g1.globo.com/economia/tecnologia/noticia/2020/08/06/valor-de-mercado-da-apple-ja-ultrapassa-o-pib-do-brasil-de-2019.ghtml>. Accessed 6 Jun. 2022.

867 VAN DER AALST, Wil; HINZ, Oliver; WEINHARDT, Christof. Big Digital Platforms: Growth, Impact, and Challenges. *Business and Information Systems Engineering*, v. 61, n. 6, p. 645–648, 2019, p. 645.

868 VARDI, Moshe Y. The winner-takes-all tech corporation. *Communications of the ACM*, v. 62, n. 11, p. 7, 2019, p. 7.

869 According to SHAPIRO, Carl; VARIAN, Hal R. *Information rules: a strategic guide to the network economy*. Boston, Mass: Harvard Business School Press, 1999, p. 45,

Some authors propose, as a starting point for confronting this hegemony, mechanisms that allow, for example, the portability of data belonging to the user of the platforms, as a way of returning the centrality of the digital transaction to the user. As happened with the telecommunications market (cell phones), data portability would give citizens more power of choice when it comes to digital platforms, increasing competition between companies and reducing the economic power of the biggest Big Techs.[870] Fukuyama, Richman, and Goel propose the creation of an intermediary layer between the user and the platform,[871] which would invariably mean some degree of direct state intervention in the digital infrastructure of the platforms. There are also advocates of a purely competitive antitrust regulatory approach to break up large companies, as was done in the past with AT&T.[872] There are also regulatory approaches concerning data and privacy, among other concerns, and in this sense the approval of more effective data protection regulations represented a major shift in the direction of regulation motivated by the rise of the big platforms,[873] complemented later with the Digital Markets Act and the Digital Services Act.

Even with recent advances, there is skepticism about the potential of regulating Big Tech, considering that such measures tend only to slow down the damage caused to society and not prevent it, which requires other approaches to tackle these dilemmas from an ethical perspective and promote user activism.[874] The law has difficulty reaching these activities through top-down intervention, and traditional regulatory techniques are losing ground to the industry itself.[875] This limited capacity to regulate technology is due to two reasons. Firstly, there is a profound asymmetry of

---

"...network effects arise when the value one user places on a good depends on how many other people are using it."

870 MARCIANO, Alain; NICITA, Antonio; RAMELLO, Giovanni Battista. Big data and big techs: understanding the value of information in platform capitalism. *European Journal of Law and Economics*, v. 50, n. 3, p. 345–358, 2020.

871 FUKUYAMA, Francis; RICHMAN, Barak; GOEL, Ashish. How to Save Democracy from Technology. *Foreign Affairs*, v. 100, n. 1, p. 98–110, 2021.

872 See Unites States. v. AT&T, Inc., 552 F. Supp. 131 (D.D.C., 1982).

873 VAN DER AALST, Wil; HINZ, Oliver; WEINHARDT, Christof. Big Digital Platforms: Growth, Impact, and Challenges. *Business and Information Systems Engineering*, v. 61, n. 6, p. 645–648, 2019, p. 646.

874 AROGYASWAMY, Bernard. Big tech and societal sustainability: an ethical framework. *AI and Society*, v. 35, n. 4, p. 829–840, 2020.

875 GUIHOT, Michael; MATTHEW, Anne; SUZOR, Nicolas Pierre. Nudging Robots: Innovative Solutions to Regulate Artificial Intelligence. *Vanderbilt journal of entertainment and technology law*, v. 20, n. 2, p. 385–456, 2017.

information between public regulatory institutions and the digital market, which prevents the authorities from revealing the fundamentals of the algorithms used in services and data processing. Secondly, traditional public policies are designed and implemented at a national or local level, while digital platforms are global.[876]

From a Gramscian point of view, state initiatives to regulate the activities of Big Tech and the development of technologies such as AI can be interpreted as the natural and expected consideration of the interests of the dominated group by the dominant group. Thus, the latter's resignation or compliance (the "compromise") would be a sacrifice in political and cultural terms in order to achieve a balance which, because it does not change the basic condition of those who make the key decisions in the economic core, does not change the hegemony and its consequences.[877] This compromised balance, however, is still a way of affirming the state's dynamic capacity to govern resilient production systems.

In geopolitical terms, the US seeks to exercise hegemony in the digital transformation of the world by dominating the forefront of information technology development within its liberal capitalist development model, especially through its private companies. A similar process can be observed in relation to China, which shares with the US the leadership role in the development and use of information technology,[878] despite the greater degree of political control characteristic of the Chinese regime. The dispute for technological hegemony is also an ideological dispute that involves some degree of justification for exercising power over the rest of the world, which transcends the actions and interests of private actors, in a process of digital colonialism.[879] The European Union, on the other hand, which does not have the same leading role as the US and China in the development of cutting-edge technologies, adopts a different strategy, compensating for its lack of leading role in technological innovation with the leading role in regulatory innovation, thus seeking to have an important and decisive

876 MARCIANO, Alain; NICITA, Antonio; RAMELLO, Giovanni Battista. Big data and big techs: understanding the value of information in platform capitalism. *European Journal of Law and Economics*, v. 50, n. 3, p. 345–358, 2020, p. 355.

877 GRAMSCI, Antonio. *Quaderni del carcere - Quaderni 1 - 5*. 2. ed. Torino: Einaudi, 1977, p. 461.

878 ANDREONI, Antonio; ROBERTS, Simon. Governing data and digital platforms: regulations, competition and industrial policies, with sectoral case studies from South Africa. *Digital Pathways at Oxford Paper Series*, n. 5, 2020, p. 18.

879 KWET, Michael. Digital colonialism: US empire and the new imperialism in the Global South. *Race and Class*, v. 60, n. 4, p. 3–26, 2019, p. 17.

influence on the core of technological economic activity through state intervention and based on legal instruments.

The hegemonic processes are presented in different vertical and horizontal facets, respectively, in the spheres of the different countries and sovereign national boundaries, or in terms of the socio-economic activities themselves, in a combination of reciprocal implications that is amplified and complexified when we take into account the international relations that are intertwined in the internal dynamics of the states.[880] In this way, ideologies born in developed countries can spread to the global periphery, influencing local interactions,[881] which social networks and globalization itself end up reinforcing.

With regard to Digital Government, the absence of clear disputes over the direction of the policy may make it seem as if there is no hegemony in progress, or that the issue is surprisingly open to any and all views as beneficial to all in order to overcome the petty and mundane dispute of interests. However, when we put the issue in the context of the spaces occupied by government and the market in social life, we see that the supposed lack of hegemony and, consequently, of a clear political direction for the Digital Government, is in fact the very expression of the hegemony of the big technology companies, who are only interested in the state as a facilitator of private activities and fulfiller of activities inherent to *laissez-faire*, as well as a client of their solutions. This may partly explain why the Digital Government political agenda has been defined in recent decades in Brazil in an inertial way and guided predominantly by the search for economic efficiency, in other words, the maximization of utility aimed at saving the state's financial resources, or those of private individuals in the activities in which they are obliged to interact with the state. Digital Government, as a re-signification of the role of the state in the lives of citizens made possible by technology capable of taking the realization and enjoyment of rights to an unprecedented level, has been sidelined by a silent political choice disguised as a consensus.

Public policies are an expression of state power and, in the case of countries like Brazil, they are instruments for overcoming underdevelopment by aiming to realize constitutionally established social rights that have been contrasted, since their inception, with the limiting and dysfunctional social

880 GRAMSCI, Antonio. *Quaderni del carcere - Quaderni 12-29*. 2. ed. Torino: Einaudi, 1977, p. 1585.

881 *Ibid.*

reality. The political direction is historically decisive in this process, as it enables great leaps in concrete evolutionary realization and, symbiotically, allows for the absorption of demands from non-hegemonic groups in a dialectical process.[882] This is also the OECD's conclusion when examining the institutionalization of decision-making processes in digital transformation in Brazil, arguing that

> [...] the inexistence of a strong digital government leadership and mandate covering also digital service policies, determines that the delivery of public services follows mostly an agency-thinking approach, which is typical of e-government rather than of a digital government approach.[883]

However, this seems to apply to digital government in general. In South Korea, for example, a country considered to be very advanced in this area, the development of Digital Government depends considerably on political leadership, in compensation for the low degree of institutionalization of bodies that formulate actions.[884] This perception can be seen even in technical studies on the application of technology in the public sector. In an engineering paper, Eunjin Koo points out that political leadership has a high impact on systems, which can evolve or regress depending on the will of the leader, adding that "it is necessary to be patient", because

882 According to BRUNET, Emiliano. Estado, Poder Político e Direito em uma época de mudanças: por que ler Gramsci? *REI - Revista Estudos Institucionais*, v. 7, n. 3, p. 880–907, 2021 when mentioning as an example what Gramsci describes of the unification of the Italian states.

883 OECD. *Digital Government Review of Brazil: Towards the digital transformation of the public sector.* Paris: OECD, 2018, p. 22.

884 CHUNG, Choong Sik. *Developing digital governance: South Korea as a global digital government leader.* London and New York: Routledge, 2020, p. 249, 254 In 2017, South Korea approved the Presidential Committee on the Fourth Industrial Revolution (PCFIR), through the Presidential Decree on the Creation and Management of the PCFIR, of August 22, 2017. The Committee has several thematic subcommittees, and is also responsible for the elaboration of policies related to Digital Government, in particular it "deliberates upon and coordinates policy measures submitted by various ministries and the committee members; organizes public campaigns related to the Fourth Industrial Revolution and encourages public participation; prepare the groundwork for regulatory and institutional reforms in support of public–private partnerships; fosters ecosystems for new industries (Special Committee on Smart Cities, Special Committee on Healthcare, etc.)". The author, however, considers that the committee did not work well due to low institutionalization.

national laws and regulations change very slowly and through very complex processes.[885]

Although it is possible to extend the criticism to different national governments and to the ideological view of the *locus* of Digital Government in development, judging by the way the OECD and the UN deal with the matter, the agenda in the European Union has produced a convergence between the political and the legal, unlike Brazil. There are two factors behind this, which are also interrelated. The first is the European Union's strategic position in the correlation of global forces on digital transformation, as a coadjutant at the technological forefront and a protagonist on the regulatory issue. In this respect, exercising this position and defining Europe's geopolitical position requires a clear definition of the political agenda so that it can be translated into regulatory initiatives capable of influencing the global debates and direction of the state-society relationship concerning information technology. The second is due to the phenomenon of the Europeanization of public policies, in the sense of processes of institutional elaboration of a set of shared procedures, rules, and guidelines with a view to their subsequent incorporation in the respective member states as part of the domestic public culture and policies.[886] Both factors have cognitive and normative expressions. Although policy analysis literature often treats both dimensions together as underpinning the fundamental social functions of integrating a community to create conditions for affirming identities, prescribing principles and methodologies for actors, managing tensions, and distributing power,[887] it may be helpful to recognize the legal-normative dimension as independent from the normative-cognitive one in the case of both the formation of a European digital transformation policy and the Europeanization of digital transformation policies.

This has resulted in the production of legislation on digital transformation and digital government that is prolific within the European Union,

885 KOO, Eunjin. *Digital Transformation of Government: From E-Government to Intelligent E-Government.* Master's thesis (Engineering and Management), Massachusetts Institute of Technology, Cambridge, 2019, p. 30.

886 For a more precise definition, according to FEATHERSTONE, Kevin; RADAELLI, Claudio M. *The Politics of Europeanization.* Oxford: Oxford University Press, 2003, p. 30, "Processes of (a) construction, (b) diffusion, and (c) institutionalization of formal and informal rules, procedures, policy paradigms, styles, 'ways of doing things', and shared beliefs and norms which are first defined and consolidated in the making of EU public policy and politics and then incorporated in the logic of domestic discourse, identities, political structures, and public policies."

887 SUREL, Yves. The role of cognitive and normative frames in policy-making. *Journal of European Public Policy*, v. 7, n. 4, p. 495–512, 2000, p. 496, 500.

but at the same time politically oriented, both in the projects based on the supranational discourse and worldview that integration represents, and in the dynamics of internalizing guidelines in the national legal systems and political agendas of the member states.

In the case of Brazil, we can also observe a prolific production of norms as a phenomenon of "hyper-normatization" with two characteristics: when the level of institutionalization is high, the norms are insufficient or inadequate to respond to the social challenges of Digital Government; when they are more adequate from the material point of view, they have a low level of institutionalization and isolation, which hinders their potential.

Considering Brazil's federal system, the low level of institutionalization of a substantial part of Digital Government policies represents a concentration of efforts and results within the same bureaucratic level of competence, which explains the relative success of federal Digital Government policies in public services under the competence of the Federal Government. In this case, policymakers enjoy sufficient autonomy to formulate a more or less coherent set of measures and put them into practice within their regular administrative structures. On the other hand, this bureaucratic isolation leads to coordination limitations and the overlapping of norms and structures within the same entity, in the absence of institutional structures that guarantee more effective instruments for coordinating not only internal initiatives, but also those external to the Federal Executive, partially causing the deleterious effects of scenarios of exaggerated autonomy.

At the other end of the spectrum, in matters that constitutionally fall outside the competence of the Federal Executive, there is a scenario of low bureaucratic autonomy in relation to potential public policy measures, which also results in low results in policies that would necessarily involve other actors who are not legally bound by the most precarious normative instruments. At the same time, depending on the part and angle of analysis of the Brazilian Digital Government, there is an inverted U-shaped relationship between the quality of government and the autonomy of the bureaucracy, in which an intermediate value of autonomy results in better results than in scenarios in which it is very low or exaggerated.[888]

Thus, the lack of political direction affects the range and scope of the Digital Government's institutional instruments, and vice versa: low institutionalization, especially of instruments for the coordination and financial structuring of policies, also weakens attempts at political direction, which

888 FUKUYAMA, Francis. *What Is Governance?* Washington, DC: Center for Global Development, 2013, p. 11.

over the years have been limited to the agenda of the state bureaucracy staff itself, within the limits of its normal administrations and competences, and dependent on scattered initiatives linked to the visions of technicians and enthusiasts within the government.

The absence of politically structured and informed purposes left the process without a compass and without coordination, and this lack or insufficiency of political direction impacts the law, because it limits the versatility of the legal instruments used in politics. They thus lack the legitimizing authorizations (translated into the rites and requirements of legitimation) needed to break through legal-institutional bottlenecks, such as, for example, transfederalist effectiveness, or the very financing and relevant positioning of the policy in the budget.

4.4 The challenges of coordination in the federal system

The problem of coordination in Digital Government issues rests on multiple factors, from pure and simple limitations in terms of the cost of structures, but mainly on the quality of decision-making, since the interests that interact in the environment of the constellation of actors tend to make the solutions optimized by the lowest common denominator.[889] The greater the complexity of the constellation of actors, the number of interests and pressures and, above all, the opportunities for vetoes that present themselves institutionally in this scenario, the more timid the outcome of the public policy will be. This is what Fritz Scharpf identified as "joint decision trap" (*Politikverflechtungsfalle*) based on the analysis of complex federalist structures such as Germany's,[890] which can also be applied to any other nation with complex federalism, such as Brazil and the United States.

In the Brazilian case, the issue of coordination between actors with multiple levels and legally affirmed autonomies goes beyond Scharpf's abstract finding, which in itself represents an *a priori* challenge.

889 HEUBERGER, Moritz. *Coordinating digital government: explaining coordination challenges regarding the digital transformation of public administration in a federal context.* PhD Dissertation (Political Science), Universität Potsdam, Potsdam, 2022, p. 14.

890 SCHARPF, Fritz W. The Joint-Decision Trap: Lessons from German Federalism and European Integration. *Public Administration*, v. 66, n. 3, p. 239–278, 1988.

Although this is not a finding that can be generalized to other areas[891], digital Government seems to be more advanced in countries with unitary forms of state, as opposed to states that adopt federalism. We can cite the example of Germany itself, which has a complex federalism and is evolving more slowly in Digital Government, compared to Scandinavian countries such as Denmark, for example, or even smaller states, such as the always mentioned example of Estonia - it should also be noted that, in these latter cases, the smaller scale is also an important factor. In Brazil, there is a gulf between the level of development in the Federal Government and in the states and municipalities. Considering only the Federal Government, the country is in the top positions in international rankings, but when you add states and municipalities to the equation, the picture changes dramatically. One question that might be asked is whether this finding is due to a pattern in the relationship between federalism and innovation in the public sector or whether it simply reflects the differences in institutional capacities between entities that have always existed in the federations. The answer is probably both.

Some issues reflect the traditional problems of federalism, such as an imbalance in the relationship between material competences and budgetary and institutional capacities, but some implications relate specifically to Digital Government policies, especially due to their character of profound transformation of administrative relations and processes, which are permanently innovative. Due to the substance and content of this public policy, material and institutional change has an even greater weight in shaping its results when compared to others, in which it already plays a fundamental role and is, therefore, the object of academic concern. This is because this is a policy that not only depends on change (as is natural to infer from any reform process), but whose object is change itself, adaptability, and the continuous incorporation of innovation into the public sector. In this sense, since federalism is a complex system of entities, competences, autonomies, centers, and decision-making processes, with a broad and complex constellation of actors, coordinating all these factors around a result that represents innovation is the main challenge.

On the other hand, in potential terms, federalism seems, from its conception, to be geared towards fostering innovation, in the sense that local autonomies will naturally be more aligned with specific needs and the

891 KINCAID, John. Economic policy-making: advantages and disadvantages of the federal model. *International Social Science Journal*, v. 53, n. 167, p. 85–92, 2001, p. 92.

flow of information, and will be better able to propose and develop new solutions to the issues that arise. At the same time, the multiplicity of decision-making centers and enabling points also multiplies the chances of any of these solutions representing a significant innovation in material or institutional terms, which could have repercussions and be replicated at a national or universal level.[892] In a situational analysis[893] of the relationship between federalism and innovation, the model's strengths, weaknesses, opportunities, and threats are identified considering the specific scenario. In management literature, strengths and weaknesses are both impacts arising from internal factors of a given model, with the former representing positive impacts and the latter representing negative impacts. Opportunities and threats also represent positive and negative impacts respectively, usually from factors external to an organization.[894]

Taking the federalist model in the context of innovation, the weaknesses are the large number of veto points throughout the decision-making process that emerge from the conjunction between the constellation of actors (especially public) and the institutionally established modes of interaction, as well as the personified expression of these veto points (the veto players), which directly or indirectly impact major changes in the political course.[895] Along the same lines, the threat is the phenomenon of non-cooperative federalism, which goes beyond the conflicts generated by the autonomy of the federal levels in formulating their own policies or in their participation in the formulation of national policies, and can also take the form of resistance of all kinds even on issues whose competence lies with the Union.[896] The strengths of federalism are the flexibility provided by the proximity of governments at regional and local level through decentralization, and the opportunities are the potential for political experimentation provided by this flexibility and the autonomy of the federal entities.

---

892 This occurs regardless of the different views on the political-legal interactions between states and the federal government around cooperation, non-cooperation or rivalry. On this matter, BULMAN-POZEN, Jessica; GERKEN, Heather K. Uncooperative Federalism Essay. *Yale Law Journal*, v. 118, n. 7, p. 1256–1311, 2008.

893 WEIHRICH, Heinz. The TOWS matrix—A tool for situational analysis. *Long Range Planning*, v. 15, n. 2, p. 54–66, 1982.

894 ANSOFF, H. Igor. Strategic issue management. *Strategic Management Journal*, v. 1, n. 2, p. 131–148, 1980, p. 136.

895 SCHMIDT, Manfred G. Thesen zur Reform des Föderalismus der Bundesrepublik Deutschland. *Politische Vierteljahresschrift*, v. 42, n. 3, p. 474–491, 2001, p. 483.

896 BULMAN-POZEN; GERKEN, *op. cit.*, p. 1263–1264.

Counterintuitively, there are arguments that question the real vocation of federalism for decentralization, despite this being one of its primary objectives. According to this view, a greater degree of decentralization can be observed in unitary states compared to federal states, when the proportional allocation of resources to local levels is analyzed.[897] This reflection is receiving renewed attention nowadays when it is inferred that technology contributes in some way to relativizing consolidated ideas about the effects of state forms. While it has traditionally been said that the federative form tends to bring government closer to local reality and people,[898] the instantaneous nature of communications and telecommunication infrastructures (and Digital Government itself) means that this question can, at the very least, be questioned, even though physical distance is only part of the concept of proximity in these cases. Also contributing to this are observations on the functioning of administrative models such as the Chinese, which, despite being a unitary state, currently has a high degree of decentralization of administrative decisions - although it can be pointed out that a significant part of the experimental reforms that China carried out took place before the decentralization movement.[899]

Beyond abstractions and generalizations about development models, it makes more sense to find out to what extent the forms of state contribute to fostering or hindering certain specific policies, and how the aptitude of these macro-institutional models impacts their results, as a starting point for a diagnosis of practical utility. In other words, it is important to know whether, for the purposes of developing efficient Digital Government policies, federalism produces the desired decentralization, whether or not this is beneficial in the specific case, and how the institutions of the federal state fit into the broad legal-institutional arrangement of the policy, limiting or enabling possibilities for institutional design, continuity or reform.

Brazilian federalism has many similarities with German federalism in terms of the implications of this dissertation. These include the institutional design at complex levels, exclusive and concurrent legislative and material

897 CROSS, Frank B. The Folly of Federalism. *Cardozo Law Review*, v. 24, n. 1, p. 1–60, 2002, p. 46–57.

898 CHEMERINSKY, Erwin. The Values of Federalism Dunwoody Distinguished Lecture in Law. *Florida Law Review*, v. 47, n. 4, p. 499–540, 1995, p. 524.

899 To the contrary, but confirming that the hypothesis is widely accepted in both China and the West, CAI, Hongbin; TREISMAN, Daniel. Did Government Decentralization Cause China's Economic Miracle? *World Politics*, v. 58, n. 4, p. 505–535, 2006.

powers, and the way in which the interests of the states are represented and balanced at Union level (in German parliamentarianism, concentrated in the *BundesRat*; in Brazil, with a presidentialist tradition inspired by the American model, in the Federal Senate). In addition, there is another parallel between the two systems represented by the historical evolution of the correlation of forces between the federal entities of different levels. This is reflected in the financial/ revenue power of each of them and, consequently, in their ability to execute material competences and influence the direction of public policy. Thus, the configuration of forces represented in the tax powers and revenue divisions present in the legal-institutional arrangement of the German Basic Law in the post-war period, which provided for the allocation of certain taxes to the Union (such as those levied on the sale of goods, for example) and others to the states (personal and corporate income tax - *Einkommensteuer* and *Körperschaftsteuer*), has undergone changes that have modified the balance initially proposed. With the *Bundesrat*'s consent, during the 1950s and 1960s, the Federal Government began to have a greater share in the apportionment of taxes that were mostly earmarked for the states and, at the same time, began to finance the states themselves through subsidies and grants. On the one hand, this favored a leveling out of regional inequalities, but on the other it made the states more financially dependent on administrative agreements with the Federal Government that were increasingly complex and detailed.[900]

In Brazil, something similar happened after the approval of the 1988 Constitution, which provided for a tax system containing different types of taxes, with different rules for collection and division between the federal levels. Some taxes were the exclusive responsibility of the municipalities (such as the Urban Property Tax and the Tax on Services), the Tax on the Circulation of Goods was the responsibility of the states (but also divided between the municipalities), and there are also federal taxes, such as the Income Tax and the Tax on Industrialized Products, which, despite being administered by the Federal Government, also have their collection divided between the states and municipalities according to constitutional rules.

In addition, however, there is the tax figure of the *social contribution*, which is the exclusive competence of the Federal Government and can be created by ordinary law, whose approval quorum is much smaller than that

900 SCHARPF, Fritz W. Recht und Politik in der Reform des deutschen Föderalismus. *In*: BECKER, Michael; ZIMMERLING, Ruth (Eds.). *Politik und Recht*. Wiesbaden: Springer-Verlag, 2006, p. 308.

of a constitutional amendment. In this way, and with a view to increasing revenue, the Federal Government started to use new social contributions (also approved by the Senate), the collection of which, unlike income tax, does not have to be shared with the other federal units. Since 1988, therefore, there has been a wide use of this expedient, which has created a substantial distortion in Brazilian fiscal federalism,[901] further aggravating the dependence of municipalities on direct subsidies from the central government, in a phenomenon with results similar to the German process.

The distortion is all the more evident considering that there is a concentration of material competences in the states and municipalities compared to the Federal Government,[902] with services such as education, sanitation, transport, among others, concentrated in them, despite the decreasing proportion in the share of public revenue. In the German case, the process provoked different reactions that created reformist tendencies over time and shaped a pendulum that alternated between centralization and decentralization of powers and organizational forms of federalism, and between a greater or lesser degree and complexity of cooperation between the entities.[903] In Brazil, this is still a long way from being resolved. Still, on the other hand, it creates additional means for the Federal Government to influence states and municipalities when it comes to public policies.

The vocation for political experimentation is of great importance in the conception of federalism. From Friedrich Hayek's liberal economic perspective, procedural experimentation can be inserted into a context of development fostered by competition, when the environment allows and encourages competitors to follow the path of innovation, with the incorporation of new practices being an essential condition for improving results and, consequently, survival in the market.[904] In an environment of federative interactions, it would be expected that the reasoning would not apply in the same way, considering the public nature of relationships and institutions. However, it has to be considered that, despite the non-market

901 ALVES, Raquel de Andrade Vieira. Federalismo fiscal e distorções do modelo brasileiro. *Revista de Finanças Públicas, Tributação e Desenvolvimento*, v. 6, n. 6, 2018.

902 IBRAHIM, Fábio Zambitte; SCHWARTZ, Gustavo Carvalho Gomes. As contribuições sociais como instrumento de fraude ao pacto federativo. *Revista Direito das Relações Sociais e Trabalhistas*, v. 3, n. 1, p. 183–206, 2017, p. 190.

903 SCHARPF, *op. cit.*, p. 307–314.

904 HAYEK, Friedrich A. von. *Der Wettbewerb als Entdeckungsverfahren.* Tübingen: Mohr, 1968, p. 10.

organization of relations, the public sphere is also subject to qualitatively and quantitatively different forms of competition, reflecting not commercial relations, but political relations and political power. In this way, to some degree, albeit less, there are potential incentives for the replication of innovative experimental solutions as a way for competitors to survive politically, the same type of coercion of behavior that Hayek referred to as more efficient than any type of command or instruction. *A contrario sensu* to his reasoning, the incentives for one competitor to abuse their position to prevent another from conducting experiments, frustrating the innovative process, will also be smaller than in a market context.[905]

In this sense, with a configuration of positive and negative incentives softened by the public nature of the institutions and actors of federalism, a space is opened up for the law to intensify or modulate the consequences of forces naturally present in the model, in a more effective way than occurs in the state-society relationship, represented by state intervention in the market, due to the lower complexity of relations, lower asymmetry of information and the diverse nature of the entities. At the same time, characteristics and behaviors that are present to a limited extent in market organization, such as aptitude for collaboration,[906] present themselves as a vocation in the constellations of actors in the model of public interactions represented by federalism. If, in the case of market competition, this results in associations for the defense of common interests - which is relevant but has less business interest in a competitive market context - in the public sphere, collaboration is the rule, or at least the vocation of the public and federalist model.

It's natural for this to be questioned by empirical observation, but the question of whether federalism works in practice to foster cooperation, especially around innovation, is different from the question of the model's vocation and potential. This then becomes less a matter of questioning the institutions themselves and more a matter of analyzing how to position and regulate the legal-institutional "gears" so that the machine performs

905 *Ibid.*

906 According to SHUBIK, Martin. Game Theory, Law, and the Concept of Competition. *University of Cincinnati Law Review*, v. 60, n. 2, p. 285–304, 1991, p. 301, the forms of collaboration between competitors are present in a market environment and can result in improved competition (in the case of cooperation), or its deterioration (in the case of collusion). But the reference here is to the nature of market institutions and their purposes or vocations, compared to other organizational forms.

the function for which it was conceived in the first place. Therefore, the question of whether a form of state - unitary or federal - has a positive or negative impact on policy reforms cannot rest solely on an abstract debate or disregard the complexity at the meso-institutional level of the organization of the different federal configurations. More important than questioning the efficiency of federalism, especially when it comes to its limitations and the fact that it can be an obstacle to innovation and institutional change, is how competences and powers are distributed among the federal entities, how financial resources are divided, and the instruments for coordination and political and regulatory integration.[907]

When jurists analyze institutional structures made up of constitutional normative texts, ordinary laws, and regulations, they tend to believe that identifying problems in the functioning of these arrangements automatically leads to the easy solution of changing the laws and structures, simply rewriting the legal syntax of the arrangements according to an idealized conception of institutional functioning, often inspired by idealizing comparative studies. Whether it's deeper reforms or simply the design and implementation of important, cross-cutting policies such as Digital Government, the learning derived from public policy case studies shows that the solutions go far beyond what legislative change can do. In fact, legislative change itself becomes very difficult without overcoming political problems beyond positive law. In this sense, we must accept the fact that federalism is endowed with complexities shaped by a process of path dependence and that, for this very reason, it cannot be altered simply by technocratic changes that ignore it, otherwise it will fail from a practical point of view.[908] This is the fundamental premise to take into account when analyzing a public policy such as Digital Government, especially with regard to the process of mapping and forward-looking institutional imagination: imagination is free to those who think, and the pen is available to those with sufficient power, but reality and its historical foundation impose conditions.

Furthermore, despite federal legal structures, centralization and decentralization can be relative. The way federalism is presented constitutionally in terms of the distribution of the material and legislative competences of the federal levels varies according to the policy being analyzed. In some

907 BENZ, Arthur. Themen, Probleme und Perspektiven der vergleichenden Föderalismusforschung. *In*: BENZ, Arthur; LEHMBRUCH, Gerhard (Orgs.). *Föderalismus: Analysen in entwicklungsgeschichtlicher und vergleichender Perspektive.* Wiesbaden: VS Verlag für Sozialwissenschaften, 2002, p. 40.

908 *Ibid.*, p. 45.

cases, the distribution of competences can mean decentralization, and in others, greater centralization. This is because, when working with the legal concepts of exclusive and concurrent competence, the Constitution may have decentralized attributions and the decision-making process considering the average of state activities, but it may have concentrated certain competences relating to one policy in the Union, and competences relating to others in the states and municipalities.

Federalism can also concentrate certain measures in the Executive Branch, which in these cases represents even greater centralization, since the distribution between branches is multiplied by the consequences of the federative structure. The fact that the expectation on a certain matter falls within the exclusive remit of the Executive Branch in the Federal Government, for example, creates disincentives for this issue to be discussed and formulated in conjunction with regional interests, due to the legal protection represented by constitutional material competence and the political discourse it supports. Or, in the worst-case scenario, this leads to legal-institutional bottlenecks, such as the prohibition of some attributions constitutionally linked to the central government being dealt with regionally, or the need for legal instruments of interaction, such as agreements or public consortia, which often require complex and multi-level procedures for their legal validity.

In these terms, the original centralization of competences at the federal level can favor decentralization because there is greater freedom in the discretionary acts of delegation and coordination. This is clearly seen in the analysis of the case of the implementation of electronic elections in Brazil and also, partially, in the CNJ's role in the process of digitizing the Brazilian justice system. In this regard, although the literature indicates that decentralization, in general, favors the generation of knowledge and efficiency in the formation of public policies that depend on this infrastructure, it is necessary to point out that there are matters in which innovation and efficiency perceive more advantages or vocations in centralized execution or formulation, due to static costs or greater institutional capacities for innovation.[909] An example of this are aspects of public policy that benefit more from standardization and use at scale, as in the case of digital systems for managing administrative processes and digital identity.

909 SAAM, Nicole J.; KERBER, Wolfgang. Policy Innovation, Decentralised Experimentation, and Laboratory Federalism. *Journal of Artificial Societies and Social Simulation*, v. 16, n. 1, 2012.

Another important aspect concerns the asymmetry of decentralization. A given field of policy formulation and implementation may be well distributed among the different federal levels in terms of material and legislative competences, with the decision-making process decentralized and, in theory, institutionally favoring experimental practice. However, in the same material field, the structures and instruments for financing the measures may be centralized in the Federal Government (or in the states, in relation to the municipalities), which prevents the federative entities from formulating or implementing public policies at regional level with the laboratory characteristics that are dear to innovation and that would do justice to the experimentalist vocation of federalism.

All these aspects are taken into account when thinking of alternatives for promoting Digital Government in Brazil, which invariably involve integrating states and municipalities into this process, through a structure (not necessarily dependent on statutory law) that neutralizes the model's weaknesses and threats and enhances its strengths and opportunities. This involves bodies with the power to centralize matters that require scale and standardization, at the same time as autonomies that are cradles of innovation, which can then be assimilated, distributed, and generalized by the centralized function and so on, in a virtuous circle.

4.5 Innovation Environment: administration in the self-regulatory logic

Public administration, considering the internal organization of governments and their relationship with the individual, has followed the cycles of transformation of society and the state mentioned above, adapting to the realities under construction. The administrative model linked to the Weberian conception of bureaucracy stands out in industrial society, as opposed to patrimonialist models based on traditional authority and typical of less complex societies. It can be said that bureaucracy, in this way, determined the predominant logic of the state in the 20th century.[910] In describing the bureaucratic model, Weber had in mind the highly disciplined and institutionalized Prussian bureaucracy through a legal system that later characterized the German *Rechtsstaat* – sometimes called a liberal autocracy – in whose environment of protection of individual rights and stability

910 FOUNTAIN, Jane E. *Building the virtual state: information technology and institutional change.* Washington, D.C: Brookings Institution Press, 2001, p. 48.

the strong industrialization and economic growth at the end of the 19th century was able to thrive.[911]

The two basic attributes of this model are its structure based on rules/commands and its hierarchical organization.[912] The first aspect also later takes the form of fundamental rights that are constitutionalized through a democratic process. Administrative law, especially in the post-World War II period, came to be characterized by the provision of legality (*Gesetzesvorbehalt*) and the guarantee of a judicial remedy (*Rechtsschutzgarantie*), with a corresponding constitutionalization.[913] The hierarchy is characterized by top-down control of the administration, with a structure organized from the national to the local level, defining and determining public policy objectives and the means to achieve them.[914] There is little discretion at the lower levels and an almost total absence of agencies or administrative organizations independent of this pyramidal structure, with the political components (ministers of state, for example) answering to Parliament.[915]

With the complexification of social and legal relations, a new type of administration has emerged, which has been identified with the very idea of regulation. Regulation can be considered a form of administration that differs from the pure bureaucratic model,[916] and consists of "mostly

911 FUKUYAMA, Francis. *Political Order and Political Decay: From the Industrial Revolution to the Globalization of Democracy*. New York: Farrar, Straus and Giroux, 2014, p. 66–67.

912 FLEISCHER, Julia. Federal Administration. *In*: KUHLMANN, Sabine *et al* (Orgs.). *Public Administration in Germany*. Cham: Palgrave Macmillan, 2021, p. 61, 66, 67.

913 SCHNEIDER, Jens-Peter. Regulation and Europeanisation as Key Patterns of Change in Administrative Law. *In*: RUFFERT, Matthias (Org.). *The Transformation of Administrative Law in Europe*. Munich: Sellier European Law Publishers, 2007, p. 310.

914 HOMSY, George C.; LIU, Zhilin; WARNER, Mildred E. Multilevel Governance: Framing the Integration of Top-Down and Bottom-Up Policymaking. *International Journal of Public Administration*, v. 42, n. 7, p. 572–582, 2019, p. 574.

915 SCHNEIDER, *op. cit.*, p. 310.

916 In essence, it is difficult to speak of pure models, not least because Weber's vision was structured in ideal types and configurations that could be abstracted. In practice, elements of patrimonialism can subsist in bureaucratic structures, just as these permeate other models considered to be neopatrimonialist. For a critical view of the dichotomy between patrimonial and bureaucratic administration, its expression in the Brazilian case and contemporary forms of neopatrimonialism, see, respectively, RUDOLPH, Lloyd I.; RUDOLPH, Susanne Hoeber. Authority and Power in Bureaucratic and Patrimonial Administration: A Revisionist Interpretation of Weber on Bureaucracy. *World Politics*, v. 31, n. 2, p. 195–227, 1979; PINHO, José Antonio Gomes de; SACRAMENTO, Ana Rita Silva. Brazil: between the modern

sector-specific rules establishing markets and specific public obligations with regard to competition and certain social interests".[917] These proactive organizational activities generally require a multidimensional balance of interests and decision-making processes in contexts of great uncertainty. In this case, the decision-making model based simply on pre-established and sufficient rules is questioned, and the increasingly uncertain environment "demands new forms of administrative decision-making, knowledge-generating monitoring procedures, as well as increased flexibility to adjust administrative decisions to new perceptions".[918]

In environments with greater dynamism, such as those observed due to the development of technology and economic activities, the clarity and stability of the application of the law based on conventions and meanings shared in everyday life is losing its place.[919] The positivist idea that the meaning of the law can simply be recognized[920] - since it is based on pre-established conventions - is becoming increasingly questionable, and the law is more often dealing with a kind of knowledge-generating infrastructure necessary for the process of generating legal knowledge,[921] such as regulatory processes. Regulatory law, then, does not imply simply restricting freedoms in order to avoid certain consequences. On the contrary, regulation organizes markets proactively, building alternatives and paths for economic activities that require some kind of intervention.[922] In other words, regulation complements the legislative and judicial processes with the institutional functions of constraining and enabling.[923]

In the current relationship between the state and the market, especially in the forms of intervention in dynamic economic activity, law comes to mean less the application of the material result of the traditional legislative

bureaucracy of Weber and resilient patrimonialism. *Management Research: The Journal of the Iberoamerican Academy of Management*, v. 13, n. 2, p. 140–159, 2015; BACH, Daniel C. Patrimonialism and neopatrimonialism: comparative trajectories and readings. *Commonwealth & Comparative Politics*, v. 49, n. 3, p. 275–294, 2011.

917 SCHNEIDER, *op. cit.*, p. 311.

918 *Ibid.*, p. 313.

919 TRUTE, Hans Heinrich. On knowledge and law: The role of law in the generation and harmonisation of knowledge. *In*: HORATSCHEK, Anna Margaretha (Org.). *Competing Knowledges - Wissen im Widerstreit.* Berlin, Boston: De Gruyter, 2020, v. 9, p. 103.

920 *Ibid.*, p. 105.

921 *Ibid.*, p. 115.

922 SCHNEIDER, *op. cit.*, p. 312.

923 See section1.9.1 above.

process (whose premise is stable or pre-established shared conventions) and more the conformation of a legal-institutional infrastructure for the generation and assimilation of knowledge, through the production of valid and effective normative determinations, which, even though they are located at an non-statutory level, often only draw their procedural legitimacy from the law[924] and their basis for validity. The institutionalization of this reflective and learning structure is essential if the rules applied in regulated sectors are to be effective, given the strength of the private or delegated activity. It can even coexist with major legal frameworks that organize sectoral public policies, configuring their legal institutions and assigning competences, but not necessarily.

Today, however, the development of new products and services in the market economy takes place in ever shorter cycles. This is partly due to the action of competitive forces themselves, which are the driving force behind the obsolescence of technology,[925] and partly because the life cycle of products related to the IT and computing sector is itself shorter than that of traditional sectors of the economy.[926] This shortening of product cycles and their technologies makes more evident the process of diminishing or disappearing clarity and stability of the knowledge and conventions on which the laws arising from the traditional legislative process are based, and it emphasizes the function of legal infrastructures in the production of knowledge. Although parliaments and courts are still central elements of the political and legal systems,[927] the law in the strict sense (statutes) is becoming a late and often inadequate instrument for shaping the conduct

---

924 Procedural legitimacy consists of precise administrative process rites that fully identify the points of interface between the Administration and the people affected by its decisions, according to SCHIRATO, Vitor Rhein. A deterioração do sistema regulatório brasileiro. *Revista de Direito Público da Economia*, v. 11, n. 44, p. 249–274, 2013, p. 261.

925 BRAUN, Christoph-Friedrich von. The Acceleration Trap. *Sloan Management Review*, v. 32, n. 1, 1990, p. 50.

926 BYUN, Jeongeun; SUNG, Tae Eung; PARK, Hyun Woo. Technological innovation strategy: how do technology life cycles change by technological area. *Technology Analysis & Strategic Management*, v. 30, n. 1, p. 98–112, 2017, p. 108.

927 Illustrative of this view is the classical Luhmann Systems Theory. In his conception, the basic element of society is communication and society is formed by systems that work based on communicative reality. In this context, there is a functional differentiation between the systems, each one having a different semantics for this communication. Within systems, organizations can be created and each system needs an organization to make a decision. Such as, for example, the court (legal system) and parliament (political system). LUHMANN, Niklas. Politische Verfassungen im Kontext des Gesellschaftssystems (1. Teil). *Der Staat*, v. 12, n. 2, p. 1–22,

performed in the context of activities involving these technologies, especially if they are eminently private activities.

This issue is not unaccompanied by disputes over visions. The limits of the administrative and interpretative role of agencies in the face of the primary legislative role of the Legislative Branch and the jurisdictional role of the Judicial Branch were the subject of a paradigmatic decision by the Supreme Court of the United States (SCOTUS) in the early 1980s, which ruled in favor of the interpretative power of agencies over the meaning of normative texts approved by the Legislative Branch.[928] This consolidated a doctrine "of implicit delegation of interpretive authority",[929] which would later come under increasing pressure for changes,[930] until, in 2024, it was revised by the SCOTUS to diminish this interpretive power of the administration.[931] From the point of view of public policy, this discussion transcends the American constitutional scenario, as it highlights a political dispute between a type of conservatism that seeks to curb the transformative power of executive government action under the argument of protecting individual rights, and a progressivism that sees flexible government action as a way of achieving material objectives and solving collective problems more quickly, in the direction of protecting social rights. In the latter case, in short, less *laissez-faire* and more government action.

In a broad sense, regulation implies, to some degree, a reduction in the private individual's sphere of freedom, and deregulation is an increase in that same sphere. From the point of view of society and the conduct of individuals, the rule is broad freedom, and only in cases where the law determines, is this freedom limited. This rule is legally expressed in the maxim "no one shall be obliged to do or refrain from doing anything except by virtue of the law", in Article 5, II of the Brazilian Federal Constitution.[932] From the state's point of view, considering an originally absolute power that

1973, p. 5; COSTA, Éverton Garcia da; COELHO, Gabriel Bandeira. Para entender a sociologia de Niklas Luhmann. *Caderno CRH*, v. 30, n. 81, p. 597–599, 2017, p. 597–599.

928 Chevron U.S.A., Inc. v. NRDC, 467 U.S. 837 (1984)

929 MERRILL, Thomas W. *The Chevron doctrine: its rise and fall, and the future of the administrative state.* Cambridge, Massachusetts: Harvard University Press, 2022, p. 81, 93–97.

930 KREPS, Sarah; KRINER, Doug. How AI Threatens Democracy. *Journal of Democracy*, v. 34, n. 4, p. 122–131, 2023, p. 124.

931 Loper Bright Enters. v. Raimondo, 544 F. Supp. 3d 82 (D.D.C. 2021)

932 In this case, 'law' has the more specific meaning of statute. In the original, "ninguém será obrigado a fazer ou deixar de fazer alguma coisa senão em virtude de lei".

cries out for limitation, the general rule in law is that of non-freedom. For Canotilho, this means a combination of two principles: the "prevalence of the law (*Vorrang des Gesetzes*) and the principle of the reservation of [statutory] law (*Vorbehalt des Gesetzes*)".[933] This conjunction can be deduced from the interpretation *a contrario sensu* of the same item II of article 5 of the Constitution, together with the caput of article 37.[934]

Thus, the process of limiting citizens' freedom is an intentional intervention[935] in the broadest sense, whose most important role today is still that of the Legislative Branch, which will provide the necessary legitimacy for this intervention.[936] However, as seen above, this regulatory process is no longer dependent solely on the legislative process, at least not directly. The advent of the regulation paradigm (especially economic regulation) allows non-statutory (subordinate legislation) regulation to reach activities more efficiently and quickly, while preserving the legitimacy of the intervention, whether through the procedural legitimacy of the institution of the rules (participation), formal legitimacy (the basis for the validity of subordinate legislation rules is found in the law and the Constitution), or material legitimacy (the result of the regulation itself, if good, generates favorable expectations in the recipients in the face of future regulations).

With regard to the state, the establishment of rules for the actions of administrators can also be seen as a regulatory process, but on a diametrically opposite spectrum (authorizing) to the regulatory process of private activities (restricting, constraining). This process deals with legal authorizations for the actions of public authorities, in other words, authorizing commands that lift cloaks of unlawfulness over conduct that is actually possible for state agents or, at least, over whose legality there are reasonable doubts that inhibit the administrator from acting, out of caution or fear of legal consequences.

---

933 CANOTILHO, José Joaquim Gomes. *Direito constitucional.* 7. ed. Coimbra: Almedina, 1993, p. 371. In the original, "prevalência da lei (Vorrang des Gesetzes) e o princípio da reserva de lei (Vorbehalt des Gesetzes)".

934 "Art. 37: The direct and indirect public administration of any of the Powers of the Union, the States, the Federal District and the Municipalities shall obey the principles of legality, impersonality, morality, publicity and efficiency, as well as the following:". In the original, "Art. 37. A administração pública direta e indireta de qualquer dos Poderes da União, dos Estados, do Distrito Federal e dos Municípios obedecerá aos princípios de legalidade, impessoalidade, moralidade, publicidade e eficiência e, também, ao seguinte:".

935 KOOP, Christel; LODGE, Martin. What is regulation? An interdisciplinary concept analysis. *Regulation & Governance*, v. 11, n. 1, p. 95–108, 2017, p. 97–98.

936 CANOTILHO, *op. cit.*, p. 371.

The authorizing regulation of the public administration can be complemented in the same way as it is in the private sphere: by the creation of a structure of incentives to achieve some goal, such as the allocation of financial resources, among other types. The combination of these factors in a legal-institutional environment leads to different emphases concerning the effects and expected behavior of the actors, which are presented differently in the public and private spheres.

In the private sphere, the combination of lower regulation, unaccompanied by incentives, results in an institutional configuration that is conducive to enabling actors' behavior. If regulation is high in a scenario with limited incentives, behavior is restricted. In the presence of strong regulation and complementary incentives, the scenario is one of promoting behavior, according to the intervention model defined by the state. And in the case of low regulation and strong complementary incentives, there is a risk scenario: the abuse of positions and powers and the exacerbation of market failures.

In the public sphere, on the other hand, less (authorizing) regulation and a lack of incentives result in a scenario of restriction, with the paralysis of creative and innovative activity. In the presence of a sufficient authorizing regulatory process but without complementary incentives, the institutional configuration makes the administration conducive to enabling the administrator's action; in other words, it allows the administrators' initiatives to be carried out, creating enabling points but without defining a clear political direction or mission. When regulation is sufficient and there are complementary incentives for administrators' actions around an agenda, the scenario is one of promotion. And when there is insufficient or inadequate authorizing regulation, with the concomitant presence of incentives, there is a risk scenario. The latter means either the possibility of actions by administrators that violate citizens' rights, or the possibility of actions that, even if they don't violate citizens' individual rights, are not in line with the law or simply with the view of external administrative control, generating possible punishments for managers and civil servants in general. The diagram below illustrates the scenarios. It is worth noting that, counterintuitively, the output configurations are not symmetrical.

Figure 2 - administration under the regulatory logic

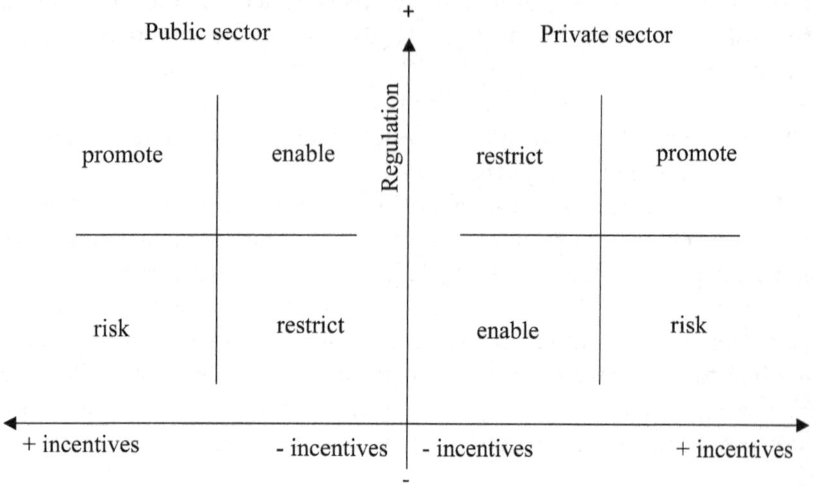

Source: Own elaboration.

Unlike what already happens in the private sector due to the regulatory model based on the rule-making power of regulatory agencies, this whole process in the public sphere is intensely and permanently dependent on the legislative process. It is not uncommon for this legislative process to be specially qualified, such as that required for the approval of complementary laws[937] or constitutional amendments, or subject to rules of competence and initiative limiting the possibilities of legislative modification, such as article 61, §1 of the Brazilian Constitution. However, there is nothing to prevent various aspects of it from also being delegated to agencies by the Legislative Branch, in the exercise of its function as a macro-institution in an experimentalist administration. In this sense, the Legislative Branch has the role of establishing guidelines and objectives, but they must not be excessive or too specific, so as not to frustrate the creativity of initiatives in the search for solutions.[938]

This type of configuration also has the advantage of shielding the actions of public managers from excessively repressive administrative external control, by representing an intermediary legitimizing body. The creation of

937 A complementary law is a type of Brazilian statutory law that requires a higher proportion of votes for its approval than an ordinary law.

938 DORF, Michael C.; SABEL, Charles F. A constitution of democratic experimentalism. *Columbia Law Review*, v. 98, n. 2, p. 267–473, 1998, p. 428.

legitimizing bodies capable of giving symbolic strength to policies created and implemented at materially weak federal levels would be achieved by stimulating a centralizing activity to coordinate efforts. It would have the power to monitor all the widespread initiatives and promote this "communication" between what is done at the top and what is done elsewhere, carrying out benchmarks that bring information from local initiatives to the coordination nucleus, incorporating them into a thesaurus of legitimate experimental initiatives, and creating a kind of seal of approval for the centralized entity. This seal would not necessarily be one of merit approval (in the sense of stating that it is a good or bad policy), but it would show that it is an innovation initiative that deserves to be tested in public administration practice and is in line with best practice. This would not confer a greater degree of legal autonomy on the controlled entities, but it would have a political effect in this sense, considering that the entity's autonomy is backed by a central coordinating body whose institutional strength and credibility guarantee the legitimacy of experimental actions.

The issue today is that administrative bodies legally have a great deal of autonomy, which the repressive culture can pejoratively perceive as an autonomy "to make mistakes" indiscriminately, the result of probable bad faith or ineptitude. However, they do not have the autonomy to create. Real autonomy to create is guaranteed through a coordinating structure within the administration that is in constant dialogue with these autonomous entities, including ensuring, through responsive means, that experimentation is carried out responsibly. At the same time, the culture of the controller is modified to look at the macro issue - how this coordination is carried out, what the metapolitical guidelines are that guide the experimentalist practice, and whether the results of those processes taken as a whole are positive - representing the full nature of innovation. In this way, the effective autonomy of the entities is achieved; in other words, the pressures of perverse incentives on the decision-making process are relieved, creating the right environment for institutional and material innovation, which, together with positive pressure instruments such as simulated competition and political scrutiny, generates innovation.[939]

In the case of digital transformation in the Brazilian public sector, this can be clearly seen in the cases analyzed of electronic elections, electronic judicial proceedings and also in the governance structure of the internet,

939 VERHOEST, Koen; VERSCHUERE, Bram; BOUCKAERT, Geert. Pressure, Legitimacy, and Innovative Behavior by Public Organizations. *Governance*, v. 20, n. 3, p. 469–497, 2007, p. 471, 472, 473, 489, 490.

albeit in different ways. With regard to the digitalization of the Judiciary, this authorizing regulatory function was delegated with the creation of the CNJ, which began to regulate the administrative and disciplinary aspects of the Judiciary. As a result, it acquired the power to deal not only with the initial digitization process but also with the ongoing incorporation of technology, issuing rules more quickly and in line with the pace of change. The political impetus came mainly at the beginning, with the creation of the full institutionalization structures that form the equilibrium and the general guidelines for action that legitimize the body's actions, while dynamic regulation was conveniently delegated so that it no longer depended on political impulses at the legislative level, as it already started from a configuration in which preferences are partially frozen.

In the case of electronic voting machines, there was no creation of a new institutional structure, nor was it delegated, in a reform process, to an entity of this kind. However, because of the particular way in which the Electoral Justice was originally organized, as well as the constitutional competences of the Superior Electoral Court - TSE stemming from historical issues, the autonomous environment for the authorizing regulation already existed, either because of the recognition of the TSE's regulatory power by the Supreme Court, or because of the strength and institutional independence of the Judiciary in relation to the other Powers and external administrative control. When this enabling environment also came to rely on complementary incentives, in particular an agenda politically fostered by the top leadership, the conditions for the effective promotion of policies were created, and the result was a direct consequence of this.

Finally, in the case of internet governance, the CGI, even without a robust legal form and without its competences being laid down in law, also had a delegated role in regulating public infrastructures for access to the internet, which was legitimized in particular by the results presented, but also by the good accommodation of the interests of the various actors in the management and decision-making structure. This was enhanced by the presence of complementary incentives, notably the financial autonomy resulting from the revenue obtained from domain registrations.

In the German experience, even considering its conservatism, some of these elements can be observed in the current model for developing Digital Government. Of particular note is the leading role that the *IT-Planungsrat* has gained over the course of its institutional trajectory as a result of strengthening the institutionalization of the previous inter-federative decision-making bodies. This coordinating, enabling, and promoting role of the

IT-Planungsrat is enhanced by the incentives provided by both the OZG and the financing structures of the policies, secured through European policies promoting the modernization of administrations, and also by the prioritization of the subject internally, with increasing dedication to the matter in political coalition agreements. Another sign of this is the NKR's recommendation to create an agency dedicated to the issue, to replace the current governance structure.[940]

Therefore, the state must be able to "regulate" itself in digital transformation processes, at least as quickly and efficiently as it is able to regulate the market. The same self-regulatory logic, already verified in the three cases analyzed, should be applied in the case of the Digital Government policies *stricto sensu* examined in chapter 2. This structure would have to be able to respond quickly and adequately to the challenges of integrating administrations and, at the same time, as Sabel and Dorf argue, be responsible for generating benchmarks and learning "through the generalization of successful local initiatives".[941] In line with what Trute says about the dynamics of regulation in general, it would be "the institutionalization of an infrastructure specifically designed for a kind of permanent knowledge production",[942] but aimed at producing knowledge about the best use of information technology in the administration, the best rules for its control, standards and good practices. They also combine elements of innovation labs and sandboxes, dealt with in sections 2.2.1.10 and 2.2.2.7, making it possible to test new regulatory approaches for the administration's own day-to-day activities. These arrangements also favor the development of digital public infrastructures with an impact far beyond the government sphere, promoting significant and rapid social transformations.[943]

---

940 NKR. *Jahresbericht 2023 des Nationalen Normenkontrollrates.* Berlin: Bundesministerium der Justiz, 2023, p. 48–49.

941 DORF; SABEL, *op. cit.*, p. 412.

942 TRUTE, Hans Heinrich. On knowledge and law: The role of law in the generation and harmonisation of knowledge. *In*: HORATSCHEK, Anna Margaretha (Org.). *Competing Knowledges - Wissen im Widerstreit.* Berlin, Boston: De Gruyter, 2020, v. 9, p. 114.

943 A good example of this kind of digital public infrastructure is PIX, an instant payment method developed by the Central Bank of Brazil which, among other effects, has contributed to a significant increase in the number of Brazilians who have a bank account. On the determinants of this policy, as well as data on its impact on Brazilian society, see SCHAPIRO, Mario G.; MOUALLEM, Pedro Salomon Bezerra; DANTAS, Eric Gil. PIX: explaining a state-owned Fintech. *Brazilian Journal of Political Economy*, v. 43, n. 4, p. 874–892, 2023.

4.6 Public services, public participation and technology as a catalyst

When it comes to public services, the field of law most often refers to a political-legal concept,[944] i.e., a collective choice about what is or is not the object of public provision expressed through the requirements of the statutory law. But the notion of public service as a factor of social cohesion and essentiality, in a sociological concept,[945] has the merit of highlighting the importance of bringing these activities closer to the real needs of the population and, consequently, the importance of integrating citizens into the decision-making and execution processes of public services beyond the structures of representative democracy. Unger argues that there is a dualism between "administrative Fordism", with the state bureaucracy providing public services of a lower quality than those offered on the market to people who have the money to buy them, and the alternative of pure and simple privatization of public services to companies interested in profiting from the activity.[946] The path to the full realization of the democratic project in this scenario would involve the state organizing, monitoring, and financing society so that it can participate in the experimental and competitive provision of public services.[947]

The consolidation of Digital Government in public administration, with legal institutions and their actors able to accommodate innovations, is part of the set of state activities that foster this dynamic capability through the effective participation of people in the direction of government, in the characterization and development of public services and in making agile and appropriate decisions. With this, there is an integration between two dimensions of democracy, "participation in decision-making and involvement in problem-solving".[948]

It is well established in the literature that citizen trust is an essential element for the success of Digital Government, as it allows people to engage more easily with online public services and accept more significant changes

944 According to JÈZE, Gaston. *Les principes généraux du droit administratif.* Paris: Lib. Marcel GIRARD, 1930, p. 7.

945 According to DUGUIT, León. *Traité de Droit Constitutionnel.* Paris: Ancienne Librairie, 1923, p. 55.

946 UNGER, Roberto Mangabeira. A constituição do experimentalismo democrático. *Revista de Direito Administrativo*, v. 257, p. 57–72, 2011, p. 69.

947 *Ibid.*

948 FREGA, Roberto. *Pragmatism and the Wide View of Democracy.* Cham: Springer International Publishing, 2019, p. 300.

in the way they relate to government.[949] Less frequently explored is the capacity of Digital Government policies to increase the general level of trust citizens have in their relations with the state due to transformations in the expectations underlying them.[950]

In this regard, in private service provision, technology catalyzes transformations in legal relationships, changing the expectations and behaviors of those involved in the relationship, and substantially increasing mutual trust. Firstly, the repercussions are the reduction of transaction costs,[951] thanks to the modification of a set of legal relationships and deals underlying a given activity. High transaction costs make it impossible or discourage the exercise of certain activities under a given legal regime. With their reduction, the expectations of the social and economic actors involved and the opportunities for contracting are significantly altered.[952] As a result of the reduction in data collection costs and their massification, the costs of contracting the use of private property rights are also affected. Algorithmic solutions for renting a house or a car, for example, have made it easier and cheaper to coordinate actions and access to each of the types of utility included in the property right, so that the sharing economy is characterized precisely by this divisibility of uses which, with artificial intelligence re-

949 In this sense, AKKAYA, Cigdem; WOLF, Dr Petra; KRCMAR, Helmut. The Role of Trust in E-Government Adoption: A Literature Review. *In*: *AMCIS 2010 Proceedings*. Lima: Association for Information Systems, 2010; DISTEL, Bettina; KOELMANN, Holger; PLATTFAUT, Ralf; *et al.* Watch who you trust! A structured literature review to build a typology of e-government risks. *Information Systems and e-Business Management*, v. 20, n. 4, p. 789–818, 2022; DISTEL, Bettina; KOELMANN, Holger; SCHMOLKE, Florian; *et al.* The Role of Trust for Citizens' Adoption of Public E-Services. *In*: BLÖBAUM, Bernd (Org.). *Trust and Communication: Findings and Implications of Trust Research*. Cham: Springer International Publishing, 2021, p. 163–184.

950 See, for instance, PUERTAS, Alejandro Moreno; TEIGLAND, Robin. The trust revolution: Blockchain's potential to resolve institutional inefficiencies?. *In*: LARSSON, Anthony; TEIGLAND, Robin (Orgs.). *Digital Transformation and Public Services*. London: Routledge, 2019, p. 277–292.

951 The notion of transaction costs was first proposed by Ronald Coase and later developed by Oliver Williamson and is defined as "the costs necessary to carry out a transaction in the market, rather than within the company", consisting of the uncertainty typical of economic relations. SALOMÃO FILHO, Calixto. *Direito Concorrencial*. São Paulo: Malheiros, 2013, p. 391–392.

952 SOUZA, Carlos Affonso Pereira de; LEMOS, Ronaldo. Aspectos jurídicos da Economia do Compartilhamento: função social e tutela da confiança. *Revista de Direito da Cidade*, v. 8, n. 4, p. 1757, 2016.

sources, can be better allocated in time and space.[953] Thus, "in the big data economy, reduced transaction costs of accessing information are increasing the potential for improved efficiency, in terms of increased room for market transactions".[954]

A particularly notable effect of this is the modification of the social function of goods through greater protection of trust.[955] By means of instruments for controlling, checking, and managing information about products and services that have only become possible on a large scale through the adoption of new technology, the trust of the parties in the legal relationship is strengthened to the point of dispensing with previously necessary care and measures, as well as altering the expectations and behavior on a cultural level of users and service providers, who have come to trust each other more. As a result, in addition to encouraging the conclusion of legal transactions that were previously more risky, there has also been a change in behavioral culture.

Several of the obligations in the contracts involved are self-executing, via *smart contracts*, defined as internet protocols created for negotiating and implementing legal transactions in which the "clauses", using machine language and without intermediaries, establish and self-execute rights and obligations between parties who don't necessarily know each other and don't need any degree of trust in each other.[956] Smart contracts may or may not be a source of law, and there are two different cases. In the first, the smart contract is linked to a traditional, separate contract between the parties and will only have the function of automatically implementing the content of the deal, providing evidence of the existence of the agreement, its content, and carrying out its execution. In the second, there is no underlying contract, in the sense of a legal instrument signed by the parties that records the terms of an agreement, and the smart contract takes on the function of providing its own legal effects, in addition to its automatic

953 MARCIANO, Alain; NICITA, Antonio; RAMELLO, Giovanni Battista. Big data and big techs: understanding the value of information in platform capitalism. *European Journal of Law and Economics*, v. 50, n. 3, p. 345–358, 2020, p. 345–346.

954 *Ibid.*, p. 346.

955 SOUZA; LEMOS, *op. cit.*

956 GOMES, Silvana Santos. Smart Contracts: legal frontiers and insertion into the Creative Economy. *Brazilian Journal of Operations & Production Management*, v. 15, n. 3, p. 376–385, 2018, p. 377.

implementation.[957] As a result, the parties to the relationship don't have to worry about each other defaulting, at least in simple services such as transportation and the leasing of goods. Lower transaction costs and reduced information asymmetry have a direct impact on the social function of property and objective good faith.[958] The effectiveness of these two legal commands is strengthened by the transformation of how economic activities and legal transactions are carried out.

As far as the public sphere is concerned, it is often pointed out that the degree of trust people have in government is related to the effective involvement of citizens in public policy processes.[959] This presupposes transparency, but simply explaining the trade-offs and conflicts surrounding a decision on the suitability of one measure over another can have the opposite effect to that intended, reducing trust in the resolution structures.[960] Transparency mechanisms must, therefore, be accompanied by ways of involving citizens in the process. This is usually attempted through mechanisms of public/popular participation and forms of direct deliberation (such as participatory budgeting, for example), which are commonly tested but rarely consolidate themselves as something viable in the long term. Participatory budgeting, which was born in the city of Porto Alegre, Brazil, has gone into sharp decline in the country, largely due to low participation.[961] In Germany, participatory budgeting is experiencing similar challenges,[962] which suggests that the problems of this form of interaction are generalizable. Despite the fascination that proposals for deliberative democracy can cause, it doesn't seem that they are a sustainable alternative for widespread adoption in a government model of effective rapprochement with citizens.

Sabel and Dorf proposed a system called *directly deliberative polyarchy* as a way for citizens to actively participate in defining and evaluating public services, with broad access to information on best practices in other

957 GOVERNATORI, Guido *et al.* On legal contracts, imperative and declarative smart contracts, and blockchain systems. *Artificial Intelligence and Law*, v. 26, n. 4, p. 377–409, 2018, p. 378.

958 SOUZA; LEMOS, *op. cit.*

959 KUMAGAI, Saki; IORIO, Federica. *Building Trust in Government through Citizen Engagement.* Washington, DC: World Bank, 2020.

960 KETTL, Donald F. *Can governments earn our trust?* Cambridge, UK: Polity, 2017, p. 59.

961 LÜCHMANN, Lígia Helena Hahn. Fatores do declínio dos Orçamentos Participativos na região sul do Brasil. *Política & Sociedade*, v. 21, n. 50, p. 206–232, 2022.

962 ZEPIC, Robert; DAPP, Marcus; KRCMAR, Helmut. E-Partizipation und keiner macht mit. *HMD Praxis der Wirtschaftsinformatik*, v. 54, n. 4, p. 488–501, 2017.

jurisdictions and structured ways of comparing solutions.[963] It would be a form of democracy based on the dynamics of governance councils for defining public choices and organizing the provision of services through the information brought by local experiences, which would favor the accountability of managers and the reaffirmation of citizens' rights.[964] The innovations created would increase the performance of problem-solving processes, contributing to more innovations in a virtuous circle of continuous exchange of information and solutions, which themselves change the way the actors behave and relate to each other.[965] This model presupposes the establishment of benchmarking practices and the creation of the complex institutions needed to carry out the surveys and monitoring. It also involves direct deliberation by users on public policy decisions within administrative agencies in the case of public services.[966]

Sabel and Dorf's proposal for a deliberative polyarchy requires political reforms that are difficult to achieve in any society. Therefore, it has an inevitably idealistic character and is the subject of numerous criticisms regarding its concrete content.[967] The idea, however, could be an inspiring seed for ways of involving citizens in public services of unprecedented proportions, given that today there is the possibility of obtaining and recirculating information mediated automatically by technology, which goes far beyond speech, opinion polling, and deliberative participation.[968] This "data polyarchy" can be complemented with other forms of passive and active participation, such as opinion polls and surveys that ask questions to better understand how citizens actually think and what they want. In this respect, data science and the technology embedded in a cell phone allow indirect questions to be asked, rather than the direct ones that are characteristic of a normal deliberative process. The problem of misreporting in opinion polls is well known, especially when it comes to sensitive questions. This concern has led researchers to develop various methods to compensate for

963 DORF, Michael C.; SABEL, Charles F. A constitution of democratic experimentalism. *Columbia Law Review*, v. 98, n. 2, p. 267–473, 1998, p. 288.

964 *Ibid.*, p. 319.

965 *Ibid.*, p. 322.

966 *Ibid.*, p. 439.

967 See, for instance, SCHEUERMAN, William E. Democratic Experimentalism or Capitalist Synchronization? Critical Reflections on Directly-Deliberative Polyarchy. *Canadian Journal of Law & Jurisprudence*, v. 17, n. 1, p. 101–127, 2004.

968 In explaining the model, the authors cite the example of defining and redefining public transport routes and characteristics, which nowadays makes frequent use of data. DORF; SABEL, *op. cit.*, p. 317.

the distortion of results, especially involving indirect questions that could guarantee more reliable results,[969] even if they themselves have flaws and do not eliminate the problem completely.[970] But beyond the issue of sensitive questions, it can be said that survey methods in general, especially opinion polls, are not perfect and can generate bad results. In addition, there is the case where citizens answer wrong on purpose, but there is also the case where they are not even aware of their preferences or in a position to make a public policy choice, even if they are very well informed.

The practice of direct democracy systems, such as participatory budgets and assemblies, is based on the formulation of direct questions and clear choices: the allocation of a resource, the decision on whether or not to do a certain piece of work, etc., which can favor this type of distortion. In a "data polyarchy", made possible by technology, the use of indirect questions for administrative decision-making becomes more feasible. In many cases, big data analysis can complement or even replace surveys[971] (and direct deliberative processes), proving to be a powerful tool for encouraging people to get involved in the process of government action[972] but in a different way from the traditional assembly. It is often said today that social networks know people better than they know themselves.[973] The prospect of the state also knowing precisely people's preferences through instruments such as these should be considered as a public policy option, as long as it is geared towards the common good and guarantees individual rights, which would already be a qualitative leap compared to what is currently practiced by the private sector.

---

969 HOFFMANN, Adrian *et al.* On the comprehensibility and perceived privacy protection of indirect questioning techniques. *Behavior Research Methods*, v. 49, n. 4, p. 1470–1483, 2017, p. 1472.

970 JERKE, Julia *et al.* Too sophisticated even for highly educated survey respondents? A qualitative assessment of indirect question formats for sensitive questions. *Survey Research Methods*, v. 13, n. 3, p. 319–351, 2019.

971 See WHITAKER, Stephan D. Big Data versus a survey. *The Quarterly Review of Economics and Finance*, v. 67, p. 285–296, 2018; CALLEGARO, Mario; YANG, Yongwei. The Role of Surveys in the Era of "Big Data". *In*: VANNETTE, David L.; KROSNICK, Jon A. (Orgs.). *The Palgrave Handbook of Survey Research*. Cham: Springer International Publishing, 2018, p. 175–192.

972 ARAGONA, Biagio; DE ROSA, Rosanna. Big data in policy making. *Mathematical Population Studies*, v. 26, n. 2, p. 107–113, 2019, p. 111.

973 PETERS, Michael A. Platform ontologies, the AI crisis and the ability to hack humans 'An algorithm knows me better than I know myself'. *Educational Philosophy and Theory*, v. 52, n. 6, p. 593–601, 2020.

In this way, the state's dynamic capability to bring public services closer to citizens lies much less in direct democracy practices, which have already proven to be problematic or excessively idealized, and more in the adoption of passive citizen participation instruments through data, which does not, *a priori*, represent an incompatibility with the system of individual rights, although it does offer challenges in the construction of legal-institutional designs that guarantee the preservation of these rights. Instead of a dreaded digital Leviathan, this would be something closer to a smart social contract in which efficiency is enhanced by trust and vice versa.

4.7 Chapter conclusion

The welfare state is a historical construction that responds to challenges related to the complexification of social and economic relations and the social conflict resulting from the unfolding of capitalism. In Brazil, it is currently facing very unique conditions of consolidation and, at the same time, the urgency of recovery, amidst a context of crises and unfavorable political and economic times. Digital Government, in this scenario, takes the form of an enabler of the state's dynamic capabilities, representing not only gains in economic efficiency provided by technology, but also a leap in quality in the relationship between citizens and government, with increasing affirmation and enjoyment of social rights. To achieve this, attention must be paid to the need for clear political direction, taking advantage of the original vocations of federalism to overcome coordination problems, as well as adopting an authorizing regulatory logic for the activities of the public administration and new ways of involving the population in the processes of formulating policies and providing public services.

As previously mentioned, Digital Government can be defined as the continuous incorporation, in the public sector, of state-of-the-art information technology with the greatest possible potential for realizing democratic opportunities and state goals. It is a notion that is part of the broader discussion about the role of the state and the quality of democracies, and aims not only to optimize economic efficiency but also the maximum realization of rights.

Innovation is central to understanding the concept, as it consists of both the advance of technology and the advance of the legal-institutional structures that make it possible to assimilate it into public power. Going down to the specific level, Digital Government has concrete expressions in the intensive use of data, citizen orientation, the idea of transparency and popular/public participation, and the integration of technology and innovation into the public policy cycle.

The plasticity of legal institutions under public law through design or reinterpretation favors greater adaptability on the part of the state, which in turn is fundamental to the success of public policies that incorporate up-to-date technology into the relationship between government and citizens. In order to overcome the paradigm of digital governments as mere optimizers of relations and services and elevate them to powerful instruments of democratic re-signification and the realization of rights, this issue must be on the horizon of policy makers, enforcers, and also controllers so that the law is a facilitator rather than an obstacle to development.

Conclusion

This dissertation began by asking how legal institutions can contribute to the development of Digital Government in Brazil to improve efficiency, transparency, and social participation, making the evolution of the state faster and less dependent on crises. The analysis of experiences and concrete cases, in the light of the theoretical framework specially shaped for the research objectives, indicates some ways of understanding the role of law in the conception of the Brazilian Digital Government.

When examining the components of the Digital Government in Brazil, its trajectory, arrangements, and developments, it can be seen that the policy is limited to a semi-institutionalized structure that has its origins in the early days of its implementation and has been reproduced, without major transformations, over the years. Even when an attempt was made to raise the level of institutionalization by passing a federal law on the subject, the result was that the law reproduced the same structures that had been in place until then, mainly neglecting federative negotiation and the distribution of competences, especially with regard to the role and importance of states and municipalities in the digital transformation process.

On an international level, Germany is contradictorily lagging behind in the digital transformation of the public sector, but with an institutional framework that is constantly evolving around concrete coordination instruments aimed at overcoming the challenges arising from the complexity of its federalism, which can serve as an inspiration for Brazil. The *IT-Planungsrat* and its executive arm, the result of a long process that involved constitutional reform, a treaty between the states, and the passing of laws by parliament, are instances of federal coordination that make structured initiatives to overcome the digital backwardness possible, such as the OZG and its "*Einer für Alle*" form of implementation. Despite its own challenges and probable insufficiency in resolving issues related to German Digital Government, as pointed out by the NKR, this structure is better able to respond to future challenges than the way in which Digital Government is organized in Brazil, i.e., in a compartmentalized way, dependent on constant exogenous impulses, and excessively linked to a model of predominance of optimization and search for economic efficiency. In the case of Germany, the issue has become important enough to be highlighted in the agreements of the government coalitions, and these political impulses have led to the formation of new balances of preferences around the issue, translated into incremental but robust institutional improvements, capable of generating endogenous impulses of their own. European practices of encouragement and promotion are also important here, with strong political affirmation through coordinative and communicative discourses on the subject of digitalization, making it a priority for European integration and cohesion, as well as programs with a substantial amount of resources earmarked for initiatives in the member states.

At the Brazilian level, the cases of digital transformation of electronic elections, the judicial process, and Internet governance also highlight legal-institutional factors that are key to the success of these policies. They must be observed in an exercise of institutional imagination of Digital Government for the future, encompassing the existence of conditions conducive to experimental practice, protection from excessively repressive external administrative control, financial autonomy, and the combination of the agendas of the bureaucracy and the leadership.

In this sense, it is proposed that the Digital Government in Brazil be the very expression of the dynamic capabilities of a digital welfare state that goes far beyond the paradigm of economic efficiency, representing a new form of relationship between citizens and government and a means of energizing citizen relations, in the full realization of the democratic project. This is achieved through arrangements that simultaneously amplify the political direction impulses around the mission of digital transformation, enhance the experimental effects of federalism by centralizing certain activities and decentralizing others, generalize experimental solutions, and regulate the administration itself to create enabling points and environments sensitive/responsive to incentives. Furthermore, it involves (self)regulating matters that pertain to the use of information technology in administrations, within the limits of guaranteeing fundamental rights, similar to the currently played by the National Council of Justice (CNJ) in the Judiciary. The creation of infrastructures for the generation of legal knowledge that favor the plasticity of state institutions and their adaptability to emerging technologies is a condition for the state to regain its leading role in mediating the public sphere and adequately fulfill its purposes.

The concrete way in which the suggestions can be assimilated has a wide range of possibilities, varying from the creation of an agency that brings together all these competences, to the expansion of competences of existing institutions, such as the National Digital Government Network, which today is a federative cooperation of a voluntary and collaborative nature, or the CGI itself, which today already has initiatives to produce content and research on the subject. These forms may have their own administrative structure or manage resources reallocated from other agencies, in unconventional organizational forms that avoid the unnecessary expenditure of resources on creating additional administrative structures. In theory, there are various ways to implement these measures, each with its advantages and disadvantages, requiring varying degrees of political and legislative effort, which should be the subject of further research.

References

AARNIO, Aulis. Paradigms in Legal Dogmatics. *In*: PECZENIK, Aleksander; LINDAHL, Lars; ROERMUND, Bert Van (Orgs.). *Theory of Legal Science: Proceedings of the Conference on Legal Theory and Philosopy of Science Lund, Sweden, December 11–14, 1983.* Dordrecht: Springer Netherlands, 1984, p. 25–38. (Synthese Library).

ABEL, Luiz Fernando. Trust in ICT for the public sector: e-voting in Brazil's 2014 election. *Planejamento e Políticas Públicas*, n. 50, 2018.

ABREU, Marjory da Costa; SILVA, Bruno. A critical analysis of "Law 4.0": The use of Automation and Artificial Intelligence and their impact on the judicial landscape of Brazil. *Revista de Direitos Fundamentais e Tributação*, v. 1, n. 3, p. 1–16, 2020.

ACKERMAN, Bruce. Constitutional Politics/Constitutional Law. *The Yale Law Journal*, v. 99, n. 3, p. 453–547, 1989.

ADAMI, Mateus Piva. *A universalização das telecomunicações no Brasil: uma análise de seus arranjos institucionais.* PhD dissertation (Economic and Financial Law), University of São Paulo, São Paulo, 2021.

AFONSO, C.A. The Internet and the community in Brazil: background, issues, and options. *IEEE Communications Magazine*, v. 34, n. 7, p. 62–68, 1996.

AHN, Michael J.; BRETSCHNEIDER, Stuart. Politics of E-Government: E-Government and the Political Control of Bureaucracy. *Public Administration Review*, v. 71, n. 3, p. 414–424, 2011.

AKKAYA, Cigdem; WOLF, Dr Petra; KRCMAR, Helmut. The Role of Trust in E-Government Adoption: A Literature Review. *In*: *AMCIS 2010 Proceedings*. Lima: Association for Information Systems, 2010.

ALANI, Mohammed M. *Guide to OSI and TCP/IP Models.* Cham: Springer International Publishing, 2014. (SpringerBriefs in Computer Science).

ALBER, Jens. Der deutsche Sozialstaat im Licht international vergleichender Daten. *Leviathan*, v. 26, n. 2, p. 199–227, 1998.

ALLEN, Hilary J. Regulatory Sandboxes. *George Washington Law Review*, v. 87, n. 3, p. 579–645, 2019.

ALMEIDA, Virgilio A. F. The Evolution of Internet Governance: Lessons Learned from NETmundial. *IEEE Internet Computing*, v. 18, n. 5, p. 65–69, 2014.

ALVARGONZÁLEZ, David. Multidisciplinarity, Interdisciplinarity, Transdisciplinarity, and the Sciences. *International Studies in the Philosophy of Science*, v. 25, n. 4, p. 387–403, 2011.

ALVES, Raquel de Andrade Vieira. Federalismo fiscal e distorções do modelo brasileiro. *Revista de Finanças Públicas, Tributação e Desenvolvimento*, v. 6, n. 6, 2018.

ALVIM, Frederico Franco; NETO, Jaime Barreiros; SANTIAGO, Marta Cristina Jesus (Orgs.). *25 Anos da Urna Eletrônica: Tecnologia e Integridade nas eleições brasileiras.* Salvador: Tribunal Regional Eleitoral da Bahia, 2021.

AMABLE, Bruno; DEMMOU, Lilas; LEDEZMA, Ivan. The Lisbon strategy and structural reforms in Europe. *Transfer: European Review of Labour and Research*, v. 15, n. 1, p. 33–52, 2009.

AMATO, Lucas Fucci. *Construtivismo jurídico: teoria no direito*. Curitiba: Juruá, 2017.

AMATO, Lucas Fucci. Justiça Social e Instituições: a visão de Unger comparada ao Liberalismo Igualitário e à Teoria Crítica. *Revista Estudos Políticos*, v. 8, n. 16, p. 90–114, 2019.

ANASTÁCIO, Kimberly. Brazil's approach to multistakeholderism: multi-participation in the Brazilian Internet Steering Committee (CGI. br). *Berkman Center for Internet & Society at Harvard University*, 2015.

ANDRADE, Maria Abad. *Verfassungsgerichtliche Entscheidungsfindung und ihre Folgen: Das Türkische Verfassungsgericht zwischen Mehrheitslogik und Konsensverfahren*. Baden-Baden: Nomos, 2020.

ANDREONI, Antonio; ROBERTS, Simon. Governing data and digital platforms: regulations, competition and industrial policies, with sectoral case studies from South Africa. *Digital Pathways at Oxford Paper Series*, n. 5, 2020.

ANDREWS, Josephine T.; MONTINOLA, Gabriella R. Veto Players and the Rule of Law in Emerging Democracies. *Comparative Political Studies*, v. 37, n. 1, p. 55–87, 2004.

ANSOFF, H. Igor. Strategic issue management. *Strategic Management Journal*, v. 1, n. 2, p. 131–148, 1980.

ANTHES, Gary. Estonia: A model for e-government. *Communications of the ACM*, v. 58, n. 6, p. 18–20, 2015.

ARAGONA, Biagio; DE ROSA, Rosanna. Big data in policy making. *Mathematical Population Studies*, v. 26, n. 2, p. 107–113, 2019.

ARANHA, Diego F.; VAN DE GRAAF, Jeroen. The Good, the Bad, and the Ugly: Two Decades of E-Voting in Brazil. *IEEE Security & Privacy*, v. 16, n. 6, p. 22–30, 2018.

ARAÚJO, Alexandra Fuchs de. *Políticas Públicas, Poder Judiciário e o Direito à Moradia*. Belo Horizonte: Forum, 2023.

ARAÚJO, Diógenes Carlos; LIMA, Alexandre; LIMA, João Pedro; *et al.* A Comparison of Classification Methods Applied to Legal Text Data. *In*: *Progress in Artificial Intelligence. EPIA 2021.* Cham: Springer, 2021, p. 68–80.

ARCOLEZE, Conrado Ferreira. O Caso Proconsult não morreu: *Faces da História*, v. 7, n. 1, p. 400–419, 2020.

AROGYASWAMY, Bernard. Big tech and societal sustainability: an ethical framework. *AI and Society*, v. 35, n. 4, p. 829–840, 2020.

ASSOUAD, Lydia; CHANCEL, Lucas; MORGAN, Marc. Extreme Inequality: Evidence from Brazil, India, the Middle East, and South Africa. *AEA Papers and Proceedings*, v. 108, p. 119–123, 2018.

ATTARD, Judie; ORLANDI, Fabrizio; SCERRI, Simon; *et al.* A systematic review of open government data initiatives. *Government Information Quarterly*, v. 32, n. 4, p. 399–418, 2015.

AVGEROU, Chrisanthi. Explaining Trust in IT-Mediated Elections: A Case Study of E-Voting in Brazil. *Journal of the Association for Information Systems*, v. 14, n. 8, p. 420–451, 2013.

AVGEROU, Chrisanthi; GANZAROLI, Andrea; POULYMENAKOU, Angeliki; *et al.* ICT and citizens' trust in government: lessons from electronic voting in Brazil. *In*: *Proceedings of the 9th conference on social implications of computers in developing countries*. São Paulo: IFIP, 2007.

ÁVILA, Thiago José Tavares; LANZA, Beatriz Barreto Brasileiro; VALOTTO, Daniel de Souza. Base Nacional de Serviços Públicos do Brasil: sistematização e interoperabilidade de informações para o Governo Digital. *Gestão.org*, v. 19, n. 2, 2021.

BACH, Daniel C. Patrimonialism and neopatrimonialism: comparative trajectories and readings. *Commonwealth & Comparative Politics*, v. 49, n. 3, p. 275–294, 2011.

BALDWIN, Robert; CAVE, Martin; LODGE, Martin. *Understanding Regulation*. New York: Oxford University Press, 2012.

BARCEVIČIUS, Egidijus; CIBAITĖ, Guoda; CODAGNONE, Cristiano; *et al. Exploring digital government transformation in the EU: analysis of the state of the art and review of literature*. Luxembourg: Publications Office of the European Union, 2019.

BARROS, Manoel Joaquim F. de; MELO, Paulo; LEFRANÇOIS, Denise A. E-citizenship: the digital cities program, a tool for a new model of citizenship in Brazil. *Journal on Innovation and Sustainability RISUS*, v. 12, n. 2, p. 30–38, 2021.

BATISTA, André Pereira; CRUZ, Cláudia Ferreira da. Digital by Default: O uso de canais de serviço por cidadãos em cidades. *In*: *XLIII Encontro da ANPAD - EnANPAD*. São Paulo: ANPAD, 2019, p. 1–17.

BAUM, Matthew A.; LAKE, David A. The Political Economy of Growth: Democracy and Human Capital. *American Journal of Political Science*, v. 47, n. 2, p. 333–347, 2003.

BAUMGARTNER, Sabrina. *Die Regierungskommunikation der Schweizer Kantone: Regeln, Organisation, Akteure und Instrumente im Vergleich*. Wiesbaden: VS Verlag für Sozialwissenschaften, 2010.

BAUMGOLD, Deborah. Hobbes's and Locke's Contract Theories: Political not Metaphysical. *Critical Review of International Social and Political Philosophy*, v. 8, n. 3, p. 289–308, 2005.

BECK, Ulrich. *Schöne neue Arbeitswelt*. Berlin: Suhrkamp, 2007.

BECK, Wolfgang. Aktuelle E-Government-Regelungen in Deutschland, Österreich und der Schweiz. *In*: STEMBER, Jürgen; EIXELSBERGER, Wolfgang; SPICHIGER, Andreas; *et al* (Orgs.). *Aktuelle Entwicklungen zum E-Government: Neue Impulse und Orientierungen in der digitalen Transformation der öffentlichen Verwaltung*. Wiesbaden: Springer Fachmedien, 2021, p. 3–28. (Edition Innovative Verwaltung).

BECKER, Gary S. Crime and Punishment: An Economic Approach. *Journal of Political Economy*, v. 76, n. 2, p. 169–217, 1968.

BEDÊ, Marco Aurélio. *Sobrevivência das Empresas no Brasil*. Brasília: SEBRAE, 2016.

BÉLAND, Daniel; LEIBFRIED, Stephan; MORGAN, Kimberly J.; *et al* (Orgs.). *The Oxford Handbook of the Welfare State*. 2. ed. Oxford: Oxford University Press, 2021.

BELLI, Luca. A heterostakeholder cooperation for sustainable internet policymaking. *Internet Policy Review*, v. 4, n. 1, p. 1–21, 2015.

BENTHAM, Jeremy. *An introduction to the Principles of Morals and Legislation.* Kitchener: Batoche Books, 2000.

BENZ, Arthur. Themen, Probleme und Perspektiven der vergleichenden Föderalismusforschung. *In*: BENZ, Arthur; LEHMBRUCH, Gerhard (Orgs.). *Föderalismus: Analysen in entwicklungsgeschichtlicher und vergleichender Perspektive.* Wiesbaden: VS Verlag für Sozialwissenschaften, 2002, p. 9–50. (Politische Vierteljahresschrift Sonderheft).

BERGER, Ariane. Die Entfesselung von D'Artagnan. *In*: SECKELMANN, Margrit; BRUNZEL, Marco (Orgs.). *Handbuch Onlinezugangsgesetz: Potenziale - Synergien - Herausforderungen.* Berlin, Heidelberg: Springer, 2021, p. 75–93.

BERGER, Peter L; LUCKMANN, Thomas. *The Social Construction of Reality. A Treatise in the Sociology of Knowledge.* London: Penguin Books, 1991.

BERNACIAK, Magdalena. *Social Dumping: Political Catchphrase or Threat to Labour Standards?* Working Paper 2012.06. Brussels: European Trade Union Institute, 2012.

BIEBER, Christoph. Wählen als elektronischer Demokratieprozess? E-Government und E-Voting als Instrumente politischer Modernisierung. *In*: SCHÜNEMANN, Wolf J.; KNEUER, Marianne (Orgs.). *E-Government und Netzpolitik im europäischen Vergleich.* 2. ed. Baden-Baden: Nomos Verlagsgesellschaft mbH & Co. KG, 2019, v. 19, p. 357–380. (E-Government und die Erneuerung des öffentlichen Sektors).

BIRD, Robert C. Pathways of Legal Strategy. *Stanford Journal of Law, Business & Finance*, v. 14, n. 1, p. 1–42, 2008.

BIRKINSHAW, Patrick J. *European Public Law: The Achievement and the Challenge.* 2. ed. Alphen aan den Rijn: Wolters Kluwer Law & Business, 2014.

BITTENCOURT FILHO, Jorge Calmon Moniz de; LOIOLA, Elizabeth R. The Public Services Provided by Brazilian Government Over the Internet. *SSRN Electronic Journal*, 2001.

BIZER, Johann. Digitale Souveränität – wer steuert, organisiert und kontrolliert die digitale Verwaltung? *In*: LÜHR, Hans-Henning; JABKOWSKI, Roland; SMENTEK, Sabine (Orgs.). *Handbuch Digitale Verwaltung.* Wiesbaden: KSV Verwaltungspraxis, 2019, p. 23–36.

BJERG, Ole. How is Bitcoin Money? *Theory, Culture & Society*, v. 33, n. 1, p. 53–72, 2016.

BOBBIO, Norberto. *Dalla struttura alla funzione.* Roma-Bari: Laterza, 2007.

BOBBIO, Norberto; MATTEUCCI, Nicola; PASQUINO, Gianfranco (Orgs.). *Dizionario di politica.* 2. ed. Torino: UTET, 1983.

BOSSE, Christian K.; DEHLING, Florian; GROEN, Eduard C.; *et al.* Auf dem Weg zu gebrauchstauglichen Datenschutzlösungen für digitale Ökosysteme. *Datenschutz und Datensicherheit - DuD*, v. 48, n. 2, p. 82–88, 2024.

BOTTA, Jonas. Der digitale Staat als gläserner Staat. Transparenz als Bedingung verfassungskonformer Registermodernisierung. *In*: KUHLMANN, Simone; DE GREGORIO, Fabrizio; FERTMANN, Martin; *et al* (Orgs.). *Transparency or Opacity: A Legal Analysis of the Organization of Information in the Digital World*. Baden-Baden: Nomos, 2023, p. 27–48.

BOUDON, Raymond. Beyond Rational Choice Theory. *Annual Review of Sociology*, v. 29, n. 1, p. 1–21, 2003.

BOUNABAT, Bouchaïb. From e-Government to digital Government: Stakes and Evolution Models. *Electronic Journal of Information Technology*, n. 10, p. 8–21, 2017.

BRAGA, André de Castro Oliveira Pereira. *O Tribunal de Contas da União inibe inovações em concessões públicas?* Master's thesis (Public Administration), FGV, Rio de Janeiro, 2015.

BRAGA, Lamartine Vieira; ALVES, Welington Souza; FIGUEIREDO, Rejane Maria Da Costa; *et al.* O papel do Governo Eletrônico no fortalecimento da governança do setor público. *Revista do Serviço Público*, v. 59, n. 1, p. 5–21, 2008.

BRANDALISE, Isabella; FERRAREZI, Elisabete; LEMOS, Joselene. *Colaboração internacional para inovação: o caso do gnova e mindlab*. Brasília: Enap, 2018.

BRASIL. *Mapa de Governo Digital*. Brasília: Secretaria de Governo Digital, 2022.

BRASIL. *Plano Diretor da Reforma do Aparelho do Estado*. Brasília: Presidência da República, 1995.

BRAUN, Christoph-Friedrich von. The Acceleration Trap. *Sloan Management Review*, v. 32, n. 1, 1990.

BRESSER-PEREIRA, Luiz Carlos. *Democracy and Public Management Reform: Building the Republican State*. Oxford: Oxford University Press, 2004.

BRESSER-PEREIRA, Luiz Carlos. Reforma gerencial e legitimação do estado social. *Revista de Administração Pública*, v. 51, p. 147–156, 2017.

BREWER, Scott. Logocratic method and the analysis of arguments in evidence. *Law, Probability and Risk*, v. 10, n. 3, p. 175–202, 2011.

BROMLEY, Daniel W; YAO, Yang. Understanding China's Economic Transformation. *World Economics-Henley on Thames*, v. 7, n. 2, p. 73, 2006.

BROWN, Archie. *The myth of the strong leader: political leadership in modern politics*. New York: Basic Books, 2014.

BRUNAZO FILHO, Amilcar; MARCACINI, Augusto Tavares Rosa. Legal aspects of e-voting in Brazil. *In*: MAURER, Ardita Driza; BARRAT, Jordi (Orgs.). *E-Voting Case Law: A Comparative Analysis*. Burlington: Ashgate, 2016, p. 65–88. (Election Law, Politics, and theory).

BRUNET, Emiliano. Estado, Poder Político e Direito em uma época de mudanças: por que ler Gramsci? *REI - Revista Estudos Institucionais*, v. 7, n. 3, p. 880–907, 2021.

BRUNKHORST, Hauke. Demokratischer Experimentalismus. *In*: BRUNKHORST, Hauke (Org.). *Demokratischer Experimentalismus: Politik in der komplexen Gesellschaft*. Frankfurt am Main: Suhrkamp, 1998. (Suhrkamp Taschenbuch Wissenschaft, 1369).

BUCCI, Maria Paula Dallari. A abordagem DPP no Brasil_Quadros analíticos. *Revista Campo de Públicas: conexões e experiências*, v. 2, n. 1, 2023.

BUCCI, Maria Paula Dallari. Estado social: uma sistematização para pensar a reconstrução. *Revista de Ciências do Estado*, v. 8, n. 1, p. 1–31, 2023.

BUCCI, Maria Paula Dallari. *Fundamentos para uma teoria jurídica das políticas públicas*. São Paulo: Saraiva, 2013.

BUCCI, Maria Paula Dallari. Law and Public Policy in Brazil and the United States: A North-South Dialogue. *SSRN Electronic Journal*, 2022.

BUCCI, Maria Paula Dallari. Quadro de referência de uma política pública: primeiras linhas de uma visão jurídico-institucional. *In*: SMANIO, Gianpaolo Poggio; BERTOLIN, Patrícia Tuma; BRASIL, Patrícia Cristina (Orgs.). *O Direito na Fronteira das Políticas Públicas*. São Paulo: Páginas e Letras, 2015, p. 7–11.

BUCCI, Maria Paula Dallari; GASPARDO, Murilo. Mapeamento de arranjos jurídico-institucionais: um roteiro metodológico para estudos das relações entre direito e política. *REI - Revista Estudos Institucionais*, v. 10, n. 1, p. 1–36, 2024.

BULMAN-POZEN, Jessica; GERKEN, Heather K. Uncooperative Federalism Essay. *Yale Law Journal*, v. 118, n. 7, p. 1256–1311, 2008.

BURCHARDT, Dana. The Functions of Law and their Challenges: The Differentiated Functionality of International Law. *German Law Journal*, v. 20, n. 4, p. 409–429, 2019.

BUTLER, Brian E. *The Democratic Constitution: Experimentalism and Interpretation*. Chicago and London: University of Chicago Press, 2017.

BYUN, Jeongeun; SUNG, Tae Eung; PARK, Hyun Woo. Technological innovation strategy: how do technology life cycles change by technological area. *Technology Analysis & Strategic Management*, v. 30, n. 1, p. 98–112, 2017.

CAI, Hongbin; TREISMAN, Daniel. Did Government Decentralization Cause China's Economic Miracle? *World Politics*, v. 58, n. 4, p. 505–535, 2006.

CAIRNEY, Paul. *Understanding public policy: theories and issues*. London: Bloomsbury Publishing, 2019.

CALLEGARO, Mario; YANG, Yongwei. The Role of Surveys in the Era of "Big Data". *In*: VANNETTE, David L.; KROSNICK, Jon A. (Orgs.). *The Palgrave Handbook of Survey Research*. Cham: Springer International Publishing, 2018, p. 175–192.

CAMARÃO, Paulo Cesar Bhering. Urna eletrônica brasileira: um projeto de sucesso. *In*: ALVIM, Frederico Franco; NETO, Jaime Barreiros; SANTIAGO, Marta Cristina Jesus (Orgs.). *25 Anos da Urna Eletrônica: Tecnologia e Integridade nas eleições brasileiras*. Salvador: Tribunal Regional Eleitoral da Bahia, 2021, p. 29–42.

CAMPANA, Priscilla de Souza Pestana. A cultura do medo na Administração Pública e a ineficiência gerada pelo atual sistema de controle. *Revista de Direito - Viçosa*, v. 9, n. 1, p. 189–216, 2017.

CAMPBELL, Donald T. Reforms as experiments. *American Psychologist*, v. 24, n. 4, p. 409–429, 1969.

CANOTILHO, José Joaquim Gomes. *Direito constitucional*. 7. ed. Coimbra: Almedina, 1993.

CAREY, George W. Separation of Powers and the Madisonian Model: A Reply to the Critics. *American Political Science Review*, v. 72, n. 1, p. 151–164, 1978.

CARSTENSEN, Helle Vibeke; BASON, Christian. Powering collaborative policy innovation: Can innovation labs help? *The Innovation Journal*, v. 17, n. 1, p. 2, 2012.

CARSTENSEN, Martin B.; SCHMIDT, Vivien A. Power through, over and in ideas: conceptualizing ideational power in discursive institutionalism. *Journal of European Public Policy*, v. 23, n. 3, p. 318–337, 2016.

CARVALHO, André Castro; VENTURINI, Otavio. A função do Código de Defesa do Usuário de Serviços Públicos (Lei nº 13.460/2017) no modelo brasileiro de controle dos serviços públicos. *Revista de Direito Administrativo*, v. 278, n. 1, p. 141–162, 2019.

CARVALHO, Lucas Borges de. Governo digital e direito administrativo: entre a burocracia, a confiança e a inovação. *Revista de Direito Administrativo*, v. 279, n. 3, p. 115–148, 2020.

CARVALHO, Marcelo Sávio Revoredo de Menezes; CUKIERMAN, Henrique Luiz. The Dawn of the Internet in Brazil. *IEEE Annals of the History of Computing*, v. 37, n. 4, p. 54–63, 2015.

CASTELLS, Manuel. *The Power of Identity*. 2. ed. Chichester: Wiley-Blackwell, 2010. (The information age: Economy, Society, and Culture).

CDU; CSU; FDP. *Koalitionsvertrag 2009-2013*. Available at <https://www.nachhaltigkeit.info/media/1272874930php6WwCER.pdf>. Accessed 26 Mar. 2024

CDU; CSU; SPD. *Koalitionsvertrag 2013-2017*. Available at <https://archiv.cdu.de/sites/default/files/media/dokumente/koalitionsvertrag.pdf>. Accessed 26 Mar. 2024

CDU; CSU; SPD. *Koalitionsvertrag 2018-2021*. Available at <https://archiv.cdu.de/system/tdf/media/dokumente/koalitionsvertrag_2018.pdf?file=1>. Accessed 26 Mar. 2024

CHEMERINSKY, Erwin. The Values of Federalism Dunwoody Distinguished Lecture in Law. *Florida Law Review*, v. 47, n. 4, p. 499–540, 1995.

CHRISTENSEN, Clayton M. *The Innovator's Dilemma: When New Technologies Cause Great Firms to Fail*. Boston: Harvard Business School Press, 1997.

CHUNG, Choong Sik. *Developing digital governance: South Korea as a global digital government leader*. London and New York: Routledge, 2020.

CLUNE, William H. A Political Model of Implementation and Implications of the Model for Public Policy, Research, and the Changing Roles of Law and Lawyers. *Iowa Law Review*, v. 69, p. 47–125, 1983.

CLUNE, William H. Legal Disintegration and a Theory of the State. *German Law Journal*, v. 12, n. 1, p. 186–205, 2011.

CODAGNONE, Cristiano; LIVA, Giovanni; GUNDERSON, Laura; *et al*. *Europe's Digital Decade and autonomy*. Luxembourg: Policy Department for Economic, Scientific and Quality of Life Policies. European Parliament, 2021.

COLLINGTON, Rosie. Disrupting the Welfare State? Digitalisation and the Retrenchment of Public Sector Capacity. *New Political Economy*, v. 27, n. 2, p. 312–328, 2022.

CORDEIRO, Caio Barros. *Desafios do Estado para a transformação digital: uma análise à luz da abordagem Direito e Políticas Públicas*. PhD Dissertation (Law), University of São Paulo, São Paulo, 2023.

CORDEIRO, Caio Barros. *Tecnologia e Estado na era digital: Transformação à luz da abordagem Direito e Políticas Públicas*. Belo Horizonte: Fórum, 2024.

CORRÊA, Priscilla Pereira da Costa. Direito e desenvolvimento e sua base teórica. *In*: PINHEIRO, Armando Castelar; PORTO, Antônio José Maristrello; SAMPAIO, Patrícia Regina Pinheiro; *et al* (Orgs.). *Reflexões sobre direito e economia*. Rio de Janeiro: FGV Direito Rio, 2020, p. 321–320.

COSTA, Éverton Garcia da; COELHO, Gabriel Bandeira. Para entender a sociologia de Niklas Luhmann. *Caderno CRH*, v. 30, n. 81, p. 597–599, 2017.

COUTINHO, Diogo R. Direito e institucionalismo econômico: apontamentos sobre uma fértil agenda de pesquisa. *Brazilian Journal of Political Economy*, v. 37, p. 565–586, 2017.

COUTINHO, Diogo R. O direito nas políticas públicas. *In*: MARQUES, Eduardo Cesar; FARIA, Carlos Aurélio Pimenta de (Orgs.). *A política pública como campo multidisciplinar*. São Paulo: Fiocruz/UNESP, 2013.

COUTINHO, Diogo Rosenthal. O Direito econômico e a construção institucional do Desenvolvimento democrático. *Rei - Revista Estudos Institucionais*, v. 2, n. 1, p. 214, 2016.

CRAWFORD, Sue E. S.; OSTROM, Elinor. A Grammar of Institutions. *The American Political Science Review*, v. 89, n. 3, p. 582–600, 1995.

CRESPO, Ricardo F. Aristotle on agency, habits and institutions. *Journal of Institutional Economics*, v. 12, n. 4, p. 867–884, 2016.

CROSS, Frank B. The Folly of Federalism. *Cardozo Law Review*, v. 24, n. 1, p. 1–60, 2002.

DALLARI, Dalmo. *Elementos de Teoria Geral do Estado*. 32. ed. São Paulo: Saraiva, 2013.

DANTAS, Adriano Mesquita. A evolução do processo brasileiro: história e perspectiva do processo judicial eletrônico. *Revista do Tribunal Regional do Trabalho da 18a Região*, v. 12, p. 177–192, 2012.

DATTA, Arijit; BHATIA, Vimal; NOLL, Josef; *et al*. Bridging the Digital Divide: Challenges in Opening the Digital World to the Elderly, Poor, and Digitally Illiterate. *IEEE Consumer Electronics Magazine*, v. 8, n. 1, p. 78–81, 2019.

D'AVINO, Marco; DE SIMONE, Valerio; IANNUCCI, Marco; *et al*. Guidelines for e-startup promotion strategy. *Journal of Technology Management and Innovation*, v. 10, n. 1, p. 1–16, 2015.

DAVIS, Lance; NORTH, Douglass. Institutional Change and American Economic Growth: A First Step Towards a Theory of Institutional Innovation. *The Journal of Economic History*, v. 30, n. 1, p. 131–149, 1970.

DE LA PORTE, Caroline; JENSEN, Mads Dagnis. The next generation EU: An analysis of the dimensions of conflict behind the deal. *Social Policy & Administration*, v. 55, n. 2, p. 388–402, 2021.

DE PAULA, Felipe. Does Brazil have a Legislative Policy? *The Theory and Practice of Legislation*, v. 4, n. 3, p. 329–353, 2016.

DE WILDE, Marc. The dark side of institutionalism: Carl Schmitt reading Santi Romano. *Ethics & Global Politics*, v. 11, n. 2, p. 12–24, 2018.

DELEON, Peter; MARTELL, Christine R. The Policy Sciences: Past, Present, and Future. *In*: PETERS, B.; PIERRE, Jon (Eds.). *Handbook of Public Policy*. London: SAGE Publications, 2006, p. 31–48.

DEMO, Pedro. Educação na nova Constituição - qualidade e democratização. *Em Aberto*, v. 7, n. 39, 1988.

DEQUECH, David. The Demarcation between the "Old" and the "New" Institutional Economics: Recent Complications. *Journal of Economic Issues*, v. 36, n. 2, p. 565–572, 2002.

DEWEY, John. *The public and its problems: An essay in political inquiry*. Chicago: Gateway Books, 1946.

DIERMEIER, Daniel; KREHBIEL, Keith. Institutionalism as a Methodology. *Journal of Theoretical Politics*, v. 15, n. 2, p. 123–144, 2003.

DIETRICH, Michael; VINJE, Thomas. The European Commission's proposal for a Digital Markets Act — In search of a 'golden standard' for appropriate ex ante regulation of large digital players. *Computer Law Review International*, v. 22, n. 2, p. 33–38, 2021.

DIMAGGIO, Paul. The New Institutionalisms: Avenues of Collaboration. *Journal of Institutional and Theoretical Economics (JITE) / Zeitschrift für die gesamte Staatswissenschaft*, v. 154, n. 4, p. 696–705, 1998.

DIMAGGIO, Paul J.; POWELL, Walter W. The Iron Cage Revisited: Institutional Isomorphism and Collective Rationality in Organizational Fields. *American Sociological Review*, v. 48, n. 2, p. 147–160, 1983.

DINIZ, Eduardo Henrique; BARBOSA, Alexandre Fernandes; JUNQUEIRA, Alvaro Ribeiro Botelho; *et al.* O governo eletrônico no Brasil: perspectiva histórica a partir de um modelo estruturado de análise. *Revista de Administração Pública*, v. 43, n. 1, p. 23–48, 2009.

DISTEL, Bettina; KOELMANN, Holger; PLATTFAUT, Ralf; *et al.* Watch who you trust! A structured literature review to build a typology of e-government risks. *Information Systems and e-Business Management*, v. 20, n. 4, p. 789–818, 2022.

DISTEL, Bettina; KOELMANN, Holger; SCHMOLKE, Florian; *et al.* The Role of Trust for Citizens' Adoption of Public E-Services. *In*: BLÖBAUM, Bernd (Org.). *Trust and Communication: Findings and Implications of Trust Research*. Cham: Springer International Publishing, 2021, p. 163–184.

DORF, Michael C.; SABEL, Charles F. A constitution of democratic experimentalism. *Columbia Law Review*, v. 98, n. 2, p. 267–473, 1998.

DOUCOULIAGOS, Hristos; ULUBAŞOĞLU, Mehmet Ali. Democracy and Economic Growth: A Meta-Analysis. *American Journal of Political Science*, v. 52, n. 1, p. 61–83, 2008.

DRAHEIM, Dirk; KRIMMER, Robert; TAMMET, Tanel. On State-Level Architecture of Digital Government Ecosystems: From ICT-Driven to Data-Centric. *In*: HAMEURLAIN, Abdelkader; TJOA, A. Min (Orgs.). *Transactions on Large-Scale Data- and Knowledge-Centered Systems XLVIII*. Berlin, Heidelberg: Springer, 2021, p. 165–195. (Lecture Notes in Computer Science).

DROR, Yehezkel. Social science meta-policy: Some concepts and applications. *In*: CHERNS, A. B.; JENKINS, W. I.; SINCLAIR, R. (Orgs.). *Social Science and Government*. London and New York: Routledge, 1972.

DUGUIT, León. *Traité de Droit Constitutionnel*. Paris: Ancienne Librairie, 1923.

DUNLEAVY, Patrick. Micro-institutions and Liberal Democracy. *Political Insight*, v. 10, n. 1, p. 35–39, 2019.

EASTON, David. The New Revolution in Political Science. *The American Political Science Review*, v. 63, n. 4, p. 1051–1061, 1969.

EHLING, Manfred; SOMMER, Bettina. Struktur und Entwicklung der Bevölkerung in Deutschland. *In*: BADURA, Bernhard; SCHRÖDER, Helmut; KLOSE, Joachim; *et al* (Orgs.). *Fehlzeiten-Report 2010: Vielfalt managen: Gesundheit fördern — Potenziale nutzen*. Berlin, Heidelberg: Springer, 2010, p. 57–67.

ERKUT, Burak. From digital government to digital governance: Are we there yet? *Sustainability*, v. 12, n. 3, p. 1–13, 2020.

ESPING-ANDERSEN, Gøsta. *The three worlds of welfare capitalism*. Reprint. Cambridge: Polity Press, 2009.

ESTONIAN ICT EXPORT CLUSTER. *X-Road - e-Estonia*. E-Estonia.Com. Available at <https://e-estonia.com/component/x-road/>. Accessed 3 Jan. 2020

EUROPEAN UNION. *2023 European Semester: Country Reports - European Commission*. Available at <https://economy-finance.ec.europa.eu/publications/2023-europea n-semester-country-reports_en>. Accessed 30 Mar. 2024

EUROPEAN UNION. *eGovernment in the European Union*. Brussels: European Commission, 2017.

EWALD, François. A Concept of Social Law. *In*: TEUBNER, Gunther (Org.). *Dilemmas of Law in the Welfare State*. Berlin, New York: De Gruyter, 2011, p. 40–75.

FALCÃO, Tiago; COSTA, Patricia Vieira da. Advances and challenges for social development in Brazil. *In*: CASTRO, Ana Célia; FILGUEIRAS, Fernando (Orgs.). *The State in the 21th century*. Brasília: Enap, 2018, p. 321–336.

FEATHERSTONE, Kevin; RADAELLI, Claudio M. *The Politics of Europeanization*. Oxford: Oxford University Press, 2003.

FENWICK, Mark; KAAL, Wulf A.; VERMEULEN, Erik P. M. Regulation Tomorrow: What Happens When Technology Is Faster than the Law. *American University Business Law Review*, v. 6, n. 3, p. 561–594, 2016.

FERNANDES, Andréa Gomes; AFONSO, José Roberto Rodrigues. e-Governo no Brasil: Experiências e Perspectivas. *Revista do BNDES*, v. 8, n. 15, 2001.

FERNANDES, Ciro Campos Christo. *Sistemas de compras eletrônicas e sua aplicação à administração pública - o caso do SIASG/Comprasnet*. Master's thesis (Business Management), FGV, Brasília, 2003.

FERRÃO, Isadora Garcia; CHERVINSKI, João Otávio; SILVA, Sherlon Almeida da; *et al*. Urnas Eletrônicas no Brasil: linha do tempo, evolução e falhas e desafios de segurança. *Revista Brasileira de Computação Aplicada*, v. 11, n. 2, p. 1–12, 2019.

FERRAREZI, Elisabete; ALMEIDA, Guilherme de Almeida. *Laboratórios de inovação: como e por que criá-los.* Brasília: Escola Nacional de Administração Pública - Enap, 2023.

FERREIRA, Antônio Sérgio Seco; NEVES, Sérgio da Cunha. Contribuições para o planejamento da integração e da publicação de informações da administração pública. *Revista de Administração*, v. 37, n. 1, 2002.

FLEISCHER, Julia. Federal Administration. *In*: KUHLMANN, Sabine; PROELLER, Isabella; SCHIMANKE, Dieter; *et al* (Orgs.). *Public Administration in Germany.* Cham: Palgrave Macmillan, 2021, p. 61–79.

FOCACCIA, Gaetano Alberto. Norme costituzionali e norme di legge anteriori. *Il Foro Italiano*, v. 79, p. 61–70, 1956.

FOUNTAIN, Chris. Famous last words. A collection of inaccurate forecasts about technology that have been made through history. *IPA Review*, v. 49, n. 1, p. 46–48, 1996.

FOUNTAIN, Jane E. *Building the virtual state: information technology and institutional change.* Washington, D.C: Brookings Institution Press, 2001.

FRAUNDORFER, Markus. Brazil's Organization of the NETmundial Meeting: Moving Forward in Global Internet Governance. *Global Governance*, v. 23, n. 3, p. 503–522, 2017.

FREDRIKSSON, Anders. Bureaucracy intermediaries, corruption and red tape. *Journal of Development Economics*, v. 108, p. 256–273, 2014.

FREGA, Roberto. *Pragmatism and the Wide View of Democracy.* Cham: Springer International Publishing, 2019.

FREITAS, Jorge Lheureux de; MACADAR, Marie Anne. The Brazilian Electronic Voting System: evolution and challenges. *In*: KRIMMER, Robert; VOLKAMER, Melanie; BRAUN BINDER, Nadja; *et al* (Orgs.). *2nd Joint International Conference on Electronic Voting.* Lochau/Bregenz: TUT Press, 2017.

FRIEDMAN, Lawrence M. Legal Culture and the Welfare State. *In*: TEUBNER, Gunther (Org.). *Dilemmas of Law in the Welfare State.* Berlin, New York: De Gruyter, 2011, p. 13–27.

FUJIWARA, Thomas. Voting Technology, Political Responsiveness, and Infant Health: Evidence from Brazil. *Econometrica*, v. 83, n. 2, p. 423–464, 2015.

FUKUYAMA, Francis. *Political Order and Political Decay: From the Industrial Revolution to the Globalization of Democracy.* New York: Farrar, Straus and Giroux, 2014.

FUKUYAMA, Francis. *What Is Governance?* Washington, DC: Center for Global Development, 2013.

FUKUYAMA, Francis; RICHMAN, Barak; GOEL, Ashish. How to Save Democracy from Technology. *Foreign Affairs*, v. 100, n. 1, p. 98–110, 2021.

GALLO, Amynthas Jacques de Moraes. Gestão Estratégica da Informação no ambiente do Governo Digital. *Revista Brasileira de Biblioteconomia e Documentação*, v. 6, n. 2, p. 3–19, 2010.

GAMBA, Giovanna Maísa. *Estratégia nacional de combate à corrupção e à lavagem de dinheiro: institucionalidade jurídica da política em rede.* Belo Horizonte, MG: Editora Fórum, 2023. (Coleção Fórum Direito e Políticas Públicas).

GARCIA, Rodrigo-Moreira. Governo eletrônico, informação e competência em informação. *Informação & Sociedade: Estudos*, v. 16, n. 2, 2006.

GASPARDO, Murilo. Democracia participativa e experimentalismo democrático em tempos sombrios. *Estudos Avancados*, v. 32, n. 92, p. 65–88, 2018.

GEIGER, Christian Philipp; LUCKE, Jörn von. Open Government and (Linked) (Open) (Government) (Data). *JeDEM - eJournal of eDemocracy and Open Government*, v. 4, n. 2, p. 265–278, 2012.

GEIS, Ralf. Das Onlinezugangsgesetz im Rechtsvergleich. *In*: SECKELMANN, Margrit; BRUNZEL, Marco (Orgs.). *Handbuch Onlinezugangsgesetz: Potenziale - Synergien - Herausforderungen*. Berlin, Heidelberg: Springer, 2021, p. 229–252.

GERLING, Rainer W. De-Mail und E-Mail made in Germany sind ein konsequenter Schritt. *Datenschutz und Datensicherheit - DuD*, v. 38, n. 2, p. 109–111, 2014.

GERRING, John; BOND, Philip; BARNDT, William T.; *et al.* Democracy and Economic Growth: A Historical Perspective. *World Politics*, v. 57, n. 3, p. 323–364, 2005.

GIDDENS, Anthony. *Central Problems in Social Theory: Action, structure and contradiction in social analysis*. London: Macmillan, 1979.

GIELEN, Nico; UPHUES, Steffen. Digital Markets Act und Digital Services Act Regulierung von Markt- und Meinungsmacht durch die Europäische Union. *Europäische Zeitschrift für Wirtschaftsrecht*, n. 14, p. 627–637, 2021.

GIL, Antônio Carlos. *Métodos e técnicas de pesquisa social*. São Paulo: Atlas, 1999.

GLASER, Hartmut; CANABARRO, Diego R. Before and after the WGIG: Twenty Years of Multistakeholder Internet Governance in Brazil. *In*: DRAKE, William J. (Org.). *The Working Group on Internet Governance: 10th anniversary reflections*. Johannesburg: APC, 2016.

GOMES, Fábio Guedes. Conflito social e welfare state: Estado e desenvolvimento social no Brasil. *Revista de Administração Pública*, v. 40, p. 201–234, 2006.

GOMES, Silvana Santos. Smart Contracts: legal frontiers and insertion into the Creative Economy. *Brazilian Journal of Operations & Production Management*, v. 15, n. 3, p. 376–385, 2018.

GONGGRIJP, Rop; HENGEVELD, Willem-Jan. Studying the Nedap/Groenendaal ES-3B voting computer: a computer security perspective. *In*: *Proceedings of the USENIX Workshop on Accurate Electronic Voting Technology*. USA: USENIX Association, 2007, p. 1. (EVT'07).

GONTIJO, Miriam. Análise da proposta brasileira de E-Governo como expressão de uma política de informação a partir do conceito de regime de informação. *Perspectivas em Ciência da Informação*, v. 7, n. 2, 2002.

GOVERNATORI, Guido; IDELBERGER, Florian; MILOSEVIC, Zoran; *et al.* On legal contracts, imperative and declarative smart contracts, and blockchain systems. *Artificial Intelligence and Law*, v. 26, n. 4, p. 377–409, 2018.

GRAMSCI, Antonio. *Quaderni del carcere - Quaderni 1 - 5*. 2. ed. Torino: Einaudi, 1977.

GRAMSCI, Antonio. *Quaderni del carcere - Quaderni 12-29*. 2. ed. Torino: Einaudi, 1977.

GRAUX, Hans. The Single Digital Gateway Regulation as an Enabler and Constraint of Once-Only in Europe. *In*: KRIMMER, Robert; PRENTZA, Andriana; MAMROT, Szymon (Orgs.). *The Once-Only Principle: The TOOP Project.* Cham: Springer International Publishing, 2021, p. 83–103.

GREEN, Leslie. The functions of law. *Cogito*, v. 12, n. 2, p. 117–124, 1998.

GRÖSCHNER, Rolf. Rechtsdogmatik. *In*: HILGENDORF, Eric; JOERDEN, Jan C. (Orgs.). *Handbuch Rechtsphilosophie.* Stuttgart: J.B. Metzler, 2021, p. 66–71.

GRYTSENKO, Ruslan. Why it is so important to keep analytics independent. What are the lessons of the scandal with the Doing Business Report? *In*: *Proceedings of the 5th International Scientific Conference.* Rome: Publisher.agency, 2023. (5).

GUIHOT, Michael; MATTHEW, Anne; SUZOR, Nicolas Pierre. Nudging Robots: Innovative Solutions to Regulate Artificial Intelligence. *Vanderbilt journal of entertainment and technology law*, v. 20, n. 2, p. 385–456, 2017.

HADDAD, Frederico. *O direito à rua: políticas públicas e a função social das vias urbanas.* Belo Horizonte: Fórum, 2022.

HALL, Peter A.; TAYLOR, Rosemary C. R. Political Science and the Three New Institutionalisms. *Political Studies*, v. 44, n. 5, p. 936–957, 1996.

HAOUACHE, Gerold. Die rechtliche Erfassung neuer Technologien zur digitalen Aufgabenerledigung der Verwaltung (E-Government/M-Government). *In*: HARTLEB, Torsten; FISCHER, Jürgen (Orgs.). *Innovative Verwaltung in Forschung und Lehre.* Baden-Baden: Nomos, 2020, p. 47–58.

HARRAß, Sven. Liquid Democracy im Feldversuch – Beteiligungsmöglichkeiten in der Enquete-Kommission „Internet und digitale Gesellschaft“ des Deutschen Bundestages. *In*: FRIEDRICHSEN, Mike; KOHN, Roland A. (Orgs.). *Digitale Politikvermittlung: Chancen und Risiken interaktiver Medien.* Wiesbaden: Springer Fachmedien, 2015, p. 485–498.

HARRY, Girvetz. Welfare State. *In*: SILLS, David (Org.). *International encyclopedia of the social sciences.* New York: Macmillan, 1968, v. 16, p. 512–521.

HART, Herbert Lionel Adolphus. *The concept of law.* 2. ed. New York: Oxford University Press, 1994.

HAURIOU, Maurice. An Interpretation of the Principles of Public Law. *Harvard Law Review*, v. 31, n. 6, p. 813–821, 1918.

HAURIOU, Maurice. *Aux sources du droit: le pouvoir, l'ordre et la liberté.* Paris, France: Bloud et Gay, 1933.

HAYEK, Friedrich A. von. *Der Wettbewerb als Entdeckungsverfahren.* Tübingen: Mohr, 1968. (Kieler Vorträge : gehalten im Institut für Weltwirtschaft an der Universität Kiel).

HAYS, Sharon. Structure and Agency and the Sticky Problem of Culture. *Sociological Theory*, v. 12, n. 1, p. 57–72, 1994.

HEALY, Deirdre; GRIFFIN, Diarmuid. Unnesting the Matryoshka Doll: An Ecological Model of Probation and Parole Decision-Making in Ireland. *Journal of Contemporary Criminal Justice*, v. 39, n. 1, p. 75–93, 2023.

HEINEN, Juliano. Acesso à informação e seus "dois maridos": duas leis em um mesmo tema – transparência e tratamento dos dados públicos. *In*: VALLE, Vanice Regina Lírio do; MOTTA, Fabrício (Orgs.). *Governo Digital e a Busca por Inovação na Administração Pública.* Kindle. Belo Horizonte: Forum, 2022.

HENKE, Wilhelm. Wandel der Dogmatik des öffentlichen Rechts. *JuristenZeitung*, v. 47, n. 11, p. 541–548, 1992.

HEUBERGER, Moritz. *Coordinating digital government: explaining coordination challenges regarding the digital transformation of public administration in a federal context.* PhD Dissertation (Political Science), Universität Potsdam, Potsdam, 2022.

HILL, Hermann. Die Kunst des Entscheidens. *Die öffentliche Verwaltung*, v. 70, n. 11, p. 433–443, 2017.

HODGSON, Geoffrey M. *The Evolution of Institutional Economics.* London and New York: Routledge, 2004.

HOEFER, Richard. Institutionalism as a Theory for Understanding Policy Creation: an Underused Resource. *Journal of Policy Practice and Research*, v. 3, n. 2, p. 71–76, 2022.

HOFFMANN, Adrian; WAUBERT DE PUISEAU, Berenike; SCHMIDT, Alexander F.; *et al.* On the comprehensibility and perceived privacy protection of indirect questioning techniques. *Behavior Research Methods*, v. 49, n. 4, p. 1470–1483, 2017.

HOMSY, George C.; LIU, Zhilin; WARNER, Mildred E. Multilevel Governance: Framing the Integration of Top-Down and Bottom-Up Policymaking. *International Journal of Public Administration*, v. 42, n. 7, p. 572–582, 2019.

HOOD, Christopher. A Public Management for All Seasons? *Public Administration*, v. 69, n. 1, p. 3–19, 1991.

HUMAN RIGHTS WATCH. *World Report 2017.* New York: Seven Stories Press, 2017.

HUSTEDT, Thurid; TREIN, Philipp. Koordination und Integration im E-Government. *In*: KLENK, Tanja; NULLMEIER, Frank; WEWER, Göttrik (Orgs.). *Handbuch Digitalisierung in Staat und Verwaltung.* Wiesbaden: Springer Fachmedien, 2020, p. 1–10.

IANNI, Octavio. O príncipe eletrônico. *Sociologias*, v. 22, n. 1, 1999.

IBRAHIM, Fábio Zambitte; SCHWARTZ, Gustavo Carvalho Gomes. As contribuições sociais como instrumento de fraude ao pacto federativo. *Revista Direito das Relações Sociais e Trabalhistas*, v. 3, n. 1, p. 183–206, 2017.

IMMERGUT, Ellen M. Historical-Institutionalism in Political Science and the Problem of Change. *In*: WIMMER, Andreas; KÖSSLER, Reinhart (Orgs.). *Understanding Change.* London: Palgrave Macmillan UK, 2006, p. 237–259.

IMMERGUT, Ellen M. Institutions, Veto Points, and Policy Results: A Comparative Analysis of Health Care. *Journal of Public Policy*, v. 10, n. 4, p. 391–416, 1990.

IMMERGUT, Ellen M. The rules of the game: The logic of health policy-making in France, Switzerland, and Sweden. *In*: STEINMO, Sven; THELEN, Kathleen; LONGSTRETH, Frank (Orgs.). *Structuring Politics: Historical Institutionalism in Comparative Analysis.* Cambridge: Cambridge University, 1992, p. 57–89.

IMMERGUT, ELLEN M. The Theoretical Core of the New Institutionalism. *Politics & Society*, v. 26, n. 1, p. 5–34, 1998.

IMMERGUT, Ellen M.; ORLOWSKI, Matthias. Veto Points and the Environment. *In*: ARMINGEON, Klaus (Org.). *Staatstätigkeiten, Parteien und Demokratie: Festschrift für Manfred G. Schmidt*. Wiesbaden: Springer Fachmedien, 2013, p. 205–217.

IOCKEN, Sabrina Nunes; GARCIA, Rodrigo Guerra. A Lei no 14.129/21 como facilitadora normativa para transformação digital e gestão do conhecimento nas organizações públicas. *In*: VALLE, Vanice Regina Lírio do; MOTTA, Fabrício (Orgs.). *Governo Digital e a Busca por Inovação na Administração Pública*. Kindle. Belo Horizonte: Forum, 2022.

JACOBY, Wade; BEHRENS, Martin. Experimentalism as a tool of economic innovation in Germany. *German Politics and Society*, v. 19, n. 3, p. 1–33, 2001.

JARDIM, José Maria. Governo eletrônico no Brasil: o portal Rede Governo. *Arquivística.net*, v. 3, n. 1, 2007.

JELLINEK, Georg. *Allgemeine Staatslehre*. Berlin, Heidelberg: Springer Berlin Heidelberg, 1929.

JELLINEK, Georg. *Verfassungsänderung und Verfassungswandlung eine staatsrechtlich-politische Abhandlung*. Berlin: Häring, 1906.

JERATH, Kavita S. *Science, Technology and Modernity: An Interdisciplinary Approach*. Cham: Springer International Publishing, 2021.

JERKE, Julia; JOHANN, David; RAUHUT, Heiko; *et al.* Too sophisticated even for highly educated survey respondents? A qualitative assessment of indirect question formats for sensitive questions. *Survey Research Methods*, v. 13, n. 3, p. 319–351, 2019.

JÈZE, Gaston. *Les principes généraux du droit administratif*. Paris: Lib. Marcel GIRARD, 1930.

JOHN, Peter. *Analyzing Public Policy*. 2. ed. London and New York: Routledge, 2013.

JONES, Steven E. *Against Technology: From the Luddites to Neo-Luddism*. New York: Routledge, 2006.

JORDÃO, Eduardo. A relação entre inovação e controle da administração pública. *A&C - Revista de Direito Administrativo & Constitucional*, v. 18, n. 72, p. 133–146, 2018.

JØRGENSEN, Rikke Frank. Data and rights in the digital welfare state: the case of Denmark. *Information, Communication & Society*, v. 26, n. 1, p. 123–138, 2023.

JØRGENSEN, Rikke Frank (Org.). *Human rights in the age of platforms*. Cambridge, Massachusetts: The MIT Press, 2019.

KATTEL, Rainer; MAZZUCATO, Mariana. Mission-oriented innovation policy and dynamic capabilities in the public sector. *Industrial and Corporate Change*, v. 27, n. 5, p. 787–801, 2018.

KECK, Otto. Der neue Institutionalismus in der Theorie der Internationalen Politik. *Politische Vierteljahresschrift*, v. 32, n. 4, p. 635–653, 1991.

KELSEN, Hans. *General theory of law and state*. Cambridge, Massachusetts: Harvard University Press, 1949.

KELSEN, Hans. *Teoria Pura do Direito*. São Paulo: Martins Fontes, 1998.

KENNEDY, Duncan; KLARE, Karl E. A Bibliography of Critical Legal Studies. *The Yale Law Journal*, v. 94, n. 2, p. 461–490, 1984.

KETTL, Donald F. *Can governments earn our trust?* Cambridge, UK: Polity, 2017.

KHALIFA, Azaddin Salem. Strategy, nonstrategy and no strategy. *Journal of Strategy and Management*, v. 14, n. 1, p. 35–49, 2020.

KINCAID, John. Economic policy-making: advantages and disadvantages of the federal model. *International Social Science Journal*, v. 53, n. 167, p. 85–92, 2001.

KITSING, Meelis. An evaluation of E-government in Estonia. *In*: *Internet, Politics and Policy 2010: An Impact Assessment*. Oxford: Oxford University, 2010.

KNAPP, Georg Friedrich. *The State theory of money*. London: Macmillan & Co, 1925.

KOO, Eunjin. *Digital Transformation of Government: From E-Government to Intelligent E-Government*. Master's thesis (Engineering and Management), Massachusetts Institute of Technology, Cambridge, 2019.

KOOP, Christel; LODGE, Martin. What is regulation? An interdisciplinary concept analysis. *Regulation & Governance*, v. 11, n. 1, p. 95–108, 2017.

KRAWIETZ, Werner. Ansätze zu einem Neuen Institutionalismus in der modernen Rechtstheorie der Gegenwart. *JuristenZeitung*, v. 40, n. 15/16, p. 706–714, 1985.

KREPS, Sarah; KRINER, Doug. How AI Threatens Democracy. *Journal of Democracy*, v. 34, n. 4, p. 122–131, 2023.

KRIMMER, Robert; PRENTZA, Andriana; MAMROT, Szymon; *et al*. The Once-Only Principle: A Matter of Trust. *In*: KRIMMER, Robert; PRENTZA, Andriana; MAMROT, Szymon (Orgs.). *The Once-Only Principle: The TOOP Project*. Cham: Springer International Publishing, 2021, p. 1–8. (Lecture Notes in Computer Science).

KRIPPENDORFF, Klaus. *Content Analysis: An Introduction to Its Methodology*. 4. ed. Los Angeles: Sage Publications, 2018.

KÜHN, Hannes. Recht als Gestaltungsinstrument einfacher, digitaler Verwaltungsleistungen – Bessere Rechtsetzung als Voraussetzung vollzugs- und digitaltauglicher Gesetze. *In*: SECKELMANN, Margrit; BRUNZEL, Marco (Orgs.). *Handbuch Onlinezugangsgesetz: Potenziale - Synergien - Herausforderungen*. Berlin, Heidelberg: Springer, 2021, p. 17–51.

KUHNLE, Stein; SANDER, Anne. The Emergence of The Western Welfare State. *In*: BÉLAND, Daniel; LEIBFRIED, Stephan; MORGAN, Kimberly J.; *et al* (Orgs.). *The Oxford Handbook of the Welfare State*. 2. ed. Oxford: Oxford University Press, 2021, p. 73–92.

KUMAGAI, Saki; IORIO, Federica. *Building Trust in Government through Citizen Engagement*. Washington, DC: World Bank, 2020.

KWET, Michael. Digital colonialism: US empire and the new imperialism in the Global South. *Race and Class*, v. 60, n. 4, p. 3–26, 2019.

LA TORRE, Massimo. Teorías institucionalistas del Derecho (esbozo de una voz de enciclopedia). *Derechos y Libertades*, v. 11, n. 14, p. 103–112, 2006.

LAIA, Marconi Martins de; CUNHA, Maria Alexandra Viegas Cortez da; NOGUEIRA, Antonio Roberto Ramos; *et al*. Electronic government policies in Brazil: Context, ICT management and outcomes. *RAE Revista de Administracao de Empresas*, v. 51, n. 1, p. 43–57, 2011.

LANDAU, Susan. Highlights from Making Sense of Snowden, Part II: What's Significant in the NSA Revelations. *IEEE Security & Privacy*, v. 12, n. 1, p. 62–64, 2014.

LARASATI, Zita Wahyu; YUDA, Tauchid Komara; SYAFA'AT, Akbarian Rifki. Digital welfare state and problem arising: an exploration and future research agenda. *International Journal of Sociology and Social Policy*, v. 43, n. 5/6, 2022.

LAZZARI, João Batista. Justiça sem papel: uma realidade dos Juizados Especiais Federais do sul do Brasil. *Revista de Doutrina da 4a Região. Porto Alegre*, n. 18, 2007.

LEE, Celia; MA, Liang. The Role of Policy Labs in Policy Experiment and Knowledge Transfer: A Comparison across the UK, Denmark, and Singapore. *Journal of Comparative Policy Analysis: Research and Practice*, v. 22, n. 4, p. 281–297, 2020.

LEE, Jooho. Exploring the Role of Knowledge Networks in Perceived e-Government: A Comparative Case Study of two Local Governments in Korea. *American Review of Public Administration*, v. 43, n. 1, p. 89–108, 2013.

LEITER, Brian. Legal Realism and Legal Doctrine. *University of Pennsylvania Law Review*, v. 163, n. 1975, p. 11, 2015.

LEONI, Francesco; CARRARO, Martina; MCAULIFFE, Erin; *et al.* Data-centric public services as potential source of policy knowledge. Can "design for policy" help? *Transforming Government: People, Process and Policy*, v. 17, n. 3, p. 399–411, 2023.

LÉVI-STRAUSS, Claude. *Tristes tropiques*. Paris: Librairie Plon, 1955.

LHOTTA, Roland. Der Staat in uns: Hermann Hellers etatistischer Neo-Institutionalismus avant la lettre. *In*: FRICK, Verena; LEMBCKE, Oliver W. (Orgs.). *Hermann Hellers demokratischer Konstitutionalismus*. Wiesbaden: Springer Fachmedien, 2022, p. 85–117. (Staat - Souveränität - Nation).

LHOTTA, Roland. Europäische Mehrebenengovernance und das Bundesverfassungsgericht. *In*: ARNAULD, Andreas von; HUFELD, Ulrich (Orgs.). *Systematischer Kommentar zu den Lissabon-Begleitgesetzen*. 2. ed. Baden-Baden: Nomos, 2018.

LHOTTA, Roland. Neoinstitutionalismus und Demokratie. *In*: LEMBCKE, Oliver W.; RITZI, Claudia; SCHAAL, Gary S. (Orgs.). *Zeitgenössische Demokratietheorie*. Wiesbaden: Springer Fachmedien, 2016, p. 127–150.

LIMA, Weldson Queiroz de. *Contribuições do SERPRO para a formação do Programa de Governo Eletrônico Brasileiro em uma perspectiva fazendária*. Specialization thesis (Public Management), Uniserpro, Porto Alegre, 2014.

LINDBLOM, Charles E. Still Muddling, Not Yet Through. *Public Administration Review*, v. 39, n. 6, p. 517–526, 1979.

LINDBLOM, Charles E. The Science of "Muddling Through". *Public Administration Review*, v. 19, n. 2, p. 79–88, 1959.

LIPSKY, Michael. *Street-level bureaucracy: Dilemmas of the individual in public service*. New York: Russell Sage Foundation, 2010.

LIU, Tze-Chang. Digital policy in European countries from the perspective of the Digital Economy and Society Index. *Policy & Internet*, v. 14, n. 1, p. 202–218, 2022.

LIVERMORE, Michael A. Rule by rules. *In*: WHALEN, Ryan (Org.). *Computational Legal Studies. The Promise and Challenge of Data-Driven Research*. Cheltenham and Northampton: Edward Elgar, 2020, p. 238–264.

LOPUCKI, Lynn M.; WEYRAUCH, Walter O. A Theory of Legal Strategy. *Duke Law Journal*, v. 49, n. 6, p. 1405–1486, 2000.

LOWNDES, Vivien; ROBERTS, Mark. *Why institutions matter: the new institutionalism in political science.* Houndmills, Basingstoke, Hampshire: Palgrave Macmillan, 2013. (Political Analysis).

LÜCHMANN, Lígia Helena Hahn. Fatores do declínio dos Orçamentos Participativos na região sul do Brasil. *Política & Sociedade*, v. 21, n. 50, p. 206–232, 2022.

LUHMANN, Niklas. Politische Verfassungen im Kontext des Gesellschaftssystems (1. Teil). *Der Staat*, v. 12, n. 2, p. 1–22, 1973.

LUHMANN, Niklas. *Sociologia do direito I.* Rio de Janeiro: Tempo Brasileiro, 1983.

LÜHR, Hans-Henning. IT-Planungsrat. *In*: KLENK, Tanja; NULLMEIER, Frank; WEWER, Göttrik (Orgs.). *Handbuch Digitalisierung in Staat und Verwaltung.* Wiesbaden: Springer Fachmedien Wiesbaden, 2020, p. 1–12.

LÜHR, Henning. Von der Konferenz „Deutschland online“ zur föderativen IT-Kooperation – Innovation und Digital Leadership im föderalen Mehrebenensystem in Deutschland. *In*: SECKELMANN, Margrit; BRUNZEL, Marco (Orgs.). *Handbuch Onlinezugangsgesetz: Potenziale - Synergien - Herausforderungen.* Berlin, Heidelberg: Springer, 2021, p. 95–116.

MACCORMICK, Donald Neil; WEINBERGER, Ota. *Grundlagen des institutionalistischen Rechtspositivismus.* Berlin: Duncker & Humblot, 1985.

MACHADO, Caio; KIRA, Beatriz; NARAYANAN, Vidya; *et al.* A study of misinformation in whatsapp groups with a focus on the brazilian presidential elections. *In*: *The Web Conference 2019 - Companion of the World Wide Web Conference, WWW 2019.* New York: Association for Computing Machinery, Inc, 2019, p. 1013–1019.

MANCIO, Sabrina Dominique Dias. *Na guerra entre cotexto e contexto, uma letra faz a diferença: as emendas de redação no texto legislativo.* Specialization thesis (Portuguese language), UniCEUB, Brasília, 2017.

MARCACINI, Augusto Tavares Rosa; JUNIOR, Irineu Francisco Barreto. Aspectos jurídicos, políticos e técnicos sobre sistemas eletrônicos de votação e a urna eletrônica brasileira. *Revista Brasileira de Estudos Políticos*, n. 118, 2019.

MARCH, James G.; OLSEN, Johan P. The New Institutionalism: Organizational Factors in Political Life. *The American Political Science Review*, v. 78, n. 3, p. 734–749, 1984.

MARCIANO, Alain; NICITA, Antonio; RAMELLO, Giovanni Battista. Big data and big techs: understanding the value of information in platform capitalism. *European Journal of Law and Economics*, v. 50, n. 3, p. 345–358, 2020.

MARGETTS, Helen; NAUMANN, Andre. Government as a platform: What can Estonia show the world. *Research paper, University of Oxford*, 2017.

MARTI, Michael D.; ESTERMANN, Beat; NEURONI, Alessia C. Die Tallinn-Prinzipien als Wegbereiter der digitalen Transformation des öffentlichen Sektors in der Schweiz. *In*: PLEGER, Lyn Ellen; MERTES, Alexander (Orgs.). *Digitale Transformation der öffentlichen Verwaltung in der Schweiz: Stand, Entwicklungslinien und Praxisbeispiele.* Wiesbaden: Springer Fachmedien, 2022, p. 299–330.

MAYNARD, Dilton C. S. An Introduction to the History of the Internet: A Brazilian Perspective. *In*: PEREIRA NETO, André; FLYNN, Matthew B. (Orgs.). *The Internet and Health in Brazil: Challenges and Trends.* Cham: Springer International Publishing, 2019, p. 15–26.

MAYNTZ, Renate; SCHARPF, Fritz W. Der Ansatz des akteurzentrierten Institutionalismus. *In*: MAYNTZ, Renate; SCHARPF, Fritz W. (Orgs.). *Gesellschaftliche Selbstregelung und politische Steuerung.* Frankfurt/New York: Campus Verlag, 1995, p. 39–72.

MAZZUCATO, Mariana; KATTEL, Rainer. COVID-19 and public-sector capacity. *Oxford Review of Economic Policy*, v. 36, n. S1, p. S256–S269, 2020.

MCDERMOTT, Patrice. Building open government. *Government Information Quarterly*, v. 27, n. 4, p. 401–413, 2010. (Special Issue: Open/Transparent Government).

MEDEIROS, Paulo Henrique Ramos; GUIMARÃES, Tomás De Aquino. A institucionalização do governo eletrônico no Brasil. *Revista de Administração de Empresas*, v. 46, n. 4, p. 1–13, 2006.

MEHR, Hila. *Artificial Intelligence for Citizen Services and Government.* Cambridge: Harvard Ash Center Technology & Democracy, 2017.

MÉNARD, Claude. Meso-institutions: The variety of regulatory arrangements in the water sector. *Utilities Policy*, v. 49, p. 6–19, 2017.

MENGER, Karl. On the Origin of Money. *The Economic Journal*, v. 2, n. 6, p. 239–255, 1892.

MERGEL, Ines. Digital Transformation of the German State. *In*: KUHLMANN, Sabine; PROELLER, Isabella; SCHIMANKE, Dieter; *et al* (Orgs.). *Public Administration in Germany.* Cham: Springer International Publishing, 2021, p. 331–355.

MERRILL, Thomas W. *The Chevron doctrine: its rise and fall, and the future of the administrative state.* Cambridge, Massachusetts: Harvard University Press, 2022.

MEYER, Heinz-Dieter. Tocqueville's Cultural Institutionalism: Reconciling Collective Culture and Methodological Individualism. *Journal of Classical Sociology*, v. 3, n. 2, p. 197–220, 2003.

MICHALLEK, Stefanie. *Funkgeräte aus den 80ern, Dokumentenversand per Fax: Bundeswehr kämpft mit veralteter Technik.* Business Insider. Available at <https://www.businessinsider.de/politik/bundeswehr-nutzt-alte-technik-enorme-investitionen-seien-noetig/>. Accessed 27 Mar. 2024

MILHAUPT, Curtis J.; PISTOR, Katharina. *Law and capitalism: what corporate crises reveal about legal systems and economic development around the world.* Chicago: University of Chicago Press, 2008.

MILL, John Stuart. *Considerations on Representative Government.* Cambridge: Cambridge University Press, 2010.

MILUTINOVIC, Petar. Digital public policy and e-Governance as factors of the enhanced socio-economic cohesion in the European Union. *Kultura Polisa*, v. 19, n. 4, p. 146–166, 2022.

MIRANDA, Antonio. Sociedade da informação: globalização, identidade cultural e conteúdos. *Ciência da Informação*, v. 29, n. 2, p. 78–88, 2000.

MONTESQUIEU, Charles L. de Secondat, Baron de La Brède et de. *O espírito das Leis.* 4. ed. São Paulo: Martins Fontes, 2000.

MOON, M. Jae; WELCH, Eric W. Same Bed, Different Dreams? A Comparative Analysis of Citizen and Bureaucrat Perspectives on E-Government. *Review of Public Personnel Administration*, v. 25, n. 3, p. 243–264, 2005.

MORAES, Alexandre de. *O direito eleitoral e o novo populismo digital. Liberdade de escolha do eleitor e a promoção da Democracia.* Thesis for full professorship (Law), University of São Paulo, São Paulo, 2024.

MOROZOV, Evgeny. *Big Tech - a ascensão dos dados e a morte da política.* São Paulo: Ubu, 2018.

MUNZER, Stephen. *Legal Validity*. Dordrecht: Springer Netherlands, 1972.

MURRAY, Thomas. Socio-Economic Rights Versus Social Revolution? Constitution Making in Germany, Mexico and Ireland, 1917–1923. *Social and Legal Studies*, v. 24, n. 4, p. 487–508, 2015.

MUSAFIR, Valeria Esther Nigri; FREITAS, Christiana Soares de. Strategies, Policies and Evaluations of Brazilian Electronic Government. *Electronic Journal of e-Government*, v. 13, n. 2, p. 136-149, 2015.

NATALI, David. The Lisbon strategy a decade on: a critical review of a multi-disciplinary literature. *Transfer: European Review of Labour and Research*, v. 15, n. 1, p. 111–137, 2009.

NIETO-MATIZ, Camilo; SKIGIN, Natán. The Unintended Consequences of Democratic Reforms: Electronic Voting and Criminal Violence in Brazil. *APSA Preprints*, 2020.

NKR. *Jahresbericht 2023 des Nationalen Normenkontrollrates.* Berlin: Bundesministerium der Justiz, 2023.

NULLMEIER, Frank. Sozialstaat. *In*: ANDERSEN, Uwe; BOGUMIL, Jörg; MARSCHALL, Stefan; *et al* (Orgs.). *Handwörterbuch des politischen Systems der Bundesrepublik Deutschland.* Wiesbaden: Springer Fachmedien, 2021, p. 836–842.

OECD. *A Caminho da Era Digital no Brasil.* Paris: Organisation for Economic Co-operation and Development, 2020.

OECD. *Digital Government Review of Brazil: Towards the digital transformation of the public sector.* Paris: OECD, 2018. (OECD Digital Government Studies Digital).

OECD. *Recommendation on Digital Government Strategies.* Paris: Public Governance and Territorial Development Directorate, 2014.

OECD. *Rethinking E-government Services: User-centred Approaches.* Paris: OECD Publishing, 2009.

OECD. *The OECD digital government policy framework: Six dimensions of a digital government.* Paris: OECD Publishing, 2020. (OECD Public Governance Policy Papers).

OETER, Stefan. *The global legal order: an international lawyers' perspective inspired by institutionalism.* Bremen: University of Bremen, Collaborative Research Center 597: Transformations of the State, 2009. (TranState Working Papers).

OFFERMAN, Theo; VAN DER VEEN, Ailko. How to subsidize contributions to public goods: Does the frog jump out of the boiling water? *European Economic Review*, v. 74, p. 96–108, 2015.

OLIVEIRA, Evandro Luiz de. Voto Eletrônico - Processo Eleitoral Brasileiro. *IP-Informática Pública*, v. 3, n. 1, p. 17–28, 2001.

OMARI, Jeffrey. Chronicles of Internet Openness: The Brazilian Case Study Articles and Essays. *Colorado Technology Law Journal*, v. 20, n. 1, p. 85–120, 2022.

OOSTVEEN, Anne-Marie. Outsourcing Democracy: Losing Control of e-Voting in the Netherlands. *Policy & Internet*, v. 2, n. 4, p. 201–220, 2010.

OSTROM, Elinor. *Governing the Commons: The Evolution of Institutions for Collective Action*. Cambridge: Cambridge University Press, 2015. (Canto Classics).

OSTROM, Elinor. Rational Choice Theory and Institutional Analysis: Toward Complementarity. *The American Political Science Review*, v. 85, n. 1, p. 237–243, 1991.

PADILHA, Felipe; FACIOLI, Lara. Colonialismo tecnológico ou como podemos resistir ao novo eugenismo digital – entrevista com Sérgio Amadeu Silveira. *Estudos de Sociologia*, v. 25, n. 48, p. 363–378, 2020.

PALLANTE, Francesco. *Il neoistituzionalismo nel pensiero giuridico contemporaneo*. Napoli: Jovene, 2008. (Memorie del Dipartimento di scienze giuridiche, ser. 5, memoria 35).

PARK, Sang Chul. The Fourth Industrial Revolution and implications for innovative cluster policies. *AI and Society*, v. 33, n. 3, p. 433–445, 2018.

PECZENIK, Aleksander. Empirical Foundations of Legal Dogmatics. *Logique et Analyse*, v. 12, n. 45, p. 32–64, 1969.

PEDERSEN, John Storm. The digital welfare state: Dataism versus relationshipism. *In*: PEDERSEN, John Storm; WILKINSON, Adrian (Orgs.). *Big Data: Promise, Application and Pitfalls*. Cheltenham: Edward Elgar Publishing, 2019, p. 301–324.

PEDERSEN, Keld. E-government transformations: challenges and strategies. *Transforming Government: People, Process and Policy*, v. 12, n. 1, p. 84–109, 2018.

PETERS, B. Guy. *Institutional theory in political science: the new institutionalism*. 4. ed. Northampton, MA: Edward Elgar Pub, 2019.

PETERS, Guy. Institutional theory. *In*: ANSELL, Christopher; TORFING, Jacob (Orgs.). *Handbook on Theories of Governance*. 2. ed. Cheltenham, Northampton: Edward Elgar Publishing, 2022, p. 323–335.

PETERS, Michael A. Platform ontologies, the AI crisis and the ability to hack humans 'An algorithm knows me better than I know myself'. *Educational Philosophy and Theory*, v. 52, n. 6, p. 593–601, 2020.

PETROVIĆ, Dragan; STEFANOVIĆ, Zoran. Methodological position(s) of institutional economics. *Facta universitatis - Series: Economics and Organization*, v. 6, n. 2, p. 105–114, 2009.

PHILBECK, Thomas; DAVIS, Nicholas. The Fourth Industrial Revolution: Shaping a New Era. *Journal of International Affairs*, v. 72, n. 1, p. 17–22, 2018.

PIERRE, Jon. Disciplinary Perspectives. *In*: PETERS, Guy; PIERRE, Jon (Orgs.). *Handbook of Public Policy*. London: SAGE Publications, 2006, p. 481–492.

PIERSON, Paul. Increasing Returns, Path Dependence, and the Study of Politics. *The American Political Science Review*, v. 94, n. 2, p. 251–267, 2000.

PIETRACCI, Luciano. *Programa gerador de declarações de imposto de renda pessoa jurídica em disquete*. Brasília: ENAP, 1997. (Concurso Inovação na Gestão Pública Federal).

PINHO, José Antonio Gomes de; SACRAMENTO, Ana Rita Silva. Brazil: between the modern bureaucracy of Weber and resilient patrimonialism. *Management Research: The Journal of the Iberoamerican Academy of Management*, v. 13, n. 2, p. 140–159, 2015.

PINTORE, Anna. Institutionalism in law. *In*: *Routledge Encyclopedia of Philosophy*. Trad. Neil MacCormick. 1. ed. London: Routledge, 2016.

POSNER, Richard A. *The economics of justice*. Cambridge, Mass: Harvard University Press, 1981.

PROLL, Eva-Charlotte. Die Umsetzung des OZGs in Deutschland. *In*: STEMBER, Jürgen; EIXELSBERGER, Wolfgang; SPICHIGER, Andreas; *et al* (Orgs.). *Aktuelle Entwicklungen zum E-Government: Neue Impulse und Orientierungen in der digitalen Transformation der öffentlichen Verwaltung*. Wiesbaden: Springer Fachmedien, 2021, p. 29–52. (Edition Innovative Verwaltung).

PUERTAS, Alejandro Moreno; TEIGLAND, Robin. The trust revolution: Blockchain's potential to resolve institutional inefficiencies? *In*: LARSSON, Anthony; TEIGLAND, Robin (Orgs.). *Digital Transformation and Public Services*. London: Routledge, 2019, p. 277–292.

RACKWITZ, Maike; HUSTEDT, Thurid; HAMMERSCHMID, Gerhard. Digital transformation: from hierarchy to network-based collaboration? The case of the German "Online Access Act". *dms – der moderne staat – Zeitschrift für Public Policy, Recht und Management*, v. 14, n. 1, 2021.

RAZ, Joseph. Legal Principles and the Limits of Law. *Yale Law Journal*, v. 81, n. 5, p. 823–854, 1971.

RAZ, Joseph. *The authority of law. Essays on law and morality*. New York: Oxford University Press, 2009.

RECK, Janriê Rodrigues; HÜBNER, Bruna Henrique. A transformação digital do Estado: digitalização do governo e dos serviços úblicos no Brasil. *Revista Eletrônica Direito e Política*, v. 16, n. 3, p. 1075–1096, 2021.

REHDER, Britta. *Rechtsprechung als Politik: der Beitrag des Bundesarbeitsgerichts zur Entwicklung der Arbeitsbeziehungen in Deutschland*. Frankfurt am Main: Campus-Verl, 2011. (Schriften aus dem Max-Planck-Institut für Gesellschaftsforschung Köln, 74).

REYNA, Justo; GABARDO, Emerson; SANTOS, Fabio de Sousa. Electronic government, digital invisibility and fundamental social rights. *Seqüência: Estudos Jurídicos e Políticos*, v. 41, n. 85, p. 30–50, 2020.

RIBEIRO, Leonardo Coelho. O direito administrativo como caixa de ferramentas e suas estratégias. *Revista de Direito Administrativo*, v. 272, p. 209, 2016.

RIKER, William H. Implications from the Disequilibrium of Majority Rule for the Study of Institutions. *The American Political Science Review*, v. 74, n. 2, p. 432–446, 1980.

RIPLEY, Randall B. Stages of the policy process. *In*: DANIEL C. MCCOOL (Ed.). *Public policy theories, models, and concepts: an anthology*. New Jersey: Prentice Hall, 1995.

RITTER, Gerhard A. *Der Sozialstaat: Entstehung und Entwicklung im internationalen Vergleich*. 3. ed. München: Oldenbourg Verlag, 2010.

RODRIGUEZ, Ricardo; WARMERDAM, John; TRIOMPHE, Claude Emmanuel. *The Lisbon Strategy 2000 - 2010 An analysis and evaluation of the methods used and result*. Brussels: European Parliament, 2010.

ROSENBLOOM, David H. Public Administration's Legal Dimensions: Three Models. *In*: MENZEL, Donalf C.; WHITE, Harvey L. (Orgs.). *The State of Public Administration: Issues, Challenges and Opportunities*. London and New York: Routledge, 2015, p. 368–387.

ROßNAGEL, Alexander; HORNUNG, Gerrit; KNOPP, Michael; *et al.* De-Mail und Bürgerportale. *Datenschutz und Datensicherheit - DuD*, v. 33, n. 12, p. 728–734, 2009.

RUDOLPH, Lloyd I.; RUDOLPH, Susanne Hoeber. Authority and Power in Bureaucratic and Patrimonial Administration: A Revisionist Interpretation of Weber on Bureaucracy. *World Politics*, v. 31, n. 2, p. 195–227, 1979.

RUIZ, Isabela; BUCCI, Maria Paula Dallari. Quadro de problemas de políticas públicas: uma ferramenta para análise jurídico-institucional. *REI - Revista Estudos Institucionais*, v. 5, n. 3, p. 1142–1167, 2019.

RUSCHEL, Aírton José; LAZZARI, João Batista; ROVER, Aires José. O processo judicial eletrônico no brasil: uma visão geral. *In*: COÊLHO, Marcus Vinicius Furtado; ALLEMAND, Luiz Cláudio (Orgs.). *Processo Judicial Eletrônico*. Brasília: OAB, 2014, p. 13–28.

RÜTHERS, Bernd. *Rechtsdogmatik und Rechtspolitik unter dem Einfluß des Richterrechts*. Trier: Institut für Rechtspolitik an der Universität Trier, 2003. (Rechtspolitisches Forum).

SAAM, Nicole J.; KERBER, Wolfgang. Policy Innovation, Decentralised Experimentation, and Laboratory Federalism. *Journal of Artificial Societies and Social Simulation*, v. 16, n. 1, 2012.

SABATIER, Paul A.; WEIBLE, Christopher M. The Advocacy Coalition Framework: Innovations and Clarifications. *In*: SABATIER, Paul (Org.). *Theories of the Policy Process*. 2. ed. London and New York: Routledge, 2007.

SAKR, Rafael Lima. Do software livre ao desafio informacional: direito e liberdade na sociedade rede. *Revista da Faculdade de Direito, Universidade de São Paulo*, v. 104, p. 617–637, 2009.

SALDANHA, Douglas Morgan Fullin; SILVA, Marcela Barbosa da. Transparência e accountability de algoritmos governamentais: o caso do sistema eletrônico de votação brasileiro. *Cadernos EBAPE.BR*, v. 18, p. 697–712, 2020.

SALES, Gabriela Azevedo Campos. *Estado social e federalismo: a institucionalização dos sistemas de políticas públicas no Brasil.* Belo Horizonte, MG: Fórum, 2023. (Coleção Fórum Direito e Políticas Públicas).

SALOMÃO FILHO, Calixto. *Direito Concorrencial.* São Paulo: Malheiros, 2013.

SAMNAKAY, Nadeem. Thinking Strategically in Federal Policy: Defining the Attributes of High-level Policies. *Australian Journal of Public Administration*, v. 76, n. 1, p. 106–121, 2017.

SANTANO, Ana. As narrativas e as necessidades: o sistema eletrônico de votação brasileiro a partir de uma análise de política pública. *A&C - Revista de Direito Administrativo & Constitucional*, v. 22, n. 88, p. 75, 2022.

SANTOS, Roberval de Jesus Leone dos. *Rede Governo: o portal de serviços e informações para o cidadão.* Brasília: Escola Nacional de Administração Pública, 2003. (Concurso Inovação na Gestão Pública Federal).

SARAIVA, André. *A Implementação do SEI - Sistema Eletrônico de Informações.* Brasília: Enap. Casoteca da Gestão Pública, 2018. (Casos Seges).

SATZ, Debra; FEREJOHN, John. Rational Choice and Social Theory. *The Journal of Philosophy*, v. 91, n. 2, p. 71–87, 1994.

SCHAPIRO, Mario G.; MOUALLEM, Pedro Salomon Bezerra; DANTAS, Eric Gil. PIX: explaining a state-owned Fintech. *Brazilian Journal of Political Economy*, v. 43, n. 4, p. 874–892, 2023.

SCHARPF, Fritz W. Die Politikverflechtungsfalle: Europäische Politik und deutscher Födemlismus im Vergleich. *Politische Vierteljahresschrift*, v. 26, p. 323–356, 1985.

SCHARPF, Fritz W. Recht und Politik in der Reform des deutschen Föderalismus. *In*: BECKER, Michael; ZIMMERLING, Ruth (Eds.). *Politik und Recht.* Wiesbaden: Springer-Verlag, 2006.

SCHARPF, Fritz W. The Joint-Decision Trap: Lessons from German Federalism and European Integration. *Public Administration*, v. 66, n. 3, p. 239–278, 1988.

SCHARPF, Fritz Wilhelm. *Games real actors play: actor-centered institutionalism in policy research.* Boulder, CO: Westview Press, 1997. (Theoretical lenses on public policy).

SCHEUERMAN, William E. Democratic Experimentalism or Capitalist Synchronization? Critical Reflections on Directly-Deliberative Polyarchy. *Canadian Journal of Law & Jurisprudence*, v. 17, n. 1, p. 101–127, 2004.

SCHEUERMAN, William E. Whistleblowing as civil disobedience: The case of Edward Snowden. *Philosophy & Social Criticism*, v. 40, n. 7, p. 609–628, 2014.

SCHIEDER, Siegfried. Institutionalismus in den Internationalen Beziehungen. *In*: SAUER, Frank; MASALA, Carlo (Orgs.). *Handbuch Internationale Beziehungen.* Wiesbaden: Springer Fachmedien, 2017, p. 177–214. (Springer Reference Sozialwissenschaften).

SCHIRATO, Vitor Rhein. A deterioração do sistema regulatório brasileiro. *Revista de Direito Público da Economia*, v. 11, n. 44, p. 249–274, 2013.

SCHMANDT, Marco; TIELKES, Constantin; WEINHARDT, Felix. Königsteiner Schlüssel verteilt Gelder und Aufgaben zwischen Bundesländern kaum nach Wirtschaftskraft. *DIW Wochenbericht*, v. 90, n. 18, p. 204–209, 2023.

SCHMIDT, Manfred G. Thesen zur Reform des Föderalismus der Bundesrepublik Deutschland. *Politische Vierteljahresschrift*, v. 42, n. 3, p. 474–491, 2001.

SCHMIDT, Vivien. Discursive Institutionalism: The Explanatory Power of Ideas and Discourse. *Annual Review of Political Science*, v. 11, 2008.

SCHMIDT, Vivien A. Reconciling Ideas and Institutions through Discursive Institutionalism. *In*: BÉLAND, Daniel; COX, Robert Henry (Orgs.). *Ideas and politics in social science research*. Oxford and New York: Oxford University Press, 2011, p. 47–64.

SCHMIDT-AßMANN, Eberhard. *Verwaltungsrechtliche Dogmatik: eine Zwischenbilanz zu Entwicklung, Reform und künftigen Aufgaben*. Tübingen: Mohr Siebeck, 2013.

SCHNEIDER, Jens-Peter. Regulation and Europeanisation as Key Patterns of Change in Administrative Law. *In*: RUFFERT, Matthias (Org.). *The Transformation of Administrative Law in Europe*. Munich: Sellier European Law Publishers, 2007, p. 307–322.

SCHREIBER, Anderson. Marco Civil da Internet: avanço ou retrocesso? A responsabilidade civil por dano derivado do conteúdo gerado por terceiro. *In*: LUCCA, Newton de; FILHO, Adalberto Simão; LIMA, Cíntia Rosa Pereira de (Orgs.). *Direito & Internet*. São Paulo: Quartier Latin, 2015, v. 2, p. 277–305.

SCHULTZ, Theodore W. Capital Formation by Education. *Journal of Political Economy*, v. 68, n. 6, p. 571–583, 1960.

SCHULZ, Sönke E. Rechtlicher Rahmen der Digitalisierung und der Online-Dienste. *In*: LÜHR, Hans-Henning; JABKOWSKI, Roland; SMENTEK, Sabine (Orgs.). *Handbuch Digitale Verwaltung*. Wiesbaden: KSV Medien, 2019, p. 159–184.

SCHULZ, Sönke E. Schulz: Der elektronische Zugang zur Verwaltung. *Recht Digital*, n. 8, p. 377–383, 2021.

SCHÜTZ, Alfred. *The theory of social action: The correspondence of Alfred Schutz and Talcott Parsons*. Bloomington: Indiana University Press, 1978.

SCHWEIGHOFER, Erich; HÖTZENDORFER, Walter. Electronic identities – public or private. *International Review of Law, Computers & Technology*, v. 27, n. 1-2, p. 230–239, 2013.

SEARLE, John R. *Making the social world: the structure of human civilization*. Oxford: Oxford University Press, 2011.

SEN, Amartya K. Rational Fools: A Critique of the Behavioral Foundations of Economic Theory. *Philosophy & Public Affairs*, v. 6, n. 4, p. 317–344, 1977.

SENSHAW, Debas; TWINOMURINZI, Hossana. Critical path-dependencies affecting digital government innovation in low-income countries: a case study from Woredas in Ethiopia. *Electronic Government, an International Journal*, v. 20, n. 1, p. 1–19, 2024.

SERAFIM, Milena Pavan; DAGNINO, Renato Peixoto. A política científica e tecnológica e as demandas da inclusão social no governo Lula (2003-2006). *Organizações & Sociedade*, v. 18, n. 58, p. 403–427, 2011.

SERPRO. *Relatório Integrado Anual*. Brasília: Escritório de Governança e Estratégia Corporativas, 2022.

SHAPIRO, Carl; VARIAN, Hal R. *Information rules: a strategic guide to the network economy*. Boston, Mass: Harvard Business School Press, 1999.

SHARON, Tamar. Blind-sided by privacy? Digital contact tracing, the Apple/Google API and big tech's newfound role as global health policy makers. *Ethics and Information Technology*, v. 23, n. Suppl 1, p. 45–57, 2021.

SHEN, Hong. China and global internet governance: toward an alternative analytical framework. *Chinese Journal of Communication*, v. 9, n. 3, p. 304–324, 2016.

SHUBIK, Martin. Game Theory, Law, and the Concept of Competition. *University of Cincinnati Law Review*, v. 60, n. 2, p. 285–304, 1991.

SIEBERT, Horst. *Der Kobra-Effekt wie man Irrwege der Wirtschaftspolitik vermeidet.* Ungekürzte Taschenbuchausg. München/Zürich: Piper, 2003. (Serie Piper: Business, Geld, Karriere).

SIEGFRIED, Tina. E-government in Germany. *In*: NIXON, Paul G.; KOUTRAKOU, Vassiliki N. (Orgs.). *E-government in Europe.* London: Routledge, 2007, p. 90–102.

SIMÃO, João Batista; RODRIGUES, Georgete. Acessibilidade às informações públicas: uma avaliação do portal de serviços e informações do governo federal. *Ciência da Informação*, v. 34, n. 2, p. 81–92, 2005.

SIMONS, Josh; GHOSH, Dipayan. *Utilities for Democracy: Why and How the Algorithmic Infrastructure of Facebook and Google Must Be Regulated.* Washington, DC: Brookings Institution, 2020. (Brookings Foreign Policy Report).

SKOCPOL, Theda; AMENTA, Edwin. States and Social Policies. *Annual Review of Sociology*, v. 12, p. 131–157, 1986.

SMITS, Jan M. What is legal doctrine? On the aims and methods of legal-dogmatic research. *In*: ROB VAN GESTEL; HANS-W. MICKLITZ; EDWARD L. RUBIN (Orgs.). *Rethinking legal scholarship: a transatlantic dialogue.* New York: Cambridge University Press, 2017, p. 207–228.

SORIANO, Fernando Hervás; MULATERO, Fulvio. Knowledge Policy in the EU: From the Lisbon Strategy to Europe 2020. *Journal of the Knowledge Economy*, v. 1, n. 4, p. 289–302, 2010.

SOUZA, Carlos Affonso Pereira de; LEMOS, Ronaldo. Aspectos jurídicos da Economia do Compartilhamento: função social e tutela da confiança. *Revista de Direito da Cidade*, v. 8, n. 4, p. 1757, 2016.

SOUZA, Matheus Silveira de. *Direito, Políticas Públicas e Educação Profissional.* Belo Horizonte, MG: Fórum, 2022.

SPD; BÜNDNIS 90/DIE GRÜNEN; FDP. *Koalitionsvertrag 2021-2025.* Available at <https://www.spd.de/fileadmin/Dokumente/Koalitionsvertrag/Koalitionsvertrag_2021-2025.pdf>. Accessed 26 Mar. 2024

SPIRO, Herbert J. Critique of Behavioralism in Political Science. *In*: VON BEYME, Klaus (Org.). *Theory and Politics/Theorie und Politik: Festschrift zum 70. Geburtstag für Carl Joachim Friedrich.* Dordrecht: Springer Netherlands, 1971, p. 314–327.

STEINMO, Sven. Historical institutionalism and experimental methods. *The Oxford handbook of historical institutionalism*, p. 108–124, 2016.

STEMBER, Jürgen; HASENKAMP, Victoria. E-Government in Deutschland: Ein Überblick. *In*: STEMBER, Jürgen; EIXELSBERGER, Wolfgang; SPICHIGER, Andreas; *et al* (Orgs.). *Handbuch E-Government: Technikinduzierte Verwaltungsentwicklung.* Wiesbaden: Springer Fachmedien, 2019, p. 31–52.

STEMBER, Jürgen; HASENKAMP, Victoria; HABBEL, Franz-Reinhard. E-Government auf den unterschiedlichen administrativen Ebenen in Deutschland. *In*: STEMBER, Jürgen; EIXELSBERGER, Wolfgang; SPICHIGER, Andreas; *et al* (Orgs.). *Handbuch E-Government: Technikinduzierte Verwaltungsentwicklung*. Wiesbaden: Springer Fachmedien, 2019, p. 183–206.

STEMBER, Jürgen; HESSE, Emanuel. Das Projekt E-Government-Modellkommunen des Bundesministeriums des Innern in Deutschland. *In*: STEMBER, Jürgen; EIXELSBERGER, Wolfgang; SPICHIGER, Andreas (Orgs.). *Wirkungen von E-Government: Impulse für eine wirkungsgesteuerte und technikinduzierte Verwaltungsreform*. Wiesbaden: Springer Fachmedien, 2018, p. 345–381.

STEPAN, Alfred. Brazil's Decentralized Federalism: Bringing Government Closer to the Citizens? *Daedalus*, v. 129, n. 2, p. 145–169, 2000.

STROMBERG, Roland N. The Philosophes and the French Revolution: Reflections on Some Recent Research. *The History Teacher*, v. 21, n. 3, p. 321–339, 1988.

SUNDFELD, Carlos Ari. Como tornar o controle eficiente? Definindo os limites do papel do Ministério Público e dos Tribunais de Contas. *In*: GIAMBIAGI, F.; FERREIRA, S.G.; HOELZ, A.A.M. (Orgs.). *Reforma do Estado Brasileiro - Transformando a Atuação do Governo*. Rio de Janeiro: GEN Atlas, 2020.

SUNDFELD, Carlos Ari. *Direito Administrativo para Céticos*. São Paulo: Malheiros, 2012.

SUNSTEIN, Cass R. On the Expressive Function of Law. *University of Pennsylvania Law Review*, v. 144, n. 5, p. 2021–2053, 1996.

SUREL, Yves. The role of cognitive and normative frames in policy-making. *Journal of European Public Policy*, v. 7, n. 4, p. 495–512, 2000.

SÜß, Rahel Sophia. Demokratie ist radikaler Experimentalismus. *In*: RAJAL, Elke; TRAFO.K; MARCHART, Oliver; *et al* (Orgs.). *Making Democracy - Aushandlungen von Freiheit, Gleichheit und Solidarität im Alltag*. Bielefeld, Germany: transcript Verlag, 2020, v. 94, p. 193–204.

SWEDBERG, Richard. On the Heuristic Role of Concepts in Theorizing. *In*: *Theory in Action. Theoretical Constructionism*. Leiden: Brill, 2017, p. 23–38.

SZIKRA, Dorottya; ÖKTEM, Kerem Gabriel. An illiberal welfare state emerging? Welfare efforts and trajectories under democratic backsliding in Hungary and Turkey. *Journal of European Social Policy*, v. 33, n. 2, p. 201–215, 2023.

TAGESSCHAU. *Wie das BAföG Studierende in den Wahnsinn treibt | akkurat*. Available at <https://www.youtube.com/watch?v=p3nY-pxOsQY>. Accessed 28 Mar. 2024

TAMANAHA, Brian Z. Understanding Legal Realism. *Texas Law Review*, v. 87, n. 4, p. 731–786, 2008.

TANGI, Luca; JANSSEN, Marijn; BENEDETTI, Michele; *et al.* Digital government transformation: A structural equation modelling analysis of driving and impeding factors. *International Journal of Information Management*, v. 60, p. 10, 2021.

TAYLOR, Matthew M. Veto and Voice in the Courts: Policy Implications of Institutional Design in the Brazilian Judiciary. *Comparative Politics*, v. 38, n. 3, p. 337–355, 2006.

TCU. *Avaliação do Programa Governo Eletrônico. Tribunal de Contas da União.* Brasília: Secretaria de Fiscalização e Avaliação de Programas de Governo, 2006. (Sumários Executivos. Nova Série).

TEIXEIRA, Lucas De Barros. Transparência algorítmica em soluções utilizadas por governos. *Revista Internacional de Debates da Administração & Públicas - RIDAP*, v. 6, n. 1, p. 1–10, 2021.

TENNER, Edward. Who's Afraid of the Frightful Five? Monopoly and Culture in the Digital Age. *Hedgehog Review*, v. 20, n. 1, p. 68–77, 2018.

TERRA, José Cláudio Cyrineu; GORDON, Cindy. *Realizing the promise of corporate portals: Leveraging knowledge for business success.* Burlington: Butterworth-Heinemann, 2003.

THALER, Richard H. Behavioral economics: Past, present, and future. *American economic review*, v. 106, n. 7, p. 1577–1600, 2016.

THELEN, Kathleen. Historical Institutionalism in Comparative Politics. *Annual Review of Political Science*, v. 2, n. 1, p. 369–404, 1999.

THOMAS, Daniel C. Explaining the negotiation of EU foreign policy: Normative institutionalism and alternative approaches. *International Politics*, v. 46, n. 4, p. 339-357, 2009.

THORNHILL, Christopher. *Democratic Crisis and Global Constitutional Law.* Cambridge: Cambridge University Press, 2021.

TOCQUEVILLE, Alexis de. *De la démocratie en Amérique.* Paris: Institut Coppet, 2012.

TOLBERT, Pamela S.; ZUCKER, Lynne G. The Institutionalization of Institutional Theory. *In*: CLEGG, Stewart R.; HARDY, Cynthia (Orgs.). *Studying Organization: Theory & Method.* London: SAGE Publications, 1999, p. 169–184.

TOLEDO, Carlos José Teixeira de. *Políticas Públicas e Valorização do Professor da Educação Básica.* Belo Horizonte, MG: Fórum, 2022.

TOMASEVICIUS FILHO, Eduardo. Marco Civil da Internet: uma lei sem conteúdo normativo. *Estudos Avançados*, v. 30, n. 86, p. 269–285, 2016.

TOMIO, Fabrício Ricardo de Limas; ROBL FILHO, Ilton Norberto. Accountability e independência judiciais: uma análise da competência do Conselho Nacional de Justiça (CNJ). *Revista de Sociologia e Política*, v. 21, n. 45, p. 29–46, 2013.

TOURAINE, Alain. An Introduction to the Study of Social Movements. *Social Research*, v. 52, n. 4, p. 749–787, 1985.

TRUTE, Hans Heinrich. On knowledge and law: The role of law in the generation and harmonisation of knowledge. *In*: HORATSCHEK, Anna Margaretha (Org.). *Competing Knowledges - Wissen im Widerstreit.* Berlin, Boston: De Gruyter, 2020, v. 9, p. 103–122. (Abhandlungen der Akademie der Wissenschaften in Hamburg).

TRUTE, Hans-Heinrich. Die demokratische Legitimation der Verwaltung. *In*: HOFFMANN-RIEM, Wolfgang; SCHMIDT-AßMANN, Eberhard; VOSSKUHLE, Andreas (Orgs.). *Grundlagen des Verwaltungsrechts.* 2. ed. München: C. H. Beck, 2012.

TRUTE, Hans-Heinrich. Die konstitutive Rolle der Rechtsanwendung. *In*: TRUTE, Hans-Heinrich; SCHMIDT-AßMANN, Eberhard; GROSS, Thomas; *et al* (Orgs.). *Allgemeines Verwaltungsrecht - zur Tragfähigkeit eines Konzepts.* Tübingen: Mohr Siebeck, 2008, p. 211–232.

TRUTE, Hans-Heinrich. Rechtliche Herausforderungen der Digitalisierung: Daten - Algorithmen - Wissen. *In*: BÄR, Christian; GRÄDLER, Thomas; MAYR, Robert (Orgs.). *Digitalisierung im Spannungsfeld von Politik, Wirtschaft, Wissenschaft und Recht*. Berlin, Heidelberg: Springer, 2018, p. 313–330.

TSE. *Relatório das Eleições 2002*. Brasília: Tribunal Superior Eleitoral, 2003.

TSEBELIS, George. Veto Players and Law Production in Parliamentary Democracies: An Empirical Analysis. *American Political Science Review*, v. 93, n. 3, p. 591–608, 1999.

ULEN, Thomas S. Rational choice theory in law and economics. *Encyclopedia of law and economics*, v. 1, p. 790–818, 1999.

UNGER, Roberto Mangabeira. A constituição do experimentalismo democrático. *Revista de Direito Administrativo*, v. 257, p. 57–72, 2011.

UNGER, Roberto Mangabeira. Legal Analysis as Institutional Imagination. *The Modern Law Review*, v. 59, n. 1, p. 1–23, 1996.

UNGER, Roberto Mangabeira. The Critical Legal Studies Movement. *Harvard Law Review*, v. 96, n. 3, p. 561–675, 1983.

UNGER, Roberto Mangabeira. *What Should Legal Analysis Become?* London: Verso, 1996.

UNITED NATIONS. *E-Government Survey 2020*. New York: Department of Economic and Social Affairs, 2020.

VALENTE, Sergio Ruy David Polimeno. Direito e políticas públicas: uma visão jurídico-institucional sobre o caso do saneamento básico no Brasil. *Rei - Revista Estudos Institucionais*, v. 5, n. 3, p. 1064–1092, 2019.

VALENTE, Sergio Ruy David Polimeno. *Políticas públicas e a visão jurídico-institucional: o caso do saneamento básico no Brasil*. Master's thesis, University of São Paulo, 2018.

VALLE, Vanice Regina Lírio do; MOTTA, Fabrício. Governo digital: mapeando possíveis bloqueios institucionais à sua implantação. *In*: VALLE, Vanice Regina Lírio do; MOTTA, Fabrício (Orgs.). *Governo Digital e a Busca por Inovação na Administração Pública*. Kindle. Belo Horizonte: Forum, 2022.

VAN DEN HOVE, Sybille; MCGLADE, Jacqueline; MOTTET, Pierre; *et al*. The Innovation Union: a perfect means to confused ends? *Environmental Science & Policy*, v. 16, p. 73–80, 2012.

VAN DER AALST, Wil; HINZ, Oliver; WEINHARDT, Christof. Big Digital Platforms: Growth, Impact, and Challenges. *Business and Information Systems Engineering*, v. 61, n. 6, p. 645–648, 2019.

VAN DIJCK, José. Governing digital societies: Private platforms, public values. *Computer Law and Security Review*, v. 36, p. 1-4, 2020.

VARDI, Moshe Y. The winner-takes-all tech corporation. *Communications of the ACM*, v. 62, n. 11, p. 7, 2019.

VASAK, Karel. A 30-year struggle; the sustained efforts to give force of law to the Universal Declaration of Human Rights. *The Unesco Courier*, p. 29–32, 1977.

VEITCH, Scott; CHRISTODOULIDIS, Emilios A.; GOLDONI, Marco. *Jurisprudence: themes and concepts*. 3. ed. London and New York: Routledge, 2018.

VELOSO, João Francisco Alves; MONASTERIO, Leonardo Monteiro; VIEIRA, Roberta da Silva; *et al.* Uma visão inicial dos subsistemas da gestão pública municipal. *In*: VELOSO, João Francisco Alves; MONASTERIO, Leonardo Monteiro; VIEIRA, Roberta da Silva; *et al* (Orgs.). *Gestão municipal no Brasil: um retrato das prefeituras*. Brasília: Ipea, 2011, p. 11–40.

VERHEYEN, Sabine; RIEKE, Katharina. E-Government in der Europäischen Union. *In*: STEMBER, Jürgen; EIXELSBERGER, Wolfgang; SPICHIGER, Andreas; *et al* (Orgs.). *Handbuch E-Government: Technikinduzierte Verwaltungsentwicklung*. Wiesbaden: Springer Fachmedien, 2019, p. 95–110.

VERHOEST, Koen; VERSCHUERE, Bram; BOUCKAERT, Geert. Pressure, Legitimacy, and Innovative Behavior by Public Organizations. *Governance*, v. 20, n. 3, p. 469–497, 2007.

VIANA, Ana Cristina Aguilar. Digital transformation in public administration: From e-government to digital government. *Revista Eurolatinoamericana de Derecho Administrativo*, v. 8, n. 1, p. 115–136, 2021.

VIANELLO, Lorenzo Córdova. Liberalismo, democracia, neoliberalismo e ingobernabilidad. *Revista Mexicana de Sociología*, v. 58, n. 4, p. 3–35, 1996.

VIEHWEG, Theodor. Systemprobleme in Rechtsdogmatik und Rechtsforschung. *In*: DIEMER, Alwin (Org.). *System und Klassifikation in Wissenschaft und Dokumentation: Vorträge und Diskussionen im April 1967 in Düsseldorf*. Meisenheim am Glan: Hain, 1968, p. 96–104.

VOLCANSEK, Mary L. Constitutional courts as veto players: Divorce and decrees in Italy. *European Journal of Political Research*, v. 39, n. 3, p. 347–372, 2001.

VON LUCKE, Jörn; GOLLASCH, Katja. *Open Government: Offenes Regierungs- und Verwaltungshandeln – Leitbilder, Ziele und Methoden*. Wiesbaden: Springer Fachmedien, 2022. (Edition eGov-Campus).

VON WRIGHT, G. H. Deontic Logic Revisited. *Rechtstheorie*, v. 4, n. 1–2, p. 37–46, 1973.

VOSS, Vivien C. Die Implementation der Europäischen Dienstleistungsrichtlinie – lessons learned im Hinblick auf das Wirksamwerden der Single Digital Gateway-Verordnung und des Onlinezugangsgesetzes. *In*: SECKELMANN, Margrit; BRUNZEL, Marco (Orgs.). *Handbuch Onlinezugangsgesetz: Potenziale - Synergien - Herausforderungen*. Berlin, Heidelberg: Springer, 2021, p. 199–225.

WAJSMAN, Samuel ZUCCARO; BLIACHERIENE, Ana Carla. Access to information, transparency and social control in Brazil. *International Journal of Open Governments*, v. 9, p. 165–190, 2020.

WALTON, Kevin. A realistic vision? Roberto Unger on law and politics. *Res Publica*, v. 5, n. 2, p. 139–159, 1999.

WASSERFALLEN, Antoine. When Asian Industry Influences Western Factories: Kanban Origins. *Ferrum*, n. 82, p. 96–103, 2010.

WEBER, Max. *Wirtschaft und Gesellschaft: Grundriss der verstehenden Soziologie*. 5. ed. Tübingen: Mohr, 1990.

WEIHRICH, Heinz. The TOWS matrix—A tool for situational analysis. *Long Range Planning*, v. 15, n. 2, p. 54–66, 1982.

WEINBERGER, Ota. Das Recht als Institutionelle Tatsache: Gleichzeitig eine Uberlegung uber den Begriff des Positiven Rechts Abhandlungen und Aufsatze. *Rechtstheorie*, v. 11, n. 4, p. 427–442, 1980.

WEINBERGER, Ota. Neo-Institutionalism: My Views on the Philosophy of Law. *In*: WINTGENS, Luc J. (Org.). *The Law in Philosophical Perspectives: My Philosophy of Law*. Dordrecht: Springer Netherlands, 1999, p. 253–272. (Law and Philosophy Library).

WEINBERGER, Ota. Verfassungstheorie vom Standpunkt des neuen Institutionalismus. *ARSP: Archiv für Rechts- und Sozialphilosophie*, v. 76, n. 1, p. 100–118, 1990.

WELSER, Marcus von. Kampf um Linux: Ist die Freiheit der Open-Source-Software bedroht? *Gewerblicher Rechtsschutz und Urheberrecht, Praxis im Immaterialgüter und Wettbewerbsrecht*, n. 7, p. 164–166, 2018.

WERNER, Petra. *Die Normentheorie Helmut Schelskys als Form eines Neuen Institutionalismus*. 1. ed. Berlin: Duncker & Humblot, 1995.

WEWER, Göttrik. Open Government als Zukunftsvision für Kommunen? *In*: ROTERS, Wolfgang; GRÄF, Horst; WOLLMANN, Hellmut (Orgs.). *Zukunft denken und verantworten: Herausforderungen für Politik, Wissenschaft und Gesellschaft im 21. Jahrhundert*. Wiesbaden: Springer Fachmedien, 2020, p. 377–391.

WHITAKER, Stephan D. Big Data versus a survey. *The Quarterly Review of Economics and Finance*, v. 67, p. 285–296, 2018.

WIENS, David. Prescribing Institutions Without Ideal Theory. *Journal of Political Philosophy*, v. 20, n. 1, p. 45–70, 2012.

WILLIAMS, Mark; VALAYER, Clementine. *Digital Government Benchmark. Study on Digital Government Transformation*. Brussels: DG Joint Research Centre. European Commission, 2018. (European Location Interoperability Solutions for e-Government).

WILLIAMSON, John. A Short History of the Washington Consensus. *Law and Business Review of the Americas*, v. 15, n. 1, p. 7–26, 2009.

WILLIAMSON, Oliver E. Transaction Cost Economics: How It Works; Where It is Headed. *De Economist*, v. 146, n. 1, p. 23–58, 1998.

WIMMER, Maria A. Once-Only und Digital First als Gestaltungsprinzipien der vernetzten Verwaltung von morgen. *In*: SECKELMANN, Margrit; BRUNZEL, Marco (Orgs.). *Handbuch Onlinezugangsgesetz: Potenziale - Synergien - Herausforderungen*. Berlin, Heidelberg: Springer, 2021, p. 145–163.

WIRTZ, Bernd W.; KUBIN, Pascal R. M. E-Government in Deutschland: Entwicklung, Barrieren und Verbesserungsansätze. *VM Verwaltung & Management*, v. 27, n. 6, p. 285–294, 2021.

WORLD BANK. *Brazil: Systematic Country Diagnostic*. Washington DC: World Bank Group, 2016.

WORLD BANK. *Training for Reform*. Washington, DC: World Bank Group, 2019. (World Bank Group Flagship Report).

XAVIER, Jean Frederick Brito. *Governo eletrônico: o cidadão e o direito de acesso à informação*. PhD Dissertation (Information Science), University of São Paulo, São Paulo, 2022.

XU, Li Da; XU, Eric L.; LI, Ling. Industry 4.0: State of the art and future trends. *International Journal of Production Research*, v. 56, n. 8, p. 2941–2962, 2018.

YANG, Kaifeng. Neoinstitutionalism and E-Government: Beyond Jane Fountain. *Social Science Computer Review*, v. 21, n. 4, p. 432–442, 2003.

YEE, Albert S. The causal effects of ideas on policies. *International Organization*, v. 50, n. 1, p. 69–108, 1996.

YÖRÜK, Erdem; ÖKER, İbrahim; TAFOYA, Gabriela Ramalho. The four global worlds of welfare capitalism: Institutional, neoliberal, populist and residual welfare state regimes. *Journal of European Social Policy*, v. 32, n. 2, p. 119–134, 2022.

ZACHER, Hans F. Der Sozialstaat als Prozeß. *Zeitschrift für die gesamte Staatswissenschaft*, v. 134, n. 1, p. 15–36, 1978.

ZAMUR FILHO, Jamil. *Processo judicial eletrônico: alcance e efetividade sob a égide da Lei No 11.419, de 19.12.2006*. PhD Dissertation (Law), University of São Paulo, São Paulo, 2011.

ZEHAVI, Amos J. Veto Players, Path Dependency, and Reform of Public Aid Policy toward Private Schools: Australia, New Zealand, and the United States. *Comparative Politics*, v. 44, n. 3, p. 311–330, 2012.

ZEPIC, Robert; DAPP, Marcus; KRCMAR, Helmut. E-Partizipation und keiner macht mit. *HMD Praxis der Wirtschaftsinformatik*, v. 54, n. 4, p. 488–501, 2017.

ВАСЛАВСКИЙ, Ян И.; ГАБУЕВ, С. В. Неоинституциональный подход как методологическая основа исследования электронного правительства. *Вестник МГИМО-Университета*, n. 6(51), p. 60–75, 2016.

Apple Wallet ID - Your Arizona ID in Apple Wallet | ADOT. Available at <https://azdot.gov/applewallet>. Accessed 3 Jun. 2022

BAföG 2022: Durchschnittlicher Förderbetrag um gut 5 % gestiegen. Statistisches Bundesamt. Available at <https://www.destatis.de/DE/Presse/Pressemitteilungen/2023/08/PD23_307_214.html>. Accessed 28 Mar. 2024

Compras.gov.br. Available at <http://www.comprasnet.gov.br/noticias/noticias1.asp?id_noticia=197>. Accessed 8 Apr. 2024

Corona-Folgen bekämpfen, Wohlstand sichern, Zukunftsfähigkeit stärken Ergebnis Koalitionsausschuss 3. Juni 2020. Available at <https://www.bmwk.de/Redaktion/DE/Downloads/E/eckpunktepapier-corona-folgen-bekaempfen.pdf?__blob=publicationFile&v=6>. Accessed 25 Mar. 2024

Corregedoria autoriza transferência eletrônica de veículos por registro civil. Portal CNJ. Available at <https://www.cnj.jus.br/corregedoria-autoriza-transferencia-eletronica-de-veiculos-via-registro-civil/>. Accessed 12 Oct. 2024

Dashboard Digitale Verwaltung. Available at <https://dashboard.ozg-umsetzung.de/>. Accessed 26 Mar. 2024

De-Mail: Der Telekom-Ausstieg und die Folgen | heise online. Available at <https://www.heise.de/news/De-Mail-Der-Telekom-Ausstieg-und-die-Folgen-6194853.html>. Accessed 22 Mar. 2024

Digitale Verwaltung. Bundesministerium der Justiz. Available at <https://www.normenkontrollrat.bund.de/Webs/NKR/DE/digitaler-und-moderner-staat/digitale-verwaltung/digitale-verwaltung_node.html>. Accessed 26 Mar. 2024

Entire population of Brazil possibly exposed in massive data leak. Cybernews. Available at <https://cybernews.com/security/brazil-data-leak-cpf-card/>. Accessed 16 Aug. 2024

Especial CNJ 1 - Conselho Nacional de Justiça desenvolve ações para acelerar processos no Judiciário (07' 00") - Rádio Câmara. Portal da Câmara dos Deputados. Available at <https://www.camara.leg.br/radio/programas/271167-especial-cnj-1-conselho-nacional-de-justica-desenvolve-acoes-para-acelerar-do-processos-no-judiciario-07-00/>. Accessed 7 May 2024

Futurium. Available at <https://futurium.ec.europa.eu/en/node>. Accessed 31 Mar. 2024

GovTech Maturity Index (GTMI) Data Dashboard. World Bank. Available at <https://www.worldbank.org/en/data/interactive/2022/10/21/govtech-maturity-index-gtmi-data-dashboard>. Accessed 20 Apr. 2024

Inforegio - Priorities for 2021-2027. Available at <https://ec.europa.eu/regional_policy/policy/how/priorities_en>. Accessed 31 Mar. 2024

Invasão hacker interrompe aula de Lewandowski com mensagens nazistas. Poder360. Available at <https://www.poder360.com.br/justica/invasao-hacker-interrompe-aula-de-lewandowski-com-mensagens-nazistas/>. Accessed 3 Jan. 2021

Joinup. Available at <https://joinup.ec.europa.eu/>. Accessed 31 Mar. 2024

Ministério do Meio Ambiente de Bolsonaro apagou 30 anos de documentos | Metrópoles. Available at <https://www.metropoles.com/colunas/guilherme-amado/ministerio-do-meio-ambiente-de-bolsonaro-apagou-30-anos-de-documentos>. Accessed 21 Aug. 2024

Plataforma Sinapses reúne 150 modelos de inteligência artificial. UNDP. Available at <https://www.undp.org/pt/brazil/news/plataforma-sinapses-reune-150-modelos-de-inteligencia-artificial>. Accessed 19 Apr. 2024

Programa Europa Digital – Conselho define a sua posição. Available at <https://www.consilium.europa.eu/pt/press/press-releases/2018/12/04/digital-europe-programme-council-agrees-its-position/>. Accessed 7 May 2024

Search | CORDIS | European Commission. Available at <https://cordis.europa.eu/search?q=contenttype%3D%27project%27%20AND%20frameworkProgramme%3D%27H2020%27%20AND%20(%27digital%27)&p=1&num=10&srt=Relevance:decreasing>. Accessed 31 Mar. 2024

Segurança das urnas eletrônicas é contestada. Jornal da USP. Available at <https://jornal.usp.br/atualidades/seguranca-das-urnas-eletronicas-e-contestada/>. Accessed 4 Oct. 2023

Structural Reform Support Programme (SRSP) - European Commission. Available at <https://commission.europa.eu/about-european-commission/departments-and-executive-agencies/structural-reform-support/structural-reform-support-programme-srsp_en>. Accessed 31 Mar. 2024

Valor de mercado da Apple ultrapassa o PIB do Brasil de 2019 | Tecnologia | G1. Available at <https://g1.globo.com/economia/tecnologia/noticia/2020/08/06/valor-de-mercado-da-apple-ja-ultrapassa-o-pib-do-brasil-de-2019.ghtml>. Accessed 6 Jun. 2022

World Bank Group to Discontinue Doing Business Report. World Bank. Available at <https://www.worldbank.org/en/news/statement/2021/09/16/world-bank-group-to-discontinue-doing-business-report>. Accessed 16 Aug. 2024

Your Europe. Your Europe. Available at <https://europa.eu/youreurope/index.htm>. Accessed 30 Mar. 2024